PREVENTING ADOLESCENT SUICIDE

Dave Capuzzi, Ph.D., N.C.C.
Professor of Counselor Education
Portland State University
Portland, Oregon

Larry Golden, Ph.D.
Professor, Counseling and Guidance Program
University of Texas at San Antonio
San Antonio, Texas

ACCELERATED DEVELOPMENT INC.
Publishers
Muncie, Indiana

PREVENTING ADOLESCENT SUICIDE

Library of Congress Number: 87-72747

International Standard Book Number: 0-915202-74-3

1 2 3 4 5 6 7 8 9 10

Printed in United States of America

Technical Development: Virginia Cooper
Tanya Dalton
Delores Kellogg
Marguerite Mader
Sheila Sheward

Order additional copies from

Accelerated Development Inc.
Publishers Tel (317) 284-7511
3400 Kilgore Avenue, Muncie, Indiana 47304

This book is dedicated with deepest appreciation

to our wives,

Celia Capuzzi

and

Meredith Norwood

PREFACE

Many people absolutely reject suicide under any circumstances. However, most of us can sympathize with the suicidal motives, let's say, of an elderly person afflicted with terminal cancer. But it disturbs the core of our being that a *child* would find this life so empty of hope that death would be preferable. Teenagers are so full of pain, pleasure, sexuality, energy, curiosity, idealism, bravado, vulnerability, rebellion, and promise!

We know that children grow with considerable ambivalence towards the awesome responsibilities of adulthood. Sexual and physical maturity thrust the child into the adult world. However, physical development belies the reality of emotional immaturity. Television and movies excite teens with a plethora of lethal images. Drug and alcohol abuse are epidemic. Families are breaking up. Adolescents simply cannot bring sufficient perspective to the problems they face. The world, itself, seems a suicidal free fall into the nuclear abyss.

While most adolescents accumulate a few psychological scars along the way, most are able to "tough it out." Why do some succumb and others survive, indeed thrive, under similar conditions? The "psychological authopsies" that follow a suicide rarely uncover a clear and reasonable motive. The questions about "Why" and "If only..." persist. Who is to blame? What could have been done? How can we recognize the signs of a suicidal crisis before it's too late? How can we intervene with a suicide attempter to preclude another, perhaps successful, attempt? How can we avoide the "cluster" effect, the rash of attempts, that often follows a suicide?

This book comes to grips with the reality of adolescent suicide. In the book are fifteen chapters organized under five major parts. The name and a synopsis of each chapter are as follows:

I. THE PROBLEM OF ADOLESCENT SUICIDE:

Chapter 1, Adolescent Suicide: An Introduction to Issues and Interventions, is an overview of the suicide problem while *Chapter 2, Societal Trends and the World of the Adolescent,* contains a discussion about changes in American society that influence adolescent development.

II. A PROFILE OF THE ATTEMPTER

This part describes individuals who are most likely to commit suicide. In *Chapter 3, Behavioral Indicators,* is established a conceptual baseline of "normal adolescent behavior" as a point of departure.

Chapter 4, Personality Variables, contains information about personality traits and disorders that contribute to adolescent suicide.

Chapter 5, Thinking Patterns and Motivation, has an explanation of how suicidal adolescents differ from their nonsuicidal peers in terms of cognitive process and motivation. Typically, suicidal thoughts are dominated by a negative view of self and pessimistic expectations for the future. Suicide is motivated by a desire to finally gain some measure of control.

In *Chapter 6, Depression,* is information that supports the view that most suicidal individuals are basically depressed. Depressed individuals feel helpless, unable to change their life circumstances.

III. ASSESSING LETHALITY

Some suicidal teens give hints that are hard to miss, such as "You're going to regret how you've treated me," "Life has no meaning anymore," or "I'm tired of living." Others become preoccupied with morbid themes. Still others give virtually no clues.

In *Chapter 7, Psychological Assessment,* is provided a comprehensive system for psychological assessment of suicidal adolescents that is useful in both assessing suicidal risk and generating appropriate treatment strategies. The "symptom clusters" that predict high risk are described.

In *Chapter 8, "Signatures" of Suicide,* are discussed the developmental problems which occur during childhood and, quite often, set the stage for an adolescent suicide. Situational "signatures," such as social isolation, are identified. No single signature is complete as a predictor, rather, the professional must be aware of the accumulation of warning signs that put adolescents at risk.

IV. PREVENTION AND INTERVENTION

Treating suicidal adolescents can be a terrible burden. The ideal, of course, is prevention rather than treatment. In Part IV are described (1) programs for suicide prevention and (2) strategies for intervention when suicide has been attempted.

In *Chapter 9, Overview of Prevention,* is proposed content for school/community based suicide prevention programs and recommendations are provided for schools and communities interested in initiating a prevention program.

In *Chapter 10, A Model Prevention Program,* is described the development of suicide prevention programs and a description of an actual program. The chapter includes ideas for networking, program expansion, and program evaluation.

Native American adolescents are at high risk for suicide attempts and completions. In *Chapter 11, Interventions with Native Americans* contains treatment issues such as intentionality and client roles as well as specific interventions.

In *Chapter 12, Interventions with College Campus Populations,* the suicide problem is viewed from the perspective of university counseling center staff. Epidemiology is reviewed—How prevalent is suicidal behavior among college students? Legal, ethical, and practical concerns which college administrators must face when dealing with a suicidal crisis are discussed.

In *Chapter 13, Crisis Intervention,* are school-based strategies for preventing adolescent suicide. Roles of teacherrs, administrators, studens, and counselors as part of a district-wide crisis intervention team are presented.

In *Chapter 14, Family Therapy and Networking,* the focus is on the use of the family therapy and professional networking. Three major sections are included: the variety of self-destructive behaviors demonstrated by adolescents, family therapy as a treatment modality with suicidal adolescents, and consultation in the treatment of the suicidal adolescent and the family.

V. LEGAL ISSUES

While Part V is comprised of only one chapter, it is of great importance. In *Chapter 15, Legal Consideratins for the Practitioner,* is the issue of whether or when the law will hold a health care practitioner responsible for a suicide. In addition, suggestions are provided for what practitioners can do during treatment to avoid law suits.

Suicide is an extreme method of ending a crisis. The person can see no other way to find relief. Usually an adolescent who attempts suicide is reaching out for help. School and community groups must plan for the increasing problem of adolescent suicide in the same way that provisions are being made for interventions related to physical and sexual abuse, and drug abuse. We must affirm the self-worth of every child by being sensitive to his or her developing individuality. We must join with our young people in creating a world that is worth living for.

Dave Capuzzi
Portland State University

Larry Golden
The University of Texas at San Antonio

TABLE OF CONTENTS

LIST OF FIGURES

LIST OF TABLES

PART I
PROBLEM OF ADOLESCENT SUICIDE

CHAPTER **1**

ADOLESCENT SUICIDE AN INTRODUCTION TO ISSUES AND INTERVENTIONS

Dave Capuzzi, Ph.D.
and
Larry Golden, Ph.D.

EDITORIAL ABSTRACT: *The purpose of this chapter is to introduce the reader to issues and interventions connected with the topic of adolescent suicide and the prevention of adolescent suicide. The developmental problems of adolescence, personality, and behavioral disorders, dysfunctional relationships and societal provocations and pending catastrophes are overviewed to provide the reader with an understanding of the adolescent suicide problem in the United States. Predicting adolescent suicide is addressed through discussion of the myths connected with adolescent suicide, signs and symptoms and a presentation of the profile of the suicidal adolescent. Prevention, crisis management, postvention, and approaches to counseling/therapy are also overviewed to provide the reader with a point of departure for the focused follow-up chapters of this book.*

> Matt Reiser had a date with Cheryl Burress last Tuesday night in Bergenfield, N.J., near New York city, but at 6:30 Cheryl called to cancel. "We can't get together tonight," she told Reiser. "We're going to visit Joe." Reiser thought he knew what she meant. Joe Major, a friend of Cheryl's, had fallen 200 feet to his death off the Palisades cliffs along the Hudson River last September in what police considered an alcohol-related accident, and Reiser figured that Cheryl was planning to visit Major's grave that night, as she had many times before. Reiser was wrong.
>
> Instead, Cheryl, 17, and her sister Lisa, 16, went driving around the Bergenfield area with two companions, Thomas Olton, 18, and Thomas Rizzo, 19. At about 3 a.m., the teenagers stopped at an Amoco station and bought $3 worth of gas for Olton's brown Camaro. They asked if they could take the hose from the station's automobile vacuum cleaner, but the attendant refused.
>
> It was a short drive from the gas station to Foster Village apartments, a housing complex. The place was well known. Garage No. 74, vacant at least a month, had been serving as a hangout where groups of Bergenfield teenagers came to drink and to smoke marijuana. The youngsters drove into the dark garage, shut the door and locked it. They left the car idling, its windows open. Then they sat back and waited.
>
> The steadily burning gasoline did its job, releasing deadly carbon monoxide fumes. Within an hour all four were dead. (Wilentz, 1987, pp. 12-13)

The story above appeared in the March 23, 1987, issue of *Time*. The day after the bodies of the four teens were found, two more adolescent girls killed themselves by the same method. One of them, Karen Logan, was found holding a stuffed animal and a rose.

Adolescent suicide has become a critical problem in the United States. Recent yearly estimates report as many as 7,000 completions and 400,000 attempts among the adolescent population in this country. Five years ago, suicide was the third leading cause of death among the 11 to 24 year age group. Now it is the second leading cause. Only accidents, usually automobile accidents, rank higher. Suicide among the nation's youth, particularly white males, jumped 40 percent during a 10 year period, 1970-1980. The full extent of the adolescent suicide problem is difficult to quantify because many suicides are reported as accidents because of family embarrassment, religious beliefs, or community discomfort.

While the statistics that describe adolescent suicide can be interpreted in various ways, the fact that more and more young people are killing themselves can only be understood in one way: as a terrible waste.

UNDERSTANDING ADOLESCENT SUICIDE

Teenagers are just starting out in life. They are anxiously and excitedly planning for career or vocation and exploring relations with the opposite sex. A small minority are planning on a suicidal career! It disturbs the core of our being that a child would find life so empty of hope that death would be preferable.

While most adolescents accumulate a few psychic scars along the way to adulthood, most can cope with the stress of daily living. In an attempt to understand the contingencies which make some adolescents vulnerable to suicide, we will explore four factors: (a) developmental problems of adolescence, (b) personality and behavioral disorders, (c) dysfunctional relationships, and (d) societal provocations and pending catastrophes.

Developmental Problems of Adolescence

With the exception of infancy, no period is so fraught with change as adolescence. Forsaking the security of childhood, the adolescent grows with considerable ambivalence towards the awesome responsibilities of adulthood. School is no longer merely a place to learn and play, but has become the training ground for earning a living and mate selection. Home is no longer the source of endless sustenance and support, but is a place to leave, a trap to struggle free of. Sexual and physical maturity propels the child into the adult world. However, physical development belies the reality of emotional immaturity. Adolescents simply cannot bring sufficient perspective to the problems they face.

Suicidal youngsters are subject to the same stressful circumstances that all adolescents are, but *more so*. These at risk teens are less resourceful in their ability to cope. During times of stress, they obsess about suicide as an escape, devoting more and more energy to planning the details of the act.

The stressful events that precipitate a suicide may not be of overwhelming proportions. Such events are failure of a subject in school, rejection by a friend, a disappointing romance, or a family argument. Even pleasurable experiences can cue suicidal fantasies. For example, high school graduation, for many, symbolizes the transition to young adulthood and the initiation of a life more independent of other family members. Even though adolescents will tell friends and family that they are thrilled to graduate, they may be apprehensive.

For teens to indulge in suicidal fantasies is not abnormal. Further, normal adolescents are easily influenced by their peers. They are in search of an identity that fits. A youngster who is "barely getting by" is especially vulnerable when another person in the immediate community commits suicide. Therefore when a suicide occurs in a school, we can expect a rash of suicidal "copycats" to follow (Berman, 1986). These multiple suicides occurring in a brief time are called "clusters."

Personality and Behavioral Disorders

In his masterpiece, *Steppenwolf*, Herman Hesse (1974) invited us to investigate the personality traits of individuals at risk of suicide, "Just as there are those who at the least indisposition develop a fever, so do those whom we call suicides, and who are always very emotional and sensitive develop at the least shock the notion of suicide."

Why do some succumb and others survive, indeed thrive, under similar environmental conditions? The "suicide note" is but a morsel of information, what Pfeifer (1986) calls "iceberg" talk. The whole truth lies deeper and is more complex.

An understanding of the "suicidal personality" begins with an understanding of depression. The majority of suicidal individuals of all ages are basically depressed (Toolan, 1984). Depressed adolescents complain of feelings of sadness, isolation, fatigue, and boredom. They may have trouble getting up in the morning, cry easily, and daydream excessively. They may suffer from melancholia, a loss of pleasure in almost everything. Depressed individuals feel helpless, unable to change their life circumstances. The consequent feelings of rage are turned inwards. However, depression may be masked by overactivity, participation in a constant round of social activities, sexual promiscuity, or drug abuse (Emery, 1983).

Holinger and Offer (1982) suggested two models: (1) competition and failure, and (2) progressive isolation. According to the first model, some teenagers who fail in the competition to play sports, earn high grades, gain entrance to good colleges, or socialize with the "right" peers, seek relief in suicidal fantasies. The pressure to achieve academically, vocationally, and socially is one that is keenly felt by adolescents. In the competition for success, some teenagers will win, some will lose, and a few of these "losers" will become suicidal. The second model envisions a fragile, isolated adolescent who bases an assessment of personal inferiority on a narrow, and thereby, distorted perspective. "Nobody wants me," becomes a pervasive theme. The individual becomes increasingly isolated and undefended against feelings of despair.

Poor problem solving ability is another characteristic of many suicidal adolescents. This trait is epitomized by a lack of resourcefulness in generating options, coping with a difficult relationship, or planning for the future.

A lack of problem solving skills is particularly troublesome in conjunction with another trait which is part of the suicidal pattern—total commitment to a relationship or a goal for the future. Suicidal adolescents develop a tunnel-visioned perspective. A relationship may become so important that other friendships are dropped; a goal may begin to dominate every decision. Commitment, total and unswerving, often becomes the theme for the patterning of daily, weekly, and monthly activities and priorities. When an important relationship ends or a goal becomes unachievable, self-esteem plummets, feelings are kept secret, achievement is roadblocked, and the behavioral repertoire becomes frozen in maladaptive patterns. The result is an escalation of stress and anxiety. Suicide becomes an extreme method of ending the crisis. The person can see no other way find relief at the time the suicide takes place (Berman, 1986).

The United States is experiencing an epidemic of drug use and abuse. Drug abuse goes "hand-in-glove" with suicide. Opportunities to experiment with marijuana, alcohol, and other drugs are presented to fifth and sixth graders in most school in this country. Suicide prone adolescents are especially vulnerable to peer pressure; it is common for parents of suicidal adolescents to report that their child seemed to lose control and judgment in the presence of peers and that they dreaded the arrival of their child's friends for an afternoon visit or a weekend stay. Since problem-solving ability, self-esteem, communication skills, etc., which may already be inadequate, are never enhanced through the use of drugs, suicide prone adolescents become even higher risks as drug experimentation and dependency increases.

From a psychoanalytic perspective, a suicide attempt is seen as an acting out of sadomasochistic excitement (Furman, 1984). Suicidal adolescents provoke rejections and misconstrue the words and behavior of others. Violence and mutual hurting provide gratification and death may take the place of surrender or orgasm (Furman, 1984).

Dysfunctional Relationships

No evidence exists that suicide is genetically inherited. Further, children have committed suicide when no apparent psychopathology is within the family. That is, some of these families are normal. However, suicide does tend to run in families, just as physical and sexual abuse does. Members of families share an emotional climate since parents model coping skills as well as high or low self-esteem. According to McAnarney (1979), "In societies where family ties are close, suicidal rates are low and and conversely, where families are not close, suicidal rates are high." A close relationship with parents has been found to be inversely related to depressive mood in adolescence (Kandel & Davies, 1982).

Poor Communications

Typically, families of suicidal youngsters are troubled by dysfunctional communication. These families report great difficulty in communicating clearly and consistently with one another (whether between parents or between parent and child). Even when the family eats breakfast or dinner together, quite often the meal is eaten in silence or with attention directed to a television program. Very often, parents have not modeled a positive, articulate communication style for their children to imitate. Parents may have little knowledge of the tribulation experienced by their adolescent child. The adolescent may have difficulty talking with peers and siblings; talking with parents may seem unthinkable. As time passes, the easier thing to do is to keep feelings buried. The suicide comes as a surprise.

A striking feature of communication in "suicidogenic families" is the presence of overt and covert messages about suicide and death (Richman, 1984). Examples of overt messages would be, "I wish you'd never been born," or "Croaking was the best thing your father ever did for this family." Covert messages, of course, are more difficult to decipher. According to Richman (1984), the isolation and loneliness of the suicidal individual is invariably related to unconscious family rules. Both an absence of any warm, parental figure with whom to identify and a sense of aloneness exists. The individual is trapped within the boundaries of the family while intimacies with persons outside are seen as a threat and, therefore, forbidden. Consequently, many suicidal adolescents have a relatively small network of social support.

Separation and Loss

Social isolation makes these adolescents vulnerable to the loss of any love object, which may trigger the suicide attempt (Rice, 1987). These youngsters are not only vulnerable to loss, they are likely to experience it. In fact, suicidal adolescents are more likely to have experienced the loss of a parent through separation or divorce by their twelfth year than "normals" (Berman, 1986). In what Litman and Diller (1985) called the "classical crisis case," even an individual with a history of normal relationships can become suicidal after a sudden loss, usually of a love relationship.

The issue of separation from loved ones is central to the adolescent experience. Adolescents are bound and determined on the road of independence from their families. However, this road can be deadly for those not prepared for the journey. Richman (1984) believed that the increase in adolescent suicide is related to growing pressure on youngsters to leave home as soon as possible. A mistake is often made by confusing *physical* separation from the family with personal autonomy. The suicidal adolescent feels expendable, yet lacks the maturity to separate and leave.

Family Disorganization

Family disorganization is widely implicated in adolescent suicide (Jacobzinner, 1965; McAnarney, 1979; Molin, 1986; Rice, 1987). Recent decades have witnessed the decline of the traditional nuclear family. The stability that this model afforded, albeit at the expense of personal freedom, has been eroded.

The role of the single parent has long been characterized by escalated responsibility, lowered income, high stress, and lack of time. A single parent may be so busy attempting to provide an acceptable standard of living for his/her children that little time can be allotted to the basics of a parent-child relationship.

Remarriage results in "blended" or "step" families. When adults who have custody of children from a previous marriage decide to form a new family, the dynamics can become unwieldy. For some adolescents, the adjustment is too difficult when faced with a "substitute" parent, new guidelines for behavior and discipline, additional siblings, less personal space, or a different home in a new neighborhood.

More and more American families are finding that two incomes are needed to support an acceptable standard of living. Parents in these dual career families may bring the stresses of employment into the family system. Less time is available to accomplish household tasks, grocery shop, schedule medical and dental appointments, and so forth. The breakdown of a car or a child's minor illness can easily disrupt a taut schedule.

Parents of adolescent children are usually between the ages of 35 and 50. As parents see their children approach the age of leave taking, they may begin the process of reassessing themselves, the familiar "mid-life crisis." They may reevaluate their career and financial status. Issues between spouses may resurface if they were not dealt with successfully earlier. Just at the time when children need more time and attention, parents may be focused on their own status and anxieties about time "running out."

Families in which physical or sexual abuse is occurring are at high risk for adolescent suicide. Children of abusive parents have not been taught to feel good about themselves and to problem-solve well. Escaping the pain of such a family atmosphere or the self-deprecating viewpoint they have internalized can be sufficient motivation for suicide.

Today, virtually all American families are at risk. Unless family members are good at managing both time and stress, saying "no" to unnecessary work-related or other responsibilities, helping one another and meeting each other's needs at the time these needs arise, the family climate may be one of tension and lack of receptiveness. Adolescents may not feel they can turn to family members for help. Parents must be alert to signs of depression and poor adjustment in themselves and their adolescent children.

Societal Provocations and Pending Catastrophes

Little if any evidence is available to link problems that threaten human society to the rise in adolescent suicides. However, negative social trends and frightening world events can engender feelings of despair in all of us. In an essay titled, *The Adolescent Philosopher in a Nuclear World*, Austin and Mack (1986) observed that traditionally the adolescent struggle has occurred in relation to a stable but progressive social order. While every generation of teenagers has faced crises (the Depression, World War II, etc.), suicide is clearly on the rise in today's generation. Therefore, a look at the formidable issues that loom large for our youth is worth taking.

Racism and Poverty

While the suicide rate is lower for Blacks than for Whites, the murder rate, specifically among young Black men, is much higher

(Cohen, 1987). Suicide and homicide are obviously different kinds of acts but depression, hopelessness, and frustration can energize either or both.

Death and Violence as a Media Theme

Recently, one of the authors saw a marquee at a San Antonio mall cinema advertising: "Black Widow," "Evil Dead 2," "Lethal Weapon," "Nightmare on Elm Street," and "Witchboard." Suicidal adolescents borrow lethal ideas and images from media sources.

Decline in the American Standard of Living

Indications are that the growth in the American economy is slowing down. Many young people can anticipate a lower standard of living than their parents because of inflation, depletion of natural resources, huge national debt, competition from abroad, bankruptcies of family farms, and so forth. The reality of the situation may be less crucial than how it is perceived. Some adolescents may fear that no matter how much effort they expend, they are destined for a bleak future.

Acquired Immune Deficiency Syndrome (AIDS)

Still unknown is how this disease will impact the psychology of adolescents. For some, fear of AIDS may relieve pressure to engage in premature sexual experimentation. It may also cause terrible anxiety about the onset of a new "Black Plague."

Nuclear War

Today's young people are aware that a nuclear war will end human civilization. As vast amounts of the earth's resources are deployed in a search for still more lethal forms of annihilation, the appearance is that the human race, itself, is suicidal. Austin and Mack (1986) quoted one youngster as saying, "My generation has been shaped not so much by the Civil Rights Movement or even by Vietnam—that's your generation. We're the generation that has nuclear weapons all around us...I would rather die trying to save the world, than just die. So that's how I'm going to live." This response holds a promise, not just for this teenager, but for all of us.

PREDICTING ADOLESCENT SUICIDE

Who is at risk for suicide? This section on prediction will (1) dispel certain myths about adolescent suicide, (2) identify signs of an impending suicide attempt, and (3) profile a "typical" adolescent suicide.

Myths

One of the first steps in understanding adolescent suicide is identifying the commonly held misconceptions about it:

> *Adolescents who talk about suicide are not serious about doing it.* Almost all suicidal adolescents have made attempts, verbally or nonverbally, to let someone else know that life seems to be too much to handle. These attempts, often barely audible or visible, are a cry for help to find options, other than death, to decrease the pain of living. Always take verbal threats seriously and never assume such threats are only for the purpose of attracting attention or manipulating others.
>
> *Suicide happens without warning.* Most suicidal adolescents give numerous hints about their suicidal thinking and intentions. Clues can be verbal or in the form of gestures, such as taking a few sleeping pills or becoming accident prone. As stress escalates and options, other than suicide, seem few, suicidal adolescents may withdraw from an already small circle of friends making it more difficult for others to notice warning signs.
>
> *Once an adolescent is suicidal, he/she must always and forever be considered suicidal.* Most adolescents are suicidal for a limited period of time. In the experience of the authors, the 24 to 72 hour period around the peak of the "crisis" is the most dangerous. If counselors and other mental health practitioners can monitor this crisis period and then get the adolescent into regularly scheduled, long-term counseling/therapy, a strong possibility is that another suicidal crisis will never occur. The more effort that is made to help an adolescent identify stressors and develop problem-solving skills during this post-suicidal crisis period and the more time that passes, the better the prognosis.

If an adolescent attempts suicide and survives, he/she will not make an additional attempt. A difference exists between the adolescent who experiences a suicidal crisis but does not attempt, and the adolescent who actually tries to bring an end to life. An adolescent who carries through with an attempt had identified a plan, had access to the means, and maintained a high enough energy level to follow through. He/she knows that a second or third attempt would be within the realm of possibility. Most likely, each follow-up attempt will be more lethal.

Adolescents who commit suicide always leave notes. Only a small percentage of adolescents who complete the act of suicide leave notes. This is a popular myth and one of the reasons why many suicides are mistakenly classified and reported as accidents.

Most adolescent suicides happen late at night. This myth is not true for the simple reason that most suicidal adolescents actually want help. Mid-to-late morning and mid-to-late afternoon are the time periods when most attempts are made because someone is more likely to be around to intervene than would be the case at night.

Never use the word "suicide" when talking to adolescents because it may "put ideas in their heads." This is simply not true; using the "word' will not motivate someone to commit suicide who is not suicidal. However, if an adolescent is suicidal, the use of the world can help him/her begin to verbalize feelings. If a suicidal adolescent thinks you know he/she is suicidal and realizes you are afraid to approach the subject, it can only contribute to feelings of despair and helplessness.

People with strong religious beliefs will not attempt suicide. This is not true. In fact, although the Catholic Church considers suicide a serious moral offense, Catholics actually attempt suicide more frequently than non-Catholics (Toolan, 1984)

Signs and Symptoms

Professionals who work with adolescents should familiarize themselves with these indications of an impending suicide attempt.

Changes in Behavior. In general, any decided change in behavior should be noted. A sudden drop in grades, difficulty with concentration, a loss of interest in hobbies, changes in sleeping and eating habits, experimentation with marijuana, running away, and sexual promiscuity can all be warning signs. Cause for concern is present when depression occurs in combination with other marked behavior change for periods lasting longer than a week. An especially important point to realize is that when an adolescent who has been struggling with periodic depressive episodes suddenly improves, a suicide attempt may be imminent. For a person who has seemed troubled for some time to improve suddenly and "magically" is unlikely. Quite often, an abrupt change in emotional tenor results after the decision about when and how to make a suicide attempt has been made.

Verbal Cues. Changes in behavior, such as the ones previously described, may be accompanied by a number of explicit verbal warnings:

"I can't go on."

"I wish I was dead."

"I'm not the person I used to be."

"There's only one way out."

"You won't be seeing me around anymore."

"You're going to regret how you've treated me."

"Life has no meaning anymore."

"I'm tired of living."

"If (such and such) happens, I'll kill myself."

"If (such and such) doesn't happen, I'll kill myself."

"I'm going *home*."

"Here take this (cassette, jewelry, etc.); I won't be needing it anymore."

Although the idiosyncratic language of the teenage community varies from year to year and from one part of the country to another, the previous statements convey that suicide is being considered as an option. Such verbalizations should cue us to pay attention and invite additional disclosures.

Themes or Preoccupations in Thinking. Listen for the themes or preoccupations that dominate the suspect individual's thinking:

Wanting to escape from a situation which seems intolerable (e.g., abuse, difficulty at school, drugs, lack of friends, etc.).

Wanting to join a friend or family member who has died.

Wanting total commitment to a relationships or a goal.

Wanting to be punished.

Wanting to avoid being punished.

Wanting revenge.

Wanting to control when death will occur.

Wanting to end an unresolvable conflict.

Wanting to become a martyr for a cause.

A Profile of the Suicidal Adolescent

To My Dearest Family,

I know that you will not understand why I've done this. Please don't blame yourselves. It has nothing to do with you. A boy who I love very much doesn't want me. I've tried everything to let him know how much I love him. I know you will think this sounds stupid, but I don't believe I can be happy without him. Everybody dies sooner or later anyways.

Love,

Alicia

Alicia slit her wrists, then called the boy who had rejected her, who, in turn, called EMS (Emergency Medical Service). The wounds were superficial.

The case of Alicia is real. Following is a description of a hypothetical case, that of the *typical* suicidal adolescent, adapted from the work of Martin (1986) and Tishler, McKenry, and Morgan (1981).

Our typical suicidal adolescent is a white 15 year old girl. Her parents are divorced and her mother works full time. Last year she earned "As" and "Bs" in school, but this year she is failing several subjects. She has excessive absences from school due to colds and flu symptoms and has been caught truant several times. Teachers describe her as lethargic and depressed. She has lost weight and complains of a loss of appetite, fatigue, and insomnia. Recently, she broke up with her boyfriend of two months. She has few if any friends and feels she cannot communicate with either parent. Her mother suffers from depression and attempted suicide a year ago. Mother and daughter quarreled shortly before the girl's drug overdose.

PREVENTING ADOLESCENT SUICIDE

In 1910, in the Austrian capital of Vienna, Sigmund Freud addressed a professional conference:

> A secondary school should achieve more than not driving its pupils to suicide. It should give them a desire to live and should offer them support and backing at a time in life at which the conditions of their development compel them to relax their ties with their parental home and their family.

Prevention in the Schools

Suicidal behavior usually has origins that are unrelated or indirectly related to events in the school (Berkovitz, 1985). For some students, however, school exacerbates suicidal despair. Competition for grades, overworked teachers who teach too many students, and, in general, the lack of a caring, personal touch are pervasive problems.

In all fairness, schools cannot be expected to cure all of society's ills. However, since virtually all children go to school, it is the logical place to start preventive programs. Schools that deter suicide would enable children to grow towards mastery and a positive view of self and the world. Children would learn to cope with stress. The curriculum would place more emphasis on cooperation and less on bruising competition. Mistakes would be regarded as opportunities for new learning. A wide range of extracurricular activities would offer alternatives to social isolation. A commitment to improving society through community service would be encouraged. Children would learn respect for the miracle of life.

Suicide prevention should be initiated on the elementary school level and continued through secondary school. Counselors should be permitted to counsel children rather than perform administrative and clerical duties. Class sizes should be reduced so teachers can develop personal relationships with pupils. Remedial reading programs could reduce academic failures. Low self-esteem and poor problem-solving skills are observed in some first and second graders. These problems are more easily resolved in the formative years.

Counselors who work with students in grades five through twelve can provide information about the signs of an impending suicidal crisis. Classroom presentations should encourage students who are concerned about themselves or their friends to ask for assistance from adults, as confidants (Ross, 1985). Not unlike the Mafia, the society of adolescents honors a sacred code of silence! In the case of a potential suicide, this commitment to keeping secrets, especially from adults, can be dangerous. Teens must be convinced that their first loyalty to a suicidal friend is to inform adults.

Teachers and administrators need inservice training. Not only must school personnel understand the dynamics of the suicidal adolescent, they must know how to make appropriate and timely referrals.

Some have cautioned that "death" education will cause suicides (Raspberry, 1987). This is not unlike the view that sex education will cause promiscuity. Until evidence exists of a cause-effect relationship, the authors strongly recommend education as a strategy for suicide prevention.

Postvention

Given the well known cluster phenomenon, the response to an actual suicide can be crucial. Postvention becomes a means of prevention both in the immediate situation and in subsequent decades and generations.

A suicide creates a state of terrible disequilibrium for the immediate family and the entire community. Unfortunately, the community is all too quick to blame the parents for causing the suicide. Questions about, "Why," are raised again and again as well as, "If only," self-reproach. Who is to blame? What could have been done to avert this death? The investigation is seldom conclusive since people rarely kill themselves for a single reason (Hill, 1984).

As many as six to ten people are affected, on a long-term basis, for each adolescent suicide attempt or completion. A necessary procedure is to offer either individual or group ("survivor groups") counseling for family members and friends of the suicide victim or attempter. On a short-term basis, hundreds of people, if not entire communities, can be in need of assistance ranging from information about the dynamics of suicide to individual or group counseling.

If a student has *attempted* suicide, best procedure is to wait a few months before starting prevention programs in the school so that the returning student will not be focused upon. Individual or group counseling can still be provided for those who need to talk about their feelings.

The end of a period of suicidal crisis or the return of an adolescent who has made an unsuccessful attempt does not mean that the problem has been resolved. The best hope for improved mental health of such an adolescent is long-term counseling focused upon overcoming low self-esteem and depression so that life and its options can be viewed differently.

TREATING ATTEMPTED SUICIDE

"Suicide is based upon a problem in the present which has its basis in unresolved crises in the past which, in turn, precipitates a major crisis, the fate of which may determine the future." (Ross, 1985, p. 400)

Crisis Management

For a short time (24 to 72 hours), the client must be directed and monitored. Definite steps must be taken to safeguard the well being of the client and expedited in an assertive manner. If a person were in an accident which resulted in a life-threatening physical injury, paramedics and emergency room physicians and nurses would act, without the permission of the patient, to save the life. Managing a suicidal crisis is no different.

When a counselor is called upon to help an adolescent in a suicidal crisis, a number of steps must be followed to ascertain the level of lethality and reduce the risk.

Be a Good Listener. Suicidal individuals may have difficulty communicating. Judgmental statements such as, "it's against the teachings of your religion" or "you can't consider suicide, it would be devastating to your family," will make it difficult, if not impossible, for rapport to develop. Convey understanding and respect for everything that is being shared. However the circumstances, concerns and feelings, they are *reality* for this client. Counselors must be able to hear how the client perceives his/her world however distorted that perception might seem.

Be Supportive. When talking with an adolescent who may be at risk, be genuinely reassuring. Avoid phony reassurance, such as, "things aren't really that bad" (for the client, things *are* bad) or "the situation will take care of itself" (circumstances usually do not become better without much effort). Being supportive means that the counselor communicates understanding, reinforces the client for seeking assistance, and outlines counseling options for the near future.

Assess Lethality. The following questions should be asked to determine the degree of risk:

1. What has happened to make life so difficult?

2. Why are you thinking of suicide?

3. Do you have a suicide plan? The more specific the client is about the method, the time, the place, and who will or will not be nearby, the higher the lethality. If the client des-

cribes a specific method, such as, an overdose of sleeping pills, using a gun or a knife, and so forth, ask if he/she has that item in a pocket or purse and require that the suicide "weapon" be left with you. Firearms and highly lethal items, however, should be handled by the police. Most adolescent clients will cooperate with reasonable docility if they feel that they are in the care of a competent and trusted adult.

4. How much do you want to live? The more difficult it is for the client to respond with conviction, the higher the risk.

5. How much do you want to die? The more the client discusses ending life, the higher the risk.

6. How frequently do periods of suicidal thinking occur? How intense are they? How long do the episodes last? The more frequent, the more intense, and the longer the length of suicidal obsessing, the more lethal the condition. During episodes of suicidal preoccupation, virtually no time and energy are available for solving problems and seeking alternatives.

7. Have you attempted suicide in the past? If the answer is "yes," the client is more lethal. The more recent the attempt, the more dangerous the current crisis.

8. Has a family member, neighbor, friend ever attempted or completed suicide? If the answer is "yes," the client is more lethal.

9. On a scale of "1" to "10," with "1" being low and "10" being high, what is the number which depicts the probability that you will attempt suicide?

10. Is there anyone to stop you? This question is important for two reasons. First, if the client had difficulty identifying anyone who would want to keep them alive, the lethality is higher. Second, an important procedure is to obtain specific information about the people identified in response to this question. Names, addresses, phone numbers, and the nature of the current or past relationship may be needed to organize a suicide watch.

Make a Decision About Intervention. If the risk factor or lethality is high, the counselor must develop a crisis management plan which must be followed until the crisis subsides and long-term counseling can be initiated. If the client is acutely suicidal, hospitalization or a suicide watch is necessary. A suicide watch is organized by contacting friends and relatives. Family members and friends take turns staying with the client until the crisis has subsided. Under no circumstances should an adolescent in crisis leave the counselor's office until arrangements have been make to monitor the client. Contacting friends, family, and so forth breaks confidentiality but, in this case, does not violate any professional code of ethics. Such steps must be taken to save the client's life.

A written contract can be used along with a suicide watch (or in place of a suicide watch if the risk is low). Such a contract should specify activities, time with friends, and so forth. The client must agree to phone if preoccupation with suicide begins.

The counselor should not assume that a high risk client will have the energy to arrive for needed counseling even when the crisis has subsided. The counselor must be willing to cancel other appointments and "drop everything" to respond to a new crisis.

Counseling/Therapy

Edwin Shneidman (1987), a professor of thanatology, conducts what he calls "psychological autopsies" of suicides. He is convinced that suicide is not a vengeful or hostile act, but rather, that people try to kill themselves to make the pain stop. Therefore, the immediate task is to reduce the pain. Shneidman will intervene with lovers, parents, teachers, whoever or whatever is causing distress. Sometimes this is sufficient. But often, beneath the immediate concern, there is deep psychic pain and unmet needs. Counseling and psychotherapy are the means to address the client's psychological problems and unmet needs. Following is a discussion of various therapeutic approaches.

Psychoanalysis

Toolan (1984) advised individual, psychoanalytically oriented therapy for both child and parents. The child needs to be separated from his/her parents in the therapeutic process in the interest of confidentiality, an especially important concern for adolescents (Toolan, 1984). Freud believed that the act of suicide was an expression of anger towards an introjected, ambivalently regarded lost object (Trautman & Shaffer, 1984). The "lost object" might well be parental love. The goal of psychoanalytic therapy, therefore, would be to bring ambivalent feelings into consciousness, to confront feelings of rejection, and to allow the client to separate from the lost object (Trautman & Shaffer, 1984). A problem here is that most adolescents are action-oriented; they are poor candidates for long-term, insight oriented psychotherapy.

Cognitive-Behavioral Therapy

Suicidal adolescents hold irrational ideas about themselves and the world. The goal of cognitive-behavioral therapy is to teach the client to test the validity of these ideas. The client is taught problem solving skills and urged to consider alternate solutions.

Suicidal individuals see only two alternatives: a total solution or a total cessation. In fact, very few of life's problems yield to a total solution; total cessation of pain, on the other hand, can be achieved by anyone with the means. The goal, obviously, is to broaden the suicidal person's constricted perspective. In a suicidal state, Shneidman (1987) believed, a person, "...cuts his or her throat and cries out for help at the same time." The individual must learn how to separate these two acts; to get help without being self-destructive. In an intervention called "stress-inoculation," solutions to difficult situations are role-played and rehearsed.

Group Therapy

Social isolation is often seen in suicidal youngsters. In group therapy, clients discover that they are not alone and that they share feelings in common with others. Further, through feedback and role-modeling, the client learns social skills. Group therapy can be an alternative to family therapy for the adolescent in florid rebellion against his/her parents (Trautman and Shaffer, 1984). On the negative side, Trautman and Shaffer (1984) are concerned that suicidal ideation and behavior could spread to all group members.

Family Therapy

According to "systems theory," a symptom in a family member is maintained by faulty family structure. Therefore, the family, not the suicidal youngster, is the "client." Blurred or rigid boundaries between family members are examined. Examples of boundary problems would be when individuation is stifled in the name of family loyalty, a child forms an alliance with one parent against another, or a child is forced to assume adult responsibilities. Communication problems are also considered. Examples of dysfunctional communication would be when conflicts are avoided at the expense of intimacy, excessive blaming keeps productive interaction to a minimum, or family secrets are kept according to powerful but unspoken rules.

At family sessions, the therapist may ask each family member about events leading up to the suicide attempt. Typically, the suicidal member will be in a "scapegoat" role. Complaints are voiced and anger escalates. However, such outbursts in a therapeutic setting are less dangerous than bottled-up rage with a subsequent decline into depression. Richman (1984) recommended that the identified suicidal member be asked, "Do you feel that the family is fed up with you?" or "Do you think that you are a burden and that they would be better off if you were dead?" Covert or overt death wishes may be voiced by family members. Alternatives, other than "being rid of" someone, that could make family life more manageable, are explored.

Relationships in dysfunctional families, indeed, in most families, are intensely ambivalent. Behind the hate is also love. Parents want their children to succeed at the same time that they fear their child's autonomy. The job of the therapist is to reframe a hopeless and hateful condition in a new light. For example, an angry outburst can be reframed as an attempt, albeit ineffectual, to communicate. Hope is the antidote to despair and the therapist's faith that a family can go beyond a suicidal crisis to renewed living is essential.

The authors regard family therapy in combination with a cognitive-behavioral approach as the treatment of choice for most suicidal adolescents. The major limitation is that families are disinclined to accept responsibility for a suicidal act and will, therefore, push for a quick repair as opposed to a long-term solution (Berman, 1986). In fact, less than half of families will return for treatment after the first session (Morrison & Collier, 1969).

Hospitalization

Unless a suicidal adolescent will agree to assume responsibility for coming to therapy sessions regularly, calling for help if needed, and taking prescribed medication, many therapists will refuse to treat outside of a hospital (Toolan, 1984). Increasingly, hospital wards are being set aside for the treatment of emotionally disturbed and misbehaving adolescents. A course of hospital treatment will be a month or longer. The patient receives a wide range of therapeutic interventions. Behavior is carefully monitored and consistently rewarded or punished. Thereby, the patient learns about the "cause and effect" of his/her behavior. Richman (1984) cautioned that discharge from the hospital for the suicidal adolescent can be experienced as a recapitulation of other separations in the past. This new separation experience must be sensitively confronted.

A suicide attempt serves to erode parental authority. Parents may fear that the act of disciplining their child will trigger another suicide attempt. Unfortunately, while hospitalization may provide some much needed respite for parents, it ultimately diminishes their power (Haley, 1980). Further, hospital care is enormously expensive.

Medication

Depressed youngsters, as opposed to those who are angry, seem to respond well to antidepressant medication. However, antidepressant medication, even when effective, takes two to three weeks to produce its full therapeutic effect (Toolan, 1984). Even when medication is effective, psychotherapy is also recommended.

SUMMARY

As a final word of caution, treating suicidal adolescents can be a terrible burden. Toolan (1984) advises that therapists not accept more than one or two acutely suicidal patients in therapy at the same time.

In summary, an adolescent who attempts suicide is reaching out for the help. School and community groups must plan, network, and fund services to cope with the increasing problem of adolescent suicide in the same way that provisions are being made for intervention related to physical and sexual abuse and drug abuse. We must affirm the self-worth of every adolescent child by being sensitive to his/her developing individuality. We must join with our young people in creating a world that is worth living for.

REFERENCES

Austin, D.A., & Mack, J.E. (1986). The adolescent philosopher in a nuclear world. In C.A. Corr & J.N. McNeil (Eds.), *Adolescence and death* (pp. 57-75). New York: Springer.

Berkovitz, I.H. (1985). The role of schools in child, adolescent, and youth suicide prevention. In M.L. Peck, N.L. Farberow, & R.E. Litman (Eds.), *Youth Suicide* (pp. 170-90). New York: Springer.

Berman, A.L. (1986). Helping suicidal adolescents: Needs and responses. In C.A. Corr & J.N. McNeil (Eds.), *Adolescence and death* (pp. 151-66). New York: Springer.

Cohen, R. (1987). Suicide defined by level of society. *San Antonio Express-News*, March 20, 7-B.

Emery, P.E. (1983). Adolescent depression and suicide. *Adolescence, 18*, 245-58.

Furman, E. (1984). Some difficulties in assessing depression and suicide in childhood. In H.S. Sudak, A.B. Ford, & N.B. Rushforth (Eds.), *Suicide in the young* (pp. 245-57). Boston: John Wright.

Haley, J. (1980). *Leaving home: The therapy of disturbed young people.* New York: McGraw-Hill.

Hesse, H. (1974). *Steppenwolf.* New York: Bantam.

Hill, W.C. (1984). Intervention and postvention in the schools. In H.S. Sudak, A.B. Ford, & N.B. Rushforth (Eds.), *Suicide in the young* (pp. 407-15). Boston: John Wright.

Holinger, P., & Offer, D. (1982). Prediction of adolescent suicide: A population model. *American Journal of Psychiatry, 139*, 302-7.

Jacobziner, H. (1965). Attempted suicides in adolescents by poisoning. *Journal of the American Medical Association, 191*(1), 101-5.

Kandel, D.B., & Davies, M. (1982). Epidemiology of depressive mood in adolescents. *Archives of General Psychiatry, 39*, 1205-12.

Litman, R.E., & Diller, J. (1985). Case studies of youth suicide. In M.L. Peck, N.L. Farberow, & R.E. Litman (Eds.), *Youth suicide* (pp. 48-70). New York: Springer.

Martin, N.K. (1986). Adolescent suicide: Myths, recognition, and evaluation. *School Counselor, 33*(4), 265-71.

McAnarney, E.R. (1979). Adolescent and young adult suicide in the United States—A reflection of societal unrest? Adolescence, 14(56), 765-74.

Molin, R.S. (1986). Covert suicide and families of adolescents. *Adolescence, 21*(81), 177-84.

Morrison, G.C., & Collier, J.G. (1969). Family treatment approaches to suicidal children and adolescents. *Journal of the American Academy of Child Psychiatry, 8*, 140-53.

Pfeifer, J.K. (1986). *Teenage suicide: What can the schools do?* Bloomington, IN: Phi Delta Kappa.

Raspberry, W. (1987). Caution is the word on death education. *San Antonio Express-News*, March 20, 7-B.

Rice, P.F. (1987). *The adolescent: Development, relationships, and cultures (5th ed.).* Boston: Allyn & Bacon.

Richman, J. (1984). The family therapy of suicidal adolescents: Promises and pitfalls. In H.S. Sudak, A.B. Ford, & N.B. Rushforth (Eds.), *Suicide in the young* (pp. 393-405). Boston: John Wright.

Ross, C.P. (1985). Teaching children the facts of life and death: Suicide prevention in the schools. In M.L. Peck, N.L. Farberow, & R.E. Litman (Eds.), *Youth suicide* (pp. 147-69). New York: Springer.

Shneidman, E. (1987). At the point of no return. *Psychology Today, March*, 54-8.

Tishler, C.L., McKenry, P.C., & Morgan, K.C. (1981). Adolescent suicide attempts: Some significant factors. *Suicide and Life-Threatening Behavior, 11*(2), 86-92.

Toolan, J.M. (1984). Psychotherapeutic treatment of suicidal children and adolescents. In H.S. Sudak, A.B. Ford, & N.B. Rushforth (Eds.), *Suicide in the young* (pp. 325–343). Boston: John Wright.

Trautman, P.D., & Shaffer, D. (1984). Treatment of child and adolescent suicide attempters. In H.S. Sudak, A.B. Ford, & N.B. Rushforth (Eds.), *Suicide in the young* (pp. 307-24). Boston: John Wright.

Wilentz, A. (1987). Teen suicide: Two death pacts shake the country. *Time, March 23*, 12-13.

CHAPTER **2**

SOCIETAL TRENDS AND THE WORLD OF THE ADOLESCENT

Jan Gill-Wigal, Ph.D.

Jan Gill-Wigal, Ph.D.

Assistant Professor
Counseling Department
Youngstown State University
Youngstown, OH 44555

Dr. Jan. Gill-Wigal is currently an Assistant Professor in the Counseling Department at Youngstown State University. She has extensive experience counseilng at the middle school, high school and college levels. She has worked in the community mental health system as well as in drug treatment. As a Psychologist in the Counseling Center at Ohio University, Dr. Gill-Wigal counseled students, taught undergraduate Psychology classes and coordinated outreach programming.

In addition to her current responsibilities, Dr. Gill-Wigal does consultation for business/industry, schools, and community organizations. She also provides inservice programs on various mental health topics such as suicide prevention, understanding adolescents, stress management, assertiveness training, time management, and human sexuality.

EDITORIAL ABSTRACT: *In this chapter are discussed societal changes and their impact on adolescent development. The rapid growth that makes adolescence a time of difficult adjustment also must interact with such powerful forces as the onset of the "information society" and its ubiquitous computers, intense competition for fewer jobs, restructuring of traditional sex roles, the threat of nuclear war, AIDS, substance abuse, and the erosion of the nuclear family. The result is that today's teenagers experience enormous stress.*

Adolescents now live in a society where technology is rapidly changing the way we live (Rice, 1981). With the advent and expansion of technology, we have evolved from an industrial to a technological society. No longer does change come slowly or are jobs stable and secure. Americans have watched their manufacturing industries contract one by one. Once productive and active industries such as steel, rubber, and automotive have laid off workers and closed plants both temporarily and permanently. Wages and benefit concessions, once unthinkable, have been willingly accepted to preserve jobs. Many skilled and unskilled men and women have lost decent paying jobs and now work for minimum wage and part-time hours. Some formerly productive workers have had to resort to welfare. Many workers trained in manufacturing found their skills obsolete as technology altered the workplace.

Finding a stable career is much more tedious and difficult than it was ten years ago. As society changes, job tasks also change. In the past, workers learned one skill which usually lasted a lifetime. Now workers in technological and information fields must acquire new skills constantly. High school graduates find themselves ill-prepared for much of the technological work available. Education and training are emphasized in most arenas. Even those in professional areas are required to take continuing education. Unfortunately, education does not guarantee job security or placement. As people become more educated the competition for jobs increases.

We now live in what has been called the "information society." The omnipresent computer stores vast amounts of information economically and efficiently. Even pre-school youngsters are exposed to computers and their use. Consequently, some degree of computer literacy has become a must for working Americans.

Adolescents feel the pressure of this push for education, skills training, and success. Often they pay an emotional price and experience psychological stress as they try to adapt to these changes (Gordon & Gordon, 1983).

Children are growing up in a world much different than that of their parents (Gordon & Gordon, 1983). In the past, the extended family offered a buffer for families experiencing disorganization or stress. Today, families have become more mobile (Hafen & Frandsen, 1986), moving frequently due to job advancement or in search of new employment. Fifty million Americans change their place of residence each year (Justice & Justice, 1979). This mobility threatens the existence of the extended family and its support (Dacey, 1982). With mobility, families seem to be experiencing more alienation and isolation (Gordon & Gordon, 1983).

In addition, the very nature of family life is changing. Robon (1987) suggested that children today are likely to experience more than one family pattern during their development. He stated that 25% of all children will be part of a remarried family and that many others will live in common-law families. Between 25% and 70% of all marriages end in divorce (Gordon & Gordon, 1983; Woodward, 1978). One of every six children live with a single parent (Dacey, 1982). Gordon and Gordon (1983, p. 179) state that "single parent families represent the fastest growing type of family unit." Often ordinary problems in nuclear families become magnified in this type of family.

Changes in the family structure are accompanied by inherent stress. Adolescents often find these changes difficult. In so-called blended or step-families the adolescent may experience difficulty adjusting to a new or substitute parent (Capuzzi, 1986). No surprise should occur when teens report often feeling alienated from their families (Dykeman, 1984). Many researchers (Peck, Farberow, & Litman, 1985; Hawton, 1982; Dykeman, 1984) have suggested that changes in the quality of family life have contributed to the rise in adolescent suicide.

Pfeffer (1985) stated that the most significant life stress is loss. Strauss (1985) reported suicidal adolescents have histories including many losses with few social supports to compensate. "Today's families are fractured and fragile and cannot meet the demands put on them" (Justice & Justice, 1979, p. 20).

Surrogate parenting has allowed previously infertile couples to conceive. Surrogating also has brought with it a host of emotional, moral, and legal dilemmas. Time has not allowed us to assess the influence of surrogating on the emotional/psychological well-being of children—very different issues from those with which our parents wrestled decades ago.

The increasing presence of women in the workplace and their assumption of more powerful economic positions also has contributed to the changing society. Use of child care facilities and the emergence of "latch key" children are some relatively new phenomena. Relationships between husband and wife have changed as have sex roles and expectations for men and women (Justice & Justice, 1979).

Teens are strongly influenced by societal expectations of the kind of work males and females should do (Rice, 1981). To find one's place as a productive, valued member of our society can be difficult and confusing.

The threat of nuclear war and international unrest hovers over mankind. Although most of us do not dwell on the possibility of nuclear annihilation, the threat is inherent. The festering conflicts in South America, Africa, and the Middle East threaten to explode in ways yet unknown. Adolescents often question social behavior and attitudes toward war. In addition, the Chernobyl disaster has illustrated that nuclear catastrophes are no longer part of the future but a real part of our present.

Coping with these changes brings confusion to the adjusting family. In many ways, "the home has become a pressure cooker" (Justice & Justice, 1979, p. 20)

THE NEW AGE ADOLESCENT

Physiological, psychological, sexual, academic, and family pressures always have been difficult during the transition from childhood to adulthood. The inherent conflicts associated with adolescence are today intensified as society passes through an era of upheaval.

Physiological Changes

At puberty, increased physical growth combines with social and cultural pressures (Golombek, 1983). Adolescents are concerned about these physiological changes, and resulting social pressures (Shertzer & Stone, 1981). They are concerned about their rate of development and how it compares with their peers. Self doubts about appearance are accentuated by the impossible physical ideal perpetuated in the media.

Teens also are reaching puberty at a younger age. This means the gap between physical changes and emotional maturity is widening (McCoy, 1982).

Psychological Changes

Adolescents strive to become independent while still maintaining some sense of security. One important developmental task of this stage is the separation from one's family. The confusing issue for adolescents, however, is that they are still dependent upon their families for their physical and psychological needs. Another cause for confusion is the mixed messages sent by families. At one point parents may call for independence and responsibility from their teens. At another they may treat their adolescent as a child. Adolescents are forced to choose between adult rules and peer rules. They find themselves struggling to resolve these issues and become autonomous. Adolescent behavior, consequently, often appears confused and inconsistent (Davis, 1983).

A sense of belonging is a pressing need for teens (Levine, 1983). In the place of family, adolescents seek acceptance from their peers. Due to insecurity, adolescents conform in attempting to emulate the group they wish to join (Sherzer & Stone, 1981). No matter the socioeconomic level, crowds or cliques are part of the adolescent world (Dunphy, 1980).

Adolescents are sensitive to criticism and rejection. Hypersensitivity is an occasional problem for teenagers. They become upset by perceived rejection. The search for identity often leaves teens feeling isolated and alone. Those that are different are often ostracized and called by slang names such as "nerd" and "geek."

Unfortunately, our society has very narrow definitions of what adolescents, of either sex, must look like. Being obese is a problem for many adolescents because they are affected by popular images of the ideal body (Rice, 1981).

Girls have difficulty coming to terms with their bodies. They may feel that their breasts are too small, thighs too big and stomachs too full. This quest for an arbitrary ideal often leaves girls unhappy and dissatisfied. Since not all girls can be "perfect," much pressure exists for them to achieve "perfection" in maladaptive ways.

Boys face different physical pressures. The adolescent male learns he has to be tall and strong. Sports, which, for good or ill, are deemed important by peers, parents, teachers, and others, are the purview of the larger, swifter, and stronger boys. Shorter, slower boys are usually left out.

Because adolescence is often an awkward physical stage for both sexes, many teenagers feel unattractive, unpopular, and unhappy. The lack of acceptance of their physical selves makes it difficult for many to achieve feelings of self worth.

Sexuality

Adolescents struggle with identity problems particularly as they relate to their sexual feelings (Finch, Poznanski, & Waggoner, 1971). They face many conflicting messages about sexuality. The media is seen to advocate sex without responsibility. Yet increasingly teens are warned of the dangers of sexuality transmitted, sometimes life threatening diseases, such as AIDS.

Many adolescents are sexually active. One-half of all teens engage in sexual intercourse before they leave high school, while births to unwed teen mothers have reached an all-time high (Gordon & Gordon, 1983).

In spite of apparent sophistication, adolescents may have little accurate sexual knowledge. They have difficulty admitting to this lack of knowledge because it can be interpreted as a sign of immaturity and social inadequacy (Anderson, 1984).

Like adults, adolescents are confused about sex role differences (Anderson, 1984). Young women are still pulled between success goals and affiliation needs. Young men are confused about their own roles and the expectation of others.

Since intimacy is one of the tasks of older adolescence, teens find the need to become involved in intimate relationships regardless of the sexual involvement.

Mood Fluctuations

Mood swings seem to be a trademark of adolescence. Internal and external events seem to have a greater impact during adolescence (Offer & Franzen, 1983). These mood fluctuations also may be a result of the confusion of sifting through old and new values and developing a style which is right for each individual.

Adolescents are present oriented. The future is now. This causes adolescents to behave impulsively, experiencing things that physically, and psychologically, they may not be ready for.

Achievement Pressures

Our society puts a premium on achievement and competition Gordon & Gordon, 1983). Making money and moving up the corporate ladder are the values of the 1980s. Adolescents are told via marketing and mass media they must achieve academic success to afford the many luxuries of our times.

Pressure exists to get into the "right" college or university. Part of the process of getting accepted means not only good grades but good test scores. We see the evidence of this in the many ACT and SAT preparation courses available both in high schools and the private sector. The emphasis on academic achievement has filtered down to pressure youth as young as three or four years old as parents push for the "right" pre-schools. The need to choose a major or enter a particular discipline of study puts added stress on adolescents seeking a college education.

Many parents, too, have high expectations for the achievement and success of their children. This comes at a time in which the upcoming generation, for the first time in the nation's history, will not achieve a higher standard of living than their parents. For adolescents, the inability to live up to parent's expectations can signify loss and can lead to depression (McCoy, 1982).

Family Conflicts

Historically, adolescents have experienced difficulty dealing with their parents. Much of this conflict arises from the natural process of forming an identity while developing values of their own. Many parents do not have the skills, time, and energy to be good listeners. Many families have difficulty sharing feelings (Capuzzi, 1986), especially positive ones. Consequently, communication problems occur between parents and their teens.

Increases in the reports of physical, sexual, and emotional abuse in our culture have been documented. More families report problems with drugs and alcohol. Approximately three million teens have problems with alcohol (McCoy, 1982). Interactions within the family are often abusive. Healthy communication and support for adolescents in families with abuse or chemical dependency problems are too frequently minimal or unavailable. Adolescents go through a naturally difficult time of testing their limits. Those from abusive families, however, must do so without the love, support, and safety net they really need.

Part of developing self identity means exploring and developing relationships with many kinds of people. Not all relationships will last. Therefore, normal adolescence also means learning to cope with loss. Loss takes many forms, such as through death, termination of a relationship, or divorce. Through dating and development of peer relationships, adolescents will naturally be forced to deal with loss. All loss is difficult. However, loss combined with the turbulance of adolescence can be particularly difficult.

WE LIVE IN A STRESSFUL SOCIETY

The rate of change in our lifestyles has increased tremendously (Dacey, 1982). The rapidity of change in society suggests a continuing increase in stress levels.

One of the shortcomings in society, has been the failure to teach stress-coping skills. Neither parents nor schools have adequately taught children and adolescents how to deal with the stressors of life in the late 20th century. Young boys are taught "big boys don't cry" and emotions exhibited by women are often seen as "weak." Consequently, the natural ways in which we deal with stress are negated. We teach people to work against natural healing, while suppressing feelings and emotions.

In this culture, apparently the inability to deal with emotional stress is considered a weakness. On the other hand, to have a physical problem is acceptable. In many cases one will get sympathy, encouragement, and support for physical ills. However to discuss psychological ills is less acceptable. To show stress is to show weakness. therefore, those under emotional stress often deny its existence.

Unfortunately, when stress is not dealt with, it takes its toll. Physically stress can aggravate many pre-existing conditions. The top selling prescription drugs in this country are used to treat conditions which are stress related. A large percentage of the visits to family physicians are stress related. For adolescents, failure to deal with stress often means an increase in psychological concerns such as depression, lethargy, anxiety, and fear. Stress may even trigger suicide attempts (Rice, 1981).

Our society endorses instant gratification. This notion is particularly reinforced for adolescents via the styles and fads they embrace. Most adolescents, like their adult counterparts, are looking for a fast, easy way to reduce stress. Because of pessimism about the future and focus on the present, many teens are searching for, and finding, momentary relief. They also are being reinforced for doing so by society. The coping mechanisms are often maladaptive. Alcoholism and other drug abuse, teenage pregnancy, eating disorders, runaways, and the perfect-child syndrome are running rampant in our society.

Ways Adolescents Choose to Cope with Stress

Society has paid little notice to the stressors adolescents experience. The exception, rather than the rule, is for parents to work with and talk to their children about coping with everyday stress. Schools are equally negligent. If anything, the emphasis in schools is moving toward a "back to basics" approach with reading, writing, and arithmetic the central focus. Consequently, teenagers are forced to find other outlets for coping with stress.

Unfortunately, many of the maladaptive ways of coping with stress have received extensive media attention. To find a magazine which does not contain full-page ads advocating the use of alcohol with friends and family is difficult to do. Often these ads are made more appealing through endorsements by celebrities and athletes. Widely watched soap operas and prime-time television advocates the virtues of sex with multiple partners and without much acknowledgement of pregnancy, disease risks, or moral issues. More than any other age group, teens are susceptible to this media bombardment. Messages about adaptive ways to deal with stressors are rare.

One of the most readily and socially acceptable ways teens maladaptively deal with stress is through the consumption of alcohol. Shertzer and Stone (1981) stated that approximately 90% of all teens have tried alcohol. It is easy to purchase, legally or illegally, in most states. Not only has a dramatic increase occurred in the use of alcohol but in the abuse as well. The National Institute on Alcohol Abuse and Alcoholism reports that 1.3 million American teens between the ages of 12 and 17 have some problem with alcohol (McCoy, 1982). Often these problems go undetected for long periods because of the availability of alcohol and its acceptance among teens and parents.

"There has been a dramatic increase in the extent of drug abuse other than alcohol," (Rice, 1981, p. 125). Many drugs have lost some of their stigma as more Americans turn to them as a means of reducing stress.

Unfortunately, drugs and alcohol do provide quick, albeit temporary, relief. Because of the focus on instant gratification, the quick relief of drugs is often seen as the only solution or as more tempting than a life-style change that includes stress reduction. Drugs also tend to loosen inhibitions. This is an attractive alternative for adolescents who are uncomfortable socially. For a few dollars they find talking, flirting, or simply being with each other easier. They allow, for a time, the avoidance of problems and the necessity of dealing with them.

Finally, in their own homes, adolescents are seeing their parents use and advocate use of alcohol and other drugs as stress reduces. It has been estimated that one-fifth of all adolescents come from homes where one or both parents have drinking problems (Hafen & Frandsen, 1986). Adolescents, then, are actually practicing what they see at home and in the media.

Teenage Pregnancy

Adolescence always has been a time to develop a sexual identity. However, many teens are using sexual activity as a way to deal with feelings of inadequacy and insecurity. They learn early that being "sexy" is often equated with being wanted. Being sexy means getting favors and compliments (Justice & Justice, 1979). Unfortunately, much of the information teens receive on developing a sexual identity is from either the popular press or each other. Consequently, teens are either uninformed or misinformed.

This lack of information may contribute to the increasing number of teen pregnancies. Births to unwed teen mothers have reached an all-time high. "Ten percent of all American teens get pregnant and six percent give birth," (Dacey, 1982, p. 256). In many high schools, it has become a status symbol to get pregnant and keep the child. Some parents and friends condone the event by having baby showers for pregnant teens. If teens keep their children, society must make changes to adapt to the developing societal patterns. Schools will need to offer tutoring and child care classes.

Many pregnant teens still seek to terminate their pregnancies. An estimated one-third of all abortions performed in the United States are on women under the age of 20. Approximately 40% of teenage pregnancies are terminated by abortion (Interdivisional Committee of Adolescent Abortion, 1987). Many women of all ages are ill-prepared to make a decision regarding abortions. Teenagers' insights are often clouded by parents, friends, and boyfriends. Many times the decision is made for them. Often, the only post-abortion counseling that is done is for birth control information.

Teens are receiving mixed messages about themselves, their sexuality, and the sex act. Unfortunately, they seem to be receiving minimal accurate information not only on the physiological aspects of sexuality but on the emotional and psychological aspects as well.

Runaways

Another way teens choose to escape a stressful situation is to physically remove themselves from it. Approximately 775,000 to 1 million teens run away annually (Shertzer & Stone, 1981; McCoy, 1982). Some of those teens are "throwaways," who, for a variety of reasons, have been told to leave or are "kicked out" of their homes. Often runaways have been abusive to or abused by their parents. Many come from homes where they have been victimized and/or exploited. The absence of communication makes them feel isolated. They believe nowhere, no place, no one is available for them to turn. So they run. With few financial resources and being emotionally ill-prepared to handle their feelings, they frequently turn to prostitution and child pornography. Escape from a perceived bad situation turns even worse.

Eating Disorders

As stated previously, teens are pressured to look like the "ideal" adolescent-male or female. For adolescent girls the pressure is to be thin. In fact, we have incorporated into our culture the saying "you can never be too rich or too thin." "Since adolescent women get so much confirmation from their appearance, they soon learn that their bodies are their mouthpiece" (Garner & Garfinkle, 1985, p. 90).

Unfortunately, adolescence is often a time of vulnerability due to such poor self-images (Gordon & Gordon, 1983). Therefore, pressure at this time to look a certain way only highlights insecurity and increases stress. An estimated one in four teenagers has trouble with some form of eating disorder. The ratio is not surprising given the premium our culture puts on youth and the social stigma against being overweight. (Garner & Garfinkle, 1985).

Eating disorders such as anorexia nervosa and bulimia are not dieting issues, however. Rather, adolescents seem to develop an eating disorder as a means of achieving a more acceptable appearance while gaining control over the stresses in their lives. Although previously considered a "female" disease, increasing numbers of males are developing eating disorders for many of the same reasons.

Perfect Child

Some adolescents deal with stressors by trying to be "perfect." These teens are fearful of making mistakes. They base their feelings, and consequently their actions about themselves on the opinion and feedback of others.

They often feel that parental love depends on their achievement (McCoy, 1982). Therefore, they push hard to succeed by their parent's standings, often negating any development of their "true" selves.

SUICIDE: THE ULTIMATE WAY OF COPING WITH STRESS

As adolescent suicides increase, more parents, teachers, and the general public are asking why so many young, capable, adolescents see suicide as their only alternative. Typically suicide is not the result of a single traumatic event. Usually a number of factors have accumulated for the adolescent with little coping skills. Suicide, then, can be seen as an act to relieve "thwarted or unfulfilled needs" (Shneidman, 1985, p. 126). It is a way out of a painful situation.

"Suicide is both a personal and social act," (Reynolds & Farberow, 1976, p. 33). In order to understand suicide we must try to understand both the adolescent and the social-cultural environment. In addition, suicide is a complex symptom evolving out of effects such as depression, anxiety, and anger (Pfeffer, 1985) in combination with environmental factors.

Recognizing the preceding as existing for teenagers, we can summarize common precipitators of adolescent suicide. We know that depression is common in adolescence (Rice, 1981). Depression is the most common factor in suicide (Hafen & Frandsen, 1986). Loneliness also is seen as a factor in suicide and chemical dependency (Dykeman, 1984). Family crisis or abuse are contributors to adolescent stress (Pfeffer, 1985). Social uninvolvement and solitary living (Trout, 1980) or at least lack of intimate involvement also may be contributors. Loss, whether it be of a person or a relationship, is a common precipitating event (Strauss, 1985) as are school difficulties and the pressure to perform. At least one in four of those adolescents who attempt or commit suicide have a parent who has attempted suicide (Hafen & Frandsen, 1986).

"Adolescents who attempt suicide also experience feelings of low self-esteem" (Capuzzi, 1986, p. 3). Because society does little to help teens feel good about themselves, teens are insecure and overwhelmed by various feelings. In fact, many adolescents have experienced one or many of the precipitators mentioned in the last paragraph. Couple the common precipitators of suicide with the lack of adaptive coping skills and one begins to see the possibility of suicide being viewed as an option by many teens.

Adolescents often have a romantic view of suicide (Dykeman, 1984). Many see it as the ultimate sacrifice or conversely, the ultimate revenge. Examples in literature, such as *Romeo and Juliet*, reinforce this notion as do many of the current examples in mass media. Those with suicidal intention may be encouraged to carry out the act because of current coverage by the media (Hawton, 1982).

Suicide can be seen as the most maladaptive means of communicating feelings of isolation, despair, fear, and anxiety. Unfortunately adolescents haven't been taught adaptive and less destructive ways of communicating these messages through living.

Suicide is one of the topics our society has tried to avoid. We simply do not have a very open attitude about death. Many adults are fearful and tend to avoid talking or thinking about death. In addition, only recently have we begun to look at ways to talk to children and adolescents about death. Rarely have parents, teachers, and teens themselves learned to talk to adolescents and each other about suicide. Only after several adolescents choose suicide do leaders in the community attempt usually to educate themselves and develop communication and "prevention plans."

REFERENCES

Anderson, P.K. (1984). *Adolescent maltreatment: Issues and program models.* (DHHS Publication No. OHDS 84-303391). Washington, DC: U.S. Department of Health and Human Services.

Capuzzi, D. (1986). Adolescent suicide: Prevention and intervention. *Counseling and Human Development*, 1-9.

Dacey, J.S. (1982). *Adolescent today* (2nd Ed.). Glenview, IL: Scott, Foresman.

Davis, P.A. (1983). *Suicidal adolescents.* Springfield, IL: Charles Thomas.

Dunphy, D.C. (1980). Peer group socialization. In R.E. Muuss (Ed.), *Adolescent behavior and society* (pp. 178-96).

Dykeman, B. (1984). Adolescent suicide: Recognition and intervention. *College Student Journal, 18*(4), 364-368.

Finch, S.M., Poznanski, E.D., & Waggoner, R.W. (1971). *Adolescent Suicide.* Springfield, IL: Charles C. Thomas.

Garner, D.M., & Garfinkel, P.E. (1985). *Handbook of psychotherapy for anorexia nervosa and bulimia.* New York: The Guilford Press.

Golombek, H. (1983). Personality development during adolescents: Implications for treatment. In B.D. Garfinkel & H. Golombek (Ed.), *The adolescent and mood disturbance* (pp. 1-14). New York: International University Press.

Gordon, S., & Gordon, J. (1983). *Raising a child conservatively in a sexually permissive world.* New York: Simon and Schuster.

Hafen, B.Q., & Frandsen, K.J. (1986). *Youth suicide: Depression and loneliness.* Evergreen, CO: Cordillera Press.

Hawton, K. (1982). Attempted suicide in children and adolescents. *Journal of Child Psychology and Psychiatry, 23*(4), 497-503.

Hawton, K., Cole, D., O'Grady, J., & Osborn, M. (1982). Motivational aspects of delicate self-poisoning in adolescents. *British Journal of Psychiatry, 141*, 286-291.

International Committee on Adolescent Abortion. (1987). Adolescent abortion psychological and legal issues. *American Psychologist, 42*(1), 73-78.

Justice, B., & Justice, R. (1979). *The broken taboo: Sex in the family.* New York: Human services Press.

Levine, S.V. (1983). Alienation as an effect in adolescence. In B.D. Garfinkel & H. Golombek (Eds.), *The adolescent and mood disturbance.* New York: International University Press.

McCoy, K. (1982). *Coping with teenage depression: A parents guide.* Bergenfield, NJ: New American Library.

Offer, D., & Franzen, S.A. (1983). Mood development in normal adolescents. In B.D. Garfinkel & H. Golombek (Eds.) (1985). *The adolescent and mood disturbance* (pp. 1-14). New York: International University Press.

Peck, M.L., Farberow, N.L., & Litman, R.E. (Eds.) (1985). *Youth suicide.* New York: Springer Publishing Company.

Pfeffer, C.R. (1985). Self-destructive behavior in children and adolescents, *Psychiatric Clinics of North America, 8*(2), 215-226.

Reynolds, D.K., & Farberow, N.L. (1976). *Suicide inside and out.* Berkley, CA: University of California Press.

Rice, F.P. (Ed.). (1981). *The adolescent.* Boston, MA: Allyn and Bacon.

Robon, B.E. (1987). Changing family patterns: Developmental impacts on Children. *Counseling and Human Development.*

Shertzer, B., & Stone, S.C. (1981). *Fundamentals of guidance* (4th ed.). Boston, MA: Houghton, Mifflin.

Shneidman, E. (1985). *Definition of suicide.* New York: John Wiley & Sons.

Strauss, M. (1985). "Acting-in" and "acting out": A comparison of dynamics in families of suicidal and delinquent young female adolescents. *Dissertation Abstracts International, 46,* 5-8.

Trout, D.L. (1980). The role of social isolation in suicide. *Suicide and Life Threatening Behavior, 10*(1), 11-21.

Woodward, K. (1978). "Saving the family." *Newsweek,* May 15.

PART II
PROFILE OF THE ATTEMPTER

CHAPTER **3**

BEHAVIORAL INDICATORS

Arlene Metha, Ph.D.
and
Helen Dunham, M.C., C.A.C.

Arlene Metha, Ph.D.

Associate Professor of Counseling Psychology
Division of Psychology in Education
Arizona State University
Tempe, AZ 85281

Arlene Metha received her B.A. degree from Arizona State University, M.A. degree from Ohio State University, and Ph.D. from the University of Southern California. She is currently an Associate Professor of Counseling Psychology in the Division of Psychology in Education at Arizona State University. Her major research has focused on adolescent suicide, in particular the gifted adolescent. During the past two years she has been studying stress, life changes, and suicide ideation among gifted adolescents. More recently, Dr. Metha (with others) was the recipient of a major endowment to study the relationship between substance abuse and suicide among teens.

She has published numerous articles and has received a number of grants to explore the topic of adolescent suicide. Dr. Metha is a member of the American Psychological Association (Divisions 17 and 35), American Association for Counseling and Development, American Association of Suicidology, American College Personnel Association, American Educational Research Association, and the National Association for Women Deans, Administrators and Counselors. She is a certified Psychologist in the State of Arizona.

Helen M. Dunham, M.C., C.A.C.

Director of Counseling
Terros Clinic
Phoenix, AZ 85017

Helen M. Dunham, M.C., C.A.C. is currently the Director of Counseling at TERROS, a non-profit mental health center, located in Phoenix, AZ. She received her Bachelors of Science degree in Psychology from Northern Arizona University in 1968 and her Masters in Counseling in 1986 from Arizona State University. Her diverse experience includes 10 years in business/industry and 9 years in the mental health field specializing in addictive behavior and suicidology.

EDITORIAL ABSTRACT: *To address adolescent behavioral indicators of suicide, it is important to first establish a conceptual baseline of "normal adolescent behavior." From this point of departure, a descriptive representation of the behavior, verbal and nonverbal, of the presuicidal adolescent can be discussed. The purpose of this chapter is to present the topic of behavioral indicators in an integrative manner by examining suicidal behavior in the context of family, school, and peer group.*

As one examines the literature concerning the behavioral indicators (clues or warning signs) of suicide, one is struck by the fact that a considerable conflict of opinion exists concerning the importance of these verbal and nonverbal clues. For example, some suicidologists believe that behavioral indicators or clues are not obvious, but others suggest that most, if not all, adolescents will give clear warning signs prior to their self-destructive behavior. The following statements exemplify the diversity of opinions concerning suicidal clues:

> The majority of adolescents who attempt suicide do not give those people around them any signals in the form of recognizable changes in behavior that the event is forthcoming. (Finch & Poznanski, 1971, p.3)

> It is impossible to crystallize a specific presuicidal syndrome that predicts if an adolescent will commit a suicidal act. (Otto, 1964, p. 387)

Contrast the two preceding statements with the three that follow:

> The teenager who has reached a point of seriously considering suicide never fails to send out warning signals. (O'Roark, 1982, p. 16)

> Of the serious suicide attempts, prodromal clues were present in over 70 percent of the cases. (Perlstein, 1966, p. 3017)

> The clues to possible suicide are thus readily available to almost any sensitive person who cares enough to see and respond to one whose life is hanging in the balance. (Parker, 1974, p. 70)

Most authors writing of suicide have devoted approximately 2 to 8 pages to the subject of behavioral indicators. The paucity of material on this topic may exist because identifying the most salient clues that could serve as reliable indicators of an individual's struggle with life and death is a difficult, if not impossible task. The purpose of this chapter is to argue that most of the literature to date has attempted to describe the "clues" without addressing the environment or setting from which they spring. To address adolescent behavioral indicators of suicide, we must first establish a conceptual baseline of "normal adolescent behavior." From this baseline a descriptive representation of the behavior, verbal and nonverbal, of the presuicidal adolescent can be posited.

The goal of this chapter is to present the topic of behavioral indicators in an integrative manner by examining suicidal behavior in the context of family, school, and peer group. Far too many writings in the past have simply listed the behavioral signs, leading readers to believe falsely that they possessed a recipe for prevention.

THE NORMAL ADOLESCENT

The adolescent has been described in history and in theory as a young person wrought with turmoil and stress who is a challenge to teachers, therapists, and particularly to parents. Plato and other Greek writers held a view of youth as a time of marked emotional upheaval. Shakespeare described Elizabethan teenagers as spending their time doing little more than "wronging the ancientry." And Anna Freud (1958) described adolescence as a period characterized as an interruption of peaceful growth (p. 255). G. Stanley Hall (1904), a pioneer in adolescent psychology, also described adolescence as time of "turmoil":

> The teens are emotionally unstable and pathic. It is a natural impulse to experience hot and perfervid psychic states, and the whole is characterized by emotionalism. (p. 74-5)

One of the major impacts of Hall's theory was to establish the belief that conflict was an inescapable component of adolescent development. In contrast, Margaret Mead (1928) challenged this theory with her anthropological account of other societies in which adolescents developed without major upheavals. Her observations and later findings contested the belief that adolescents and those around them must experience "storm and stress."

Without question for some, adolescence is a difficult and stressful time. For others, it is a relatively smooth transition between childhood and adulthood. For many researchers the important question is not whether turmoil does or does not exist, but whether or not it is correct to expect that every adolescent will pass through a tumultous period. Offer, Ostrov, and Howard (1981) suggested that the prevailing attitude is questionable:

> The often-cited attitudes that such adolescents are "going through a stage," or that he or she "will outgrow this," may harm the teenager. A disturbed youngster is done no service when his mood swings are inaccurately seen as predictable, his negative affect as typical, and his extreme rebellion as understandably normal. Even more ironically, no good comes of seeing an adolescent's disturbed adjustment as confirmation of a theory about how normal adolescents feel and behave. Instead, we should ask, "How does this adolescent compare to others who cope successfully?" (p. 93)

Without a depiction of the normal adolescent, a danger exists of overlooking and minimizing true adolescent disturbance and passing it off as mere transitory pubertal reactions. This is of particular concern for mental health practitioners involved with potentially suicidal adolescents.

One attempt to clarify true disturbance and distinguish it from normal adolescent behavior was that of Oldham (1980). He reviewed several longitudinal studies of patient and nonpatient adolescents and found that normal adolescents manifested the following behaviors:

1. Most adolescents maintained psychic equilibrium while struggling with the developmental tasks.

2. Adolescent development was generally associated with successful family adjustment.

3. Turmoil was normatively manifested in mild forms of depression and minor disagreements with authority figures.

Other reviewers, such as Coleman (1979), Ellis (1979), and Rutter (1980), essentially arrived at the same conclusions as Oldham. Rather than saying that all adolescents experience a great deal of stress and disturbance, probably a more accurate statement would be that some adolescents experience a great deal of stress and disturbance, some very little, and the others a moderate amount. Of the disturbed adolescents who were studied by Ostrov, Offer, and Hartlage (1984), the prevalence of disturbed adolescents warranting psychiatric intervention ranged from 10 to 30%; onephalf of those identified by the researchers as needing psychiatric intervention were not recognized by adult family members as needing help.

Offer, Ostrov, and Howard (1984) studied large groups of normal adolescents from a variety of cultures. Their depiction of normal adolescents in our culture, in the 1980s, was of adolescents who reportedly enjoyed life and were happy most of the time. They felt that others treated them fairly, and they believed they could control themselves in ordinary life situations. They also felt relaxed under usual circumstances. Most felt proud of their physical development and believed they were strong and healthy. They reported pleasure from doing a job well, were positive about their future careers, and wished not to be supported for the rest of their lives. Most saw themselves making friends easily and believed they would be successful both socially and vocationally. The majority stated that for them having a friend of the opposite sex was important and most were not afraid of their sexuality. They did not report major difficulties with their parents or other intergenerational conflicts in the present, nor did they perceive any major difficulty in the past or expect any major changes in the future. They saw themselves as capable of coping with new situations, enjoyed challenges, and tried to learn in advance about novel situations. Most were optimistic, confident, and liked to put things in order. They expressed a willingness to do the work necessary to achieve, and if they failed, believed they could learn from the experience. Finally, normal adolescents did not see themselves having psychopathological symptoms and on the whole, saw themselves as having no major problems.

These researchers also found gender differences but no significant age variations. The girls exhibited more negative feelings about their moods and described themselves as more lonely, sad, and vulnerable to being hurt. They felt less positive about their body changes and body image than the boys. The girls professed stronger social values, were more empathic and concerned about the welfare of others, and exhibited a need to express the truth. They also had stronger ties to family and friends. Lastly, the girls expressed a preference for the work ethic. The boys on the other hand, showed more autonomy, were less other-directed, and demonstrated a willingness to stop short of nothing if someone wronged them. They saw themselves as leaders and were less attached to their relatives and friends. In general, the girls reported strong coping abilities, but not as strong as those described by their male counterparts.

Offer, Ostrov, and Howard (1984) did not find the normal adolescent in the throes of turmoil, and they felt that these adolescents adjusted adequately. They concluded:

> The vast majority of those teenagers function well, enjoy good relationships with their families and friends, and accept the values of the larger society. In addition, most report having adapted without undue conflict to the bodily changes and emerging sexuality brought on by puberty. The only notable symptom that we encountered among normals was a situation-specific anxiety that normal adolescents can handle without undue trauma. (p. 12)

We have focused on the normal adolescent to establish a baseline for comparison. As mentioned earlier, a relatively large number of disturbed adolescents often go unnoticed and can be described as the "quietly disturbed." Ostrov et al. (1984) stated that "members of this group often become known only when they emerge from their quietness and loneliness with a sudden desperate act such as suicide or homicide" (p. 73). Perhaps the inability to assess these teenagers as disturbed is a result of promulgating the belief that they are just "going through a stage, and they will eventually snap out of it."

Adults must learn to listen with empathy to adolescents' descriptions of their internal and external worlds. They must compare the description of the adolescent population of one generation with that of another, and whenever possible, consider the changes in an adolescent's behavior over time. Otherwise, there is always the danger of minimizing an adolescent's distress and possible desperate plea for help.

THE NORMAL FAMILY

Critical to the development of the adolescent is the family system, and specialists in adolescent psychology have come to recognize the need to look at adolescent development within the context of the family (Carter & McGoldrick, 1980; Haley, 1973; Minuchin, 1974). In this section we are interested in providing a behavioral baseline of the normal family. We believe that the suicidal adolescent often develops within a dysfunctional family system; thus, knowledge of the normal family system may provide an important backdrop for better understanding the suicidal youngster.

Westley and Epstein (1969) identified several family variables associated with the mental health of adolescents. For example, they found couples with happy and healthy teenagers felt emotionally close, met each other's needs, encouraged positive self-images in each other, were clear about their identities, and saw their children as distinct from themselves. Other predictors of positive family mental health were a balanced division of labor and acceptance of parental roles.

Beyond the basic task of assuring physical survival of family members, Lewis, Beavers, Gossett, and Phillips (1976) stated that the well-functioning family had the capability of providing each family member with the optimal balance of separateness and attachment required for attainment of individual developmental goals. These researchers referred to separateness as the ability to experience oneself as a differentiated person, autonomously functioning and responsible for one's own life. They referred to attachment as the ability to relate to others, to make commitments, and to exercise the capacity for initimacy. Lewis et al. also found that normal parents were authoritative but not authoritarian; they were in charge but without rigid rules that applied at all times. Even though other relationships were important, no competing parent-child coalitions were found in the optimal families. These families were also characterized by high levels of autonomy along with high levels of closeness. Problems were usually solved efficiently by negotiation, and if a compromise could not be reached, the parents traditionally had the last word. Empathic responses and affectionate messages were common; the family mood was one of warmth, humor, and optimism. When tensions, disagreements, and family losses occurred, the optimal families appeared to know how to cope.

As a result of the National Family Strengths Research Project, Stinnett (1983) reported six qualities present in strong families.

1. Members express a great deal of appreciation for one another.
2. Family members make the effort to structure their lifestyles so that they have time to spend together.
3. Direct communication is an important component.
4. Promotion of each other's happiness and well-being takes precedence.
5. Commitment to a spiritual life-style is important.
6. An ability to cope with crisis is a high priority.

With a brief background of the so-called "normal adolescent" and "normal family," we can now turn to identification of the pre-suicidal adolescent.

IDENTIFYING THE PRE-SUICIDAL ADOLESCENT

The precursors to suicide have been termed "prodromal clues," which are considered to be important predictors of a potential suicide (Shneidman, 1965).

In reading the list of psychological indicators remember that if an adolescent exhibits any of the clues that are described, such clues should not be extrapolated immediately to mean that the adolescent is at risk for suicide. Deykin (1984) suggested that adolescents who display such clues may merely be exhibiting manifestations of so called "normal" adolescent development. Or the behavioral clues may be appropriate responses to certain situational stressors. According to Deykin, one or two behaviors or symptoms of a brief duration should not be construed automatically as pre-suicidal indicators. However, if the youth displays these behaviors over a period of several weeks, he/she may very well be issuing "a cry for help" as a prelude to a self-destructive act.

Parker (1974) summarized the tenuous interpretation of such clues:

> While some authorities feel that more clues are likely given by younger rather than older persons, and by the attempters more often than those determined to die, the consensus is still that in virtually all, the desire for life is as strong as any impulse to die. Hearing, seeing, and responding with helpful concern can make all the difference. (p. 70)

In the following sections of this chapter, the verbal and nonverbal warning signs or clues will be presented within the context of psychosocial, familial, psychiatric, and situational indicators of suicide.

PSYCHOSOCIAL INDICATORS OF ADOLESCENT SUICIDE

The psychosocial indicators of adolescent suicide pertain to the social influences as well as psychological processes that influence an individual's behavior. The following psychosocial indicators will be examined: (1) poor self-esteem and feelings of inadequacy, (2) hypersensitivity and suggestibilty, (3) the need to achieve perfection, (4) a sudden change in social behavior, such as giving away a prized possession, (5) rapid deterioration of performance or attendance in school, and (6) underachievement and learning disabilities.

Poor Self-Esteem and Feelings of Inadequacy

Low self-esteem traditionally has been described as a component of personality and/or depression (Pearlin & Schooler, 1978; Rosenberg, 1965). Self-esteem also has been viewed as a predictor or barometer of an individual's ability to cope with life stress (Dohrenwend & Dohrenwend, 1981; Hughes & Gove, 1981; Lin, Dean, & Ensel, 1986; Wheaton, 1983). According to Rosenberg (1965), low self-esteem implies "self-rejection, self-dissatisfaction, and self-contempt" (pp. 30-1). In short, poor self-esteem breeds feelings of inadequacy.

In an exploratory study of adolescent suicide attempters, Tishler and McKenry (1983) found that adolescent suicide attempters displayed significantly less self-esteem than nonattempters.

Hypersensitivity and Suggestibility

Husain and Vandiver (1984) stated that the adolescent who is hypersensitive and suggestible may be at risk for suicide. Other researchers have studied the phenomenon of suggestion, imitation, and contagion and have reported that imitative learning is influenced by a number of factors such as characteristics of the model, rewards associated with the observed behavior, identification with the decedent, etc. (Bandura, 1977; Gould & Shaffer, 1986; Phillips & Carstensen, 1986).

Although examination of the role of imitation and suggestibility in adolescent suicide is still in its infancy, the data appear sufficient to conclude that presenting media coverage of suicide within an aura of romanticization may be dangerous, particularly to youth who are most vulnerable (Gould & Shaffer, 1986; Phillips & Carstensen, 1986).

Perfectionism

One of the subpopulations of youth who are most susceptible to perfectionism are gifted adolescents. Delisle (1984) suggested that a link exists between giftedness and suicide which is often manifested in the form of an overwhelming desire to achieve perfection. He also pointed out that additional stressors are placed on gifted youngsters which put them at high risk: self and societal expectations, the feeling that one's gifts and talents can and should benefit society, and the strain of being intellectually capable while at the same time often socially immature.

Leroux (1986) summarized the "catch-22" situation that some gifted adolescents find themselves in:

> Gifted youngsters can have an overly demanding image of self because of their personal high expectations. When a discrepancy occurs between ideal self-aspiration, unrealistic goals, and low self-esteem, there is the potential for high risk. (p. 77)

Sudden Change in Social Behavior

Most experts agree that an important danger sign for suicide can be a sudden change in social behavior. For example, if an adolescent gives away his/her most prized possessions, such as a favorite collection of music tapes, a stereo, or a musical instrument, it could be a clue that the individual is contemplating the severing of social ties and ultimately, the severing of life.

Academic Deterioration

Suicidal adolescents have typically demonstrated greater withdrawal from and less involvement with the milieu than is true for non-suicidal adolescents (Berman, 1986). Teachers and counselors are in a good position to note any sudden or rapid deterioration of performance or attendance in school. Such a decline in performance may be attributed to a number of problems such as school phobia, disruptive interpersonal behavior, or a general preoccupation with emotional concerns and conflicts.

Although Sartore (1976) did not find a correlation between failure in school and suicide, he did suggest that school failure may lead to loneliness; loneliness, in turn, can prompt depression, which is associated with suicide.

In a study of adolescents 12 to 18 years of age who had been admitted to a hospital because of self-destructive behavior or strong suicidal threats, Gispert, Wheeler, Marsh, and Davis (1985) found that of the 80% who were enrolled in school, 45% were typically truant or did not attend school at all and only 50% were at the appropriate grade level.

Underachievement and Learning Disabilities

The youngster who consistently experiences feelings of failure despite expending effort and a desire to succeed, will often experience learned helplessness--a belief that failure cannot be avoided (Hiroto & Seligman, 1975; Maier & Seligman, 1976; Seligman, 1975). Thomas (1979) identified these negative self-attributes as typical of individuals who have been identified as learning disabled. According to Thomas, the learning disabled individual tends to attribute his/her failures to a lack of ability rather than a lack of effort.

Peck (1985) reported that in a 1978 study of adolescents under the age of 15 who had committed suicide, 50% had been diagnosed as learning disabled. The following vignette presented by Peck illustrates such a victim:

> A typical case example of a youngster in this category is that of 13-year-old Michael, the oldest of two children. Michael came from an intact middle-class family in southern California. As a fourth grader he had been diagnosed as hyperkinetic, placed on Ritalin, and entered into a special treatment program. While this helped somewhat with his disruptive behavior, his ability to concentrate was still limited. Michael was described as having a very poor frustration level and would frequently show aggressive behavior toward his peers. He was teased for his bad temper. By the time he had reached the seventh grade, he had rather poor relationships with his peers, except for one friend. He was involved in an intense, rebellious, independent struggle on the one hand, yet overly dependent on his family on the other. As a result he always seemed to be fighting with his family. He would

frequently express feelings of unhappiness and dissatisfaction with his life to people around him. After no particular precipitating stress, approximately two weeks before his thirteenth birthday, he found his father's gun and shot himself in the head. (p. 116)

TABLE 3.1
Psychosocial Indicators of Adolescent Suicide

Indicators	Evidence/Description
1. Poor self esteem and feelings of inadequacy.	Typically manifested by an element of personality or depression; a predictor of the ability to cope with life stress.
2. Hypersensitivity and suggestibility	Often manifested in the form of imitation which may be associated with suicide contagion.
3. Perfectionism	Often evident among gifted adolescents who feel the need to fulfill societal expectations.
4. Sudden change in social behavior.	Often manifested in giving away one's prized possessions.
5. Academic deterioration	Exhibits itself by sudden and rapid deterioration of performance or attendance in school
6. Underachievement and learning disabilities	Identified by feelings of failure, learned helplessness, negative self attitudes. Often evidenced by attribution of failure to a lack of ability rather than a lack of effort.

Sources: Delisle, 1984; Dohrenwend & Dohrenwend, 1981; Gould & Shaffer, 1986; Husain & Vandiver, 1984; Pearlin & Schooler, 1978; Peck, 1985; Phillips & Carstensen, 1986; Rosenberg, 1965; Sartore, 1976; Seligman, 1975; Thomas, 1979.

FAMILIAL INDICATORS OF ADOLESCENT SUICIDE

The familial indicators of adolescent suicide pertain to some of the origins of suicidal crisis that emanate from the interaction of the adolescent and his/her family. The following familial indicators will be examined: (1) disintegrating family relationships, (2) economic difficulties and other family stresses, (3) child and adolescent abuse, (4) ambivalence between dependence on family vs. independence, (5) running away, (6) unrealistic personal or parental expectations, and (7) a family history of suicidal behavior.

Disintegrating Family Relationships

A finding common to many studies of attempted suicide in adolescents is that in a significant number of cases there is a history of a disintegrating family or broken home (Bergstrand & Otto, 1962; Hawton, 1986; Jacobs, 1971; Walker, 1980).

Hoff (1978) presented the following vignette that describes how a disintegrating family relationship can precipitate a suicide attempt:

> Sally, age 16, made a suicide attempt by swallowing six sleeping pills, which is a medically non-serious attempt. Though she contemplated death, she also wanted to live. That is, she hoped that the suicide attempt would bring about some change in her miserable family life so that she could avoid the last resort of suicide itself. Before her suicide attempt, Sally was having trouble in school, she ran away from home once, experimented with drugs, and in general engaged in behavior that brought disapproval from her parents.
>
> All these behaviors are Sally's way of saying "Listen to me," "Can't you see that I'm miserable...that I can't control myself...that I can't go on like this anymore?"
>
> Sally had been upset for several years by her parents' constant fighting and favoritism among the children. Her father drank heavily and frequently was away from home. When Sally's school counselor had recommended family counseling, they refused out of shame. Her acting out was really a cry for help. (p. 115)

Tishler, McKenry, and Morgan (1981) found over half (52%) of the adolescents they studied who had made a suicide attempt identified parental problems as the reason for their attempt. Crumley (1979) studied 40 adolescent patients who had attempted suicide and found a similar pattern, with 32% of the adolescent suicide attempters reporting family discord, primarily through divorce.

In a study by Toolan (1968), of approximately 900 children and adolescents who were hospitalized for suicide threats or attempts, an impressive number came from disorganized homes; fewer than one-third resided with both parents. Toolan also found that fathers were significantly absent from the homes of the suicidal youth.

Hawton, O'Grady, Osborn, and Cole (1982) studied 50 adolescents, including 45 girls aged 13 to 18 who had taken overdoses; these researchers found that ¾ of the adolescents had difficulties with one or both parents. The adolescents also complained about their inability to discuss their problems with their parents, especially with their fathers. These data are consistent with other similar studies (Garfinkle & Golombek, 1983; Jacobs, 1971; Rohn, Sarles, Kenny, Reynolds, & Head, 1977).

Economic Difficulties and Other Family Stresses

At times of great family stress (e.g., unemployment, recurring illness of a parent or sibling, alcoholism, etc.), the relatives of the adolescent often will no longer be able to function as usual, and may feel obligated to either attempt to maintain their own defenses or keep up a false appearance that "everything is okay." According to Richman (1986), once this state of intolerable stress is achieved, the family is no longer helpful to the suicidal adolescent, and the teenager is left not only to face his/her own despair and self-hate but also to face the cumulative despair of others. The accumulation of economic difficulties and family stresses can place the vulnerable adolescent in a very precarious emotional state.

Other family stresses with which many adolescents find difficult to cope include parental loss and general conflict with parents. In an examination of parental loss as a mediating variable for suicide, Stanley and Barter (1970) found that the child's age at the time of loss was the pivotal mediating variable, rather than the occurrence or nonoccurrence of loss. These researchers reported that 16 of the 17 adolescents they studied who had attempted suicide had lost one or both parents before age 12.

Crook and Raskin (1975) broadened the notion of parental loss to include divorce, desertion, and separation, in addition to death of a parent; all were described as correlates of a suicide attempt.

Several studies have included information concerning the importance of parental conflict in adolescent suicide. Schrut (1964) found that ambivalence toward the child by the parents, alcohol abuse by parents, marital discord, economic stressors, hypercritical discipline, and "coldness" differentiated suicide attempters from non-attempters. In a study of female teens, Cantor (1976) suggested that this conflict may have led to an inability to request parental help. Her findings were similar to those of Grollman (1971) and Teicher (1970), who also reported parental conflict was a mediating variable in adolescent suicide.

Child and Adolescent Abuse

For the suicidal adolescent, sexual abuse, physical harm, or emotional abuse may become "the straw that broke the camel's back." Shafii, Carrigan, Whittinghill, and Derrick (1985) found that a parental history of emotional problems, abusiveness, and absence were all significant factors for children and adolescents who had committed suicide.

Egeland, Cicchetti, and Taraldson (1976) found that among families in which child or adolescent abuse occurred, a higher-than-average degree of frustration was present in addition to many stressors including marital discord, high unemployment, and alcohol abuse. With the adolescent in particular, many incidents of physical abuse were outcomes of the parent's reactions to the youth's acting out behavior such as fighting, sexual promiscuity, or aggression (Herrenkohl, Herrenkohl, & Egolt, 1983).

Kosky (1983) reported a history of child abuse for 60% of the children who had made attempts on their lives but for only 4% of the nonsuicidal psychiatrically ill children.

Roberts and Hawton (1980) found an interesting link between child abuse and suicide among parents rather than adolescents. They found that in 29% of the families with reported child abuse, one or both parents had attempted suicide.

Ambivalence Between Dependence vs. Independence

In a comprehensive study of 100 families with suicidal members, Richman (1971) identified 14 characteristics or patterns common to families with suicidal members, and that collective set of patterns he called "the suicidal family system." Of the 14 patterns, the following five touch on the conflict between an adolescent's desire for independence and a tremendous need for dependency.

1. **Intolerance for Separation:** For a suicidal family, the idea of separation becomes a very threatening possibility. According to Richman, a reason for this heightened sensitivity to separation may be that a majority of suicidal families have experienced more incidents of loss or separation than their non-suicidal family counterparts.
2. **Symbiosis without Empathy.** A unique characteristic of the suicidal family is the exploitation of the suicidal individual by other family members. Because the family cannot perceive the suicidal individual as a separate entity, the needs of the suicidal member are not recognized or acknowledged.
3. **Fixation upon Infantile Patterns.** Because growth, maturity, and change are often equated with loss and separation, the suicidal family will encourage and foster a fixation on the earlier stages of the adolescent's development to prevent the ultimate loss or separation.
4. **Fixation upon Earlier Social Roles.** According to Richman, a characteristic of suicidal families that is similar to their fixation upon an earlier infantile pattern is their tendency to identify with and act out earlier social roles to preserve the security of an earlier life period.
5. **Closed Family System.** Because any change will lead to disequilbrium and will affect or threaten the established family system, the suicidal family will exhibit a

low tolerance for contacts outside the traditional family.

Even though several writers have stated that the period of adolescence need not be one of turbulence and great emotional stress (Douvan & Adelson, 1958; Josselson, 1980; Mead, 1939), most writers of adolescent psychology would agree that because adolescents in our society remain "in the nest" longer than is true in other societies, this probably makes it all the more essential for them to establish some elements of a separation between their own world and the world of their parents (Gleitman, 1986).

Running Away

Adolescents often have difficulty communicating their thoughts and feelings with an adult. As a result, adolescents may communicate their distress silently by running away. Peck and Litman (1975) have reported that 60% of runaway youth cite difficulty in communicating with parents, and 90% of suicidal teens claim that their families do not understand them.

English (1973) concluded that adolescents run away from home for the following reasons: (1) getting out of a destructive family situation, as in the case of a girl who ran away to avoid sexual advances of a family member; (2) running away with the thought of bettering the family situation; and (3) trying to escape from an unsharable problem such as pregnancy.

Homer (1974) classified runaway girls as "run from's" who were running away because they were unable to resolve their anger and conflict at home and "run to's" who were seeking something outside the home such as sex, drugs, liquor, or escape from school. Homer found a number of these adolescents who are "run from's" were attempting to escape from an intolerable situation at home.

Sabbath (1969) described the runaway as the "expendable child," typically a depressed youngster who becomes so much of a disturbance to the family that the family members want the child to leave and literally drive the child away.

Unrealistic Personal And Parental Expectations

Victoroff (1983) described how some children may be victimized by the exploitative plans and ambitions of their parents. For example:

> A junior high girl seemed to have talent as a singer. Her ambitious mother pressed her to learn voice. She was never permitted friends, social interaction with her peers, physical recreation, or dates with boys. Her time was taken up either with school or with voice instruction. Her mother reacted to the girl's failure to win an important contest by berating her with accusations that she had failed to prepare herself adequately, concluding with: "I gave up my life for you, and this is the thanks I get." The girl died of injuries suffered when she jumped out the window of the apartment house where she had lived with her mother. (p. 56)

To the casual observer, the appearance may be that adolescent suicidal behavior is closely related to actual or anticipated academic failure. In reality, one often finds that the real pressure did not emanate from the school but rather from the unrealistic or extraordinarily high standards that many youth tend to internalize in order to meet or satisfy parental demands.

Family History of Suicidal Behavior

The probability of suicide increases among adolescents with a parent or relative who has committed suicide. Murphy and Wetzel (1982) studied family histories of 127 patients hospitalized following a suicide attempt. Among the suicide attempters with a diagnosis of primary affective disorder, 17% gave a family history of suicide, 17% a family history of suicide attempt, and 4% a family history of suicide threat. In a similar study, Tishler, McKenry, and Morgan (1981) also found that 22% of 108 adolescent suicide attempters treated at a children's hospital emergency service reported that "at least one family member had exhibited suicidal behavior" (p. 88).

Roy (1983) corroborated Tishler, McKenry, and Morgan's findings and found that among psychiatric patients with a family history of suicide, approximately 50% had attempted suicide at least once. Roy also found that the age of the child at the time of the parent's suicide was critical. For example, of the patients who were less than 11 years old at the time of their parent's suicide, ¾ of these patients attempted suicide. Victoroff (1983) suggested that exposure to suicide of a relative, friend, or peer increases the suicide potential for the survivor.

TABLE 3.2
Familial Indicators of Adolescent Suicide

Indicators	Evidence/Description
1. Disintegrating family relationships	Often manifested via family discord and conflict, broken homes, disorganized or disengaged families, and parental loss through death, divorce, or separation.
2. Economic difficulties and family stresses	Evidenced by cumulative life stress, in particular unemployment, alcoholism, family illness, etc.
3. Child and adolescent abuse	Manifested in sexual abuse, physical harm or emotional abuse which often emanates from parent's reactions to youth's acting out behavior, sexual promiscuity and aggression.
4. Ambivalence of dependency vs. independence	Evidenced by an inability to tolerate separation, symbiosis without empathy, fixation on infantile patterns of past, fixation on earlier social roles and closed family system.
5. Running away	Evidenced by an avoidance of a destructive family situation, hoping to better the plight of the family, or trying to escape from an unsharable secret. Includes "running from" and "running to" behavior.
6. Unrealistic parental demands	Manifested in the exploitation of youth by ambitious parent's unrealistic or extraordinary expectations.
7. Family history of suicide.	Manifested in a suicide or suicide threat from a family member or significant other.

Sources: Crook & Raskin, 1975; Egeland, Cicchetti, & Taraldson, 1976; Hawton, 1986; Herrenkohl, Herrenkohl, & Egolt, 1983; Homer, 1974; Jacobs, 1971; Murphy & Wetzel, 1982; Peck & Litman, 1975; Richman, 1971; Richman, 1986; Tishler, McKenry, & Morgan, 1981; Roy, 1983; Victoroff, 1983.

PSYCHIATRIC INDICATORS OF ADOLESCENT SUICIDE

The following psychiatric indicators of adolescent suicide will be examined: (1) prior suicide attempt; (2) any talk of suicide or self-harm; (3) preoccupation with death, including essays, poems, or other written work that openly or implicitly consider suicide; (4) repeated episodes of serious self-destructive ideation; (5) dare-devil or self-abusive behavior; (6) open signs of mental illness such as delusions and hallucinations; (7) an overwhelming sense of guilt and shame; (8) obsessional self-doubt; (9) phobic anxiety; and (10) clinical depression.

Prior Suicide Attempt

One of the most revealing signs of suicidal risk is a prior suicide attempt. Grollman (1971) reported that 12% of those individuals who attepted suicide will try again and succeed within a period of two years.

Berman (1986) described the adolescent suicide attempter as an individual who is extremely vulnerable. According to Berman, "once despairing enough to jeopardize one's life even without the intent to die, the likelihod of future and perhaps more lethal suicidal behavior increases" (p. 157).

A prior suicide attempt is perhaps the singlemost significant predictor of suicidal behavior for all groups.

Any Talk of Suicide or Self-Harm

Another very revealing sign of suicidal risk includes any talk or verbalization of suicide or self-harm. Moldeven (1985) suggested that an adolescent suicide might be prevented if a family is able to recognize certain clues in the adolescent's communication. These might include repeated talk of death or suicide threats. Examples of such remarks actually made by individuals who later took their own lives were as follows:

> "My family would be better off without me."
>
> "I'm going to end it all. I can't stand this any more."
>
> "I don't want to be a burden." (pp. C-21 and C-22)

"I won't be around much longer for you to put up with me."

The research data concerning verbalizations or talk of self-harm clearly questions the myth that adolescents who talk about suicide seldom commit suicide.

Preoccupation With Death, Including Essays, Poems, and Other Written Work That Openly or Implicitly Consider Suicide

O'Roark (1982) suggested that suicidal teens frequently will "become preoccupied with the notion of death in music, art, poetry, or journals they write" (p. 22). Parachini (1984) quoted Cantor who suggested that if an abrupt redirection of interest to literature that deals with depression and self-destruction has occurred, then a parent should ask his/her daughter/son about the reasons for the change in reading habits. English and art teachers need to be particularly mindful of hints or clues of a preoccupation with death in the adolescent's school related assignments.

Repeated Episodes of Serious Self-Destructive Ideation

Richman (1986) pointed out that "everything else can be present, but if the suicidal intent is absent then there will be no suicide. The explicit suicidal reaction can range from those fleeting thoughts that are virtually universal to a careful plan such as the purchase of a gun" (p. 67).

In a study of 132 adolescents, Friedrich, Reams, and Jacobs (1982) reported that suicidal ideation was a highly different phenomenon than depression and that the severity of suicidal ideation was related to family social climate. Although no clear evidence is available of an association between suicide ideation and suicide attempt, or between suicide ideation and a suicide gesture, sufficient evidence appears to suggest that suicidal ideation accompanied by depression does correlate highly with suicidal behavior (Goldberg, 1981; Vandivort, Locke, & Locke, 1979).

When considering the issue of suicide ideation, those of us who work with adolescents should not be influenced by a false sense of security when a teenager denies having any suicidal thoughts or ideas. According to Fawcett, Scheftner, Clark, Hedeker, Gibbons, and Coryell (1987), more than one-half of the patients they studied who died by suicide within six months of assessment reported mild or no suicidal ideation.

Dare-devil or Self-Abusive Behaviors

Adolescents with poor impulse control are also at risk for suicide and may be responding to a particularly stressful situation (Husain & Vandiver, 1984). Their response to the stressor(s) may be a mask or camouflage for a potential suicide attempt. Concerning the dare-devil phenomenon, many teenagers are desperately ambivalent about taking their life and they initiate a dangerous course of action that they may or may not carry to completion. That course of action is very much contingent upon their impulse control at the moment (Coleman, Butcher, & Carson, 1984).

Gordon (1986) described the period of adolescence as one of "risk-taking" and drew a comparison between high risk activities and death fears:

> Descriptions of the emotions experienced in situations of high risk are similar to descriptions of sexual feelings--exhilaration, sensations of danger, heightened physical awareness, exquisite sensation, suspension of logical thought, lack of anxiety, and testing of physical limits. Sexual feelings and death fears are hidden in ordinary situations. Dangerous situations stimulate both. High risk activities are ways of testing the body, while still remaining cloaked in the remnants of belief in immortality. At the same time, such activities may provide an outlet for sexual tensions and fears. (p. 27)

Open Signs of Mental Illness Such as Delusions or Hallucinations

The research concerning the association between mental illness and suicide behavior is mixed. Some researchers have claimed that only a small proportion of suicidal adolescents suffer from mental illness. For example, researchers have studied the details of 320 cases of suicide among high school students and concluded that only 10% "were already of unsound mind"

(Parachini, 1984, p. 17). Hawton and associates (1982) found that among adolescent suicide attempters, a psychiatric disorder was rare, although almost 25% had seen a psychiatrist at some time. They did find that a small group of the adolescents appeared to be developing severe depressive symptoms, but these symptoms were typically of a transient nature.

Other researchers, such as Seiden (1969), have suggested that depression and schizophrenia are two mental disorders that are frequently associated with suicide. (The relationship of clinical depression to adolescent suicide is discussed in greater detail in a later section of this chapter.) Toolan (1962) and Balser and Masterson (1959) have provided additional support for a positive relationship between schizophrenia and suicidal tendencies in adolescents.

Overwhelming Sense of Guilt or Shame

Feelings of guilt or shame usually arise from a behavior that is contrary to one's ethical principles and involves both a sense of devaluation and concern growing out of a fear of punishment (Coleman, Butcher, & Carson, 1984). For example, the adolescent who is fearful of facing parents because of an unwanted pregnancy or contemplated abortion may experience an overwhelming sense of guilt or shame which could precipitate a serious depressive episode or suicide attempt.

Obsessional Self-doubt

Some adolescents may exhibit an overanxious behavior that resembles obsessional self-doubt. Such adolescents may also exhibit perfectionistic ideas and become obsessed over disappointing others, particularly their parents. Coleman, Butcher, and Carson (1984) illustrated such behavior in the following vignette:

> Cindy, an overweight eleven-year-old girl, was taken to the emergency room of a hospital following an "attack" of dizziness, faintness, and shortness of breath. She believed she was having a heart attack because of discomfort she was experiencing in her chest. Cindy had a long history of health problems and concerns and was a frequent visitor to doctors. She had missed, on the average, three days of school a week since school had begun four months before. Cindy was viewed by her mother as a "very good girl" but "sickly." Cindy was very good about helping around

the house and with her two younger sisters. She seemed very conscientious and concerned about doing things right but seemed to lack self-confidence. She always checked out things with her mother, sometimes several times. She was particularly concerned about safety, and would, for example, ask her mother frequently if the kitchen stove was turned off right.

Cindy would become extremely fearful at tiems, often for no external reason. For example, on one clear summer day a few months before, she had become panicked over the possiblity that a tornado might strike and had insisted that her family take shelter for several hours in the basement. (p. 560)

Phobic Anxiety

Anxiety disorders are among the most common psychological disorders and according to Price and Lynn (1986) have been experienced by an estimated 2 to 4 percent of the general population. One category of anxiety disorders includes phobic disorders. The following vignette is interesting because it not only involves an example of a phobic anxiety experienced by an adolescent that culminated in a suicide attempt, but also illustrates how a suicide attempt can become a method of manipulation. Toolan (1968) suggested that the suicide attempt may be a way "to manipulate another, to gain love and affection, or to punish another" (p. 222). Often these feelings are directed toward the parents. To illustrate such manipulation, Toolan provided the following vignette:

> A 16-year-old girl...had withdrawn from school because of a school phobia. She insisted upon her mother's being continually in attendance and accompanying her wherever she wished to go. The mother had taken a leave of absence from her job to be with her daughter. When she announced that she planned to return to work, the girl slashed her wrists. The attempt produced the desired effect, as the mother then continued to stay home. (p. 222)

Clinical Depression

Depression has been considered one of the most important single prodromal syndromes for suicide; according to Shneidman (1965), depression occurs to some degree in approximately one third of all suicides.

Tishler and associates (1981) studied 108 adolescents who had attempted suicide and found that the majority were depressed. Depression which is masked as boredom, restlessness, or delinquent behavior should be targeted as a sign of possible suicidal risk (Husain & Vandiver, 1984).

The symptoms of depression in youth will vary with the developmental level of the adolescent and the youth's ability to tolerate pain. According to Greuling and DeBlassie (1980), in early adolescence depression is often masked by acting-out or delinquent behavior, but the older adolescent is more apt to choose drugs, alcohol, and sex as a means of avoiding painful depressive feelings.

Not all writers describe depression as one of the key predictors of suicide, particularly for youth. For example, according to Gispert and associates (1985), the relationship between depression and suicide remains unclear. They noted that although depressed patients are at risk for suicide, depressed adolescents have not yet been established necessarily suicidal.

Frazier (1985) differentiated between regular depression and clinical depression. According to Frazier, regular depression describes a normal mood that includes the ups and downs, the disappointments and losses, and the good and bad days that affect all adolescents. Clinical depression, on the other hand, is a more serious depression with persistent signs and symptoms that usually last for at least two weeks.

Clinical depression may manifest itself according to a number of dimensions which include the following: persistent change in mood; sadness as a dominant mood; change in sleep habits; change in appetite; change in appearance or grooming; change in activity or energy level; feeling of emptiness in life; feelings of hopelessness, helplessness, and worthlessness; loss of ability to experience pleasure from normally enjoyable activities; problems in judgment or memory; deficient problem-solving skills or cognitive rigidity; psychosomatic or psychogenic illness; unexplained impulsive behavior and low level of frustration tolerance; anger, rage, or hostility; acting out behaviors; withdrawal from or lack of involvement with, usual peer group; and loneliness.

According to Price and Lynn (1986), in order for a diagnosis of a depressive symptom to occur, at least four of the above dimensions must be present.

Hipple and Cimbolic (1979) recommended that counselors be alert to the different manifestations of depression and its relationship to suicide. They particularly cautioned counselors to be attentive to the period when the depression appears to subside. According to Hipple and Cimbolic, during this leveling off period the adolescent regains the necessary psychic energy to become acutely suicidal.

TABLE 3.3

Psychiatric Indicators of Adolescent Suicide

Indicators	Evidence/Description
1. Prior suicide attempt	Manifested by a prior suicide threat or gesture.
2. Verbalization of suicide or talk of self-harm	Often manifested in talk of death or suicide threats
3. Preoccupation with death	Manifested in a preoccupation with the topic of death in music, art, poetry, or journals.
4. Repeated episodes of serious self-destructive ideation	Manifested by fleeting thoughts of suicide or a careful plan.
5. Dare-devil or self-abusive behavior	The dare-devil phenomenon is often exhibited through an impulsive, dangerous course of action.
6. Open signs of mental illness	Manifested as delusions or hallucinations via schizophrenic reactions.
7. Overwhelming sense of guilt or shame	Typically exhibited in a fear of punishment emanating from some behavior that is contrary to one's convictions.
8. Obsessional self-doubt	Often demonstrated via obsession over disappointing parents.

9. Phobic anxiety	Manifested in an anxiety disorder that includes various types of fear responses.
10. Clinical depression	Usually evidenced by a number of signs including hopelessness, change in appetite, problems in judgment and memory, cognitive rigidity, psychosomatic illness, substance abuse, withdrawal, loneliness, etc.

Sources: Blatt, D'Afflitti, & Quinlan, 1976; Brennan & Auslander, 1979; Crancer & Quiring, 1970; Frederick, 1977; Gernsbacher, 1985; Grollman, 1971; Jacobs, 1971; Lester & Beck, 1975; Perlstein, 1966; Richman, 1986; Shneidman, 1965; Shneidman, 1987; Toolan, 1968; Victoroff, 1983.

SITUATIONAL INDICATORS OF ADOLESCENT SUICIDE

The situational indicators of adolescent suicide concern major life events that may be cumulative and that cause certain emotional and/or physiological types of distress. This group of life change events includes a variety of personal, social, family, and occupational life changes that require an adjustment on the part of the adolescent. A number of researchers have studied the effects of stressful life events on the individual (Coddington, 1972; Holmes & Rahe, 1967; Johnson & McCutcheon, 1980; Siegel, Johnson, & Sarason, 1979; Yeaworth, York, Hussey, Ingle, & Goodwin, 1980). They have found that life stress or life change events can have a significant impact on the physical, social, and psychological well being of the adolescent. Similarly, a number of suicidologists have identified situational crises or life change events as important in the etiology of suicide. For example, Birtchnell (1970 found that suicide attempters had experienced a recent death of a parent more often than other psychiatric patients. Other studies have found a relationship between suicide attempts and the number of stressful life events. For example, Paykel, Prusoff, and Myers (1975) looked at life events experienced within the six months prior to a suicide attempt, and they found that suicide attempters reported four times as many stressful life events as did the general population and 1½ times as many as were reported by depressed patients prior to the onset of their depression.

Gispert et al. (1985) reported that the adolescents they studied who had attempted suicide had experienced a significant number of major life events (stressors) during their lives, and especially during the month prior to the suicide attempt.

Other studies have examined the relationship between life events and suicide ideation. In an investigation that included 207 high school seniors and 901 college students, Wright (1985) found that over 10% of the high school students and over 6% of the college students reported serious suicidal thoughts. In both groups, students who considered suicide tended to perceive themselves as having a history of family stress at the time of the suicide ideation.

In a study by Cohen-Sandler, Berman, and King (1982), suicidal children were found to have experienced significantly higher levels of stress during the 12 months prior to admission to a hospital than either the depressed children or children who displayed other types of psychotic difficulties. The suicidal children were found to have experienced such events as birth of a sibling, separation or divorce of parents, marriage of a parent, hospitalization of a parent, or psychological trauma such as observing the death of a family member or peer. In short, the data seem to demonstrate a relationship between cumulative life change and suicidal tendencies (Johnson, 1986; Paykel, 1974).

TABLE 3.4

Situational Indicators of Adolescent Suicide

Indicators	Evidence/Description
1. Life events and adolescent suicide	Manifested in the relationship between stressful life events and suicide attempt, suicide ideation, and suicidal tendencies.

Sources: Birtchnell, 1970; Burns & Geist, 1984; Coddington, 1972; Coddington, 1979; Cohen-Sandler, Berman & King, 1982; Ferguson, 1981; Gersten, Langer, Eisenberg, & Orzeck, 1974; Greenberg, Siegel, & Leitch, 1983; Hawton, 1986; Johnson & McCutcheon, 1980; Johnson, 1986; Pantell & Goodman, 1983; Paykel, Prusoff, & Myers, 1975; Wright, 1985; Yeaworth, York, Hussey, Ingle, & Goodwin, 1980.

SUMMARY

Adolescents experience stress and depression as frequently as adults. However, they tend to handle their stress and pain differently. Many teenagers perceive their emotional pain as acute, overwhelming, and unending. Although some of these adolescents may exhibit a number of behavioral indicators of suicide, the majority probably will not attempt nor commit suicide. On the other hand, we must constantly be mindful and sensitive to what might be a direct "cry for help."

A number of verbal and nonverbal warning signs or clues to adolescent suicide have been presented in this chapter, including psychosocial, familial, psychiatric and situational indicators. Tables 1 through 4 summarize some of the more salient aspects of those behavioral clues. What is particularly important about each of these indicators is that they may serve as a benchmark for parents, teachers, and counselors who may suspect that a certain adolescent is at risk for suicide. By having such a comparative benchmark of potential suicidal behavior, we are in a better position to not only recognize serious problems early, but to recommend the most effective intervention for our troubled youth.

REFERENCES

Balser, B.H., & Masterson, J.F., Jr. (1959). Suicide in adolescence. *American Journal of Psychiatry, 116*(5), 400-4.

Bandura, A. (1977). *Social learning theory.* Englewood Cliffs, NJ: Prentice-Hall.

Bergstrand, C.G., & Otto, U. (1962). Suicidal attempts in adolescence and childhood. *Acta Paediatrica, 51*, 17-26.

Berman, A. (1986). Helping suicidal adolescents: Needs and responses. In C.A. Corr & J.N. McNeil (Eds.). *Adolescence and death.* New York: Springer Publishing Company.

Birtchnell, J. (1970). The relationship between attempted suicide, depression and parent death. *British Journal of Psychiatry, 116*, 307-13.

Blatt, S.J., D'Afflitti, J.P., & Quinlan, D.M. (1976). Experiences of depression in normal young adults. *Journal of Abnormal Psychology, 85*, 383-9.

Bruns, C., & Geist, C.S. (1984). Stressful life events and drug use among adolescents. *Journal of Human Stress, 9*, 135-9.

Brennan, T., & Auslander, N. (1979). Adolescent loneliness: An exploratory study of social and psychological predisposition and theory (Vol. 1). National Institute of Mental Health, Juvenile Problems Division, Grant NO. R01-MH289 12-01, Behavioral Research Institute.

Cantor, P.C. (1976). Personality characteristics found among youthful female suicide attempters. *Journal of Abnormal Psychology, 85*(3), 324-9.

Carter, E.A., & McGoldrick, M. (Eds.). (1980). *The family life cycle: A framework for family therapy.* New York: Gardner Press.

Coddington, R.D. (1972). The significance of life events as etiological factors in the diseases of children: A study of a normal population. *Journal of Psychosomatic Research, 16*, 205-13.

Coddington, R.D. (1979). Life events associated with adolescent pregnancies. *Journal of Clinical Psychiatry, 40*, 180-5.

Cohen-Sandler, R., Berman, A.L., & King, R.A. (1982). Life stress and symptomatology: Determinants of suicidal behavior in children. *Journal of the American Academy of Child Psychiatry, 21*, 178-86.

Coleman, J.C. (1979). Current contradictions in adolescent theory. In S. Chess & A. Thomas (Eds.), *Annual progress in child psychiatry and child development.* New York: Brunner/Mazel.

Coleman, J.C., Butcher, J.N., & Carson, R.C. (1984). *Abnormal psychology in modern life.* Glenview, IL: Scott, Foresman and Company.

Crancer, A., & Quiring, D. (1970). Driving records of persons hospitalized for suicidal gestures. *Behavioral Research Highway Safety, 1*, 33-42.

Crook, T., & Raskin, A. (1975). Association of childhood parental loss with attempted suicide and depression. *Journal of Consulting and Clinical Psychology, 43*(2), 277-82.

Crumley, F.E. (1979). Adolescent suicide attempts. *Journal of the American Medical Association, 241*, 2404-7.

Delisle, J.R. (1984, August). *Suicide and the gifted adolescent: Causes for concern.* Paper presented at the meeting of the American Psychological Association, Toronto, Canada.

Deykin, E.Y. (1984). Assessing suicidal intent and lethality. *Educational Horizons, 62*(4), 134-7.

Dohrenwend, B.S., & Dohrenwend, B.P. (1981). Life stress and illness: Formulation of the issues. In B.S. Dohrenwend & B.P. Dohrenwend (Eds.), *Stressful life events and their contexts.* New York: Prodist.

Douvan, E., & Adelson, J. (1958). The psychodynamics of social mobility in adolescent boys. *Journal of Abnormal and Social Psychology, 56,* 31-49.

Egeland, B., Cicchetti, D., & Taraldson, B. (1976, April 26). Child abuse: A family affair. *Proceedings of the N.P. Masse Research Seminar on Child Abuse,* 28-52. Paper presented Paris, France.

English, C.J. (1973). Leaving home: A typology of runaways. *Society, 10*(5), 22-4.

Ellis, E.H. (1979). Some problems in the study of adolescent development. *Adolescence, 14*(53), 101-9.

Fawcett, J., Scheftner, W. Clark, D., Hedeker, D., Gibbons, R., & Coryell, W. (1987). Clinical predictors of suicide in patients with major affective disorders: A controlled prospective study. *American Journal of Psychiatry, 144,* 35-40

Ferguson, W.E. (1981). Gifted adolescents, stress, and life changes. *Adolescence, 16*(64), 973-85.

Finch, S.M., & Poznanski, E.O. (1971). *Adolescent suicide.* Springfield, IL: Charles C. Thomas.

Frazier, S.H. (1985, June). *Task force on youth suicide.* Paper presented at the meeting of the National Conference on Youth Suicide, Washington, D.C.

Frederick, C.J. (1977). Advances in suicidology. In A. Griffin & D. Switzer (Eds.), *Preventing the youthful suicide.* Symposium presented at the Suicide Prevention of Dallas and Southern Methodist University, Dallas, Texas.

Freud, A. (1958). Adolescence. *Psychoanalytic study of the child, 13,* 255-79.

Friedrich, W., Reams, R., & Jacobs, J. (1982). Depression and suicidal ideation in early adolescents. *Journal of Youth and Adolescence, 11*(5), 403-7.

Garfinkle, B.D., & Golombek, H. (1983). Suicide behavior in adolescence. In H. Golombek & B.D. Garfinkle (Eds.), *The adolescent and mood disturbance.* New York: International Universities Press.

Gernsbacher, L.M. (1985). *The suicide syndrome.* New York: Human Sciences Press, Inc.

Gersten, J.C., Langer, T.S., Eisenberg, J.G., & Orzeck, L. (1974). Child behavior and life events: Desirable change or change per se. In B.S. Dohrenwend & B.P. Dohrenwend (Eds.), *Stressful life events: Their nature and effects.* New York: John Wiley.

Gispert, M., Wheeler, K., Marsh, L., & Davis, M.S. (1985). Suicidal adolescents: Factors in evaluation. *Adolescence, 20*(80), 753-61.

Gleitman, H. (1986). *Psychology.* New York: W.W. Norton & Company.

Goldberg, E.L. (1981). Depression and suicide ideation in the young adult. *American Journal of Psychiatry, 138*(1), 35-40.

Gould, M.S., & Shaffer, D. (1986). The impact of suicide in television movies: Evidence of imitation. *The New England Journal of Medicine, 315*(11), 690-4.

Gordon, A.K. (1986). The tattered cloak of immortality. In C.A. Corr & J.N. McNeil (Eds.), *Adolescence and death.* New York: Springer.

Greenberg, M.T., Siegel, J.M., & Leitch, C.J. (1983). The nature and importance of attachment relationships to parents and peers during adolescence. *Journal of Youth and Adolescence, 12,* 373-86.

Greuling, J.W., & DeBlassie, R.R. (1980). Adolescent suicide. *Adolescence, 15*(59), 589-601.

Grollman, E.A. (1971). *Suicide-prevention, intervention, postvention.* Boston: Beacon Press.

Haley, J. (1973). *Uncommon therapy: The psychiatric techniques of Milton H. Erickson, M.D.* New York: Norton.

Hall, G.S. (1904). *Adolescence: Its psychology and its relations to physiology, anthropology, sociology, sex, crime, religion, and education, vol. 2.* New York: D. Appleton.

Hawton, K. (1986). *Suicide and attempted suicide among children and adolescents.* Beverly Hills, CA: Sage Publications.

Hawton, K., O'Grady, J., Osborn, M., & Cole, D. (1982). Adolescents who take overdoses: their characteristics, problems and contacts with helping agencies. *British Journal of Psychiatry, 141,* 118-23.

Herrenkohl, R.C., Herrenkohl, E.C., & Egolf, B.P. (1983). Circumstances surrounding the occurrence of child maltreatment. *Journal of Counseling and Clinical Psychology, 51*(3), 424-31.

Hipple, J., & Cimbolic, P. (1979). *The counselor and suicidal crises.* Springfield, IL: Charles C. Thomas.

Hiroto, D.S., & Seligman, M.E. (1975). Generality of learned helplessness in man. *Journal of Personality and Social Psychology, 31,* 311-27.

Hoff, L.A. (1978). *People in crisis: Understanding and helping.* Menlo Park, CA: Addison-Wesley.

Holmes, T.H., & Rahe, R.H. (1967). The social readjustment rating scale. *Journal of Psychosomatic Research, 11*, 213-8.

Homer, L.E. (1974). The anatomy of a runaway. *Human Behavior, 3*(4), 37.

Hughes, M., & Gove, W.R. (1981). Living alone, social integration, and mental health. *American Journal of Sociology, 87*(1), 48-74.

Husain, S.A., & Vandiver, T. (1984). *Suicide in children and adolescents.* New York: S P Medical & Scientific Books.

Jacobs, G. (1971). *Adolescent suicide.* New York: Wiley-Interscience.

Johnson, J.H. (1986). *Life events as stressors in childhood and adolescence.* Beverly Hills, CA: Sage Publications.

Johnson, J.H., & McCutcheon, S.M. (1980). Assessing life stress in older children and adolescents: Preliminary findings with the Life Events Checklist. In I.G. Sarason & C.D. Spielberger (Eds.), *Stress and Anxiety.* Washington, D.C.: Hemisphere.

Josselson, R. (1980). Ego development in adolescence. In J. Adelson (Ed.), *Handbook of adolescent psychology.* New York: Wiley.

Kosky, R. (1983). Childhood suicidal behavior. *Journal of Child Psychology and Psychiatry, 24*, 457-68.

Leroux, J.A. (1986). Suicidal behavior and gifted adolescents. *Roeper Reviews, 9*, 77-9.

Lester, D. & Beck, A.T. (1975). Suicidal intent, medical lethality of suicide attempt, and components of depression. *Journal of Clinical Psychology, 31*(1), 11-2.

Lewis, J.M., Beavers, W.R., Gossett, J.T., & Phillips, V.A. (1976). *No single thread: Psychological health in family systems.* New York: Brunner/Mazel.

Lin, N., Dean, A., & Ensel, W. (Eds.). (1986). *Social support, life events, and depression.* Orlando, FL: Academic Press.

Maier, S.F., & Seligman, M.E. (1976). Learned helplessness: Theory and evidence. *Journal of Experimental Psychology: General, 105*, 3-46.

Mead, M. (1928). *Coming of age in Samoa.* New York: Morrow.

Mead, M. (1939). *From the south seas: Studies of adolescence and sex in primitive societies.* New York: Morrow.

Minuchin, S. (1974). *Families in family therapy.* Cambridge, MA: Harvard University Press.

Moldeven, M. (1985). *Military-civilian teamwork in suicide prevention.* Las Vegas, NV: Meyer Moldeven.

Murphy, G.E., & Wetzel, R.D. (1982). Family history of suicidal behavior among suicide attempters. *The Journal of Nervous and Mental Disease, 170*(2), 86-90.

Offer, D., Ostrov, E., & Howard, K. (1981). *The adolescent: A psychological self-portrait.* New York: Basic.

Offer, D., Ostrov, E., & Howard, K. (1984). The self-image of normal adolescents. In D. Offer, E. Ostrov, & K. Howard (Eds.), *Patterns of adolescent self-image: New directions for mental health services.* San Francisco: Jossey-Bass.

Oldham, D.G. (1980). Adolescent turmoil: A myth revisited. In M. Bloom (Ed.), *Life span development: Bases for preventive and interventive helping.* New York: Macmillan.

O'Roark, M.A. (1982). The alarming rise in teenage suicide. *McCalls, 109*(4), 14, 16, 22, 120.

Ostrov, E., Offer, D., & Hartlage, S. (1984). The quietly disturbed. In D. Offer, E. Ostrov, & K. Howard (Eds.), *Patterns of adolescent self-image: New directions for mental health services.* San Francisco: Jossey-Bass.

Otto, U. (1964). Changes in the behavior of children and adolescents preceding suicidal attempts. *Acta Psychiatrica Scandinavica, 40,* 386-400.

Pantell, R.H., & Goodman, B.W. (1983). Adolescent chest pain: A prospective study. *Pediatrics, 71,* 881-6.

Parachini, A. (1984, August 19). Potential suicides often give warning signals. *Los Angeles Times,* pp. 1-2, 14-9.

Parker, A.M. (1974). *Suicide among young adults.* New York: Exposition Press.

Paykel, E.S. (1974). Life stress and psychiatric disorder: Applications of the clinical approach. In B.S. Dohrenwend & B.P. Dohrenwend (Eds.), *Stressful life events: Their nature and effects.* New York: John Wiley.

Paykel, E.S., Prusoff, B.A., & Myers, J.K. (1975). Suicide attempts and recent life events. *Arch General Psychiatry, 32,* 327-33.

Pearlin, L.I., & Schooler, C. (1978). The structure of coping. *Journal of Health and Social Behavior, 19*(1), 2-21.

Peck, M. (1985). Crisis intervention treatment with chronically and acutely suicidal adolescents. In M.L. Peck, N.L. Farberow, & R.E. Litman (Eds.), *Youth Suicide.* New York: Springer Publishing Company.

Peck, M., & Litman, R. (1975). Current trends in youthful suicide. *Tribuna Media.*

Perlstein, A.P. (1966). Suicide in adolescence. *New York State Journal of Medicine, 66*(23), 3017-20.

Phillips, D.P., & Carstensen, M.S. (1986). Clustering of teenage suicide after television news stories about suicide. *The New England Journal of Medicine, 315*(11), 685-9.

Price, R.N., & Lynn, S.J. (1986). *Abnormal psychology.* Chicago, IL: The Dorsey Press.

Richman, J. (1971). Family determinants of suicidal potential. In D. Anderson & L. McClean (Eds.), *Identifying suicide potential.* New York: Behavioral Publication.

Richman, J. (1986). *Family therapy for suicidal people.* New York: Springer Publishing Company.

Roberts, J., & Hawton, K. (1980). Child abuse and attempted suicide. *British Journal of Psychiatry, 137*, 319-23.

Rohn, R.D., Sarles, R.M., Kenny, T.J., Reynolds, B.J., & Head, F.P. (1977). Adolescents who attempt suicide. *Journal of Pediatrics, 90*, 636-8.

Rosenberg, M. (1965). *Society and the adolescent self-image.* Princeton, NJ: Princeton University Press.

Roy, A. (1983). Family history of suicide. *Archives of General Psychiatry, 40*, 971-4.

Rutter, M. (1980). *Changing youth in a changing society.* Cambridge, MA: Harvard University Press.

Sabbath, J. (1969). The suicidal adolescent--The expendable child. *Journal of the American Academy of Child Psychiatry, 8*(2), 272-89.

Sartore, R.L. (1976). Students and suicide: An interpersonal tragedy. *Theory into Practice, 15*(5), 337-9.

Schrut, A. (1964). Suicidal adolescents and children. *Journal of American Medical Association, 188*, 1103-7.

Seiden, R.H. (1969). *Suicide among youth.* Public Health Service Publication, No. 1971.

Seligman, M.E. (1975). *Helplessness.* San Francisco, CA: Freeman.

Shafii, M., Carrigan, S., Whittinghill, J.R., & Derrick, A. (1985). Psychological autopsy of completed suicide in children and adolescents. *American Journal of Psychiatry, 142*(9), 1061-4.

Shneidman, E. (1987). At the point of no return. *Psychology Today, 21*(3), 54-8.

Shneidman, E. (1965). Preventing suicide. *American Journal of Nursing, 65*(5), 111-6.

Siegel, J.M., Johnson, J.H., & Sarason, I.G. (1979). Life stress and menstrual discomfort. *Journal of Human Stress, 5*, 41-6.

Stanley, E.J., & Barter, J.T. (1970). Adolescent suicidal behavior. *American Journal of Orthopsychiatry, 40*(1), 87-96.

Stinnett, N. (1983). Strong families: A portrait. In D. Mace (Ed.), *Prevention in family services: Approaches to family wellness.* Beverly Hills, CA: Sage.

Teicher, J.D. (1970). Why do adolescents kill themselves? *National health program reports.* Washington, D.C.: U.S. Government Printing Office.

Thomas, A. (1979). Learned helplessness and expectancy factors: Implications for research in learning disabilities. *Review of Educational Research, 49*, 208-21.

Tishler, C.L., & McKenry, P.C. (1983). Intrapsychic symptom dimensions of adolescent suicide attempters. *The Journal of Family Practice, 16*(4), 731-4.

Tishler, C.L., McKenry, P.C., & Morgan, K.C. (1981). Adolescent suicide attempts: Some significant factors. *Suicide and Life Threatening Behavior, 11*(2), 86-92.

Toolan, J.M. (1962). Suicide and suicidal attempts in children and adolescents. *American Journal of Psychiatry, 118*(8), 719-24.

Toolan, J.M. (1968). Suicide in children and adolescence. In H.L.P. Resnik (Ed.), *Suicidal Behaviors.* Boston: Little, Brown, and Company.

Vandivort, B.S., Locke, B.S., Locke, B.Z. (1979). Suicide ideation: Its relation to depression, suicide and suicide attempt. *Journal of Life Threatening Behavior, 9*(4), 205-18.

Victoroff, V.M. (1983). *The suicidal patitent: Recognition, intervention, management.* Oradell, NJ: Medical Economics Books.

Walker, W.L. (1980). Intentional self-imagery in school age children. *Journal of Adolescence, 3*, 217-28.

Westley, W.A., & Epstein, N.B. (1969). *The silent majority.* San Francisco: Jossey-Bass.

Wheaton, B. (1983). Stress, personal coping resources, and psychiatric symptoms: An investigation of interactive models. *Journal of Health and Social Behavior, 24*, 208-29.

Wright, L.S. (1985). Suicidal thoughts and their relationship to family stress and personal problems among high school seniors and college undergraduates. *Adolescence, 20*(79), 575-80.

Yeaworth, C.R., York, J., Hussey, M.A., Ingle, M.E., & Goodwin, T. (1980). The development of an adolescent life change event scale. *Adolescence, 15*, 91-8.

CHAPTER **4**

PERSONALITY VARIABLES

Sharla P. Nichols, M.Ed.
and
Daniel Fasko, Jr., Ph.D.

Sharla P. Nichols, M.Ed.

Elementary School Counselor
El Dorado Public Schools
El Dorado, AR 71730

Sharla P. Nichols received a Master of Education from Southern Arkansas University in 1985, with certification in both Elementary and Secondary School Counseling. She is currently employed as Elementary School Counselor for Hugh Goodwin and Southside Elementary Schools in the El Dorado, Arkansas, Public Schools. Ms. Nichols is presently serving as Elementary School Level Vice-President of the Arkansas School Counselor Association.

Daniel Fasko, Jr., Ph.D.

Assistant Professor of Education
Morehead State University
Morehead, KY 40357

Dr. Dan Fasko received a Bachelor of Arts degree in psychology from Seton Hall University in South Orange, NJ in 1970. He obtained a Master of Science degree in general applied psychology in 1974 from the University of Bridgeport, in Bridgeport, CT. Dr. Fasko was awarded the Doctor of Philosophy in educational psychology from Florida State University in Tallahassee, FL in 1983. He is presently Assistant Professor of Education at Morehead State University in Morehead, KY, where he teaches courses in educational psychology and advanced human growth and development. Previously, he was Assistant Professor of Psychology at Southern Arkansas University in Magnolia, AR. His research interests are in the areas of teacher questioning activities, student attending behaviors, and improving academic performance. He has published and presented in the areas of teacher questioning, health education, mental retardation and adolescent suicide probability. Dr. Fasko is a reviewer for the *Educational Psychologist* and is also a book reviewer for the *Journal of Sex Education and Therapy*. He holds memberships in the Southwest Educational Research Association, American Psychological Association (Division 15), the American Educational Research Association (Divisions C, E, and K), the Southwestern Psychological Association, the Arkansas Psychological Association, and the Mid-South Educational Research Association.

EDITORIAL ABSTRACT: *This chapter is one of importance to the practicing school, mental health, or licensed counselor working with potentially suicidal adolescents. The chapter reviews the literature relating to the personality traits that contribute to adolescent suicide, makes recommendations for understanding the potentially suicidal adolescent, and discusses possible prevention measures.*

Adolescent suicide is not a new problem. In fact, some 2,500 years ago in the Greek city of Miletus, suicide preventive measures were being practiced by the government due to an epidemic of suicide by hanging among young women. Pleas from family and friends were useless in halting the outbreak. The city officials ordered that the bodies of all these young women who hanged themselves be carried to their burial directly through the marketplace—a humiliation which finally brought the epidemic under control (Freese, 1979).

While the suicide rate for adolescents seems to vary slightly across the United States, Kubler-Ross (1983) reported that in some communities in which she has worked, up to 30% of the teenagers have attempted or committed suicide. The methods used most by adolescents attempting suicide are, from most to least common: drug overdose, wrist laceration, hanging, and jumping from heights or motor vehicles (Garfinkel, Froese, & Hood, 1982). Berman and Carroll (1984) suggested that the "modal" adolescent attempt is an ingestion of pills, mostly analgesics, with the majority of these attempts in the home.

A great benefit would be achieved if researchers could identify a personality profile of the suicidal adolescent. A youngster who fit the description could then be categorized "at risk," and appropriate preventive measures taken. Several attempts have been made at specifying the "typical" suicidal adolescent's personality. For example, Petzel and Riddle (1982) concluded that suicidal adolescents are shy, self-conscious, inclined to overreact, worry, and indulge in self-pity. These adolescents are also immature in understanding, attitudes, judgement, lacking in self-confidence, and react emotionally rather than intellectually. They have inadequate recreational outlets, are indecisive about the future, and have trouble controlling their impulsivity. On the other hand,

Crumley (1979) reported that the "typical" young suicide attempter is a girl who is depressed, impulsive, and has a history of drug abuse. She also has a tendency to react severely to loss and has poorly controlled rage.

Obviously, no consensus has yet been reached as to the true "typical" personality profile of the suicidal adolescent. However, researchers have generally agreed on several characteristics which seem to be common to many suicidal adolescents. Depressive personality, low self-esteem/self-concept, hopelessness and helplessness "loner" personality, dependency, impulsivity, low frustration tolerance, aggressive/acting out personality, cognitive rigidity, obsessive/compulsive personality, and borderline personality are some of the more common characteristics discussed.

Unfortunately, the rate of suicide for adolescents is steadily increasing, while that of other age groups has remained stable. A way of prediction must be found and prevention methods utilized if this serious problem is to be dealt with successfully.

The preservation of life is an important value in our society, particularly the lives of our young people. Therefore, of primary importance is to find a way to control and/or reduce this problem.

This chapter's three-fold purposes are (1) to review the literature and determine possible personality traits that contribute to adolescent suicide, (2) to make recommendations for understanding adolescent suicide probability, (3) and to discuss available preventive measures. Of the personality factors associated with suicide attempts, depression is the one most commonly discussed.

RESEARCH ON PERSONALITY TRAITS AND WHO IS AT RISK

Personality Traits

Depressive Personality. Most researchers agree that depression is significantly related to suicidal behavior in some manner. For example, Grueling and DeBlassie (1980) reported that depressive symptoms are found in 40% of adolescent suicide attempters, but this could be much higher because truancy, disobedience, increased risk-taking, and other forms of acting out can be behavioral symptoms of depression, and thus go unrecognized as such. Toolan (1975) stated that "...the vast majority of youngsters who threaten suicide or attempt suicide are depressed to a significant degree..." (p. 341). Depression may be the result of a loss of some type, but often the depression is characterological in nature, according to Finch and Poznanski (1971).

Lending support to these assertions is a study by Pfeffer, Plutchik, Mizruchi, and Lipkins (1986). Three groups of children were assessed to identify factors associated with suicidal behavior. One hundred and one children were administered specially devised research instruments, which included a spectrum of suicidal behavior scale, a spectrum of assaultive behavior scale, a precipitating events scale, general psychopathology (recent and past) scales, a family background scale, a child's concept of death scale, an ego functioning scale, and an ego defense scale. In all three groups (psychiatric inpatients, outpatients, and nonpatients), recent and past depression were significantly associated with suicidal behavior.

A highly significant correlation was found between depression and suicide ideation as a presenting symptom in a study of 900 adolescent inpatients from 1974 to 1982 (Rosenstock, 1985). In an earlier study of depressive personality types, results appeared to indicate that students who agreed with suicidal behaviors were more depressed than those who agreed less often with suicidal behaviors (Stillion, McDowell, & Shamblin, 1984).

Few authorities dispute the existence of depression as a contributing factor in adolescent suicide. The area of dissention lies in the manner and extent depression is involved. According to McCoy (1982), virtually all adolescents who attempt suicide are significantly depressed. But LaDame and Jeanneret (1982) considered depressive illness to be only one of a trio of major predictive factors in suicide prevention. They felt that adolescents who had symptoms of depressive illness, alienation, and/or anxiety should be considered "at risk." In fact, Kovacs, Beck, and Weissman (1975) found depression second only to hopelessness in effectively predicting suicide.

One analysis of the family histories of suicidal adolescents appears to link a family history of depressive illness to suicidal behavior in youngsters (Friedman, Corn, Hurt, Fibel, Schulick, & Swirsky, 1984). On the other hand, Hendin (1975) described the depression of a suicidal adolescent as "a form of protective deadness" which is actually a way of coping with life (p. 334). This theory becomes more plausible when we consider that many adolescents make suicide attempts after a depression has apparently lifted.

Depression was also a major theme in the story of Vivienne Loomis, a girl who took her life at the age of fourteen. Her poetry and papers told of her intense depression and lack of self-esteem (Mack & Hickler, 1981).

Low Self-Esteem/Self-Concept. Vivienne's feeling of worthlessness is typical of suicidal adolescents. Several researchers have discussed this aspect of adolescent suicide. Often the acting-out behaviors of many suicidal adolescents are the youngster's defense against his/her underlying feelings of worthlessness (Sheras, 1983). "Poor self-image" was reported by Faigel (1966) to be useful in assessing the possibility of suicidal behavior. Based on their own clinical experience with suicidal clients, Cull and Gill (1982) included "negative self-evaluation" as one of the four subscales on their Suicide Probability Scale. Low self-esteem, according to Stein and Davis (1982), should be addressed as a characteristic which would predispose a particular adolescent to suicidal behavior.

Some studies have attempted to establish concretely a relationship between self-concept and suicide probability. One study using measures of self-report indicated that students who agreed with suicidal behaviors tended to have lower self-esteem than those who agreed less often with suicidal behavior (Stillion et al., 1984).

A distorted self-concept, with its accompanying low self-esteem, includes unrealistic self-expectations, which can increase distress in the adolescent as these expectations are not validated (Glaser, 1978). According to Freese (1979), a loss of self-esteem is often the precipitating factor in teenage suicide. On the other hand, Toolan (1975, 1981), considered low self-esteem to be an important symptom of depression. He was of the opinion that depression is the major precipitating factor in adolescent suicide, and therefore, low self-esteem is strongly related to suicide probability.

Hopelessness/Helplessness. Other influential personality characteristics appear to be hopelessness and helplessness. Hopelessness is reported by Orbach (1984) as most characteristic of suicidal children; Peck (1983) considered hopelessness to be one of several major contributing factors for suicidal individuals. When studying the families of suicidal adolescents, Friedman et al. (1984) noted the extreme degree of hopelessness the children were experiencing, especially those whose parents were chronically depressed. In fact, the Suicide Probability Scale (Cull & Gill, 1982) included a "hopelessness" subscale; apparently the authors felt this characteristic to be a significant factor in suicidal ideation. However, this subscale also contains items more relevant to depression, loneliness, and helplessness.

Kovacs et al. (1975) concluded that suicide, for whatever purpose, is best predicted by the extent of hopelessness the individual is experiencing. In fact, this study indicated that hopelessness is a much better predictor of suicide than is depression. When hospitalized suicidal adolescents were compared with hospitalized nonsuicidal adolescents and nonhospitalized coping adolescents a significantly greater degree of hopelessness was revealed in the suicidal group than in the other two groups. The suicidal adolescents also experienced a significantly greater feeling of a lack of control over their environments. These children also expressed despair as a justification for suicide more often than did either of the other two groups (Topol & Reznikoff, 1982).

A stage theory introduced by Jacobs (1971) recognizes five progressive stages for understanding the events leading to adolescent suicidal behavior. The fourth of these five stages is a loss of hope, which is in turn used by the adolescent as a justification of the suicidal act (the fifth stage). Tabachnick (1981) noted that whether one is studying adolescence or one is studying suicide, hopelessness and helplessness are important issues.

Feelings of helplessness may be a greater factor in suicides than any other feelings. Cull and Gill (1982) stated that the lack of a sense of control over one's physical and psychological well-being can result in a suicide attempt. In his study on fatalistic attitudes and youth suicide, Peck (1983) noted that suicidal behavior often occurs when the individual is experiencing feelings of helplessness, along with loneliness and isolation. Some adolescents do not have adequate coping skills, according to Freese (1979), which makes them feel helpless; after a series of events involving feelings of helplessness, they begin to experience hopelessness. Hopelessness, Freese believed, is an important precipitating factor in adolescent suicide. One interesting study on suicidal adolescents indicated that these youngsters displayed constricted problem-solving abilities when compared to psychiatric nonsuicidal and normal adolescents (Levenson & Neuringer, 1971).

In a discussion of gifted students, Delisle (1986) indicated that one of the four major issues of gifted adolescent suicide attempters is the frustration that results from understanding adult situations and world events, but being impotent to effect change. This is a type of helplessness peculiar to the gifted child, but no less influential in suicide probability.

Underlying all the other feelings involved, Schneidman (1987) stated that what exists is "a sense of powerlessness and impotence, and the feelings that no one can help with this pain, and that there is nothing to do except commit suicide" (p. 57).

"Loner" Personality. Is loneliness a pre-existing personality set in some children which makes them more prone to suicidal behavior? Or is loneliness something that these youngsters create for themselves out of their depression and self-imposed isolation? Authorities are divided on this issue.

The developmental period of adolescence is a time when many suicidal elements become magnified. Loneliness is an example of one of these. A child who is predisposed to be a loner will find this characteristics much more exaggerated during adolescence. As acute loneliness seems to be related to suicidal behavior in general, and as adolescence exacerbates the problem, a predisposition for suicidal behavior is more present at this time (Hafen, 1972). This view is shared by Tabachnick (1981), who also pointed out that loneliness is an issue in the study of both adolescence and suicide.

Peck (1981) claimed to have identified a high-risk personality type called the loner. These young people have no close relationships and an inability to communicate. They are usually male, have feelings of sexual inadequacy, and are under high parental pressure for success.

When 299 suicidal patients were analyzed by Kiev (1977), several different profile-types emerged. One of these, *Type V*, was the social isolate. He noted that these individuals attempted suicide at a distance from others and did not make any effort to be rescued.

In addition, Stein and Davis (1982) noted that suicidal adolescents generally appear to have an "overwhelming sense of isolation and aloneness" (p. 353). Peck (1983) also observed that suicidal behavior is often precipitated by experiences of isolation and loneliness. Sommer (1984) proposed that adolescent suicidal behaviors are associated not only with disturbed family relationships, but with isolation and alienation as well. Alienation also was singled out by LaDame and Jeanneret (1982) as one of the major predictive factors in suicide prevention, along with depressive illness and anxiety.

Dependency. Another possible factor frequently mentioned in suicide research is the dependent personality. When Kiev (1977) analyzed 299 suicidal patients, he found that one of the seven profiles that emerged contained the passive-aggressive and passive-dependent personality disorders.

In a study of youthful female suicide attempters, Cantor (1976) found that these individuals appeared to have high succorant need (i.e., requiring that others assist them when they are troubled) coupled with an inability to reach significant others. Perhaps the dependent personality uses the suicide attempt as a means of meeting both of these needs: the significant others will probably respond, and in doing so will provide for these succorant needs.

Unfortunately, dependency seems to be fostered by some types of therapy (Schwartz, 1979). The nurturance and acceptance often given in crisis counseling is reinforcing to the dependent personality, and teaches them that attempting suicide is indeed a method of coercing assistance and coping with others. Prolonged hospitalization seems to be especially dangerous because it encourages dependency, according to Schwartz. To this type of personality, suicide becomes more inevitable as suicidal behaviors are consistently "reinforced."

Impulsivity. The single largest group of suicidal teenagers is that of the impulsive character disorder (Greuling & DeBlassie, 1980). This personality type has frequently been discussed in studies on suicide (e.g., Shaughnessy & Nystul, 1985; Freese, 1979; Kiev, 1977). Those youngsters who think things through seem to be less likely to commit suicide than those with impulsive personality traits and characteristics, according to Shaughnessy and Nystul (1985). Freese (1979) also noted that young people with suicidal tendencies habitually react to stress without thinking things through. Most suicide attempts are not premeditated, according to Kiev (1977), but are impulsive reactions associated with psychological distress and other factors.

The theory that suicide is fundamentally an impulsive act is the basis for the practice of crisis intervention with suicidal individuals. Crisis intervention therapists generally agree that a crisis interval is relatively short, and that if an individual can be kept alive through this period, the desire for cessation of pain (through suicide) will pass. Impulsive persons, however, do not stop to reflect that the crisis will pass, and so make a suicide attempt (Rosenkratz, 1978).

Various studies have supported this idea. When Toolan (1975) analyzed 102 suicidal adolescents who were hospitalized in 1960, immaturity and impulsivity were markedly evident. Lending additional support is a study on young female suicide attempters by Cantor (1976). When she compared suicide attempters with those who frequently considered suicide and those who rarely thought about it, the attempters appeared to be more impulsive than the nonsuicidal subjects.

Some interesting findings emerged when researchers completed a longitudinal study using data from the Terman Genetic Studies of Genius. The Terman Studies covered sixty years and amassed an enormous amount of data about the gifted individuals it followed from childhood through their adult lives. Tomlinson-Keasey, Warren, and Elliott (1986) compared the files of three groups of women from this study: a group who committed suicide, a group who died of natural causes, and a group who were still living in 1964. Among other things, they found that the suicide group had previously received higher ratings on impulsivity.

Impulsivity also may be exaggerated during adolescence along with other suicidal elements, such as loneliness and hypersensitivity (Hafen, 1972). Children who are already predisposed to impulsivity may exhibit an extreme intensification of that facet of their personality when they reach their teen years. Perhaps that is why for the impulsive personality, the adolescent period appears to be the most conducive to suicidal behavior.

What is not clear is just where impulsivity fits into the puzzle of circumstances surrounding a suicide attempt. Does the individual make the attempt because of a single impulsive decision? Or does a life-long pattern of impulsive decision-making lead to the depression and hopelessness which constrict the individual's coping abilities? Kiev (1977) stated that the individual with a lifelong history of impulsive behavior is particularly at risk for suicide. But not all researchers believe impulsivity is involved in suicidal behavior; in fact, Jacobs (1971) hypothesized that suicidal behavior is not impulsive, but is simply the final stage of a long, drawn-out sequence of events leading up to its ultimate conclusion.

Low Frustration Tolerance. Perhaps adolescents who engage in suicidal behavior have a very low tolerance for frustration. Low frustration tolerance appears to be one factor that can precipitate an impulsive act of suicide (Kiev, 1977). Cantor's (1976) study on youthful female suicide attempters indicated that an inability to tolerate frustration appeared to characterize the females who attempted suicide.

Acting Out/Aggressive. Acting out behaviors, such as delinquency, disobedience, and truancy, and aggressive behaviors, such as fighting, are frequently present in adolescents who attempt suicide. Opinion is divided as to the role of these characteristics. Are they manifestations of other factors, such as depression, or are they separate indicators of suicide potential?

According to Marohn, Locke, Rosenthal, and Curtiss (1982), suicide, homicide, and accidental death are three components of violent death and appear to be related. The case histories of five behaviorally disordered and delinquent adolescents suggest that youngsters with these characteristics may be at particular risk for one of the three forms of violent death.

Acting out behaviors were significantly correlated with a presenting problem of attempted suicide in a study of nine hundred youngsters at Houston International Hospital Adolescent center. The attempters had a history of problems with school and uncooperative behavior, as well as somatic complaints and loss of appetite (Rosenstock, 1985). Kiev (1977) referred to the delinquent with low frustration tolerance as at high risk for suicide, adding that while the risk is higher in youth it decreases with age.

Aggression appeared to be greater in suicidal individuals in a study by Geller and Atkins (1978). Rorschach inkblots were used to compare suicidal inpatients and nonsuicidal controls. In a report on youthful female suicide attempters, Cantor (1976) suggested that these individuals may use the suicide attempt as an aggressive act intended to provoke guilt and sympathy in their parents.

Other authorities (e.g., Toolan, 1975; Pfeffer, Plutchik, & Mizruchi, 1983) feel that these behaviors are merely manifestations of other problems. Delinquency and other acting-out behaviors may actually be masks for depression, according to Toolan (1975), particularly in early adolescence. A study by Pfeffer et al. (1983) of 102 children indicated that while many suicidal children display intense depression, others show less depression but much more intense aggression. Perhaps this aggressive behavior is merely their method of expressing depression.

Cognitive Rigidity. While some question exists as to whether acting out and aggression are primary or secondary factors in the potentially suicidal individual, the rigidity of the cognitive processes seems to play a direct role in this personality. Schneidman (1987) advised us to be alert for constricted, either-or type thinking when screening for suicidal potential, as well as previous episodes of disturbance and the person's way of coping with psychological pain.

A study by Neuringer (1964) supports this idea. When suicidal individuals were compared to psychosomatic and to normal subjects using two different problem-solving tests in combination, the suicidal group was found to be more cognitively rigid than the other two groups.

Suicidal, chronically ill, and normal children were compared by Orbach (1984), who found that the suicidal children were cognitively more rigid than were the other groups. This is consistent with the findings which emerged when suicidal and nonsuicidal psychiatric patients were compared on measures of rigidity, field dependence, and impulsivity. Among these measures, only cognitive rigidity discriminated the suicidal group from the nonsuicidal one (Patsiokas, Clum, & Luscombe, 1979). Perhaps this cognitive rigidity, which constricts one's problem-solving ability, is actually the precursor of the helplessness described earlier.

Borderline Personality. Other authorities (e.g., Snyder, Pitts, & Pokorny, 1986) have suggested that borderline personality is a possible predisposing trait for suicide. Data were collected from 4,800 consecutive admissions to a Veteran's Hospital from 1972-1974. A psychiatric rating scale was administered to all of those admitted in an effort to find a way to predict suicide in a psychiatric population. Those individuals with borderline subscale scores in the moderate to severe range appeared to have a greater history of suicide attempts.

In summary, of the eleven personality traits discussed that seem most prevalent in the research on suicidal adolescents, depression, impulsivity, low self-concept/self-esteem, and hopelessness/helplessness have received the most attention.

Who Is At Risk?

Several groups have been identified as having exceptionally high risk for suicide. These include substance abusers, college students, and those who have made previous attempts.

Substance Abusers. Substance abusers are frequently considered to be a particularly high-risk group. Drug abuse has complicated adolescence, according to Miller (1981), and made young people more vulnerable to suicidal behavior. On the other hand, the same factors which lead a person to excessive use of alcohol and drugs also may lead a person to commit suicide

(Greuling & DeBlassie, 1980). Impulsivity is a trait that many substance abusers have in common with those who attempt suicide. With teen alcoholism on the rise, a relationship may exist between this and the rising adolescent suicide rates.

Alcoholism tends to increase depression, which may be another reason why alcoholics are more suicidal than others (Freese, 1979). However, drugs and alcohol may be a way adolescents attempt to avoid facing their depressive feelings (Toolan, 1975). When the substances are no longer enough, the adolescent could make a suicide attempt. A study by McHenry, Tishler, and Kelley (1983) indicated that adolescent drug use and abuse is closely related to suicidal behaviors.

College Students. Another high-risk group may be those young people attending college. Price and Lynn (1981) indicated that college students are twice as likely to commit suicide as their same-age counterparts.

A suggestion has been that college students exhibiting suicidal behavior may be afraid of having an independent existence, and graduating from college has the power to free them from their "emotionally dead" relationships with their parents (Hendin, 1975). Suicide may be a way or resolving this dilemma.

Previous Attempters. One of the most important of the high-risk groups includes those who have made previous attempts. Of those who complete suicide, two-thirds have made previous attempts. An individual who has attempted suicide appears to be 64 times more likely to complete suicide than the general population (Freese, 1979).

An unsuccessful attempt can be considered a "cry for help," which, if it is not heard, can lead to more lethal attempts. If these individuals do not receive help, they may increase the lethality of their attempts to the point of death (Farberow & Schneidman, 1965).

Thus, substance abusers, college students, and previous attempters all appear to be at special risk for suicidal behavior.

APPLICATION

Self-concept and Suicide Probability

Do gifted adolescents have more problems with self-concept and social adjustment than their nongifted counterparts? Or do gifted youngsters have less trouble with self-concept and social image? If these children have low self-concept, are they then more likely to display suicidal behavior? Supporting the first view, Betts (1986) indicated that the social and emotional needs of gifted adolescents often are not being met, resulting in a lack of self-confidence and self-esteem. On the other hand, Ludwig and Cullinan (1984) indicated that gifted elementary students show fewer behavior problems than their nongifted classmates. However, in a review of the literature, Delisle (1986) reported that gifted young people are especially susceptible to making suicide attempts.

In light of the previous research, the following study by Nichols and Fasko (1986) was conducted with two purposes in mind: (1) to evaluate self-concept as one possible factor in adolescent suicide, and (2) to determine whether gifted adolescents have lower self-concepts (and therefore higher suicide probability) than their nongifted counterparts.

Method

Subjects. A total of 44 students, aged 12 through 17 years, were included in this study: twenty-five nongifted students, obtained from a program for disadvantaged high school students at a regional university in Arkansas and from classes at a public elementary school in rural Arkansas (13 white, 12 black; 14 female, 11 males); and nineteen musically gifted students, who were obtained from a similar program for gifted and talented students (19 white; 11 males, 8 females) at this same university.

Instruments. The instrument selected to measure suicide probability was the *Suicide Probability Scale* (SPS) by Cull and Gill (1982). This appeared to be a reliable instrument with a test-retest r=.92; its scores, which range from 0 to 99 on the Subclinical (low probability) scale used in this study, indicate level of probable suicidal behavior. That is, the higher the score, the more probable an individual will attempt suicide. Cross-validation studies indicated that the SPS correctly identified normal, psychiatric inpatient, and suicide attempter groups with an 84% to 88% accuracy rate.

The *Tennessee Self-Concept Scale* (TSC) by Fitts (1964), an instrument with a reported reliability coefficient of .92 for the Total Positive score was selected for measurement of self-concept. The range of scores on the TSC is from 150 to 450: the higher score indicating a more positive self-concept. Cross-validation studies also indicated that the TSC discriminated well between a hospital group, a community mental health center group, and a VA psychiatric group.

Procedure. A randomly selected group of high school students entering the regional university's special program were administered the *Tennessee Self-Concept Scale.* Within two weeks these students were administered the *Suicide Probability Scale.* The same procedure was used for those sixth grade students who were randomly selected at the beginning of the school term. The following summer, the entire class of 19 students enrolled in a university program for musically gifted high school students were administered the TSC and SPS on one day during the first week of the program.

Results

For the gifted and talented group, the results indicated a significant negative correlation between self-concept and suicide probability ($r=-.74$, $p < .05$). That is, the higher the reported self-concept, the lower the suicide probability. Scores on the TSC ranged from 253 to 398 with a mean and standard deviation of 331 and 41, respectively. For the SPS, the scores ranged from 1 to 28 with a mean of 7 and a standard deviation of 9.

For the nongifted group, the results also indicated a significant negative correlation between self-concept and suicide probability ($r=-.56$, $p < .05$). On the TSC the scores ranged from 250 to 398 with a mean and standard deviation of 322 and 43, respectively. For the SPS, the scores ranged from 1 to 14 with a mean of 6 and a standard deviation of 4. These results can be seen in Table 4.1.

TABLE 4.1

Pearson Correlations for the Tennessee Self-Concept and Suicide Probability Scales for Both Groups

Sample	N	r
Nongifted	25	-.56*
Gifted	19	-.74*

Note. * $p < .05$

To determine whether the TSC and SPS scores were different between the groups, t-tests were computed. The means, standard deviations, and t-test results can be seen in Tables 4.2 and 4.3.

TABLE 4.2

Means and Standard Deviations for the Tennessee Self-Concept and Suicide Probability Scales for both Groups

		TSC		**SPS**	
Sample	N	M	s.d.	M	s.d.
Nongifted	25	322	43	6	4
Gifted	19	331	41	7	9

TABLE 4.3

T-test for the Tennessee Self-Concept and Suicide Probability Scales for Both Groups

Source	t	omega²
TSC	-.71	.01
SPS	-.47	.02

Note. $p > .05$

The results indicated no significant differences between the groups on the TSC ($t=-.71$, $p > .05$) and the SPS ($t=-.47$, $p > .05$). However, there was a significant $F=10.3$ ($p < .05$) indicating that there was a differential variability in the responses to the SPS. That is, the gifted students appeared to be more consistent in their responses than were the nongifted students.

Discussion

The present study does not support the notion that gifted students have lower self-concept and, therefore, higher suicide probability than nongifted students. In fact, because no significant differences were identified in the average scores of the two groups, this study also lends no support to the idea that the gifted have less problems related to self-concept than their nongifted peers, and are therefore at lower risk for suicide. It must be pointed out, however, that the gifted group contained only Caucasian students while the nongifted group was more heterogeneous as to race. One might have expected this factor to have made a greater difference in the two groups.

Interestingly, though, personality traits such as "ego strength" appear to characterize creative people within a specific intellectual discipline (Gardner, 1983). However, there were no differences in ego strength/self-concept between the musically talented group and the nongifted group in this study. According to Gardner (1983) "music is a separate intellectual competence" (p. 122), which, one may assume, is different from an academic intellectual competence. Perhaps differences would have been in self-concept and suicide probability between the gifted and nongifted groups if the gifted group included academically (e.g., mathematically) talented students.

However, the results of this study do support the idea that adolescents who have lower self-concepts have a higher suicide probability. As has been stated previously, several authorities (Faigel, 1966; Cull & Gill, 1982; Stein & Davis, 1982; Stillion et al., 1984) indicated their belief that suicidal adolescents have a low self-concept. A study by Stillion et al. (1984) yielded similar results when self-report measures indicated that students who agree with suicidal behavior had lower self-esteem than those who agreed less often.

IMPLICATIONS

Although this study may be limited by the fact that it utilized a small sample of subjects, the results of this study can still help those who work with young people in determining which individuals are most likely to attempt suicide. For example, adolescents with low self-concept may be more likely to attempt suicide than those who have a higher self-concept. Those students who appear to have a lower self-concept could be considered "at risk," and the *Suicide Probability Scale* could then be administered to them. The schools that routinely administer self-concept scales could screen for those students with low scores and then give them the *Suicide Probability Scale.*

At present, the best prevention of suicide is public awareness of the determinants and warning signs of possible suicidal intent.

Teachers are in an advantageous position to spot a suicidal youngster. Often parents do not notice behavioral changes or are reluctant to admit that anything is wrong other than "growing pains." When students' grades begin to fall and they begin to withdraw from friends and activities, the teacher should take a closer look at those students and perhaps offer them an opportunity to talk.

All school counselors need to be aware of the warning signs of suicide and crisis intervention techniques. Often the counselor is the person parents or teachers turn to when they notice "something wrong" with the student. One might be wise, however, to move cautiously with the excessively dependent personality, since some evidence (Schwartz, 1979) is present that some crisis intervention therapies tend to reinforce suicidal behavior in these personality types.

By knowing what characteristics are most typical of suicide attempters (or those who think about suicide), we can investigate and take preventive measures with those adolescents who display these characteristics, thereby extending some hope of reducing the rate of adolescent suicide.

AUTHOR NOTES

We appreciate the valuable comments of Dan Ford and Ed Kardas on an earlier draft of this manuscript. We also thank Carman Wistrand for her help in preparing this manuscript.

REFERENCES

Berman, A., & Carroll, T. (1984). Adolescent suicide: A critical review. *Death Education, 8,* 53-64.

Betts, G. (1986). Development of the emotional and social needs of gifted individuals. *Journal of Counseling and Development, 64,* 587-9.

Cantor, P. (1976). Personality characteristics found among youthful female suicide attempters. *Journal of Abnormal Psychology, 85,* 324-9.

Crumley, F.E. (1979). Adolescent Suicide Attempts. *Journal of the American Medical Association, 241,* 2404-7.

Cull, J., & Gill, W. (1982). *Suicide Probability Scale Manual.* Los Angeles: Western Psychological Services.

Delisle, J. (1986). Death with honors: Suicide among gifted adolescents. *Journal of Counseling and Development, 64,* 558-60.

Faigel, H. (1966). Suicide among young persons: A review of its incidence and causes, and methods for its prevention. *Clinical Pediatrics, 5,* 187-90.

Farberow, N., & Schneidman, E. (Eds.). (1965). *The cry for help.* New York: McGraw-Hill.

Finch, S., & Poznanski, E. (1971). *Adolescent suicide.* Springfield, IL: Thomas.

Fitts, W. (1964). *Tennessee Self-Concept Scale.* Nashville, TN: Counselor Recordings and Tests.

Freese, A. (1979). *Adolescent suicide: Mental health challenge.* USA: Public Affairs Committee, Inc.

Friedman, R., Corn, R., Hurt, S., Fibel, B., Schulick, J., & Swirsky, S. (1984). Family history of illness in the seriously suicidal adolescent: A life-cycle approach. *American Journal of Orthopsychiatry, 54,* 390-7.

Gardner, H. (1983). *Frames of mind.* New York: Basic Books.

Garfinkel, B., Froese, A., & Hood, J. (1982). Suicide attempts in children and adolescents. *American Journal of Psychiatry, 139,* 1257-61.

Geller, A., & Atkins, A. (1978). Cognitive and personality factors in suicidal behavior. *Journal of Consulting and Clinical Psychology, 46,* 860-8.

Glaser, K. (1978). The treatment of depressed and suicidal adolescents. *American Journal of Psychotherapy, 32,* 252-69.

Greuling, J., & DeBlassie, R. (1980). Adolescent suicide. *Adolescence, 15,* 589-601.

Hafen, B.Q. (Ed.). (1972). *Self-destructive behavior.* Minneapolis: Burgess.

Hendin, H. (1975). Growing up dead: Student suicide. *American Journal of Psychotherapy, 29,* 327-39.

Jacobs, J. (1971). *Adolescent suicide.* New York: Wiley-Interscience.

Kiev, A. (1977). *The suicidal patient.* Chicago: Nelson-Hall.

Kovacs, M., Beck, A., & Weismann, A. (1975). The use of suicidal motives in the psychotherapy of attempted suicides. *American Journal of Psychotherapy, 29,* 363-8.

Kubler-Ross, E. (1983). *On death and dying.* New York: MacMillan.

LaDame, F., & Jeanneret, O. (1982). Suicide in adolescents: Some comments on epidemiology and prevention. *Journal of Consulting and Clinical Psychology, 5,* 355-66.

Levenson, M., & Neuringer, C. (1971). Problem-solving behavior in suicidal adolescents. *Journal of Consulting and Clinical Psychology, 37,* 433-6.

Ludwig, G., & Cullinan, D. (1984). Behavior problems of gifted and nongifted elementary school girls and boys. *Gifted Child Quarterly, 28,* 37-9.

Mack, J., & Hickler, H. (1981). *Vivienne: The life and suicide of an adolescent.* Boston: Little, Brown, & Co.

Marohn, R., Locke, E., Rosenthal, R., & Curtiss, G. (1982). Juvenile delinquents and violent death. *Adolescent Psychiatry, 10,* 147-70.

McCoy, K. (1982). *Coping with teenage depression.* New York: The New American Library.

McHenry, P., Tishler, C., & Kelley, C. (1983). The role of drugs in adolescent suicide attempts. *Suicide and Life-threatening Behavior, 13,* 166-75.

Miller, D. (1981). Adolescent suicide: Etiology and treatment. *Adolescent Psychiatry, 9,* 327-42.

Neuringer, C. (1964). Rigid thinking in suicidal individuals. *Journal of Consulting Psychology, 28,* 54-8.

Nichols, S., & Fasko, D. (1986, March). *The relationship between self-concept and adolescent suicide probability.* Paper presented at the annual meeting of the Eastern Educational Research Association, Miami Beach, FL.

Orbach, I. (1984). Personality characteristics, life circumstances, and dynamics of suicidal children. *Death Education, 8,* 37-52.

Patsiokas, A., Clum, G., & Luscombe, R. (1979). Cognitive characteristics of suicide attempters. *Journal of Consulting and Clinical Psychology, 7,* 478-84.

Peck, D. (1983). The last moments of life: Learning to cope. *Deviant Behavior, 4,* 313-42.

Peck, M. (1981). The loner: An exploration of a suicidal subtype in adolescence. *Adolescent Psychiatry, 9,* 461-6.

Petzel, S., & Riddle, M. (1982). Adolescent suicide: Psychosocial and cognitive aspects. *Adolescent Psychiatry, 9,* 343-98.

Pfeffer, C., Plutchik, R., Mizruchi, M., & Lipkins, R. (1986). Suicidal behavior in child psychiatric inpatients and outpatients and in nonpatients. *American Journal of Psychiatry, 143,* 733-8.

Pfeffer, C., Plutchik, R., & Mizruchi, M. (1983). Suicidal and assaultive behavior in children: Classification, measurement, and interrelations. *American Journal of Psychiatry, 140,* 154-7.

Price, R., & Lynn, S. (1981). *Abnormal Psychology in the Human Context.* Homewood, IL: Dorsey Press.

Rosenkrantz, A. (1978). A note on adolescent suicide: Incidence, dynamics, and some suggestions for treatment. *Adolescence, 13,* 209-13.

Rosenstock, H. (1985). Depression, suicide ideation, and suicide attempts in 900 adolescents: An analysis. *Crisis, 6,* 89-105.

Schneidman, E. (1987). At the point of no return. *Psychology Today, 21,* 54-9.

Schwartz, D. (1979). The suicidal character. *Psychiatric Quarterly, 51,* 64-70.

Shaughnessy, M., & Nystul, M. (1985). Preventing the greatest loss-suicide. *The Creative Child & Adult Quarterly, 10,* 164-9.

Sheras, P. (1983). Suicide in adolescence. In C. Walker & M. Roberts (Eds.), *Handbook of Clinical Child Psychology.* New York: John Wiley.

Snyder, S., Pitts, W., & Pokorny, A. (1986). Selected behavioral features of patients with borderline personality traits. *Suicide & Life-threatening Behavior, 16,* 29-39.

Sommer, B. (1984). The troubled teen: Suicide, drug use, and running away. *Women and Health, 9,* 117-41.

Stein, M., & Davis, J. (1982). *Therapies for adolescents.* San Francisco: Jossey-Bass.

Stillion, J., McDowell, E., & Shamblin, J. (1984). The suicide attitude vignette experience: A method for measuring adolescent attitudes toward suicide. *Death Education, 8,* 65-81.

Tabachnick, N. (1981). The interlocking psychologies of suicide and adolescence. *Adolescent Psychiatry, 9,* 399-410.

Tomlinson-Keasey, C., Warren, L., & Elliott, J. (1986). Suicide among gifted women: A prospective study. *Journal of Abnormal Psychology, 95,* 123-30.

Toolan, J. (1975). Suicide in children and adolescents. *American Journal for Psychotherapy, 29,* 339-45.

Toolan, J. (1981). Depression and suicide in children: An overview. *American Journal of Psychotherapy, 35,* 311-21.

Topol, P., & Reznikoff, M. (1982). Perceived peer and family relationships, hopelessness, and locus of control as factors in adolescent suicide. *Suicide and Life-threatening Behavior, 12,* 141-50.

CHAPTER **5**

THINKING PATTERNS AND MOTIVATION

Patricia Velkoff, M.S.
and
Thomas J. Huberty, Ph.D.

Patricia Velkoff, M.S.
Department of Counseling and Educational Psychology
Indiana University

Patricia Velkoff is a doctoral student in the Department of Counseling and Educational Psychology at Indiana University. Following her particular interests in human development and family therapy, she is completing a dissertation in the area of childhood depression. She has been Assistant Director of the Center for Human Growth, a campus/community counseling center, and Clinic Coordinator of the Institute for Child Study, a training and research center which offers diagnosis and remediation to children with various academic and behavioral difficulties.

She is currently a psychology intern at the Philadelphia Child Guidance Clinic, which offers specialized training in structural family therapy.

Ms. Velkoff has given a number of presentations in the areas of group therapy, emotional development, and depression. Her interest in adolescent suicide stems from a broader interest in depression, particularly as it affects children. Her continuing research activities are exploring the interface between cognitive and emotional development among young people.

Thomas J. Huberty, Ph.D.

Assistant Professor
Department of Counseling and Educational Psychology
Indiana University
Bloomington, IN 47405

Thomas J. Huberty received his Ph.D. in School Psychology from the University of Missouri-Columbia in 1980. Work experiences include community mental health settings, pediatrics, and facilities serving the developmentally disabled. Areas of specialization are in psychological assessment and intervention of children and adolescents with social-emotional difficulties.

He is a consultant to school systems concerning the identification and treatment of students experiencing emotional problems. He has made several presentations at national conventions concerning the psychological assessment of emotionally handicapped children and adolescents. Primary teaching responsibilities are the training of school psychologists. He has written and conducted research on anxiety in children and the relationships of cognitive-affective factors to learning. Of particular interest is the degree to which depressive behavior in children and adolescents affects cognitive ability and performance.

EDITORIAL ABSTRACT: *The purpose of this chapter is to explain how the thinking and motivational patterns of suicidal adolescents are different in quality from those of the non-suicidal adolescent. The reader will find the discussions of cognitive distortions and motivational factors particularly helpful since these discussions help direct and focus observation and assessment during counseling and/or therapy. Suggestions and guidelines for assisting adolescent clients in the process of correcting cognitive distortions and increasing motivation are also provided.*

Research has shown that the thought patterns and motivations of suicidal adolescents distinguish them from their non-suicidal peers along a number of definable dimensions. While adolescents who attempt suicide are often subject to high levels of life stress, equally well established now is that in addition to external problems, the suicidal adolescent's thoughts are different in quality and quantity from those of the normally functioning or non-suicidal adolescent. The cognitive and motivational characteristics of these young people are not only correlated with the suicide attempt, but are in many cases causally related. In coming to understand the phenomenon of adolescent suicide, an equally important aspect is to attend not only to external stressors but also to the adolescent's internal state of mind.

While knowledge of cognitive and motivational factors is helpful to mental health professionals in understanding the suicidal adolescent, they also have been shown to be excellent, and even essential, targets for the treatment and prevention of suicidal and parasuicidal behavior. Cognitive and motivational perspectives provide an excellent framework, then, for developing intervention, treatment, and prevention strategies.

REVIEW OF RELATED LITERATURE

An assumption of the present chapter is that motivational and cognitive states have a great deal to do with how one feels and behaves. The decision to take one's own life will be discussed from two points of view which initially may appear to be incompatible. A *cognitive* viewpoint assumes that suicidal individuals develop a particular cognitive framework which makes suicide, an unthinkable option for most people, appear to be a visible solution to the pains encountered in living. From this perspective, suicidal behavior is seen as a cognitively distorted means of dealing with difficult situations. A *motivational* viewpoint, on the other hand, assumes that all emotions, including those that lead an individual to attempt suicide, are adaptive and designed ultimately to regulate one's energy and perceptions and to facilitate social interaction. While the cognitive viewpoint sees suicide as resulting from maladaptive cognitions, the motivational viewpoint sees suicide, like all behavior, as ultimately adaptive.

That human thoughts and feelings are subjective allows for the reconciliation of these two different ways of understanding suicidal behavior. Every individual develops a unique perspective on the world based on an individual evaluation of experience. A personal reality is created which is an individualized understanding of how the world works. Because of this personal perspective, people are capable of having inaccurate thoughts and of initiating a maladaptive execution of the adaptive function. Inaccuracy can occur either in cognitions (e.g., "I believe that this escape into death will make me happier") or in motivation (e.g., "The only path toward survival is to get out of this intolerable situation by dying"). Suicidal behaviors, then, are believed to be based on distortions of either thought or motivation or both, and are not considered to be a normal function of adolescence, or indeed of any other age.

Cognitive Theory

Depression is the most common psychological feature associated with adolescent suicide. The estimate is that between 45% and 75% of those who commit or attempt suicide show previous signs of depression (Avery & Winokur, 1978). While depression and suicide are certainly not identical, the thought processes of suicidal individuals have a great deal in common with those of depressed individuals.

Several current theories of depression stress the role of cognitive factors in the development of depression. Two theories in particular, Beck's Cognitive Distortion Theory and Lazarus's Cognitive Appraisal Theory, explain the integral relationship between an individual's thought processes and his/her feelings.

Beck's Cognitive Distortion Theory. The Cognitive Distortion Theory of depression (Beck, 1974, 1983) provides a framework for understanding suicidal ideation. Beck proposes that depressed and suicidal individuals develop a mental framework for evaluating events that he calls the "negative cognitive triad." The triad consists of a negative view of the self, the *world*, and the *future*. Regarding the *self*, suicidal individuals believe that they are not adequate to cope with life's problems. They find justification for believing that they are defective in comparison to others and unable to appropriately set and attain goals for themselves. Regarding *others*, they view obstacles and difficulties as insurmountable and they tend to view demands made on them as being overwhelming. And regarding the *future*, they believe that no possible positive end can come to their current problems and pain and that a continuing cycle of failure is inevitable.

This negative belief system becomes pervasive, coloring the person's thoughts and leading to a negatively-biased overreaction to life events (Saklofske & Janzen, 1987). The negative distortion of reality is then applied as a way of understanding whatever happens in the individual's environment, regardless of the positive or negative valence of the original situation.

What results is a state of withdrawal and lack of initiative, since the individual believes that all aspects of life are destined to result in undesirable consequences. In his recent writings, Beck (1983) stated that these distorted psychological processes occur in conjunction with parallel biochemical processes, resulting in a state of "learned helplessness" such as that described by Seligman (1975). The reformulated model of learned helplessness (Abramson, Seligman, & Teasdale, 1978) holds that a sense of lack of control is increased when the individual believes that negative events are due to personal characteristics (internal as opposed to external events), temporally stable events, and global situations. When the individual believes that good events can be explained by external, unstable, and specific causes, perhaps depression results (Seligman, Abramson, Semmel, & VonBaeyer, 1979), although further research is needed in this area. The central variable is the degree of control which the individual believes that he/she is able to exert in the situation.

Lazarus' Cognitive Appraisal Theory. According to Cognitive Appraisal Theory (Lazarus, 1975), people define their emotional states only after they have some salient thoughts about the matter at hand. Rather than focusing on the antecedent emotions to depression, as Beck does, Lazarus (Lazarus, Kanner, & Folkman, 1980) stated that emotion is determined by the individual's anticipation of the outcome of his/her actions. Lazarus also sees emotions as having a signaling function, alerting the organism to the need for the alleviation of stress and the development of coping activities. From this point of view, depression and suicidal ideation can be seen as having a potentially positive function, that of alerting the individual to the seriousness of the situation and to the need for action to alleviate stress.

For both Beck and Lazarus, depressive and suicidal feelings are said to be the result of how one thinks about oneself and the surrounding social and physical world. Cognitive processes are seen by both theorists as an integral component of the development of all emotional states, including depression, which commonly precede suicidal behavior.

Motivational Theory

A motivational theory of emotion has been proposed by Izard and his colleagues (Izard, 1977; Izard & Schwartz, 1986). Depression and the underlying motivation for suicide is viewed as essentially adaptive, providing signals to oneself and to others about what is needed for survival. As stated previously, in the case of suicide these motivations can be distorted so that survival of the individual is actually jeopardized rather than facilitated. Nevertheless, the drive toward suicide, as opposed to the act itself, is seen from a motivational perspective as being a drive toward the preservation of life.

Within Izard's framework, suicidal ideation is seen as providing feedback both to *oneself* and to others. To *oneself*, the message is that a need exists for remedy of the current situation. Thoughts and behaviors are activated which can lead to the removal of stress, the restoration of peace, the recollection of prior ways of coping, and other life-preserving functions. Social withdrawal, which frequently accompanies depression and precedes suicide, can be seen as an adaptive removal of negative stimuli and a means of distancing oneself from intolerable pain and stress. If the adolescent believes that he/she is in an intolerable and unchangeable environmental situation, the motivation to withdraw can be understood as an attempt at self-preservation, even though suicide is an extreme, permanent, and ultimately distorted form of this function. Suicidal behavior also can be seen to have a social and communicative function of signaling to *others* the depth of the adolescent's distress and need for relief. In this sense, suicidal behavior signals to those who care about the adolescent the desperate and immediate need for caretaking and for social bonding.

Suicide, then, can be seen as a distorted form of adaptation, an expression of the adolescent's motivation to live by communicating to oneself the need to withdraw from pain and to conserve energy, and by signaling to others a pressing, even desperate, need for help. Cases of depression in a five-year-old boy (Giancotti & Vinci, 1986) and a six-year-old boy (O'Connor, 1986) have recently been described in just these terms, with an emphasis on the adaptive function of the depression which serves to protect the child from further pain. In this way, suicide is seen as a tendency toward life and not toward death, a way of mobilizing individual and collective energy to reduce overwhelming pain and in fact save the life of the individual.

Thinking Patterns of the Suicidal Adolescent

Suicidal ideation and behavior are not normal parts of adolescence but result from distorted cognitions that lead the adolescent to a depressive, helpless, and hopeless world view. Novick (1984) has emphasized that adolescent suicide attempts are the final act in a disturbance dominated by depression and feelings of abnor--mality. The mentality of suicidal and non-suicidal adolescents differ, then, along a number of definable dimensions, both cognitive and motivational.

Cognitive Content and Processes of Suicidal Adolescents. Researchers who have traced the cognitive history of adolescent suicide attempters have usually discovered a pattern of negative cognitions which applies to all, or nearly all, aspects of the adolescent's life. Little that the adolescent perceives or thinks escapes this bleak mentality that casts a dark and pessimistic shadow over everything.

This negative overview in turn leads to a series of negative distortions which color how the suicidal adolescent behaves, whether this involves learning in school, interacting with peers and family, or making simple daily decisions. Low self-esteem and self-defeating thoughts are common, creating a dominant framework for dealing with the world that is gloomy and pessimistic. The positive potential inherent in various situations is ignored, while the negative potential becomes magnified to the point that it is all-encompassing. Single difficult situations, for example performing poorly in a class or the breakup of a relationship, may be magnified to color the adolescent's entire self-image with visions of failure and pessimism.

Cognitive Distortions. While most adolescent develop ways of thinking based on the surrounding reality, suicidal adolescents distort their perceptions and thoughts to coincide with this negative mentality. While close scrutiny reveals that such a negative mentality cannot be entirely substantiated by reality, these individuals often are unable to recognize the distortions without help from someone more objective. These distortions can be categorized along a number of dimensions.

One important dimension is the *all-or-nothing thinking* in which the suicidal adolescent engages. Situations are seen as polarized, and options are thought to be either black or white. The underlying distortion behind this kind of thinking is a difficulty in perceiving subtlety and complication in a situation.

Another prominent characteristic of suicidal thought is *overgeneralization*, which lead the adolescent to take a single event and mentally magnify it so that it seems to apply to many other situations. An adolescent who is teased by a classmate might tell himself/herself that everyone in the school dislikes him/her, thus distorting a single event as evidence for a much more general pattern. An example of overgeneralization would be changing the statement: "I'm not a good basketball player" into the statement: "I'm a complete failure."

Suicidal adolescents also are seen to select a single negative detail in their life and to perseverate in their thinking about it. Over time, this single event can dominate their thoughts to the exclusion of other more healthy thoughts, a process which is often referred to as a *mental filter*. For example, adolescents often perseverate about situations involving peer relationships, since these are especially crucial during the adolescent years.

They also have a tendency to *disqualify the positive,* rejecting positive experiences and insisting that they are unimportant. This can be seen in the selective perception and attention of the adolescent for negative details, or more overtly in statements which indicate that all the positive events in the world cannot make up for one negative event.

Catastrophizing is another cognitive characteristic of the suicidal adolescent. Through this way of thinking, adolescents exaggerate the importance or consequences of negative events. Examples of this kind of thinking are embodied in the statements: "If Mary leaves, I'll never be happy again" and "If I don't make the cast of the play, I'll never be able to hold my head up again."

Distortions are also evident in the way an adolescent labels, or rather mislabels, the meaning of events. Instead of saying, "I made a mistake," the suicidal adolescent is likely to conclude that "I am a loser." This labeling process creates a more negative meaning than the original situation warrants and can facilitate other negative thoughts which go well beyond the stimulus event.

Suicidal adolescents often see themselves as the cause of negative events, such as the divorce of their parents, when in fact true responsibility lies beyond their own control. This is known as *personalization,* and is somewhat more common in younger adolescents but can be found in individuals of all ages.

Finally, *cognitive rigidity* is often present, so that suicidal adolescents become set in a way of viewing themselves and the world and obstinately retain this view despite contradictory evidence. Such cognitive rigidity often incorporates elements of all or many of the distortions just described and can lead to an obstinate retention of cognitions which are inaccurate, inflexible, or simply inappropriate for the situation at hand.

While a grain of truth is in each of these distortions (e.g., a single negative event may indeed be only one in a series of negative events which the individual has experienced), what makes them distortions is their application to situations in which they are inappropriate through selective attention, misattribution, and similar alterations in the perception of reality. In fact, the very "grain of truth" allows one to maintain a distortion; otherwise, the false or distorted aspect of it would become apparent immediately and be easy to dislodge. In working with the cognitive distortions of suicidal adolescents, one must be ready to recognize both the truth of the individual's situation (e.g., this is in fact one in a series of problems) and also the degree to which the person's thinking is negatively altered.

Self Defeating Cycle. These cognitive distortions can lead to a self-perpetuating cycle of self-defeating thoughts and reduced motivation to perform well (a "what's the use?" attitude), on the assumption that effort cannot lead to an improvement in one's situation. And the reduced effort leads in turn to poor performance, reinforcing the adolescent's view that effort is not rewarded and that he/she is incompetent and worthless. This can be schematically represented as follows:

negative cognitions—> poor expectations of success

reduced effort—> reduced performance

reduced self-esteem—> negative cognitions...

Increased social self-isolation often follows, accompanied by a sense that others cannot understand the depth of one's feelings. Unfortunately, this isolation most often leads to an accelerated cycle of self-defeat and negative thoughts, since isolated adolescents reduce their own chances of discovering that others both understand and care about the pain that they are feeling. The pattern, then, is of a self-defeating cycle. Over a period of time, negative causes and negative effects succeed each other alternatively. One cause provokes an effect, and that effect becomes the cause of another effect, perpetuating a cycle of gloom and self-defeat.

Involuntary Versus Voluntary Thought Processes. Depressed adolescents will normally experience a drop in school performance and will withdraw from activities which they previously found enjoyable. While the temptation is to press the adolescent to improve school performance, the evidence is that reduction in motivation and performance is not entirely deliberate. As the adolescent's depression continues and/or increases, he/she will lose the ability to concentrate and will be unable to complete tasks which require sustained effort (Kaslow, Rehm, & Siegel, 1984;

Raskin, Friedman, & DiMascio, 1982), Perceptual flexibility and abstract thinking also have been shown to be negatively affected by depression (Raskin, Friedman, & DiMascio, 1982), as have performance on cognitive tasks requiring perceptual organization and mental alertness (Kaslow, Rehm, & Siegel, 1984). Levenson and Neuringer (1971) have pointed out that suicidal adolescents have a generally diminished problem-solving capacity for a wide variety of tasks.

Slow performance is also a common characteristic of depression (Kaslow, Tanenbaum, Abramson, Peterson, & Seligman, 1983), although at this time the reason is unclear as to whether this is due to lower expectations for performance, higher criteria for success, preference for punishment over reward (Kaslow, Rehm, & Siegel, 1984), or decreased time perspective and goal orientation (Corder, Shorr, & Corder, 1974).

Clearly, based on these findings, depression can have a devastating effect on the adolescent's academic performance. What is more, apparently some contributing factors, such as an inability to concentrate and reduced problem-solving skills, are not experienced by the adolescent as being voluntary. Yet, despite the presence of involuntary thought processes, those who work with suicidal adolescents would do well to remember that cognitions are effective as the focus of both short-term intervention and long-term treatment. Even involuntary aspects of one's thinking, such as slowed performance and difficulties in concentration, can be altered through systematic and patient work on the adolescent's thought processes.

Motivational Factors of the Suicidal Adolescent

A bewildering array of external stressors have been linked to adolescent suicide, including rising divorce rates, single parent households, population growth, reduced family support, and the pressure on teenagers to succeed in the face of national economic difficulties (Children, Youth, and Families, 1984). However, professionals who work with younger people also come in contact with adolescents who may be experiencing a number of significant stressors but are not turning to suicide as a means of coping either with environmental problems or with developmental changes. Suicide is not a rational act in response to an impossible situation but is an irrational act reflecting a state of mind which is, at least temporarily, imbalanced. One must look beyond external factors such as stressful life events in coming to understand suicidal behavior, and focus on what motivates the young person to contemplate this extreme act.

Motivation can be defined as action which is directed toward achieving a goal, and which consists of both drives and reinforcing consequences. As such, motivation serves to activate both internal resources and external communicative functions with the anticipated outcome of reaching one's goals. A motivation toward suicide can be understood within this framework as fulfilling three primary functions: first, an *avoidance* function which protects the individual from pain; second, a *control* function by which the adolescent attempts to regain control of himself/herself and of the environment; and third, a *communicative* function which signals to others a need for help and for reduced environmental pressure.

The Avoidance Function. As stated previously, suicidal adolescents often experience a series of highly stressful situations: parental divorce, school failure, sexual maturation and physical changes, as well as new relationship roles, to name only a few. Even when these stresses are not extreme or unusual by any objective criteria, the suicidal adolescent may experience them as being overwhelming. Whether the stress is objectively verifiable or only subjectively perceived, however, the adolescent will be motivated to avoid negative situations that are perceived to be either too psychologically painful or simply unchangeable by any personal effort.

In support of this notion, Hawton, Cole, O'Grady, and Osborn (1982) conducted a study of 50 adolescents who had attempted suicide. Specifically, they looked at the reasons given by these young people after the attempt. For 42% of the group, the attempt was designed to "get relief from a terrible state of mind," and 42% also said that they wished to "escape for a while from an impossible situation." These reasons reflect the function of avoidance, the need to escape a situation which is perceived to be intolerable but from which there appears to be no other relief.

The Control Function. Suicidal adolescents are also motivated to gain control of themselves and to gain some degree of control of environmental events. This control is linked to the perceived loss of contingent reinforcement and a sense of hopelessness.

Perceived Loss of Contingent Reinforcement. Contingent reinforcement means that positive feedback from the environment is perceived to depend on (be contingent upon) one's own actions. The sense of an environment which is responsive to one's actions begins at a very early age and is central to the development of a sense of self-efficacy. Individuals vary considerably in the degree to which they feel a need for control and in their threshhold for tolerating being out of control. What is more, the life situations of individuals vary considerably in the degree to which control of reinforcement is actually possible. Irrespective of the environmental situation, however, each individual can be considered to have a subjective range of acceptable contingency, a range of perceived control which may vary around an optimal level for that individual. Variations of perceived control which lie at or above the person's essential control level lead to a sense of mastery; variations which fall below the essential level leave the person feeling helpless and hopeless, unable to adequately influence the results of his/her actions.

Helplessness versus Hopelessness. The perception that one has some degree of control over the reinforcing consequences of one's action is an important factor in the development of depression, an effect which has been shown to hold both for adults (Abramson, Seligman, & Teasdale, 1978) and for adolescents (Rholes, Blackwell, Jordan, & Walters, 1980). What is more, the sense of control is better understood not in objective terms but in subjective terms. A distinction between helplessness and hopelessness is useful in understanding this difference between perceived and actual control.

Studies of attribution have made a distinction between locus of causality, which can be either internal or external, and degree of controllability of the situation (Weiner, 1979). For example, if an adolescent of above average intelligence is failing a class, he/she may determine that the cause of failure is both internal ("I caused this myself by skipping class and not doing my homework" and controllable ("If I start studying, I can get better grades"). An adolescent of below average intelligence who has struggled through elementary school to barely keep up may discover that high school work is beyond his/her ability to perform. This adolescent may decide that the cause of failure is external ("The work is too hard for me") and uncontrollable ("I can't do well even when I try").

The distinction between causality and control is a useful one when attempting to understand the cognitive or attributional style of the suicidal adolescent. Attribution refers to the individual's belief in whether locus of control is due to his/her own effort or due to external factors. A sense of external causality can lead to a sense of hopelessness, a feeling that the situation will remain as it is, and that no hope of remedy is possible. A sense of lack of control, on the other hand, can lead to a sense of helplessness, a feeling that one cannot have an impact on the situation. While helplessness does not rule out the possibility of some eventual change in the situation, hopelessness can produce a sense of despair, a belief that no hope for relief is possible in the future. This sense of hopelessness is more likely to result in suicidal ideation and behavior than the sense of helplessness.

Research has supported this distinction in that a relationship exists between high depression scores, low income, and external locus of control (Lefkowitz, Tesiny, & Gordon, 1980; Mullins, Siegel, & Hodges, 1985). These findings support the theoretical position that an inability to effect change in the environment can lead to an increased sense of hopelessness, culminating in depressive or suicidal behavior. At the same time, income was found to account for only a small amount of the variance in depression, so that other factors, including attributional style, also must contribute to the sense of hopelessness.

The Communicative Function. In addition to the motivation to avoid pain, the suicidal adolescent is also motivated to communicate to others the need for help and for reduced stress. In the study by Hawton and associates (Hawton et al., 1982), many adolescents regarded their suicide attempts as a communicative act, a way of commanding attention. In this study, 42% said that they wished to "make people understand how desperate you were feeling;" 32% agreed that they wanted to "make people sorry for the way they have treated you, frighten or get back at someone;" 26% attempted suicide to "try to influence some particular person to get them to change their mind;" and 18% said that they wanted to "seek help from someone." This demand for responsiveness from others is an effort to regain contingent reinforcement which was lost, either in fact or in the perception of the adolescent is as though the adolescent were saying: "You haven't been listening to me, but I'll force you to listen now."

Research data have shown that parents and teachers often do not notice the signs of depression and suicidal ideation in their adolescents (Rutter, Graham, Chadwick, & Yule, 1976). If significant figures in the adolescent's life are not perceiving their despairing emotional state, they are also likely to be unresponsive to it. Numerous possible reasons for this lack of perception can be hypothesized, but the central point is that the adult's unawareness may lead to a lack of contingency in which the adolescent's misery receives no response from significant figures in the adolescent's life.

Peck (1982) has found that the parents of suicidal children and adolescents are often unable to accept the young person's feelings of misery, depression, or frustration, probably due to their own difficulty in coping with these painful feelings. In the face of emotional expression from their stressed or unhappy adolescent, these parents may either ignore or deny the pressure and strength of these feelings, or they may respond with overt hostility. This lack of acceptance may in turn lead to a sense of rejection and worthlessness, further contributing to the sense of depression and hopelessness and to social self-isolation.

Suicidal attempts also may be an indirect attempt to communicate with others with whom the adolescent is angry. In a comparison of 40 suicidal and 40 nonsuicidal psychiatric patients, Kincel (1981) found that in contrast to nonsuicidal psychiatric patients, suicide attempters experienced a higher intensity of aggression which they directed at themselves. Kincel concluded that inhibited aggression, or aggression which was not appropriately directed toward others, was an important characteristic of suicidal individuals. Similarly, Pfeffer (1984) stated that suicide attempts are often an effort to inflict pain on those who are seen to be the causes of pain for the adolescent. From this perspective, suicide can be seen as an attempt to communicate anger, but from an assumption that a direct expression of anger is unacceptable.

APPLICATIONS

Since the thought processes and motivations of the adolescent have been shown to have significant bearing on the development of depression, a treatment that focuses on cognitions and motivations can be highly effective whether used alone as the central focus of treatment or in conjunction with another treatment strategy. Behavioral, physiological, and traditional therapeutic strategies all have been successfully combined with cognitive and motivational interventions.

In practice, the simultaneous application of several approaches can contribute significantly to the success of any one element of the treatment plan. In working on the adolescent's way of thinking, non-cognitive approaches can have a positive effect upon cognitive-motivational processes. Similarly, cognitive strategies can lead to improvements in physiological symptoms and conduct problems. For example, a behavioral intervention might include graded task assignments through which the adolescent engages in an increasing variety and number of success-producing situations. Success achieved in these behavioral assignments can in turn lead to a decrease in negative cognitions and an increase in self-esteem. In the same way, techniques which lead to a decrease in suicidal ideation relate to a corresponding increase in appropriate cognitive functioning. The importance of three aspects cannot be overemphasized: the tailoring of the therapy to needs of the particular adolescent, the situation in which the adolescent operates, and the specific strengths of the therapist. Once these areas have been taken into consideration, a variety of techniques can be combined to produce maximum improvement in the adolescent's situation.

Research on Cognitive and Motivational Therapy

A number of studies have demonstrated the effectiveness of cognitive and motivational interventions in the treatment of depression. These two approaches therefore can offer concrete help to professionals in understanding and treating suicidal ideation and actions among adolescents.

Cognitive Therapy. Cognitive therapy is designed to teach the adolescent to recognize and challenge negative attitudes and beliefs. A number of studies have shown that cognitive therapy with adults is equally or more effective in the treatment of depression in comparison to other intervention strategies. A study by Rush and associates (Rush, Beck, Kovacs, & Hollon, 1977) showed that cognitive therapy was more effective than tricyclic antidepressant therapy with adult psychiatric patients, and that this effectiveness persisted even after a year from the beginning of treatment. For outpatient treatment, both McLean and Hakstian (1979) and Blackburn and colleagues (Blackburn, Bishop, Glen, Whalley, & Christie, 1981) found cognitive therapy to be superior to other forms of treatment.

Various cognitive techniques also have been studied in pre-test/post-test designs. Attribution retraining has been shown to be effective for both adults (Miller & Norman, 1979) and children (Dweck, 1975; Dweck & Repucci, 1973). Problem-solving strategies (Klein & Seligman, 1976), redecision therapy (Campos, 1986), and rehearsal of the relationship between thoughts and feelings (Mosak, 1985) are specific cognitive techniques which have been shown to be effective in working with depressed individuals.

Motivational Therapy. Motivational strategies have been found to be effective in helping individuals achieve a sense of control. Since the function of suicidal ideation is primarily that of signaling to the adolescent and to others the need for relief from stress and pain, two motivational strategies in particular can help to move the adolescent beyond the sense of immobility and self-isolation and into a more active involvement with others: social skills training and activity increase programs.

Poor or inappropriate social skills are common associated features of depression in young people (Helsel & Matson, 1984). The goal of social skills training is primarily to help the child or adolescent to develop, practice, and gain ease in exhibiting skills which lead to smooth and satisfying social relationships. In studies comparing individual therapy with social skills training (Hersen, Bellack, & Himmelhoch, 1980; Wells, Hersen, Bellack, & Himmelhoch, 1979), the latter has been shown to be effective in improving confidence and assertiveness. The use of peer-pairing also has been used as a way of improving the social skills and self-confidence of isolated children (Mervis, 1985).

Disinterest and lethargy in the suicidal adolescent are usually maintained by a combination of fatigue, the expectation of unsuccessful outcomes, reduced pleasure in activities. Activity increase programs are designed to gradually increase the adolescent's activity level through the use of a variety of incentive techniques. Studies have consistently shown the effectiveness of activity increase programs with depressed adults (Grosscup & Lewinsohn, 1980; Turner, Ward, & Turner, 1979; Zeiss, Lewinsohn, & Munoz, 1979).

Cognitive Intervention Strategies

Cognitive interventions are designed to challenge maladaptive cognitions as being distortions of reality and to help the client substitute new interpretations of the world. This is accomplished through a three stage process: assessing depressive cognitions, learning to self-monitor cognitions, and learning to develop self-control over cognitions. (See Figure 5.1.)

Stages	Intervention Strategies
Assessment of Depressive Cognitions	Personality questionnaires Self-report inventories Behavior rating Scales MMPI Multiple Approaches: observation interviews inventories self report adult reports
Self-Monitoring Of Cognitions	Self-assessment Self-recording checklist wrist-counter golf scoring counter
Development of Self-Control	Substituion of pleasant thoughts Self-control strategies Attribution training Cognition rehearsal of alternate thoughts

Figure 5.1. Cognitive intervention strategies for use with suicidal adolescents.

Assessment of Depressive Cognitions. A variety of personality questionaires, self-report inventories, and behavior rating scales are available to aid the therapist in the assessment of the adolescent's depressive thoughts. Older adolescents might be given the Minnesota Multiphasic Personality Inventory (MMPI), which includes a Depression scale that can provide information about the adolescent's cognitive state. While behavior rating scales might be helpful in establishing the presence, intensity, or classification of depressive symptomatology, they typically offer little help in describing cognitive content. For this reason, self-report measures that assess cognitive content are more likely to be the instruments of choice. When assessing depression as a syndrome or disorder, however, multiple approaches should be used, including observation, interviews, inventories, self-report measures, and information from parents and teachers.

One of the most challenging assessment tasks is the delineation of the cognitions of the depressed or suicidal adolescent. If dysfunctional cognitions are presumed to be causal in the development of adolescent depression and suicide, then valid and reliable methods to assess these cognitions are necessary. Kendall and Korgeski (1979) suggested that the assessment of cognitions serves two purposes. First, it provides a thorough description of the role or roles that cognitions play in behavior. Second, it allows the therapist and client to examine the effectiveness of various treatment methods chosen to change negative cognitions. While the initial assessment work of the therapist may be effective in accomplishing this first function, the second function can be best accomplished by the client through a variety of self-monitoring techniques. Beyond helping with the ongoing therapy process, training in self-monitoring techniques can leave the client with skills that have wide applicability to personal improvement in other areas and at other times in the individual's life.

Self-Monitoring of Cognitions. As a part of the assessment and treatment process, adolescents are taught to systematically monitor their own thoughts and behaviors. Self-monitoring involves asking the adolescent to be attentive to specific thoughts and behaviors that occur and to keep a record of them. Not only does self-monitoring accomplish the purposes suggested by Kendall and Korgeski (1979), but it may be therapeutic simply by making client aware of their dysfunctional cognitions. As a mere function of this increased awareness, the adolescent may be inclined to decrease the frequency with which the thoughts and behaviors occur.

Self-monitoring has two components, *self-assessment* and *self-recording*. *Self-assessment* refers to an individual's evaluation of his/her own behavior to determine if a particular behavior has occurred. For self-assessment to be effective, adolescents must be able and willing to examine their own thoughts and, more specifically, be able to reliably identify them. The majority of adolescents are able to identify and report on dysfunctional or negative thoughts if provided with specific guidance.

The second component of self-monitoring, *self-recording*, involves devising a method to enable the adolescent to record dysfunctional thoughts. The most common method of recording self-monitored thoughts is using a frequency count of the thoughts that occur within specified time periods, such as a morning, a day, or a week. To facilitate the usefulness of the recording process, the therapist will want to help the adolescent identify the most salient cognitions that he/she is experiencing, such as "I feel worthless" or "I want to kill myself." The three primary criteria for choosing which thoughts to record are they should be distinct from each other, identifiable, and lend themselves to reliable reporting. Using these criteria, the therapist and client can work together to develop both a list of the cognitions to be monitored and a reliable method for recording them.

While a wide variety of recording methods can be used, the optimal recording method is one which accomplishes the objective of recording with the greatest efficiency and ease of use. This is particularly important for suicidal adolescents, since they may have lowered energy or coping resources than the average adolescent. If a frequency count of distorted cognitions is needed, a *checklist* which gives a frequency count of how often the thoughts occur can be efficient. At the end of a specified time period, the frequencies can be tabulated to determine the cognitions that occurred most often. A *wrist-counter* or *golf scoring counter* can also be used, so that the adolescent activates the counter each time a negative cognition occurs.

Frequency counts are excellent sources of information about the suicidal adolescent's cognitive state, and any method that the therapist and adolescent can devise that will allow for easy recording of occurrences is recommended. The potential advantages of this approach are fivefold:

1. the client is actively involved in the assessment and treatment process from the beginning,
2. baseline data about negative cognitions can be obtained prior to the beginning of formal treatment,
3. the self-monitoring process may be therapeutic in itself, through the adolescent's increased awareness of cognitions and subsequent reduction of them,
4. recording of thoughts during and after treatment can be used as a criterion for changes in cognitions, and
5. clients will increase the self-examination of their distorted thoughts.

Developing Self-Control of Cognitions. A variety of self-control strategies are available that are effective in the treatment of the distorted cognitions that accompany suicidal ideation. While the present chapter cannot cover all possible self-control strategies, four techniques have been selected for discussion based on their applicability to suicidal adolescents and on the fact that they are widely accepted and well researched. These four strategies are substitution of pleasant thought, self-control strategies, attribution training, and cognitive rehearsal of alternate thoughts.

Substitution of Pleasant Thoughts. Suicidal adolescents are likely to have a vast repertoire of negative thoughts which dominate their cognitive set. Pleasant thoughts are rare or entirely absent, so that the adolescent engages in a self-perpetuating cycle of depressive cognitions. The method of substituting pleasant for unpleasant thoughts operates on the assumption that these two kinds of cognitions cannot occur simultaneously.

To implement this approach, the adolescent and therapist develop a list of pleasant thoughts based upon the adolescent's past history and preferences. The adolescent is then instructed to recall one of these pleasant thoughts at the time that a negative one is experienced. Through the process of repetition and continual replacement of the negative thoughts, the adolescent reduces the quantity and quality of negative cognitions in the repertoire and replaces them with positive thoughts. Obviously, the adolescent must be willing to participate and be at a level of cognitive ability to reflect on his/her own thinking processes. While little empirical evidence is available concerning the effectiveness of this technique with children and adolescents, it has proven to be effective with adults and may be particularly useful with older adolescents or with those who are at higher levels of cognitive development.

Self-control Strategies. A number of self-control techniques have been developed based on Rehm's (1977) model of depression, and include some of the ideas of Beck's (1974) cognitive therapy ideas, Kanfer's (1971) self-control theory, and Seligman's (1975) helplessness perspective. Rehm viewed depressed persons as having self-control deficits in six cases:

1. a tendency to attend to negative events or to selectively attend to positive events,
2. selective monitoring of immediate (as opposed to delayed) reinforcement,
3. setting excessively high self-evaluative standards,
4. making inaccurate attributions of responsibility for personal behavior,
5. inadequate self-reinforcement, and
6. excessive self-punishment.

The therapeutic approach suggested by Rehm is based on the assumption that deficits occur at one or more of these six levels, and that intervention efforts must address these deficits in terms of their degree of severity and their contribution to the depressive or suicidal pattern.

From this perspective, adolescents are taught to monitor the positively balanced behaviors and cognitions that are associated with improved mood. Emphasis is placed both on attending to the positive aspects of experience and on appreciating the value of delayed reinforcement. Excessively high personal standards are examined and the adolescent is taught to set limited, realistic, and attainable goals. Since most suicidal adolescents have a tendency to attribute success and failure only to themselves regardless of the actual situation, this strategy teaches them to place responsibility where it is appropriate. Finally, they are taught how to reinforce themselves appropriately and to reduce self-punishing thoughts and behaviors.

Attribution Training. The research and clinical work on helplessness has focused primarily on assessment and treatment of maladaptive attributions of success and failure. Seligman (1981) has described four therapeutic techniques that are useful in reducing depressive and suicidal ideation: environmental enrichment that reduces the probability of negative outcomes and increases the likelihood for improved outcomes subsequent to one's efforts; personal control training that emphasizes changing people's expectations from uncontrollability to controllability; resignation training that proposes to make highly desired outcomes less desirable; and attribution retraining that helps people attribute failure to more external, unstable, and specific factors and success to more internal, stable, and global ones. Attribution retraining has been shown to be effective in reducing the negative cognitive sets of depressed individuals by altering feelings of helplessness and expectations for success (Klein & Seligman, 1976; Miller & Norman, 1979).

Cognitive Rehearsal of Alternate Thoughts. Cognitive rehearsal is similar to the substitution of pleasant for unpleasant thoughts by focusing on instruction to the adolescent in creating different thinking patterns. The therapist works with the suicidal adolescent to develop a repertoire of new and adaptive thoughts to augment and eventually replace the negative thoughts that he/she might have. The adolescent then rehearses these thoughts and associated statements that are incompatible with current dysfunctional thoughts. As the frequency of adaptive thoughts increases through rehearsal, negative cognitions decrease in frequency, intensity, and duration.

Motivational Intervention Strategies

As stated earlier, suicidal ideation and behavior can be seen as an attempt to adapt to very stressful and painful circumstances. The avoidance of pain is a natural human response. Before contemplating suicide, the adolescent will often have tried other forms of withdrawing from pain which have not proven successful: social withdrawal, verbal hostility, or the like. When these coping methods fail to bring relief, suicide may be seen as the only viable alternative for maintaining survival. While the logic of this choice may be incomprehensible to most adolescents, remember that the suicidal adolescent is most likely operating from a base of several distorted cognitions that make this form of reasoning appear reasonable, at least temporarily.

From the perspective of working with the suicidal adolescent, motivation is an essential factor to consider in the selection, planning, and implementation of intervention techniques. Lack of motivation of the depressed adolescent is usually evident in behavioral indicators such as decreased socialization, withdrawal from usual activities, passivity, and an unwillingness to initiate new activities. When combinations of these behaviors become a characteristic mode of operating for the adolescent, they are indications that the adolescent's environment is perceived to be unrewarding in any positive sense of the word.

Motivation and Reinforcement. Two primary motivational explanations exist for this constellation of behaviors. First, the adolescent may be unable or unwilling to exert effort, perhaps because of intellectual of physical limitations. Second, and perhaps more commonly, the adolescent's past experiences may not have been reinforced so that efforts are not seen as leading to positive outcomes. This latter explanation, known as a low rate of response-contingent positive reinforcement, is a primary means of understanding depressive and suicidal behavior and is often a pattern that results from excessive punishment experiences (Lewinsohn & Hoberman, 1982; Lewinsohn & Shaw, 1969).

These low rates of positive reinforcement are usually associated with social skill deficits which limit the individual's opportunities for positive experiences. Although individual suicidal adolescents may receive positive input from others, the more common pattern is for them to isolate themselves and to be avoided by others. When they do have opportunities for positive experiences, cognitive distortions often lead them to ignore or discount the positive aspects of these events. Consequently, the number and quality of social experiences declines, leading to a maintenance, or even increase, of depressive symptoms. This in turn can lead adolescents to reduce their motivation either to exert effort or to change their behavior in ways that might improve the situation.

A number of approaches are available for increasing the motivation of the depressed or suicidal person. Included in this section will be a discussion of two that have been shown to be most effective: activity level increase strategies, and social skills training.

Activity Level Increase Strategies. The assumption behind various activity level increase programs is that behavior that is either intrinsically or potentially reinforcing is not being produced. The process normally begins with a careful monitoring of the adolescent's mood and activity level to obtain baseline and a standard against which subsequent progress can be measured. Behaviors that are or have been intrinsically rewarding or will produce external reinforcement are identified. Attention is given to both positive and negative mood states, and the specific activities and thoughts that are associated with each are identified. Assessment of these behaviors can be done through interviews, past histories, or self-report measures, such as the Children's Reinforcement Survey Schedule for Children (Cautela, 1977) or the Reinforcement Survey Schedule for Adults (Cautela & Kastenbaum, 1967).

Once these activities and moods have been identified, the treatment plan involves the therapist and client establishing several activities for the adolescent to engage in that have a high probability of being intrinsically rewarding or of eliciting reinforcement from others. In some cases, particularly with less motivated adolescents, external or self-reinforcement procedures may be helpful adjuncts for initiating and maintaining effort in the activities. The use of the Premack principle (that is, requiring the performance of a less desired behavior prior to engaging in a more preferred behavior) may be particularly helpful (Kaslow & Rehm, 1983). Therapy then focuses on increasing activities that can result in positive reinforcement and decreasing activities that are associated with negative mood. Additionally, the therapist and adolescent work together to establish environmental contingencies that can reinforce positive behaviors and reduce or eliminate the reinforcement of negative behaviors.

For activity level increase programs to be effective, the adolescent must be able to perform the skill or behavior being suggested. The therapist must distinguish between those adolescents who are unable to perform an activity because they lack the skill, and those who have the skill but who are not performing the activity currently, perhaps because of anxiety or a lack of motivation. Skills training may be a more appropriate choice for the former group, while activity increase strategies may be most beneficial for the latter group.

Social Skills Training. For a variety of personal and social reasons, the suicidal adolescent may have deficient social skills that interfere with the performance of appropriate interpersonal behaviors. While social skills deficits can be a significant problem at any age, they may be especially problematic during adolescence when peer relationships are of particular importance. The development of appropriate social interaction skills can fit well with the needs of the adolescent.

During social skills training, clients are taught appropriate social behaviors and how to assert themselves in interpersonal problem-solving situations. The methods used have considerable variability and have been explored in a number of studies both with adults and children. Role playing, modeling, feedback, direct instruction, observation, homework, and graded task assignments are the major techniques that have been reported. While social skill deficits often accompany depressive and suicidal ideation, the training of social skills generally has been less effective than more complex cognitive or behavioral interventions.

Indications and Counterindications

Before choosing to focus on the adolescent's adaptive motivations and thoughts, therapists are well advised to assess the appropriateness of this approach for the specific adolescent with whom they are working. Cognitive and motivational therapies assume that the client is both willing and able to participate in the planning and implementation of a treatment plan, a condition which may not be met by all suicidal adolescents. Several reasons may exist for an adolescent's inability or unwillingness to cooperate in a cognitive-motivational therapy approach: cognitive developmental level, severity of current impairment, lack of intellectual and/or social skills, and environmental reinforcement of depression.

Cognitive Developmental Level. Many intellectual, biological, social, and emotional changes occur during the period of childhood through adolescence. Some of the most dramatic changes occur in the qualitative aspects of cognitive functioning. By adolescence, young people show an increasing ability to demonstrate cognitive functioning that is very different from the patterns that are evident in childhood. Young children are concrete in their thought processes, interpreting events on the basis of environmental events and then reacting on the basis of that interpretation. Thinking and reasoning are directly tied to the child's immediate circumstances and do not include the abstract thought processes characteristic of adults. By contrast, adolescents generally show the ability to think abstractly, to anticipate future events, to generate potential alternative actions in response to a situation, to engage in hypothetical-deductive reasoning, and to reflect upon and analyze their own thinking patterns.

Self-reflective Thought. This last characteristic of adolescent thinking, the ability to engage in self-reflection, is essential to the success of cognitive intervention approaches. For adolescents who cannot reflect upon and evaluate their own cognitions, techniques requiring insight into thought processes will be difficult or impossible to implement effectively. On the other hand, the presence of these higher-level thinking skills indicates a good prognosis for the application of cognitive interventions.

Anticipation of the Future. Depressed individuals frequently are unable to anticipate future events and often see the future in negative ways. Regardless of whether this impairment is a cause or a result of the depression, an inability to project into the future and evaluate alternatives nevertheless represents a cognitive dysfunction which will attentuate progress during cognitive therapy.

Some would debate as to whether young children can fully experience hopelessness or helplessness, since they lack the ability of adults to project themselves into the future and then conclude that little change will be possible. As formal operations emerge in adolescence, however, anticipation of the future becomes possible, as do the experience of helplessness and hopelessness. In working with suicidal adolescents, the therapist will want to assess each individual for their formal level of cognitive development. When formal operational thought and the ability to anticipate the future are not present, therapeutic efforts directed toward age-appropriate facilitation of coping strategies are likely to be the most effective approach.

Severity of Current Impairment. The therapist will also want to assess the adolescent's current level of functioning in several areas. The third edition of the Diagnostic and Statistical Manual of Mental Disorders (American Psychiatric Association, 1980) suggested that the therapist assess the client's "highest level of adaptive functioning (for at least a few months) during the past year" (p. 28). This can provide useful information about the individual's current and past severity of impairment, with implications both for the choice of intervention methods and for prognosis during the course of treatment.

Severity is usually assessed in three major areas of the adolescent's life: academic and/or occupational functioning, social relationships, and use of leisure time (American Psychiatric Association, 1980). In cases of severe depression, these three areas may be impaired to the point that the adolescent is not able to mobilize sufficient personal resources to participate fully in the therapy process. In these situations, non-cognitive forms of therapy may again be more effective initially than cognitive therapy.

Lack of Intellectual and Social Skills. The adolescent also may lack either the intellectual or the social skills that are necessary for participation in the treatment process. In terms of intellectual skills, mental retardation and some forms of learning disabilities generally would make cognitive interventions a poor choice of treatment strategy. Again, biological therapy or behavioral approaches are likely to be considerably more effective with these clients.

In terms of social skills, significant deficits can be due to social or cultural isolation of either the adolescent or of the entire family, and this can lead to significantly impoverished skills. Social skills deficits are generally responsive to social skills training and activity increase programs, as described above.

Environmental Reinforcement. Suicidal adolescents sometimes operate in situations which serve to maintain their suicidal ideation or behavior. Overt or covert reinforcement of depressive behavior can come from family, relatives, friends, or individuals in the adolescent's school or social life. While reinforcement is rarely intentional or even conscious on the part of those who are engaging in it, it can serve to maintain both high levels of depression and suicidal behavior of the adolescent. Progress in therapy may not be possible until changes are made in these reinforcing situations.

Finally, these factors may exist in combination, making progress through cognitive or motivational therapy slow or impossible. Cognitive therapy is unlikely to have any significant impact when any of these factors is operating either alone or in combination. If the therapist determines that these or similar difficulties are present, work might best begin with efforts to alleviate the effects of these external problems through biological or behavioral treatment before attempting to introduce a cognitive-motivational approach.

IMPLICATIONS

The authors have taken the position that an understanding of cognition and motivation is central to understanding, assessing, and treating the suicidal adolescent. Ultimately, the interventions chosen should be based upon knowledge of the types of techniques, the efficacy, the therapist's own therapeutic skills and orientations, and, most importantly, the characteristics and needs of the adolescent. The majority of research evidence has indicated that cognitive and behavioral techniques have both immediate and long-term effectiveness, with implications for assessment and treatment selection.

Assessment

When working with suicidal adolescents, it must be remembered that their behaviors cannot be considered without also referring to their social and familial circumstances. Most suicidal adolescents are living at home, and members of the immediate and extended family can be valuable resources in developing intervention plans. Alternately, these family members may be contributing in significant ways to the problems that the adolescent is facing. In either case, involvement of the family can be useful in determining both the source of the difficulties, the specific contributions of various family members, and potential solutions. Evidence is now available that a substantial number of depressed adolescents have at least one parent with an affective disorder (Cytryn & McKnew, 1974; McKnew, Cytryn, Efron, Gershon, & Bunney, 1979). In the event that the adolescent's suicidal behavior is related to family stresses and problems, family intervention should be considered.

Individual assessment of the adolescent should be done using a *multimethod, multitrait, multisource, and multisetting approach* that includes systematic consideration of personal, social, and academic functioning. Relevant information can be obtained from interviews with parents, teachers, family members, and others who have knowledge of the adolescent. Formal and informal psychological assessment may be helpful if done in such a way as to provide information about cognitive-motivational characteristics, rather than simply for purposes of classification. The data obtained throughout the assessment process should be designed to provide information about the cognitive, affective, motivational, behavioral, and academic functioning of the adolescent.

Selecting Intervention Strategies

The selection of appropriate intervention strategies is a complex process and is determined through consideration of a number of factors. While some form of intervention with the adolescent's cognitive and motivational systems is usually indicated, a number of other factors must be taken into account when deciding on the strategy which will bring about optimal results for any individual adolescent. The following ten questions are designed to address the primary decision points in the assessment and intervention process. They provide a systematic guideline for determining the most effective intervention approach in working with a particular suicidal adolescent.

1. *Is the behavior related to problem within the family?*

If the answer is "yes," then an appropriate starting point would be family assessment and intervention, with additional help and support for the adolescent. If the answer is "no," or if appropriate family intervention is not possible, then focus on the adolescent is appropriate.

2. *Is the adolescent's suicidal behavior being overtly or covertly reinforced by external factors?*

Possibly the adolescent's suicidal ideation and/or behavior are being reinforced by the behavior of others, for example, by parents. If such a relationship exists, an important procedure is to work with the contingencies that are operating to maintain the behavior, for example, parental attention.

3. *Is the behavior secondary to another, more serious problem?*

If suicidal behavior is a manifestation of another physical or mental disorder, such as psychosis or substance abuse, then treatment of these problems is indicated, perhaps in addition to cognitive-motivational interventions.

4. *What is the adolescent's level of cognitive development?*

If the adolescent does not demonstrate a basic level of formal operational thought through the ability to anticipate future outcomes, to generate alternatives, and to reflect on his/her own thought processes, then complex cognitive interventions are not indicated initially. For these adolescents, behavioral approaches such as activity increase strategies are more likely to be helpful in the beginning stages.

5. *Does evidence exist of significant cognitive distortion as the major problem?*

If cognitive distortions such as low self-esteem, catastrophic thinking, overgeneralization, and all-or-none thinking are evident, cognitive interventions are indicated.

6. *Does a depressive attributional style prevail?*

If depressive attributions are central, helplessness therapy with an emphasis on altering dysfunctional attributions of negative events from internal to more external causes is indicated.

7. *Are social skills deficits evident?*

Significant social skills deficits are likely to be associated with depressed and suicidal behavior that lead to low levels of positive reinforcement. If these factors are predominant, then strategies designed to improve social functioning by increasing positive reinforcement from the environment are indicated.

8. *Are self-monitoring deficits evident?*

If the adolescent shows deficits in the ability to monitor both overt behavior and cognitions, strategies to improve these abilities are indicated. The type and intensity of the deficits are important to determine from both assessment and intervention perspectives.

9. *Are overt behavior and interpersonal functioning impaired?*

If the types of behaviors are deficient, then activity increase approaches are indicated. These approaches also are particularly appropriate if the adolescent lacks the ability to use or profit from more complex cognitive methods.

10. *Does the adolescent exhibit a deficiency in the ability to demonstrate self-reinforcement for positive behavior?*

If the adolescent has been unable to engage in self-reinforcement because of cognitive distortions, depressive attributional style, or other similar factors, self-reinforcement can be the most appropriate focus of treatment. Strategies should include helping the adolescent to recognize and respond to positive experiences when they occur, create positive experiences when possible, and establish a personal schedule of reinforcement so that positive experiences are rewarded.

The foregoing questions are not intended to be either exhaustive or mutually exclusive. They are guidelines that can contribute to a systematic and personalized assessment and treatment approach in working with a particular suicidal adolescent. In providing a basic outline for assessing and choosing treatment approaches, these questions can contribute to a thorough and individualized approach to working with a specific adolescent.

CONCLUSION

Suicidal adolescents differ from their nonsuicidal peers in the content of their thoughts, thought processes, and motivations. Their feelings, thoughts, and behavior are dominated by a predominantly negative view of themselves and by pessimistic expectations for the future. Suicidal talk, gestures, and acts can be understood as attempts to escape from intolerable pain, to regain control of the environment, and to mobilize internal and external resources to deal with difficulties. Therapists who understand the internal dynamics of the suicidal adolescent can utilize this information in evaluating the individual's degree of risk, available resources, and personal strengths and limitations. This information is central in the construction of a treatment plan which is tailored to the adolescent's specific abilities and needs.

In determining an appropriate intervention strategy, the therapist is well advised to consider a broad range of factors which can facilitate or inhibit the treatment process. Family functioning, external reinforcement for suicidal behavior, other mental and physical conditions, cognitive development and style, and personal skills and motivations are all integral elements in a thorough assessment process. When all of these factors are taken into consideration, the therapist has an increased chance of developing a therapeutic program which will lead to a reduction of suicidal ideation and behavior as well as to other improvements in the adolescent's functioning.

At the same time, no general planning approach is possible in the treatment of suicidal ideation or behavior. Instead, the information from various assessment and therapeutic techniques are assessed for their applicability in working with the individual client, and combined in a specific way that meets the specific needs, strengths and limitations of the individual adolescent. To the degree that a wide variety of relevant factors are taken into account throughout the process, intervention is more likely to be successful. In practice, the usual procedure is to implement several different approaches at various stages in the treatment process in order to maximize the effectiveness of therapy with a suicidal adolescent.

REFERENCES

Abramson, L.Y., Seligman, M.E.P., & Teasdale, J.D. (1978). Learned helplessness in humans: Critique and reformulation. *Journal of Abnormal Psychology, 87*, 49-74.

American Psychiatric Association. (1980). *Diagnostic and statistical manual of mental disorders* (3rd ed.). Washington, D.C.: American Psychiatric Association.

Avery, D., & Winokur, G. (1978). Suicide attempted, suicide, and relapse rates in depression. *Archives of General Psychiatry, 35*, 749-753.

Beck, A.T. (1974). The development of depression: A cognitive model. In R.J. Friedman & M.M. Katz (Eds.), *The Psychology of Depression: Contemporary Theory and Research.* New York: Wiley.

Beck, A.T. (1983). Cognitive therapy of depression: New perspectives. In P.J. Clayton & J.E. Barrett (Eds.), *Treatment of Depression: Old Controversies and New Approaches* (pp. 265-90). New York: Raven Press.

Blackburn, I.M., Bishop, S., Glen, A.I.M., Whalley, L.J., & Christie, J.E. (1981). The efficacy of cognitive therapy in depression: A treatment trial using cognitive therapy and pharacotherapy, each alone and in combination. *British Journal of Psychiatry, 139*, 180-9.

Campos, L.P. (1986). Empowering children: Primary prevention of script formation. *Transactional Analysis Journal, 16*, 18-23.

Cautela, J.R. (1977). *Behavior analysis forms for clinical intervention.* Champaign, IL: Research Press.

Cautela, J.R., & Kastenbaum, R. (1967). A reinforcement survey schedule for use in therapy, training, and research. *Psychological Reports, 20*, 1115-30.

Children, youth, and families: 1983, A year-end report on the activities of the select committee on children, youth, and families. (March, 1984). U.S. House of Representatives. 98th Congress, 2nd session. Washington, D.C.: U.S. Government Printing Office.

Corder, B.F., Shorr, W., & Corder, R.F. (1974). A study of social and psychological characteristics of adolescent suicide attempters in an urban, disadvantaged area. *Adolescence, 9*, 1-16.

Cytryn, L., & McKnew, D.J. (1974). Factors influencing the changing clinical expression of the depressive process in children. American *Journal of Psychiatry*, 131, 879-81.

Dweck, C.S. (1975). The role of expectations and attributions in the alleviation of learned helplessness. *Journal of Personality and Social Psychology*, 31, 674-85.

Dweck, C.S., & Repucci, N.D. (1973). Learned helplessness and reinforcement responsibility in children. *Journal of Personality and Social Psychology, 25,* 109-16.

Giancotti, A., & Vinci, G. (1986). A major depression of psychogenic origin in a five-year-old. *American Journal of Orthopsychiatry, 56,* 617-21.

Grosscup, S.J., & Lewisohn, P.M. (1980). Unpleasant and pleasant events and mood. *Journal of Clinical Psychology, 36,* 252-9.

Hawton, K., Cole, D., O'Grady, J., & Osborn, M. (1982). Motivational aspects of deliberate self-poisoning in adolescents. *British Journal of Psychiatry, 141,* 286-91.

Helsel, N.J., & Matson, J.L. (1984). The assessment of depression in children: The internal structure of the Child Depression Inventory. *Behavior Research Therapy, 22,* 289-98.

Hersen, M., Bellack, A.S., & Himmelhoch, J.M. (1980). Treatment of unipolar depression with social skills training. *Behavior Modification, 4,* 547-57.

Izard, C.E. (1977). *Human emotions.* New York: Plenum.

Izard, C.E., & Schwartz, G.M. (1986). Patterns of emotion in depression. In M. Rutter, C.E. Izard, & P.B. Read (Eds.), *Depression in young people: Developmental and clinical perspectives* (pp. 33-70). New York: Guilford.

Kanfer, F.H. (1971). The maintenance of behavior by self-generated stimuli and reinforcement. In A. Jacobs & L.B. Sachs (Eds.), *The Psychology of Private Events: Perspectives on Covert Response Systems.* New York: Academic.

Kaslow, N.J., & Rehm, L.P. (1983). Childhood depression. In R.J. Morris & T.R. Kratochwill (Eds.), *The Practice of Child Therapy* (pp. 27-51). New York: Pergamon.

Kaslow, N.J., Rehm, L.P., & Siegel, A.W. (1984). Social-cognitive and cognitive correlates of depression in children. *Journal of Abnormal Child Psychology, 12,* 605-20.

Kaslow, N.J., Tanenbaum, R.L., Abramson, L.Y., Peterson, C., & Seligman, M.E. (1983). Problem-solving deficits and depressive symptoms among children. *Journal of Abnormal Child Psychology, 11,* 497-501.

Kendall, P.C., & Korgeski, G.P. (1979). Assessment and cognitive-behavioral interventions. *Cognitive Therapy and Research, 3,* 1-22.

Kincel, R.L. (1981). MMPI indicators of the suicide attempt: Study of depressive serious suicide attempters and depressive non-suicidal patients. In J.P. Soubrier, & J. Vedrinne (Eds.), *Depression et Suicide: Aspects Medicaux, Psychologiques, et Socio-culturels* (pp. 847-50). New York: Pergamon Press.

Klein, D.C., & Seligman, M.E.P. (1976). Reversal of performance deficits and perceptual deficits in learned helplessness and depression. *Journal of Abnormal Psychology, 85,* 11-26.

Lazarus, R.S. (1975). A cognitively oriented psychologist looks at feedback. *American Psychologist, 30,* 553-61.

Lazarus, R.S., Kanner, A.D., & Folkman, S. (1980). Emotions: A cognitive-phenomenological analysis. In R. Plutchik & H. Kellerman (Eds.), *Theories of Emotion* (Vol. I, pp. 189-217). New York: Academic.

Lefkowitz, M.M., Tesiny, E.P., & Gordon, N.H. (1980). Childhood depression, family income, and locus of control. *Journal of Nervous and Mental Disease, 168,* 732-5.

Lewinsohn, P., & Hoberman, H. (1982). Depression. In A. Bellack, M. Hersen, & A. Kazdin (Eds.), *International Handbook of Behavior Modification and Therapy* (pp. 397-431). New York: Plenum.

Lewinsohn, P., & Shaw, D. (1969). Feedback about interpersonal behavior as an agent of behavior change: A case study in the treatment of depression. *Psychotherapy and Psychosomatics, 17,* 82-88.

Levenson, M., & Neuringer, C. (1971). Problem-solving behavior in suicidal adolescents. *Journal of Consulting and Clinical Psychology, 37,* 433-6.

McKnew, D.J., Cytryn, L., Efron, A.M., Gershon, E.S., & Bunney, W.E. (1979). Offspring of patients with affective disorder. *British Journal of Psychiatry, 134,* 148-52.

McLean, P.D., & Hakstian, A.R. (1979). Clinical depression: Comparative efficacy of outpatient treatments. *Journal of Consulting and Clinical Psychology, 47,* 818-36.

Mervis, B.A. (1985). The use of peer-pairing in child psychotherapy. *Social Work, 30,* 124-8.

Miller, I.W., & Norman, W.H. (1979, December). Reattribution training with depressed patients. Paper presented at the meeting of the Association for the Advancement of Behavior Therapy, San Francisco, CA.

Mosak, H.H. (1985). Interrupting a depression: The pushbutton technique. *Individual Psychology: Journal of Adlerian Theory, Research, & Practice, 41,* 210-4.

Mullins, L.L., Siegel, L.J., & Hodges, K. (1985). Cognitive problem-solving and life event correlates of depressive symptoms in children. *Journal of Abnormal Child Psychology, 13,* 305-14.

Novick, J. (1984). Attempted suicide in adolescence: The suicide sequence. In H.S. Sudak, A.G. Ford, & N.B. Rushforth (Eds.), *Suicide in the Young* (pp. 115-37). Boston: John Wright PSG, Inc.

O'Connor, K. (1986). The interaction of hostile and depressive behaviors: A case study of a depressed boy. *Journal of Child and Adolescent Psychotherapy, 3,* 105-8.

Peck, M. (1982). Youth suicide. *Death Education, 6,* 29-47.

Pfeffer, C.R. (1984). Clinical assessment of suicidal behavior in children. In H.S. Sudak, A.B. Ford, & N.B. Rushforth (Eds.), *Suicide in the Young* (pp. 171-82). Boston: John Wright PSG, Inc.

Raskin, A., Friedman, A.S., & DiMascio, A. (1982). Cognitive and performance deficits in depression. *Psychopharmacology Bulletin, 18*(4), 196-202.

Rehm, L.P. (1977). A self-control model of depression. *Behavior Therapy, 8,* 787-804.

Rholes, W.S., Blackwell, J., Jordan, C., & Walters, C. (1980). A developmental study of learned helplessness. *Developmental Psychology, 16,* 107-24.

Rush, A.J., Beck, A.T., Kovacs, M., & Hollon, S.D. (1977). Comparative efficacy of cognitive therapy and pharmacotherapy in the treatment of depressed outpatients. *Cognitive Therapy Research, 1,* 17-37.

Rutter, M., Graham, P., Chadwick, O., & Yule, W. (1976). Adolescent turmoil: Fact or fiction? *Journal of Child Psychology and Psychiatry, 17,* 35-56.

Saklofske, D.H., & Janzen, H.L. (1987). Children and depression. In A. Thomas & J. Grimes (Eds.), *Children's Needs: Psychological Perspectives.* Washington, D.C.: National Association of School Psychologists.

Seligman, M.E.P. (1975). *Helplessness: On depression, development, and death.* San Francisco: Freeman.

Seligman, M.E.P. (1981). A learned helplessness point of view. In L.P. Rehm (Ed.), *Behavior Therapy for Depression.* New York: Academic.

Seligman, M.E.P., Abramson, L.Y., Semmel, A., & VonBaeyer, C. (1979). Depressive attributional style. *Journal of Abnormal Psychology, 88,* 242-7.

Turner, R.W., Ward, M.F., & Turner, J.D. (1979). Behavioral treatment for depression: An evaluation of therapeutic components. *Journal of Clinical Psychology, 55,* 166-75.

Weiner, B. (1979). A theory of motivation for some classroom experiences. *Journal of Educational Psychology, 71,* 3-25.

Wells, K.C., Hersen, M., Bellack, A.S., & Himmelhoch, J. (1979). Social skills training in unipolar nonpsychotic depression. *American Journal of Psychiatry, 136,* 1131-2.

Zeiss, A.M., Lewinsohn, P.M., & Munoz, R.F. (1979). Nonspecific improvement effects in depression using interpersonal skills training, pleasant activity schedules, or cognitive training. *Journal of Consulting and Clinical Psychology, 47,* 427-39.

CHAPTER **6**

DEPRESSION

J. Jeffries McWhirter, Ph.D.
and
Timothy J. Kigin, Ph.D. Candidate

J. Jeffries McWhirter, Ph.D.

Professor
Division of Psychology in Education
Arizona State University
Tempe, AZ 85281

J. Jeffries McWhirter is a Professor in the Counseling Psychology program in the Division of Psychology in Education at Arizona State University. He received his Ph.D. in counseling psychology in 1969 from the University of Oregon. Prior to receiving his doctorate, he was graduated from St. Martin's College (Olympia, Washington) and holds masters degrees from Oregon State University and the University of Oregon.

Dr. McWhirter is the author of 16 books, monographs, and training manuals and over 50 articles which have been published in such journals as *The Counseling Psychologist, Small Group Behavior, Journal of Counseling Psychology, The School Counselor, Journal of Clinical Psychology, Counselor Education and Supervision, Journal of Learning Disabilities, Journal of Family Counseling* and the *Personnel and Guidance Journal.* He is a member of the American Association for Counseling and Development and the American Psychological Association.

He has been a visiting (summer) professor to eighteen universities including the University of Toronto, The University of Navarra (Spain), The University of Maine, the University of Victoria, and the University of Vermont. In 1977-78 he was a Senior Fulbright-Hays Scholar to Hacettepe University, Ankara, Turkey, and in 1984-85 a Fullbright Senior Scholar to Catholic College of Education-Sydney and Western Australia College of Advanced Education.

In addition to his work in suicide prevention, his areas of special interest include small group research, family counseling and parent education, counseling theory and practice, learning disabilities, and international aspects of counseling.

Timothy J. Kigin, Ph.D. Candidate

Counseling Psychology
Arizona State University
Tempe, AZ 85281

Tim Kigin first became interested in working with children and adolescents while he was an undergraduate at the University of Notre Dame. He received his B.A. in psychology in 1971, and then spent three years teaching emotionally disturbed children at a private day-treatment facility in Phoenix, Arizona. In 1974 he enrolled in graduate school at Western Washington University in Bellingham, Washington. He received an M.S. in psychology in 1976, and then worked two years as a caseworker for the Washington State Division of Developmental Disabilities.

In 1978 Mr. Kigin accepted a position as a vocational counselor for the special services office of the Bellingham school district. Working primarily with high school aged special education students, he provided assessment and counseling services related to both career and personal/social issues. In 1985 Mr. Kigin was accepted into the doctoral program in counseling psychology at Arizona State University. He continues to enjoy working with children, adolescents, and families, and has developed a particular interest in adolescent depression and suicide. Upon completion of his doctorate, Mr. Kigin intends to practice psychotherapy in a community setting.

EDITORIAL ABSTRACT: *Even though depression is the most common symptom experienced by adolescents who are suicidal, one would make a mistake to assume that a linear relationship exists between depression and suicide. The link between these two variables is not straightforward and, sometimes, suicide occurs in the absence of depression. The purpose of this important chapter is to examine the relationship between depression and suicide for adolescents and to provide descriptions of depression, its causes, and treatment approaches.*

Depression is thought to have a close relationship with suicidal behavior. Studies reviewed by Shaffer (1986) indicate, for example, that a majority of adult suicides were depressed before their death. In light of the close link between adult suicide and depression, researchers have become increasingly aware of the need to assess the nature of this relationship for child and adolescent populations (Hawton, 1986). This is particularly true for adolescents, who have experienced significant increases in the reported incidence of both depression and suicide in recent years (Gallemore & Wilson, 1972; Garrison, Schoenback, & Kaplan, 1985).

Research concerning adolescent depression is still in its infancy. Studies regarding the incidence of depression among adolescent clinical populations yield estimates that range from 3% to 33% (Robins, Alessi, Cook, Poznanski, & Yanchyshyn, 1982). Research concerning the incidence and severity of depressive symptoms in normative populations is scarce and beset with methodological difficulties, but does seem to indicate that adolescent depression is a significant problem (Garrison et al., 1985). For example, Reynolds (1983) found that 34% of a large sample of high school students were at least mildly depressed.

Depression is the most common symptom experienced by adolescents who are suicidal (Husain & Vandiver, 1984). However, to assume that a linear relationship exists between depression and suicide would be erroneous. Hawton (1986) stated that the link between these two variables was straightforward, and noted that sometimes suicide occurs in the absence of depression. Davis (1983) concurred, and also pointed out that adolescent depression does not always manifest itself the same way it does in adults.

Leonard (1974) concluded that depression and suicide both appear to be multidimensional, independent factors, and present a complex relationship. The purpose of this chapter is to examine this relationship for adolescents by providing a description of depression, its causes, and treatment approaches.

REVIEW OF RELATED LITERATURE

Definition and Classification Issues

Ever since Hippocrates (3rd century B.C.) invented the term "melancholia" to connote depressive symptoms, the concept of depression has been subject to ongoing evolution and perennial controversy, with definition and classification issues serving as consistent focal points.

One problem results from the use of the term to describe a mood, a symptom, a syndrome, and a nosologic disorder (Carlson & Garber, 1986; Coyne, 1986; Levitt, Lubin, & Brooks, 1983). The issue is one of definitional scope. As a mood or a single symptom, depression refers to an emotional state experienced by most people that is not necessarily pathological. This is contrasted with depression as a syndrome, which "...implies more than an isolated dysphoric mood, and occurs in combination with other symptoms to form a symptom-complex or syndrome. When this clinical syndrome is characterized by a particular symptom picture with a specifiable course, duration, outcome, response to treatment, and potential familial, psychological, and biological correlates, then it is referred to as a discrete nosologic entry or disorder" (Carlson & Garber, 1986, p. 400). The question becomes, "Should we limit the term 'depression' to those people suffering from a discrete nosologic disorder?" If we do, how do we describe the other "merely miserable" people who we have excluded from the "depressed" category (Coyne, 1986)?

Another question is whether depressed mood in normal persons is quantitatively or qualitatively different from the "clinical depression" experienced by hospitalized patients. The former view, termed the "continuity hypothesis," assumes that depression exists at opposite ends of a continuum. The latter perspective, however, views clinical depression as being distinct and discontinuous from normal sadness and depressed affect. As Coyne

(1986, p. 4) noted, "The controversy is likely to continue until either questions about the etiology of depression are resolved or unambiguous markers of depression are identified."

Attempts to specify the definitional boundaries and etiology of depression have occurred as a part of a larger effort to classify mental illness. The prototype for modern classification systems of psychopathology was developed by Emile Kraepelin in the 1890s. Kraepelin believed that mental illness could be divided into separate disease entities, each with a specific etiologic agent and course. Kraepelin's system offered psychiatry a paradigm for the conceptualization of psychiatric illness, and its philosophy of discontinuities between disorders had a significant effect on the direction of research (Gilbert, 1984).

The evolution of the diagnostic nomenclature of depression has involved continued efforts to differentiate among subtypes of the disorder. Classification systems have been proposed based on severity (neurotic vs. psychotic depression), symptom clusters (agitated vs. retarded), presumed cause (endogenous vs. reactive), age of onset (involutional depression), presence of mania (unipolar vs. bipolar), and presence of non-affective psychiatric illness (primary vs. secondary) (Hudgens, 1974, p. 39). These systems are based on divergent orientations and do not meld together.

The dominant classification system for the last three decades has been the *Diagnostic and Statistical Manual of Mental Disorders* (DSM-III). Although it contains elements of the above classification systems, it represents a concerted effort to avoid the controversies surrounding these systems. As Levitt et al. (1983, p. 50) noted, "The guiding purpose behind this major revision was to provide clear and exhaustive descriptions of the various diagnostic categories without assuming or supporting any particular theoretical orientation." Coyne (1986, p. 12) agreed and added that "In considering depression, the authors of DSM-III attempted to sidestep a number of longstanding controversies, including that of whether there is a continuum or a discontinuity between normal mood and clinical depressions, as well as that of the role of precipitation life circumstances in distinguishing among types of depression."

DSM-III encompasses depression in two main categories. Under "Major Affective Disorder" are included two subcategories,

Major Depression and Bipolar Disorder. Both involve the presence of the full syndrome, the major distinction between the two being the presence of a manic episode in the latter. The second category is "Other Specific Affective Disorders." Under this heading are included Cyclothymic Disorder and Dysthymic Disorder. These are both conditions in which mood disturbance has been chronic or intermittant for at least two years, although not severe enough to warrant a diagnosis of Major Affective Disorder. The third category, "Atypical Affective Disorders," provides subcategories for those affective disorders which cannot be classified under either of the two previous headings. Included here are Atypical Bipolar Disorder and Atypical Depression.

Space does not permit a discussion of the symptoms and diagnostic criteria for each of the various depressive disorders. However, Getz, Allen, Meyers, and Linder (1983, pp. 56-7) have developed a list of symptoms that generally describe the depressed client:

1. The client's mood is characterized by hopelessness and sadness, often with anxiety and agitation.

2. Some clients lose their appetite and as a result have a significant weight loss. Others experience an increase in appetite when depressed and gain weight.

3. Sleep disturbance takes various forms. Some clients may have difficulty falling asleep, others wake up early in the morning, some are restless, and some sleep during the day and stay awake at night.

4. The depressed client almost always complains of low energy and constant fatigue. This is not necessarily related to sleep and even when he/she has had an adequate amount of sleep, the person is likely to feel tired upon awakening.

5. Problems with attention, concentration, memory, and ability to think clearly are almost always present to some degree.

6. A pattern of decreased effectiveness at school, work, or home is typical in an assessment of daily activities.

7. The depressed client expresses a loss of interest and enjoyment of activities once found pleasurable.

8. Feelings of inadequacy, self-deprecation, and low self-esteem are common.

9. Social withdrawal results from a lack of interest in other people as well as the belief that no one else would want to associate with him/her.

10. Increased irritability is generally reported by the client or by family and friends.

11. The depressed client's thought processes and physical movement are slower (i.e., psychomotor retardation).

12. The depressed client is often preoccupied with thoughts of death of suicide.

The developers of DSM-III felt that the current state of knowledge was not sufficient to warrant classification of psychopathology based on etiology. By focusing on precise clinical description, they "allow investigators from various theoretical backgrounds to use DSM-III with major emphasis on objective, behavioral descriptions of symptoms" (Levitt et al., 1983, p. 51).

Causes of Depression

A number of etiological and conceptual models of depression have been developed. In most cases the primary emphasis has been placed upon adult depressive reactions (Erickson, 1987; Schwartz & Johnson, 1985).

Psychoanalytic Models of Depression. Psychoanalytic models provided an early conceptual base for later theory building. According to Becker (1974), the roots of the classical psychoanalytic position on depression are found in the works of Abraham, Freud, and Rado. Further theorizing was completed by such notables as Melanie Klein of the English school of psychoanalysis and Carl Jung. More recent contributions have been made by John Bowlby, as well as by representatives of both the ego-analytic and neo-analytic schools (cf. Becker, 1974 and Gilbert, 1984).

Because of the divergent schools within the psychoanalytic perspective, our discussion will center on the classical analytic position. A distinction is made between grief and melancholia, the former being a normal response to loss of a love object and the latter involving an intensely ambivalent love-hate relationship with the love object. Additionally, in melancholia the loss may be more imagined than real, and the individual may be unclear as to what was actually lost as a result of the object having been withdrawn into the unconscious.

Individuals predisposed toward melancholia exhibit high dependency needs, a result of fixation at the oral stage of development. Dependency arouses frustration and hostility toward the focus of the dependency. Since overt expression of hostility would endanger the relationship, the negative feelings are repressed. If the love object is lost, the individual attempts to regain it via the process of identification. That is, an attempt is made to reincarnate it as an incorporated feature of the melancholics's personality. The hostility originally felt toward the love object is through identification redirected or converted into self hostility. This "anger turned inward" causes a catastrophic diminution of self esteem and depression ensues.

Although psychoanalytic models had an early impact on the study of depression, they did not generate much empirical research nor were they successful in developing specific treatment procedures. The most influential approaches to depression are those that have demonstrated some success in treatment. These approaches fall into two general categories: behavioral models and cognitive models (Lewisohn & Hoberman, 1985).

Behavioral Models of Depression. Behaviorists view depression as a function of inadequate or insufficient reinforcement (Ferster, 1973, 1974) which may result from environmental changes, loss of the person who provided reinforcement, or the individual's inability to arrange for positive reinforcement. This position and the psychoanalytic perspective both view depression as a result of significant loss (Kovacs & Beck, 1977; Schwartz & Johnson, 1985).

Lewinsohn and his associates have refined the behavioral model into a social learning theory of depression. Lewinsohn suggested that depressive behaviors are "...a direct result of a reduction in the rate of response-contingent reinforcement. Thus, the relative presence or absence of reinforcing events is postulated as playing a major role in the development and maintenance of depression" (Lewisohn & Hoberman, 1985, p. 176).

Lewinsohn contended that either too little positive reinforcement or too much punishment can result in depression. Further, positive reinforcement is a function of three variables: "(1) the number of events which are potentially reinforcing to the individual; (2) the number of potentially reinforcing events which are available in the individual's environment; and (3) the social skill by which the individual elicits these available reinforcers" (Levitt, Lubin, & Brooks, 1983, p. 73). Similarly, punishment or aversive events "...play a role in depression when aversive events occur at a high rate; when the individual has a heightened sensitivity to aversive events; and lastly, if the individual lacks the necessary coping skills to terminate aversive events" (Lewisohn & Hoberman, 1985, p. 176).

Finally, Lewinsohn suggested a feedback loop that serves to maintain depression. Although depressive behaviors are initially elicited by the low rate of reinforcement, those same behaviors are then reinforced through concern, interest, or sympathy on the part of significant others. Finally, the depressive behaviors ultimately causes these people to begin avoiding the depressed person, positive reinforcement is further reduced, and the depression is accentuated (Lewinsohn & Hoberman, 1985).

Cognitive Models of Depression. Whereas behavioral models cite the primacy of reinforcement in depression, cognitive models emphasizes the role of cognitions. Aaron Beck, Martin Seligman, and Lynn Rehm are major contributors to the cognitive perspective.

Beck (1967) emphasized an interactive relationship between cognition and affect. Cognitions or automatic thoughts occur prior to an individual's response. If one's cognitions are inaccurate or distorted, the ensuing affective response will be inappropriate. Beck (1967) contended that the dysphoria or sadness associated with depression derives from a person's tendency to interpret experiences as deprived, deficient, or defeated. Thus depression is a function of negative cognitions.

Beck and his associates (Beck, Rush, Shaw, & Emery, 1979) described three cognitive structures important to depression: the cognitive triad, schemas, and cognitive errors. The cognitive triad are three thought patterns that account for negativistic ideation: a negative view of self; of the world, and of the future.

Beck's (1967) concept of schemas is similar to personality traits in that they represent a stable cognitive pattern. Everyone molds raw data into meaningful schemas to organize and predict experience. Depressives, however, develop certain superordinate schemata that they use to filter and distort environmental stimuli. These thought patterns generally involve a perjorative self view, and serve to mold stimuli in a direction that is consistent with that view.

Dysfunctional or negative schemas result in and are maintained by faulty information processing. These systematic errors in the logic of the depressive's thinking are labeled "cognitive errors." They are automatic and involuntary and are heavily relied upon by the depressive in evaluating experience. The result is thinking that is extreme, negativistic, categorical, absolute, and judgmental (Levitt et al., 1983; Lewinsohn & Hoberman, 1985).

Seligman (1974, 1975) formulated the "learned helplessness" model of depression. He contended that depression occurs in individuals who perceive themselves as lacking control over environmental rewards and punishers.

Seligman emphasized the self-defeating attributional style of the depressed individual. Attributions are postulated to vary along three major dimensions: internal versus external, stable versus unstable, and global versus specific. Individuals make internal attributions when they feel responsible for the outcome of an event, and external attributions when they feel it was caused by others. Stable attributions occur when the individual feels that the causes of the event will remain constant, as opposed to transitory. Finally, global attributions are made when the individual believes that event outcomes will impact upon all areas of existence, while specific attributions are made when causes are thought to be "situation-specific" (Kaslow & Rehm, 1983).

Seligman postulated that depressed persons tend to make attribution for failure that are internal, stable, and global. In contrast, their attributions for success tend to be external, unstable, and specific. The result, according to Kaslow & Rehm (1983, p. 31) is "an insidious attributional style that filters failure in such a way as to produce the affective, motivational, and self-esteem deficits associated with depression." Lewinsohn & Hoberman (1985) cited preliminary evidence in support of this proposed relationship between attributional style and degree of depression, although data for younger populations are lacking.

Rehm (1977) has developed a theory of depression that presents it as a problem of self control. He suggested that depressives exhibit deficits in three important cognitive process: self-monitoring, self-evaluation, and self-reinforcement. Depressives monitor their own behavior in two characteristic ways: They attend selectively to negative outcomes, and also to immediate versus delayed reinforcement outcomes. They thus lack "...a future perspective and are trapped by immediate consequences and outcomes" (Gilbert, 1984, p. 68). As a result, they develop negative views of themselves, the environment, and the future.

Depressives also have maladaptive methods of self-evaluation. They either make external attributions for negative events, while viewing such adversity as beyond their control, or they may make internal attributions for these same events, while viewing themselves lacking the skills to change anything. In addition, they tend to set very high standards for positive self evaluation, while exhibiting quite low thresholds for negative self evaluation. As a result, they suffer from reduced self esteem and increased feelings of helplessness (Lewinsohn & Hoberman, 1985).

Although comprehensive intervention strategies have not been generated two additional models of depression need to be mentioned in this section. The biological and life stress models of depression each provide information that is useful.

Biological Models of Depression. Biological models of depression can be divided into two main categories, those which focus on the biochemical correlates of depression and those which emphasize the role of genetic factors. Much of the biochemical research has centered on the actions neurotransmitters and their interactions with antidepressant medications. Some evidence is present to indicate that abnormalities in the metabolism of neurotransmitters exist in depressives and can be counteracted via antidepressant drugs. However no indication has been made as to whether the abnormalities are a primary cause of the depression or a secondary correlate (Kashani, Husain, Shekim, Hodges, Cytryn, & McKnew, 1981; Snyder, 1975).

The role of genetics in depression has been expanded primarily via twin and adoption studies of adult populations. Research reviewed by Kashani et al. (1981) indicates an average concordance rate of 76% for affective disorders in monozygotic twins, versus a rate of 19% for dizygotic twins. Similarly, adoption studies have demonstrated an increased rate of depression in adoptees whose biological parents suffered from an affective disorder. Although several theories have been promoted, the exact nature of genetic transmission has not yet been determined. In addition, the role of genetic factors in the etiology of depression for adolescents has not been systemtically researched. Descriptive research does indicate however, that depressed young people often have depressed parents (Schwartz & Johnson, 1985).

The Life Stress Model. According to the life stress model, depression is at least partially a result of environmental stresses or major life changes that necessitate readjustment (e.g., job loss, divorce, death in the family, and so on). Research reviewed by Kashani et al. (1981) and Schwartz and Johnson (1985) indicates that life stress may be a contributing factor, although not a primary cause, in depression for all age groups. However, the specific life stresses for young people may be different from those for adults.

The theories and conceptual models discussed above vary widely with respect to emphasis, scope, and empirical foundations. In addition, while some seek primarily to describe the disorder, others have evolved treatment interventions consistent with their theoretical underpinnings. These interventions will be discussed in a later section of this chapter.

Depression During Adolescence

No consensus has been obtained concerning adolescent depression. Classical psychoanalytic theory provided the first perspective. According to this view, "...the mechanisms of depression require a differentiated and strong ego, as well as a strong and functioning superego. Neither of these entities is thought to be present before late adolescence or early adulthood" (Garrison, Schoenbach, & Kaplan, 1985, p. 61). As a result, the existence of depressive disorders during childhood and early adolescence becomes suspect.

The psychoanalytic concept of "adolescent turmoil" also has had a significant impact on models of depression. According to this formulation all adolescents go through a period of developmental turmoil which resembles psychopathology, and which can be attributed to the naturally occurring phenomena of ego regression. Inner unrest, deviant behavior, and personality upheaval are considered normal manifestations of the developmental period. As a result, the significance of depressive symptoms becomes questionable, giving "...rise to the contention that, although depressive symptoms may be common during adolescence, they are a normal part of development and, therefore, clinically unimportant" (Garrison et al., 1985, p. 62). As Robbins and Kashani (1986) noted, clinicians who adhere to this perspective consider the absence of symptoms of adolescent turmoil to be pathologic.

The psychoanalytic model of depression was predominant for years. As a result, childhood and early adolescent depression was discounted, while during later adolescence, it was virtually ignored. More recently, however, resurgence of interest has occurred in the study of depression across all age groups.

In the 1960s the concept of "masked depression" gained popularity. According to this model, depression does occur in both childhood and adolescence but in many cases is not expressed overtly. Rather, it is masked by "depressive equivalent" or behaviors/symptoms such as hyperactivity, irritability, aggressiveness, delinquency, somatic and hypochondriacal complaints, anorexia nervosa, obesity, poor school performance, school phobia, loss of initiative, social withdrawal, and difficulty in sleeping (Carlson, 1981; Carlson & Cantwell, 1980; Davis, 1983; Husain & Vandiver, 1984).

The concept of masked depression has proven to be both controversial and difficult to validate. Carlson and Cantwell (1980), Cytryn, McKnew, and Bunney (1980), and Kovacs and Beck (1977) have been among those who are primarily responsible for its refutation. Based on their review of the literature, Kovacs and Beck (1977) concluded that "masking behaviors" are better conceptualized as presenting complaints. Carlson and Cantwell (1980) concurred and added that since these presenting complaints often meet the criteria for other disorders, particularly behavior disturbances, they may divert attention away from the concomitant depression. "To an alert clinician conducting a thorough interview, however, the depression will not be masked" (p. 449).

Cytryn et al. (1980) carried the above thought a step further by cautioning the clinician to ascertain which features dominate: the depressive equivalents or the depressive symptoms. If for example "...acting out behavior predominates and the depression seems secondary and of lesser magnitude in the clinical picture, the child should be diagnosed as having a conduct disturbance with depressive features...On the other hand, if the child fits the established criteria for a depressive disorder, that should be the primary diagnosis, with other diagnostic features stated as ancillary" (p. 23).

Adolescent turmoil also has been refuted by recent investigators (Rutter, Graham, Chadwick, & Yule, 1976). Weiner (1975, p. 101) summarized his review of the literature by noting "...that there is no common picture of adolescent turmoil simulating psychopathology, that adolescents display no greater incidence of psychological disruption or instability than is normatively found among adults, and that there is no basis for blandly expecting a troubled adolescent to grow out of his adjustment difficulties." Garrison et al. (1985, p. 63) reviewed additional research and concluded that "...many types of adolescent disturbance are not, as often presupposed, merely benign, transitory phenomena, but tend to foreshadow important psychiatric maladjustments in adulthood."

With the demise of masked depression and adolescent turmoil as explanations for depressive symptomology, acceptance is present that depression exists across all age groups. As Reynolds (1984, p. 172) noted, "The current general consensus among researchers (e.g., Carlson & Cantwell, 1980; Cytryn, McKnew, & Bunney, 1980; Puig-Antioch, 1982), is that the manifestation of depression in children and adolescents is similar to that found in adults. Consequently, adult criteria for the diagnosis of depression are viewed as appropriate and applicable to children and adolescents."

The *Research Diagnostic Criteria* (RDC) (Spitzer, Endicott, & Robins, 1978) and the DSM-III have gained wide acceptance as the primary diagnostic classificatory systems for use by researchers and clinicians. The RDC, which provides greater specificity within the category of major depressive disorder, is used primarily in research settings. DSM-III, which basically contains the RDC with some modifications, is geared more toward clinical use. DSM-III is currently considered to be a valid system for use in diagnosing both child and adolescent depression (Cytryn et al., 1980; Pfeffer, 1986; Reynolds, 1984; Robbins & Kashani, 1986; Weiner, 1983).

DSM-III supports the perspective that affective disorders are consistent across age groups. It does, however, provide age-specific associated features for prepubertal children, adolescent boys, and elderly adults when defining "major depressive episode," as well as minor variations in adolescent onset and social behavior for Dysthmic disorder.

Adolescent depression has thus run the gamut from being either denied or considered clinically unimportant, to being accepted as an affective disorder which impacts on the individual longitudinally. Nevertheless, the disorder continues to be under-recognized and relatively neglected in the research literature (Kandel & Davies, 1982; Poznanski, 1984). In addition, many studies are beset by methodological and definitional problems, particularly for research which deals with epidemiological and demographic variables. For example, the reported prevalence of adolescent depression varies significantly across studies. The discrepancies may be caused by sampling differences, variations in assessment techniques, and by ambiguity regarding diagnostic criteria.

Sampling Differences. As Reynolds (1985) noted, most of the data concerning depression in children and adolescents is based upon "convenience samples," with subjects from various in- or out-patient treatment settings. In addition, subject age varies widely across studies, with some samples composed of both children and adolescents. Therefore, not surprisingly, results are disparate and generalization of findings to the normative population are problematic. Also, relatively few studies have used "nonclinical" or normal samples.

Assessment Differences. Considerable variation in the methods and modalities is used to assess depression among adolescents. Even where the same measure is used, cut-off scores for levels of depression vary.

Diagnostic Criteria. Although the RDC and DSM-III provide formal criteria for the diagnosis of depression, only recently has a consensus been achieved concerning the appropriateness of using these systems with child and adolescent populations as previously noted. Subjective and non-standardized diagnostic criteria are prevalent in the literature with the resulting ambiguity of research findings.

The distinction between depression as a symptom vs. depression as a syndrome is also important within this context. Whereas some studies have addressed the prevalence of various symptoms of depression, others are concerned with the incidence of depressive syndromes. Since the diagnostic criteria for the latter are more rigorous than for the former, disparate incidence rates should not be surprising. With these cautions and limitations in mind, a summary of representative research findings seems in order.

Summary of Research Findings

Clinical Populations. King and Pittman (1969) found that 26.6% of a sample of adolescent psychiatric patients fit the diagnosis for depression based on criteria consistent with DSM-III and RDC.

Carlson and Cantwell (1980) found that 28% of a sample of adolescent inpatients and outpatients met DSM-III criteria for a depressive disorder.

Strober, Green, and Carlson (1981) found that 25.6% of a sample of adolescent psychiatric patients received a diagnosis of major depression based on DSM-III criteria.

Robbins, Alessi, Cook, Poznanski, and Yanchyshyn (1982) found that 27% of a sample of adolescent psychiatric inpatients fulfilled RDC criteria for major depressive disorder.

Normal Populations. Albert & Beck (1975) found that 36.5% of a sample of 7th and 8th grade students at a suburban parochial school were moderately or severely depressed as measured by the short form of the *Beck Depression Inventory* (BDI-S, Beck & Beck, 1972).

Rutter, Graham, Chadwick, and Yule (1976) in a rural English sample of 14 and 15 year olds, found that 20.8% of the boys and 23% of the girls reported often feeling miserable or depressed.

Kandel & Davies (1982) administered a 6-item self report inventory to a large sample of 13 to 19 year old adolescents. The estimated rate of major depressive disorder ranged from 13% to 28%, depending upon the cut-off score selected.

Reynolds (1983) administered a modified version of the BDI to a large sample of 13 to 18 year old adolescents. Application of Beck's (1967) cut-off criteria for moderate and severe depression yielded a prevalence rate of 18%.

Kaplan, Hong, and Weinhold (1984) administered the BDI to a large sample of junior and senior high school students. Application of Beck's cut-off criteria for moderate and severe depression yielded a prevalence rate of 8.6%.

Demographic Trends. (Cf. Reynolds, 1985; Robbins & Kashani, 1986): *Age:* The incidence of depression seems to increase with age, with a significant elevation at the onset of puberty. *Gender:* Although numerous studies with adult populations report a higher prevalence of depressive disorders among females, consistent findings have not been achieved with adolescents. Reynolds (1983) did report a strong gender difference in his study with girls manifesting greater depressive symptomology than boys. Kandel and Davies (1982) reported similar results.

Ethnic and Socioeconomic Status (SES): Although these variables have not yet been systematically addressed for adolescent populations, Kaplan et al. (1984) did report higher depression scores among the lower social class adolescents in their sample.

The previous information is evidence that depression is a major mental health problem for adolescents. The significance of the problem becomes even more apparent when the nature of the relationship between depression and suicide is examined for adolescent populations.

Depression and Suicide During Adolescence

Depression is a strong contributing factor to suicidal behavior in adults (Carlson & Cantwell, 1982). According to Guze and Robins (1970) completed suicide is 30 times more prevalent among adults suffering from primary affective disorders than it is among the general population. Similarly, studies reviewed by Morgan (1979) indicated that 50% of the adults who commit suicide show signs of depressive illness. Depression is also the most common diagnosis among adults who attempt suicide (Weissman, 1974). Studies reviewed by Pfeffer (1986) indicate that somewhere between 35% and 80% of adult suicide attempters are depressed at the time of the attempt.

Less agreement exists regarding the relationship between depression and suicide for younger populations. Early researchers (Balser & Masterson, 1959; Bender & Schilder, 1937; Despert, 1952; Schilder & Weschler, 1934) concluded that depression was not an important factor in the suicidal behavior of children or adolescents. Only recently has this perception changed. Indeed, research concerning the relationship between adolescent depression and suicide is still in its infancy. In addition most studies suffer from the same weaknesses that were mentioned earlier. Although to make any global summary statements concerning the data is difficult, research does point out some interesting trends.

Completed Suicide. In one of the few studies dealing with completed suicide, Shaffer (1974) found that 42% of a sample of 12 through 14 year old suicide victims (N = 30) showed signs of depression. Carlson and Cantwell (1982) noted that Shaffer was unable to interview surviving relatives of the victims and thus had to rely upon official records in the collection of his data. As a result, the percentage of depressive symptoms may be an understatement.

Clinical Populations—Attempted Suicide. Crumley (1979) examined the clinical diagnoses of 42 adolescent suicide attempters from his private psychiatric practice between 1972 and

1978. Using DSM-III diagnostic criteria, he found that 80% of the sample suffered from syndromes characterized by depressive episodes or depressed mood. Major depression was the predominant diagnosis, accounting for 60% of the total sample. In addition, personality disorders were diagnosed for 65% of the subjects, with Borderline Personality Disorder (BPD) the most frequent (55% of the sample). All but two of the subjects who were diagnosed as suffering from BPD were also diagnosed as suffering from a depressive disorder. It should be noted that girls outnumbered boys in this study by a ratio of 2.6 to 1.

Friedman, Clarkin, Corn, Arnoff, Hurt, and Murphy (1982) provided additional data concerning the interrelationships among affective disorders, BPD, and suicidal behaviors. Their sample consisted of 76 adolescents who had recently been discharged from a psychiatric hospital. Fifty-two percent of the subjects fulfilled the diagnostic criteria for depression, and 22% met the specific criteria for major depression. With one exception, all subjects who had attempted suicide were depressed. BPD was diagnosed for 16% of the sample, and every one of the individuals in this category also met the criteria for an affective disorder. In addition, every affective/borderline subject in the sample had attempted suicide, with those in the major depression category making both more frequent and more lethal attempts. The researchers concluded that adolescents who manifest this dual diagnosis are at very high risk for successful suicide.

Garfinkel, Froese, and Hood (1982) examined emergency room admissions at a pediatric hospital over a 7-year period and found 505 children and adolescents who had attempted suicide. Consistent with Crumley's (1979) data, girls outnumbered boys by a ratio of approximately 3 to 1. Results showed that 55.3% of the subjects exhibited dysphoric affect.

Clinical Populations—Suicidal Attempts and Suicidal Ideation. Carlson and Cantwell (1982) assessed the correlates of both suicidal ideation and suicidal attempts for a sample of 102 psychiatrically referred children and adolescents. The subjects were interviewed and administered the *Child Depression Inventory* (CDI) (Kovacs & Beck, 1977). Severe suicidal ideation was found to increase around puberty and to correlate with increasingly severe depression. Forty-five subjects exhibited no suicidal ideation, another 45 had some suicidal thoughts, and 12 seriously felt like killing themselves. Subjects in the latter group were rated as seriously depressed and 83% of them met the diagnostic criteria for major affective disorder. The frequency of affective disorder diagnosis was significantly higher for this group than for either of the two other groups (33% for those with some suicidal thoughts, and 1% for those who exhibited no suicidal ideation). Finally, results indicated that 63% of the subjects with depressed CDI scores were suicidal, as compared to 34% who were suicidal but not depressed. As a result, Carlson and Cantwell (1982, p. 365) concluded that "there is a direct association between feeling depressed (as reported by CDI and interview) and feeling suicidal."

Twenty-two of Carlson and Cantwell's (1982) subjects indicated that they had previously made a suicide attempt. A majority of these (17) were adolescents. Eleven subjects were hospitalized as a result of their suicide attempts and they were significantly more depressed than nonhospitalized attempters. Eight of the 11 hospitalized attempters met the diagnostic criteria for major affective disorder, as opposed to 3 of 11 for the nonhospitalized group. As a whole however, depressed subjects who make suicidal attempts were barely more common than attempters who were not depressed (as measured by the CDI). Carlson and Cantwell (1982) concluded therefore, that the relationship between suicide attempts and depression is not as clear as that between suicidal ideation and depression.

Brent, Kalas, Edelbrock, Costello, Dulcan, and Conover (1986) examined the relationship between psychopathology and suicidal behaviors for a sample of 231 psychiatrically referred children and adolescents. Each subject received a structured interview. Results indicated that components of depression were the most significant correlates of both suicidal ideation and attempts. Brent et al. (1986, p. 672) concluded that: "Either depression plays a larger role in youthful suicidal behavior than heretofore realized, or these findings may be attributable to the characteristics of this psychiatrically referred sample."

Clinical Populations—Lethality of Suicide Attempts. Gispert, Wheeler, Marsh, and Davis (1985) examined the medical charts of 82 adolescents (ages 12 to 18 years) admitted to a hospital adolescent unit because of suicidal threats or attempts.

Depression (as measured by the CDI) was found to be positively correlated with suicidal risk. That is, subjects who were more depressed, were also more intent on killing themselves and had a clearer perception of the lethality of their methods.

Robbins and Alessi (1985) examined the relationship between depressive symptoms and suicidal behavior in a sample of 64 hospitalized adolescent psychiatric patients (ages 13 to 18). Subjects participated in a structured interview and were administered the *Schedule of Affective Disorders and Schizophrenia* (SADS; Spitzer & Endicott, 1977). Results were consistent with those of Gispert et al. in that depressive symptomology was positively associated with suicidal behavior, particularly lethality of attempt. Specifically, 83% of the subjects who made medically serious attempts met the diagnostic criteria for major depressive disorder.

Normative Populations—Suicide Attempts and Suicidal Ideation. Smith and Crawford (1986) examined the relationship between depression and suicidal behaviors for a sample of 313 high school students. Each subject completed both the BDI and a survey of suicide-related behaviors, and were divided into four mutually exclusive groups: Nonsuicidal (n = 117), Ideators (n = 117), Planners (n = 46), and Attempters (n = 33). The BDI was then used to identify those in each group who were markedly depressed (score of 21 or above). Smith and Crawford (1986, p. 31) summarized: "Only 1.7% of the Nonsuicidal group scored as markedly depressed, compared to 11.1% of the Ideators, 32.6% of the Planners, and 42.4% of the Attempters. Approximately 14.1% of the total high school group presented themselves as significantly depressed. Depression was more common among females (18.5%) than among males (5.6%)."

Although the above findings are preliminary and skewed toward clinical populations, they suggest that depression is a significant contributing factor to adolescent suicide.

Some researchers, while admitting the link between depression and suicide, assert that a third parameter, hopelessness, is a better predictor of suicidal behaviors (Hawton, 1986). The relationship between hopelessness and suicidal ideation/attempt was first reported for adults (Beck, Kovacs, & Weismann, 1975) and has not been consistently replicated for younger populations (Kazdin, French, Unis, Esveldt-Dawson, & Sherick, 1983; Carlson & Cantwell, 1982). Nevertheless, to continue to pay particular attention to this variable would be wise. Hopelessness emerges as the primary cognitive component of depressive symptomology and suicidal behavior.

In summary, the relationship between depression and suicide during adolescence is not straightforward. Suicidal behavior may result from depression, but an adolescent need not be depressed for suicide to occur. Also, all depression does not lead to suicide. Depression remains, however, the most common denominator in both suicide attempters and completers. Thus, the presentation of depressive symptoms should be taken seriously and should alert significant others to the possibility for self-destruction.

ASSESSMENT/TREATMENT/PREVENTION

Therapeutic intervention for the depression and suicidal adolescent involves the implementation of strategies that impinge upon both. *Without question an initial emphasis must be placed upon suicide prevention.* Once the risk of imminent suicide has been diminished, the depression can be more safely treated. Intervention strategies tailored to contend with the initial suicidal crisis are examined elsewhere in this text. Therefore, we will emphasize those strategies developed for depression. Please note, however, that these strategies comprise only part of the treatment package necessary for the suicidally depressed adolescent. The section will be divided into three subsections: Assessment, Treatment, and Prevention.

Assessment

Assessment measures, the first step in the intervention process, can be used to screen at-risk populations, to assess the level of depression in already identified clients, or to judge the effectiveness of intervention strategies. According to Reynolds (1984, p. 173-4), two primary approaches exist to the assessment of depression: "The first approach focuses on the assessment of the clinical syndromes or symptom clusters which comprise the diagnostic classifications of depression such as DSM-III's major depressive disorder. The second assessment approach views depression from a depth or severity perspective without the specification of symptom-clusters. Assessment of depression in this context is typically expressed by a score continuum which may be translated into levels ranging from nondepressed through severely depressed." Reynolds (1984) noted that most instruments developed to assess adolescent depression follow the second approach.

Instruments designed to assess depression in children and adolescents have been developed within the last decade. A number of formats have been used, including self report inventories and interview schedules. Interest in childhood depression has been greater than for adolescents resulting in less instruments for adolescents although a number of measures span both developmental stages. Also, some instruments for adults also have been found to be appropriate for adolescents (Reynolds, 1985).

Self-Report Measures. Two instruments developed by Beck and his associates have been found to be useful with young clients. The first, the *Beck Depression Inventory* (BDI) (Beck, Ward, Mendelson, Mock, & Erbaugh, 1961) is frequently administered to adolescents (Reynolds, 1985). The inventory consists of 21 items and yields a single score that reflects the test-taker's position relative to four levels of depressive symptomology (nondepressed, mild depression, moderate depression, severe depression). The second instrument, the *Child Depression Inventory* (CDI) (Kovacs & Beck, 1977; Kovacs, 1981), was modified from the BDI into child appropriate language. It contains 27 items and has been administered to clinical and normative samples containing subjects from ages 6 to 17 (Kaslow & Rehm, 1983).

One measure, the *Reynolds Adolescent Depression Scale* (RADS) (Reynolds, 1981), has been developed specifically for adolescents. It consists of 30 items, and like the BDI and CDI, it follows a self report format.

Interview Measures. The *Schedule for Affective Disorders and Schizophrenia* (SADS) (Spitzer & Endicott, 1977) is a semi-structured interview instrument designed primarily to differentiate between depressed and nondepressed adults. It has also been used with adolescents (Reynolds, 1985). In addition, the *Kiddie-SADS* (Puig-Antioch & Chambers, 1978) has been derived from the SADS, for use with children ages 6 to 16. Both instruments yield DSM-III diagnoses for a number of categories (Kolko, 1987).

The *Hamilton Depression Rating Scale* (HDRS) (Hamilton, 1960) is a 17-item instrument designed to measure depressive symptomology. It has achieved wide use with adults and is also appropriate for adolescents. The HDRS is primarily a measure of severity of clinical depression which "allows the user to probe for psychotic or delusional symptoms which are precluded when one uses self-report measures such as the BDI of RADS" (Reynolds, 1985, p. 155).

Treatment

Depression treatment has traditionally been the domain of psychiatry and the therapy of choice frequently has been pharmacological interventions. More recently, however, other treatment methods have been established. This subsection will review strategies representative of both the pharmacological and the psychological approaches to treatment.

Pharmacological Interventions. Trycyclilc antidepressants have been prescribed for young patients since the 1960s (Hodgman, 1985). Monoamine oxidase inhibitors and lithium carbonate also have also been used, although to a lesser degree (Reynolds, 1985). In spite of frequent clinical use, the effectiveness of antidepressants has not yet been established via controlled research, although uncontrolled studies have claimed positive results (Robbins & Kashani, 1986).

The use of antidepressants in treating the adolescent who is both depressed and suicidal must be carefully monitored, particularly for the client who has a history of alcohol abuse. Antidepressant medications may enhance the depressant effects of alcohol, thus increasing the dangers of a suicide attempt (Medical Economics Company, 1987).

Behavioral Approaches. Behavioral strategies have been developed for the treatment of depression. Two approaches are social skills training and activity level increase programs.

Social skills training approaches are based on the premise that depression results from the absence of social skills that elicit positive consequences from others. The goal is to enhance those skills that elicit reinforcement (Lewinsohn, Biglan, & Zeiss, 1976) with training packages including modeling, role playing, feedback, instruction, situation logs, and homework practice. Specific skills (eye contact, posture, or voice quality) or improvement of interpersonal style are the focus of treatment (Kaslow & Rehm, 1983). Although social skills training has been heavily researched for adult populations, neither the prevalence of social skills deficits not the efficacy of social skills training have been systematically assessed for adolescents.

Activity level increase programs are also based on the premise that depression results from low levels of environmental reinforcement. Depression is further conceptualized, however, as a reduction in activity. The assumption is that the individual has the necessary social skills, but is not doing enough to be reinforced (Kaslow & Rehm, 1983). Activity level increase programs are thus based on the rationale that an increase in pleasant or rewarding activities will be accompanied by an increase in the level of response-contingent reinforcement, and that this in turn, will result in a reduction in the symptoms of depression.

Kaslow and Rehm (1983, p. 30) indicated that the following program components are typically included in activity programs: "(1) monitoring mood and activity level in order to obtain a baseline, (2) identifying positive activities in an individual's repertoire that correlate with daily pleasant mood, (3) instigating increases in those activities that are potentially reinforcing, (4) decreasing negative activities that correlate with negative mood, and (5) setting up environmental contingencies to reinforce increased positive and decreased negative activity." Strategies to increase positive activities include scheduling activities, pairing more frequent positive behaviors with those which are less probable (the Premack principle), or providing reinforcement programs which are either self-managed or externally controlled. Again, research assessing the efficacy of activity level increase programs has been conducted primarily with adults and has yielded only partially successful results (Kaslow & Rehm, 1983).

Cognitive Approaches. Strategies for the treatment of depression have been based upon cognitive models. Beck and his colleagues (1979) have developed an intervention package based on automatic negative cognitions with the goal to assist the client in identifying certain assumptions and themes that support recurrent patterns of negative thinking.

Beck contended that cognitive therapy should contain both behavioral and cognitive strategies and that the former should be a priority early in treatment because depressed clients often experience difficulty moving directly into cognitive tasks. The importance is to quickly establish positive activities and to preclude withdrawal. Lewinsohn and Hoberman (1985) summarized the techniques that are utilized toward these ends: graduated task assignments, activity schedules, mastery and pleasure rating, assertiveness training, behavioral rehearsal, and role playing.

After some success, the emphasis is moved to cognitive distortions which are primarily responsible for maintaining the depressive state. Kaslow and Rehm (1983, p. 31) summarized the cognitive techniques that are used to assist the client in identifying, reality-testing, and modifying these distortions: "(1) recognizing the connection between cognition, affect, and behavior, (2) monitoring negative automatic thoughts, (3) examining evidence for and against distorted automatic thoughts, (4) substituting a more reality-oriented interpretation for distorted cognitions, and (5) learning to identify and modify dysfunction beliefs." Cognitive therapy findings have been generally positive (Kolko, 1987), although few studies have assessed the approach for adolescents.

Seligman's learned helplessness model also has a cognitive base, and it too has yielded a treatment approach (Seligman, 1981). According to this model, depression is the result of faulty attributions of control and efficacy (Kolko, 1987). Proposed treatment strategies included: (1) environmental enrichment—to increase desired outcomes while decreasing unwanted ones; (2) personal control training—to foster expectations of control; (3) resignation training—to reduce preference for unobtainable outcomes; (4) attribution retraining—to replace unrealistic attributions with realistic ones. Only a few actual applications have been made of this approach, however, and no reports concerning adolescent populations.

The final cognitive approach is based on Rehm's self-control model of depression. Recommended treatment, as summarized by Kolko

(1987, p. 156), involves training in activities such as "monitoring positive events and self statements, engaging in those behaviors and thoughts associated with positive affect, emphasizing long-term positive consequences and development of achieveable goals, making more legitimate attributions, and providing more frequent self-reinforcement." Unfortunately, no reports are available of the use of self control therapy with depressed children or adolescents. Kaslow and Rehm (1983) believed, however, that the model might be useful in teaching skills for avoiding depression, and that it thus has promise as a primary prevention procedure.

Family Approaches. Adherents of the "systems" perspective view the depressed adolescent as evidence that the family may be malfunctioning. The adolescent might for example, be playing a "sick" role in a homeostatic although maladaptive family system. Thus, one can expect other family members to resist any change in the adolescent. As a result, involvement of the entire family in the treatment intervention becomes a necessity (Guttman, 1983).

The role of the family in the successful treatment of the depressed adolescent remains crucial. Robbins and Kashani (1986) noted that the clinician must be aware of both the effect of the client on the family, as well as the effects of the family members on the client. *Family support and nurturance which would effectively relieve "normal" sadness are ineffective for the depressed adolescent.* As a result, depression becomes a significant stressor, even to psychologically healthy family. Intervention thus must include and be sensitive to each family member. The effects of other family members upon the depressed adolescent are probably most significant in those cases where one of the parents also suffers from an affective disorder. Robbins and Kashani (1986, p. 79) pointed to the negative impact depressed parents have upon their children. These authors concluded that "Interventions clearly have to include appropriate treatment of the parent's affective disorder as well as identification and treatment of the secondary pathologic interactions." Research reviews (Reynolds, 1985) indicate that a significant proportion of depressed adolescents have a family history of affective disorders.

A Multimodal Perspective. The treatment approaches discussed thus far each emphasize a different facet of the individual's life experience. Because of multiple etiologies and resulting complexity of depression (Petti, Bornstein, Delamater, & Conners, 1980), one is not surprised to find that each strategy can claim some success. Therefore, the most effective means of treating depression might involve a concerted multimodal approach, i.e., a structured combination of these strategies.

The multimodal approach is actually used quite often in clinical settings (e.g., co-application of pharmacological and psychological treatments). Multimodal models have been minimally researched for younger populations although in one relevant study, Petti et al. (1980) made use of dynamically-oriented psychotherapy, social skills training and antidepressant medication in their treatment of a 10 year old depressed girl. Although their findings demonstrated the efficacy of the multimodal therapy, the contributions and interactions among the components were not delineated.

Intervening in the School Setting. The increasing rates of both depression and suicide among adolescents suggests that prevention and intervention might be effected in the school setting. Since school personnel spend considerable time with adolescents, this approach seems to have merit. School counselors and school psychologists should take the lead in this endeavor.

Forrest (1983) promoted a multimodal model of prevention and intervention for use by school counselors. His approach allows the counselor to investigate and treat the major components of depression. Included in the investigation phase of the intervention are the following strategies:

assessment of the cognitive-affective characteristics of the student;

examination of environmental stressors that may contribute to the onset of depression; and

assessment of the coping behaviors possessed by the student.

Treatment interventions are

1. cognitive strategies such as

   self-esteem building,
   self-control training,
   and cognitive restructuring.

2. behavioral interventions such as
   social skills training and
   activity level increase programs.

Forrest thus proposes that the school counselor consider a wide range of intervention techniques in treating the depressed adolescent.

Coats and Reynolds (1983) provided some data on school intervention in a study that evaluates the treatment of depressed adolescents. Thirty moderately and severely depressed subjects were randomly assigned to a cognitive-behavioral treatment (derived from the models of Beck, Lewinsohn, & Rehm), a relaxation treatment, or a wait-list control group. Both treatment conditions provided reduction in depression. Reynolds (1985, p. 168) interpreted these results as indicating "that moderate and severe levels of depression in adolescents can be effectively treated by psychologists in the school setting." Although Reynolds' findings are preliminary, they point toward the school as a logical site for the treatment of adolescent depression.

Prevention

Prevention is divided into two subcategories: primary prevention and secondary prevention.

Primary Prevention. Primary prevention involves the removal of those factors that cause a disorder. Although uncertainty regarding the etiology of depression makes this a difficult task, some researchers have begun to address it. Reynolds (1985, p. 170), for example, indicated that he was developing "a multicomponent affective curriculum to promote the prevention of depression in adolescents."

Secondary Prevention. The major component of secondary prevention is early detection and treatment. Individuals who have primary contact with the adolescent becomes crucial. As Robbins and Kashani (1986) noted, teachers, social workers, school nurses, pediatricians, and general practitioners fall into this category, and would logically serve as primary referral sources. Reynolds (1985) indicated that early detection also would be facilitated via the use of screening techniques. In light of the low cost, brevity, and group administration formats found in assessment instruments, the screening of entire schools becomes feasible.

Although approaches to both primary and secondary prevention are still in the early stages of development, the latter seem to show more promise. School personnel need to take a leadership role in this important endeavor. One can anticipate that schoolwide programs of early detection and treatment for adolescent depression will lower the suicide rate for that population.

CONCLUSIONS/IMPLICATIONS

Hopefully, this chapter has provided relevant information and generated important questions concerning adolescent depression and suicide. Depression is emerging as a major mental health problem among adolescents with manifestations similar to adults. In addition, important links exist between depression and suicide among adolescents. Data clearly indicate the increased potential for suicidal behaviors in the presence of depressive disorders.

Continued research is critical. The relative absence of data for normative populations needs to be remedied, to achieve a better perspective concerning the incidence of depression among adolescents and its relationship to suicide. Systematic exploration of the various models of depression is also needed. Of course, a related effort to evaluate the efficacy of various treatment strategies for adolescents should be a high priority.

Public education is needed regarding adolescent depression with parents and school personnel the primary targets. To do so is particularly crucial given the lack of recognition of adolescent depression (Friedman et al., 1982; Husain & Vandiver, 1984). The problem is further exacerbated by substance abuse. According to Hodgman (1985) many adolescents participate in substance abuse to cope with depression. This process of "self medication" affects accurate diagnosis and treatment.

Even though depression does not necessarily lead to suicide, and an adolescent need not be depressed for suicide to occur, depressive symptoms should alert others to the possibility for self-destructive behavior. Depression has a catastrophic effect on the adolescent and those around him/her, even without suicide. Thus, prevention and early intervention strategies are important. The school setting is the logical site for these endeavors, with school counselors and school psychologists the likely candidates for leadership roles.

REFERENCES

Albert, N., & Beck, A.T. (1975). Incidence of depression in early adolescence: A preliminary study. *Journal of Youth and Adolescence, 4,* 301-7.

Balser, B., & Masterson, J. (1959). Suicide and adolescents. *American Journal of Psychiatry, 116,* 400-7.

Beck, A.T. (1967). *Depression: Causes and treatment.* Philadelphia: University of Pennsylvania Press.

Beck, A.T., & Beck, R.W. (1972). Screening depressed patients in family practice: A rapid technique. *Postgraduate Medicine, 52,* 81-5.

Beck, A.T., Kovacs, M., & Weissman, A. (1975). Hopelessness and suicidal behavior: An overview. *Journal of the American Medical Association, 234,* 1146-9.

Beck, A.T., Rush, A.G., Shaw, B.F., & Emery, G. (1979). *Cognitive therapy for depression.* New York: Guilford.

Beck, A.T., Ward, S.H., Mendelson, M., Mock, J., & Erbaugh, J. (1961). An inventory for measuring depression. *Archives of General Psychiatry, 4,* 561-71.

Becker, J.C. (1974). *Depression: Theory and research.* New York: John Wiley.

Bender, L., & Schilder, P. (1937). Suicidal preoccupation and attempts in children. *American Journal of Orthopsychiatry, 7,* 225-34.

Brent, D.A., Kalas, R., Edelbrock, C., Costello, A.J., Dulcan, M.K., & Conover, N. (1986). Psychopathology and its relationship to suicidal ideation in children and adolescence. *Journal of the American Academy of Child Psychiatry, 25*(5), 666-73.

Carlson, G.A. (1981). The phenomenology of adolescent depression. *Adolescent Psychiatry, 19,* 411-21.

Carlson, G.A., & Cantwell, D.P. (1980). Unmasking masked depression in children and adolescents. *American Journal of Psychiatry, 137*(4), 445-9.

Carlson, G.A., & Cantwell, D.P. (1982). Suicidal behavior and depression in children and adolescents. *Journal of the American Academy of Child Psychiatry, 21,* 361-8.

Coats, K.I., & Reynolds, W.M. (1983). A comparison of cognitive-behavioral and relaxation therapies for depression with adolescents. Manuscript submitted for publication.

Coyne, J.C. (1986). Ambiguity and controversy: An introduction. In J.C. Coyne (Ed.), *Essential papers on depression*, pp. 1-22. New York: New York University Press.

Crumley, F.E. (1979). Adolescent suicide attempts. *Journal of the American Medical Association, 241*, 2404-7.

Cytryn, M.D., McKnew, D.H., & Bunney, W.E., Jr. (1980). Diagnosis of depression in children: A reassessment. *American Journal of Psychiatry, 137*(1), 22-5.

Davis, P.A. (1983). *Suicidal adolescents.* Springfield, IL: Charles C. Thomas.

Despert, J. (1952). Suicide and depression in children. *Nervous Child, 9*, 378-84.

Erickson, M.T. (1987). *Behavior disorders in children and adolescents.* Englewood Cliffs, NJ: Prentice-Hall.

Ferster, C.B. (1973). A functional analysis of depression. *American Psychologist, 28*, 857-70.

Ferster, C.B. (1974). Behavioral approaches to depression. In R.J. Friedman & M.M. Katz (Eds.), *The psychology of depression: Contemporary theory and research.* New York: Winston-Wiley.

Forrest, D.V. (1983). Depression: Information and interventions for school counselors. *The School Counselor*, March, 269-79.

Friedman, R.C., Clarkin, J.F., Corn, R., Arnoff, M.S., Hurt, S.W., & Murphy, M.C. (1982). DSM-III and affective pathology in hospitalized adolescents. *Journal of Nervous and Mental Disease, 170*(9), 511-21.

Gallemore, J.L., & Wilson, W.P. (1972). Adolescent maladjustment or affective disorder? *American Journal of Psychiatry, 129*, 608-12.

Garfinkel, B.D., Froese, A., & Hood, J.C. (1982). Suicide attempts in children and adolescents. *American Journal of Psychiatry, 139*(10), 1257-61.

Garrison, C.Z., Schoenbach, V.J., & Kaplan, B.H. (1985). Depressive symptoms in early adolescence. In A. Dean (Ed.), *Depression in multidisciplinary perspective* (pp. 60-82). New York: Bruner/Mazel.

Getz, L., Allen, D.B., Meyers, R.K., & Linder, K. (1983). *Brief counseling with suicidal persons.* Lexington, MA: D.C. Heath.

Gilbert, P. (1984). *Depression: From psychology to brain state.* London: Lawrence Erlbaum Associates Ltd.

Gispert, M., Wheeler, K., Marsh, L., & Davis, M. (1985). Suicidal adolescents: Factors in evaluation. *Adolescence, 20*(80), 753-62.

Guttman, H.A. (1983). Family therapy in the treatment of mood disturbance in adolescence. In H. Golombek & B. Garfinkel (Eds.), *The adolescent and mood disturbance*, pp. 263-72. New York: International Universities Press.

Guze, S., & Robins, E. (1970). Suicide and primary affective disorders. *British Journal of Psychiatry*, 117, 437-8

Hamilton, M. (1960). A rating scale for depression. *Journal of Neurology, Neurosurgery, and Psychiatry, 23,* 56-62.

Hawton, K. (1986). *Suicide and attempted suicide among children and adolescents.* Beverly Hills, CA: Sage Publications.

Hodgman, C.H. (1985). Recent findings in adolescent depression and suicide. *Developmental and Behavioral Pediatrics, 6*(3), 162-70.

Hudgens, R.W. (1974). *Psychiatric disorders in childhood.* Baltimore: Williams & Wilkins.

Husain, S., & Vandiver, T. (1984). *Suicide in children and adolescents.* New York: SP Medical & Scientific Books.

Kandel, D.B., & Davies, M. (1982). Epidemiology of depressive mood in adolescents. *Archives of General Psychiatry, 39,* 1205-12.

Kaplan, S.L., Hong, G.K., & Weinhold, C. (1984). Epidemiology of depressive symptomology in adolescents. *Journal of the American Academy of Child Psychiatry, 23*(1), 91-8.

Kashani, J.H., Husain, A., Shekim, W.O., Hodges, K.K., Cytryn, L., & McKnew, D.H. (1981). Current perspectives on childhood depression: An overview. *American Journal of Psychiatry, 138*(2), 143-53.

Kaslow, N.J., & Rehm, L.P. (1983). Child depression. In R.J. Morris & T.R. Kratochwill (Eds.), *The practice of child therapy,* pp. 27-51. New York: Pergamon Press.

Kazdin, A.E., French, N.H., Unis, A.S., Esveldt-Dawson, K., & Sherick, R.B. (1983). Hopelessness, depression, and suicidal intent among psychiatrically disturbed children. *Journal of Consulting and Clinical Psychology, 51,* 504-10.

King, L.J., & Pittman, G.D. (1969). A six year follow-up of sixty-five adolescent patients: Predictive value of presenting clinical picture. *British Journal of Psychiatry, 115,* 1437-41.

Kolko, D.J. (1987). Depression. In M. Herson & V.B. Van Hassalt (Eds.), *Behavior therapy with children and adolescents: A clinical approach,* pp. 137-83. New York: John Wiley & Sons.

Kovacs, M. (1981). Rating scales to assess depression in school-aged children. *Acta Paedopsychiatrica, 46,* 305-15.

Kovacs, M., & Beck, A.T. (1977). An empirical-clinical approach toward a definition of childhood depression. In J.G. Schulterbrandt & A. Raskin (Eds.), *Depression in childhood: Diagnosis, treatment, and conceptual models,* pp. 1-25. New York: Raven Press.

Leonard, C.V. (1974). Depression and suicidality. *Journal of Counseling and Clinical Psychology, 42*(1), 91-104.

Levitt, E.E., Lubin, B., & Brooks, J.M. (1983). *Depression: Concepts, controversies, and some new facts.* Hillsdale, N.J: Lawrence Erlbaum Associates.

Lewinsohn, P.M., Biglan, A., & Zeiss, A.M. (1976). Behavioral treatment of depression. In P.O. Davidson (Ed.), *The behavioral management of anxiety, depression and pain.* New York: Brunner/Mazel.

Lewinsohn, P.M., & Hoberman, H.M. (1985). Depression. In A.S. Bellack, M. Herson, & A.E. Kazdin (Eds.), *International handbook of behavior modification and therapy* (student edition), pp. 173-207. New York: Plenum Press.

Medical Economics Company. (1987). *Physician's desk reference (41st ed.).* Oradell, NJ: Author.

Morgan, H.G. (1979). *Death wishes? The understanding and management of deliberate self-harm.* New York: John Wiley & Sons.

Petti, T.A., Bornstein, M., Delamater, A., & Conners, S.K. (1980). Evaluation and multimodality treatment of a depressed prepubertal girl. *Journal of the American Academy of Child Psychiatry, 19,* 690-702.

Pfeffer, C.R. (1986). *The suicidal child.* New York: Guilford Press.

Poznanski, E. (1984). Depressed children. In N.R. Bernstein & J. Sussex (Eds.), *Handbook of psychiatric consultation with children and youth,* pp. 319-30. New York: SP Medical & Scientific Books.

Puig-Antioch, J. (1982). The use of RDC criteria for major depressive disorder in children and adolescents. *Journal of the American Academy of Child Psychiatry, 21,* 291-3.

Puig-Antioch, J., & Chambers, W. (1978). *The Schedule for Affective Disorders and Schizophrenia for School-Age Children* (Kiddie-SADS). New York: New York State Psychiatric Institute.

Rehm, L.P. (1977). A self-control model of depression. *Behavior Therapy, 8,* 787-804.

Reynolds, W.M. (1981). *Reynolds Adolescent Depression Scale.* (Available from William M. Reynolds, Department of Educational Psychology, University of Wisconsin, Madison, WI 53706.)

Reynolds, W.M. (1983, March). *Depression in adolescents: Measurement, epidemiology, and correlates.* Paper presented at annual meeting of the National Association of School Psychologists, Detroit.

Reynolds, W.M. (1984). Depression in children and adolescents: Phenomenology, evaluation and treatment. *School Psychology Review, 13*(2), 171-82.

Reynolds, W.M. (1985). Depression in childhood and adolescence: Diagnosis, assessment, intervention strategies and research. In T.R. Kratochwill (Ed.), *Advances in school psychology: Volume IV*, pp. 133-89. Hillsdale, NJ: Lawrence Erlbaum Associates.

Robbins, D.R., & Alessi, N.E. (1985). Depressive symptoms and suicidal behavior in adolescents. *American Journal of Psychiatry, 142*(5), 588-92.

Robbins, D.R., Alessi, N.E., Cook, S.C., Poznanski, E.O., & Yanchyshyn, G.W. (1982). The use of diagnostic criteria (RDC) for depression in adolescent psychiatric inpatients. *Journal of the American Academy of Child Psychiatry, 21*(3), 251-5.

Robbins, D.R., & Kashani, J.H. (1986). Depression in adolescence. In *Advances in adolescent mental health volume 1, part b*, pp. 59-89. Greenwich, CT: JAI Press.

Rutter, M., Graham, P., Chadwick, O., & Yule, W. (1976). Adolescent turmoil: Fact or fiction? *Journal of Child Psychology and Psychiatry, 17*, 35-56.

Schilder, P., & Weschler, D. (1934). The attitudes of children toward death. *Journal of Genetic Psychology, 45*, 406-18.

Schwartz, S., & Johnson, J.H. (1985). *Psychopathology of childhood* (2nd ed.). New York: Pergamon Press.

Seligman, M.E.P. (1974). Depression and learned helplessness. In R.J. Friedman & M.M. Katz (Eds.), *The psychology of depression: Contemporary theory and research*, pp. 83-125. New York: John Wiley & Sons.

Seligman, M.E.P. (1975). *Helplessness: On depression, development, and death.* San Francisco: Freedman.

Seligman, M.E.P. (1981). A learned helplessness point of view. In L.P. Rehm (Ed.), *Behavior therapy for depression*, pp. 123-41. New York: Academic Press.

Shaffer, D. (1974). Suicide in childhood and early adolescence. *Journal of Child Psychology & Psychiatry, 15*, 275-91.

Shaffer, D. (1986). Developmental factors in child and adolescent suicide. In M. Rutter, C.E. Izard, & P.B. Read (Eds.), *Depression in young people*, pp. 383-96. New York: The Guilford Press.

Smith, K., & Crawford, S. (1986). Suicidal behavior among "normal" high school students. *Suicide and Life Threatening Behavior, 16*(3), 313-25.

Snyder, S.H. (1975). Biology. In S. Perlin (Ed.), *A handbook for the study of suicide*, pp. 113-28. New York: Oxford University Press.

Spitzer, R.C., & Endicott, J. (1977). *Schedule for Affective Disorders and Schizophrenia* (SADS) (3rd ed.). New York: New York State Psychiatric Institute, Biometrics Research.

Spitzer, R.L., Endicott, J., & Robins, E. (1978). Research diagnostic criteria: Rationale and reliability. *Archives of General Psychiatry, 35*, 773-82.

Strober, M., Green, J., & Carlson, G. (1981). Utility of the Beck Depression Inventory with psychiatrically hospitalized adolescents. *Journal of Consulting and Clinical Psychology*, 49, 482-3.

Weiner, A.S. (1983). Emotional problems of adolescence: A review of affective disorders and schizophrenia. In C.E. Walker & M.C. Roberts (Eds.), *Handbook of clinical child psychology*, pp. 741-58. New York: John Wiley & Sons.

Weiner, I.B. (1975). Depression in adolescence. In F.F. Flach & S.C. Draghi (Eds.), *The nature and treatment of depression* (pp. 99-117). New York: John Wiley & Sons.

Weissman, M.C. (1974). Epidemiology of suicide attempts, 1960-1971. *Archives of General Psychiatry, 30*, 737-46.

PART III
ASSESSING LETHALITY

CHAPTER **7**

PSYCHOLOGICAL ASSESSMENT

Fred L. Alberts, Jr., Ph.D.

Fred L. Alberts, Jr., Ph.D.

Chief, Psychological Services
Tampa General Hospital
Tampa, Florida

Dr. Alberts is Chief of Psychology and Neuropsychology at The Tampa General Hospital, Tampa, Florida. In addition to his hospital practice, he maintains an independent practice in child and family psychology. He received his doctorate from the University of Southern Mississippi and completed his internship in clinical psychology at The Devereux Foundation, Devon, Pennsylvania. He served as Director of Children's Services at Northside Centers, Inc., where he directed a number of innovative intervention projects for children and adolescents. He is consulting psychologist to the Family Protection Team of the Child Abuse Council. He is co-editor, with Dr. Gregory G. Wilkins, of *Software Reviews of Microcomputer Applications in Mental Health.* His latest book, *Psychological Assessment: A Primer for Health and Allied Health Professionals,* is scheduled for release early next year. Dr. Alberts also has published numerous scientific articles in the area of clinical neuropsychology, clinical child psychology, cognitive re-training, psychodiagnostics, and applications of computer technology in mental health.

EDITORIAL ABSTRACT: *A comprehensive psychological assessment of suicidal adolescent patients provides a wealth of data that is useful in both the assessment of suicidal risk and generating appropriate treatment strategies. In this chapter are described the "system clustors" that present a picture of adolescents at high risk for suicide. A case study, including a psychological report, serves as an illustration.*

The identification and assessment of suicide potential is *the* essential component in managing and treating suicidal adolescent patients. The assessment process begins at the time a mental health or health care provider becomes aware of a patient's suicidal thoughts, intentions, gestures, and/or attempts. Because of the necessity of on-going assessment in suicidal adolescent patients, the line between assessment and intervention is rarely clear. Unfortunately, often the urgency to see the patient and to initiate intervention takes priority over a thorough and formal psychological assessment. In this chapter are considered interview and assessment strategies, as well as the more thorough and preferred formal psychological assessment.

When the mental health provider's skills do not include formal psychodiagnostic training and experience, referral should be made to a psychologist for a complete examination. The history, life stressors, family dynamics, and suicidal potential of the patient must be fully assessed by a qualified psychologist. Less formal rating scales and interview formats may be utilized by staff at various levels of training and across all disciplines, assuming their familiarity with the instruments, recognitions of the psychometric limitations, and when the information is used in consultation with other professionals for discussion of the patient's status.

CONDUCTING THE INTERVIEWS

Parent Interview

A thorough history of the patient obtained from parents or the primary caretaker is most desirable. Although it is not always possible, a parent interview can be obtained in most cases when adolescents present for either outpatient or inpatient treatment. In many cases, parents will require some immediate intervention as they are often in distress and anxious regarding their child's current emotional condition and safety. The experienced therapist will recognize the parents' need to share their anxieties and fears and afford the time necessary prior to conducting the history.

Many formats for obtaining a thorough history exist. Some history forms designed to be completed by parents provide limited information due to the nature of the instrument. That is, when a "yes" or "no" response to an item is viewed as acceptable or the parent is required to merely "check" items on a symptom list, the qualitative and dynamic aspects may be lost. These "checklists" or "parent questionnaires" are excellent adjuncts to the interview, but should not be considered a replacement for a thorough history.

Asking a series of questions in a structured but open-ended format related to the child's background and development provides the interviewer with considerable information to be used in assessing the patient's status. During the history, the following factors should be addressed:

1. Presenting Problems/Current Status
    a. Parents' description of presenting problems
    b. Overall emotional status
    c. Changes in behavior
    d. History of suicide gestures/attempts
    e. Statements regarding death wish
2. Family Constellation
    a. Mother (natural, step-, age, occupation, education, health)
    b. Father (natural, step-, age, occupation, education, health)
    c. Length of marriage
    d. History of divorce, separation, or marital discord
    e. Relationship with extended family
    f. Ages, sex of siblings
    g. Relationship with siblings.
3. Clinical Impressions of the Parents
    a. History of learning and/or emotional problems
    b. Alcohol/drug abuse history
    c. Emotional status
    d. Clinical impressions impacting child
    e. Too much/too little involvement with child

4. Developmental History
   a. Pre-, peri-, and post-natal factors
   b. Feeding
   c. Developmental milestones
      1) Motor
      2) Language
      3) Socialization
      4) Daily living
      5) Unusual behaviors
   d. 1st two years of life
   e. Pre-school factors

5. Medical History
   a. Medical problems
   b. Accidents, injuries
   c. Last physical examination
   d. Sex education
   e. Adjustment to adolescence
   f. Speech, hearing, vision
   g. Fevers
   h. Unconsciousness
   i. Seizure history
   j. Complaint of dizziness, headaches, poor sleep

6. Academic History
   a. Day-care
   b. Pre-school
   c. Kindergarten
   d. Schools (public, private)
   e. Special classes
   f. Adjustment to kindergarten and 1st grade
   g. School performance

7. Interpersonal Factors
   a. Friends
   b. Small groups/large groups/loner
   c. Leader/follower
   d. Adults/peers

8. Home Environment
   a. Own room/share with sibling/other
   b. Hobbies (casual, physical)
   c. Television
   d. Movies

e. Dating
f. Allowance
g. Curfews/bedtimes
h. Responsibilities around the home

This information lays the foundation against which the current symptoms will be viewed. The emotional turmoil, the internal and external presses, and family dynamics are to be assessed. Extracting information from parent interview data and formulating preliminary hypotheses of underlying psychodynamics are sometimes made difficult by defensive parents attempting to disown any responsibility for suicidal behavior of the patient. Thus, the therapist must be more investigative and ask proper questions in order to see the entire clinical picture. Section 1 of the Family History should determine the array of presenting problems/symptoms and the emotional overlay and resultant behaviors. The use of symptom checklists or child questionnaires can certainly highlight presenting concerns. However, a careful interviewing style not only establishes a chronology of symptoms, but also allows qualification and discussion of the symptoms in the context of current behaviors. Regardless of the technique decided upon, the interviewer must assess how the behaviors, based upon parent report, may be symptomatic of suicidal behavior and/or potential. Some symptoms will be obvious while others are more subtle. Based upon the scientific literature, most suicidal patients give "clues". Their world is not always responsive to the clues, but the clues typically exist. Clues may be verbal or non-verbal. Evidence of a significant depression and feelings of helplessness, hopelessness, and haplessness are among the most dramatic symptoms found among suicidal patients. Not all victims of suicide are depressed, but depression is most often associated with suicidal feelings. For years opinions have differed as to the manner in which depression manifests itself differently in children/adolescents and adults. A growing concensus is occurring that depression does not have differing manifestation in adolescents and adults (American Psychiatric Association, 1986; Yanchyshyn & Robbins, 1983). More overt verbal clues may include words of warning such as, "I'd be better off dead", "There's nothing left to live for", etc. These clues are given to a variety of individuals in the adolescent's life including teachers, boyfriends/girlfriends, coaches, as well as parents. In assessing the level of depression and related emotional factors based on parent report, the therapist should look for the presence of symptom clusters of anxiety, crying spells, lethargy, difficulty with concentration and/or irritability. The therapist should determine the presence of sleep disturbance (too much, too little), appetite disturbance (too much, too little), somatic symptomotology, physical complaints in the absence of organic origin, loss of interest in activities, and poor self-concept.

Sudden changes in behavior have been associated with suicide attempts and eventual suicides. These behavioral changes include, but are not limited to, interpersonal difficulties, withdrawing from social activities, and generally isolating one's self from the world. Verbal and non-verbal expression of a poor self-concept or self-pity also emerge. Assessment of any dysfunction in the home and/or school, the presence of increased aggressive behaviors, accident proneness, and moodiness should be made. In summary, in addition to a good developmental history, the therapist will want to obtain answers to the following questions.

1. What is your child's current emotional status. Is he/she depressed? Have you seen evidence of feelings of helplessness, hopelessness, and/or haplessness?
2. Have dramatic changes occurred in your child's behavior or personality?
3. What is the history of suicide threats, gestures, and/or attempts?
4. Has the patient made statements or shown other indicators of a wish to die?
5. Have any uncharacteristic behaviors occurred to suggest that the child is making any "final arrangements"?

Interviewing the Patient

Regardless of whether or not the individual conducting the interview will be the professional providing the intervention, the establishment of a pre-therapeutic relationship is essential if the clinical interview is to add to the assessment process. If one conceptualizes that suicidal behavior is a "cry for help" or a communication of internal pain, then the adolescent needs to be provided with a strong helping professional. Encouraging the patient to see the therapist as a "pal" or peer offers little to one in distress. The signal is clear and the response should be clear.

Adolescent suicidal behavior must be taken seriously, and intervention by peers, inexperienced therapists, or those not having experience with children and adolescents should be avoided. Thus, establishing a relationship is the first order of business. The therapist must avoid the temptation of being seen as a "buddy" and must resist being addressed on a first name basis for the purpose of establishing a relationship. The relationship must be viewed by the patient as a response to a "cry for help" by an individual who is capable of responding to that need. As a group, suicidal adolescents are angry at the world, angry at themselves, and are often embroiled in much emotional turbulence. Thus, establishing the relationship is often difficult unless the patient views the helping professional as non-judgmental, capable of being of assistance, and trusting.

The issue of confidentiality and the therapist's responsibilities should the patient indicate immediate danger to himself or others must be addressed. In the context of a crisis interview, discussion of the therapist's responsibility is not typically at issue, since the implication is that the therapist will take some action. In the case of a crisis interview, a structured interview format is inappropriate. Perhaps even making notes during an extremely emotional interview may be seen by some as inappropriate. However, basic aspects of the adolescent's functioning, thinking, feeling, and relating need to be assessed. In many cases, the use of a standard interview format is not only appropriate but most desirable. Figure 7.1 is a standard interview format used by this author with adolescents. It contains nothing particularly novel, but it allows organization and provides cues to items that are sometimes otherwise omitted.

Information about "presenting problems" may be obtained by parents, teachers, siblings, babysitters, etc., but the experience of this author is that the best report of what is actually happening is the adolescent's report. That is not to say that it will not sometimes be colored by defenses, embellished for manipulation, or minimized for escape from an uncomfortable situation. But, on the whole, the "presenting problems," those issues of concern to the patient in distress, are most accurately delineated by the patient. Also, when discrepancies occur between reports (e.g., parent and child), immediate hypothesis testing may begin. For example, is the parent minimizing a significant dysfunction in order to reduce his/her anxiety about the situation? Is the parent's anger at the child so intense that the parent attributes all of the difficulties to

CLINICAL INTERVIEW—ADOLESCENT

Name: ________________ Age: ___ Patient #: ______ Date: ________

PRESENTING PROBLEM:

ACADEMIC:

INTERPERSONAL:

FAMILY:

EMOTIONAL:

Mental Status

Life Stressors

Suicidal History

Ideation

Gestures

Attempts

Friends/Family History

Figure 7.1. A clinical interview format to be used with adolescents.

MEDICAL:

Last Physical

Last Physician Appointment

Physical Condition

Appetite

Sleep Patterns

Significant Illness/Injury History

Tobacco

Alcohol

Drugs

INTERESTS:

Casual

Hobbies

Social

Physical

Television/Music

Other

ACCOMPLISHMENTS:

STRENGTHS: **WEAKNESSES:**

BEHAVIORAL OBSERVATIONS:

Figure 7.1. Continued.

the child? Is the child exaggerating a conflict in order to avoid age-appropriate responsibilities? Is the child deliberately attempting to twist the truth in order to triangulate the situation and have others in conflict, thereby changing focus from the patient? A number of hypotheses may be generated and tested as more data are collected. Another valuable aspect is to ask, "Why treatment now?", as most clinical cases will have more than just a recent history. Ask the patient about his/her academic history and functioning. Pay attention to how the patient views the academic arena. For example, is it a place where he/she feels good? Are there any successes? Are the failure experiences overwhelming? Does the history reflect difficulties due to repeated change of schools and why the changes? The therapist should ask about grades, favorite/least favorite subjects, whether or not the patient is in a special school and or special classes, attachment to certain teachers, current pass/fail status, etc. Attempt to assess whether or not the academic program meets the individual's need.

Assessment of interpersonal functioning is essential. Does the patient have a group of friends? Does the patient prefer to be alone? Does the patient actually prefer to be with others, but feel like an outcast? Another significant area for assessment in suicide potential is the functioning of the family. What is the patient's relationship with the mother and father? How does the patient relate to siblings? Are divorce, separation, or adoption issues emerging with the onset of adolescence?

Prior to formal psychological assessment, the therapist, through interviewing, may conduct a brief mental status exam and attempt to assess the patient's current levels of anxiety, tension, and depression. The history of previous counseling and/or hospitalization is also useful.

One myth is that asking questions about suicidal thoughts, gestures, and intentions might increase the patient's tendency to act on the impulse, or "put the idea into his/her head". The patient's report is a crucial element of the suicide assessment and must be considered carefully. More often, discussion of the suicidal thoughts reduces the anxiety associated with them. The therapist will want information on the history and certainly the current presence of suicidal ideation, gestures, and attempts.

The patient's physical status, as reported by the patient, needs to be part of the assessment. Also determine when the last physical examination was conducted and if referral for physical examination is required. Often, suicidal patients have uncharacteristically made a number of trips to the physician's office prior to a suicide attempt. Physical complaints and illnesses should be assessed. The therapist should ask the patient about appetite and sleep patterns. The patient's report or evidence of self-inflicted wounds should be explored. The extent to which the patient is involved in drug and/or alcohol use has been shown to be of significance in suicidal patients, and should be discussed and assessed. What is the length of use, age at which regular use began, and the patient's reason for use? In the case of severely depressed adolescents, the use of alcohol and drugs is often a self-medication and not merely the result of peer pressure.

Another appropriate area for questioning is whether the patient has received any awards, special recognition, for his/her accomplishments. How the patient spends time outside of school should be evaluated, as lethargy, withdrawal, and isolation are symptom clusters for the depressed and suicidal. This is not to identify "introverts" as depressed or suicidal, but excessive withdrawal is a clear danger signal. This author often asks the patient to list "strengths" and "weaknesses." This is a revealing technique in which, using the patient's report, the self-concept and self-perceived abilities can be assessed. For the more concrete or intellectually limited, substitute the question, "What are three things you like (and do not like) about yourself?"

FORMAL PSYCHOLOGICAL ASSESSMENT

While formal psychological assessment can aid in identifying potentially suicidal patients, its greatest utility is in clarifying the amount of emotional turmoil and identifying dynamics and issues to be addressed through intervention. Demographic and behavioral variables and their relationship to effected suicide have been long established and reported in the classic works of Farberow and Schneidman (1957; 1961).

The purpose of psychological testing is to enable the psychologist to sample or measure, in a standard fashion, behaviors of the patient and to predict behaviors. The "sampling" of behaviors should be a comprehensive approach including parent interview, teacher interview, clinical interview, behavioral observations, review of records, intelligence testing, academic testing, neuropsychological screening testing, and social/emotional (personality) testing. This is particularly recommended with suicidal patients, because possibly a number of disorders may be present leading to a suicide attempt. Depression, of course, is one of the most common, and suicidal behavior is often found in the presence of depression. Neurological dysfunction, psychosis, toxic states (drug or alcohol), and a number of other interpersonal and intra-psychic dysfunctions are also possible factors in suicidal behavior. Thus, the thorough examination goes beyond assessment of depression. The intelligence test is conducted to assess how the individual processes information and to offer an estimate of the cognitive capability of the patient. Academic assessment is conducted, and a comparison among intellectual capability, achievement levels, and school performance should be made. Neuropsychological screening and referral for further evaluation, if indicated, should be a part of the assessment.

CLINICAL CASE EXAMPLE: THE CASE OF S.D.

Integrating psychological interview and assessment data is the final step in formulating treatment recommendations and generating a written report. Figure 7.2 is a summary of psychological findings in the case of S.D., a thirteen-year-old Caucasian male referred for evaluation due to changes in his behavior and concern regarding his emotional status, having lived in an abusive home most of his life. (Figure 7.2 is included at the end of this chapter.)

The background information provided by the grandmother contains a number of "danger signals" that suggest a child at risk, as well as the need for further psychological evaluation. The following are the danger signals revealed during the history:

1. S.D. has received little affection.
2. Parental communication has often been punitive.
3. S.D. continues to have difficulty relating effectively with peers.
4. S.D. is depressed.
5. S.D. is seen as having difficulty concentrating.

The behavioral observations revealed considerable anxiety and tension. His range of emotions were reported as being limited and serious. The formal psychological assessment confirmed the grandmother's impression that S.D. has difficulty concentrating. Academically, he is functioning at a level fairly consistent with intellectual expectancies as this appears to be one of the few areas where S.D. receives any gratification, as his gratification is *dependent* upon the acceptance and acknowledgements of others. The danger signals revealed through the formal assessment include the clusters of his living with a considerable amount of pain and anger, self-devaluation, poor judgment and decision making ability under stress, propensity to get "caught up" in affective situations, and the tendency to over-internalize and constrain his feelings.

Clearly S.D. is in distress and intervention is required. Although concern regarding suicidal risk was revealed, the patient is not seen as being in immediate danger, due to the fact that he was essentially "crying for help" without suicidal gestures or attempts. He was open to psychotherapy, and should be able to establish a good working relationship with a therapist. He's in pain, he wants help and he is not so impulsive or so distressed to suggest that he is in any immediate danger. As an outpatient, however, his progress must be monitored consistently and carefully.

TRANSLATING INTERVIEW AND TEST DATA TO TREATMENT RECOMMENDATIONS

Assessment of Degree of Risk

A number of psychological variables have been discussed in this chapter and throughout this book that are related to suicidal behaviors. The reader is cautioned that not just one variable, demographic or psychological, is associated with suicidal behavior.

Of utmost importance, of course, is the articulated intention of suicide. The mere thinking of suicide is not necessarily a high risk factor, as adolescents commonly have suicidal fantasies at one time or another in their development (Cantor, 1976). However, when the ideation is combined with a method, and the patient has the means, and has articulated a plan, then obviously this represents a high risk. When the factors represent a rather high risk, the patient's life stressors and coping mechanisms should be simultaneously assessed in order to render a level of risk for the patient. Some adolescent patients in crisis will appear to require hospitalization, but with proper crisis intervention and contract with a therapist may return to a previously "normal" level of adaptive functioning within a short period of time. Individuals with extremely poor problem-solving ability may present in distress, but with some directive counseling emphasizing alternatives to suicide, the patient is able to be maintained on an outpatient basis and return to "normal" functioning within a few days, following a crisis event. Many times the patient has become frustrated because strategies to cope and to problem-solve have been unsuccessful. Additionally, suicide is triggered in some individuals by a specific event such as, death of a loved one, a debilitating illness or injury, or significant disruption in the family or job. Whenever possible, consultation with a colleague or supervisor is strongly recommended when assessing the degree of suicidal risk.

Outpatient vs. Inpatient

When the assessment of an acutely suicidal patient has been made, the result is generally voluntary or involuntary admission to a psychiatric hospital or other treatment facility. These facilities provide an environment in which the goal is to stabilize the patient for return to the community or to be referred for other community programs. Drug and alcohol rehabilitation are often part of the treatment. Unless acutely suicidal, hospitalization is not the only treatment alternative for suicidal patients. Hospitalization is the choice when the patient, in spite of outpatient intervention, fails to see alternatives to the suicidal plan.

Outpatient treatment for suicidal patients requires good initial assessment and continued re-assessment. The therapist must develop a plan of action that may include a contract with the patient.

Medication

The suicidal patient presents a particular problem in regard to assessment for the advisability of psychotropic medication. On the one hand, anti-anxiety and/or anti-depressants may assist in stabilizing the patient; however, the risk of overdose and self-destructive use in combination with other drugs and alcohol exists. The same criteria used to determine the appropriateness for referral for medication assessment as used with non-suicidal patients may be utilized, but a risk/benefit must be addressed, and most preferably in consultation with a colleague or supervisor.

SUMMARY

Comprehensive psychological assessment of suicidal adolescent patients provides a wealth of data that is extremely helpful in both the assessment of suicidal risk and generating appropriate treatment strategies. Although psychological testing can be helpful and certainly aids in treatment planning, no one test, technique, or psychological variable can singly identify suicidal adolescent patients. "Symptom clusters," heavily dependent on demography, patient's previous levels of functioning, coping strategies, ability to problem-solve, and suicidal history, serve as the best source of data for assessing and managing suicidal patients.

REFERENCES

American Psychiatric Association (1986). *Diagnostic and statistical manual of mental disorders—revised.* Washington, D.C.: Author

Cantor, P. (1976). Personality characteristics among youthful female suicide attempters. *Journal of Abnormal Psychology, 85*, 324-329.

Farberow, N.L., & Shneidman, E.S. (Eds.) (1961). *The Cry for Help.* New York: McGraw-Hill.

Shneidman, E.S., & Farberow, N.L. (1957). *Clues to Suicide*, New York: McGraw-Hill.

Yanchyshyn, G.W., & Robbins, D.R. (1983). The assessment of depression in normal adolescents: A comparison study. *Canadian Journal of Psychiatry, 28*, 522-526.

CASE EXAMPLE
PSYCHOLOGICAL REPORT

NAME: S.D.

DATE OF BIRTH: August 1, 1974

AGE: 13-1

EDUCATION: 8.1

DATE OF ASSESSMENT: September 15, 1987

REASON FOR REFERRAL

S.D. was referred for psychological evaluation in order to assess his overall intellectual, academic, and personality functioning to aid in planning.

BACKGROUND INFORMATION

The background information for this evaluation was provided by review of available records and by interview of S.D.'s maternal grandmother, Mrs. L. S.D. is currently in the custody of his grandmother. S.D. and his younger brother (age 9) were placed in Mrs. L.'s custody last year, following their parents' divorce. The marriage was described as a very unstable and violent marriage, resulting in S.D. and his brother being placed in temporary shelter. According to the record, both S.D. and his brother witnessed considerable abuse of their mother by Mr. F. Mrs. F. was hospitalized due to her emotional condition and subsequently committed suicide. Mrs. L. states that she feels that the boys were subjected to very traumatic incidents involving the abuse of their mother by the father. Mr. F. has intentions of gaining custody. Mrs. L. notes that her grandchildren will often hide when their father comes to visit, so that they will not be forced to go with him.

Figure 7.2. Clinical Case Example: The Case of S.D.

Mrs. L. describes S.D. as extremely passive, and he will often allow his younger brother and much smaller friends to beat up on him. He shares his feelings only occasionally. S.D. is often picked on at school by the other children and has been frequently referred to as a "nerd." She states that he has attempted to socialize with a group of friends more recently, but he still has considerable difficulty in relating to them.

Mrs. L. reported a fairly normal developmental history with the exception of a problem with S.D.'s occasionally passing out between the ages of one and five. Medical assessment, including a CAT Scan did not reveal the etiology of the spells. Mrs. L. was not aware of any other significant medical or developmental difficulties.

Mrs. L. did not report knowledge of any previous suicidal gestures, intentions, or attempts by S.D. She does, however, describe him as depressed and a child who seems to "have his mind on other things." She is concerned that he may be suicidal.

EXAMINATION PROCEDURES:

Wechsler Intelligence Scale for Children—Revised;
Wide Range Achievement Test—Revised;
Metropolitan Achievement Test, Advanced 1, Form JS;
Rorschach Inkblots;
High School Personality Questionnaire;
Bender Visual Motor Gestalt Test;
Draw-A-Person (Story);
House-Tree;
Sentence Completion;
Review of Records;
Interview of Maternal Grandparent;
Clinical Interview.

Figure 7.2. Continued.

RESPONSE TO EVALUATION

S.D. is a thirteen-year-old Caucasian male who came willingly with the examiner to the examination room. He was neatly and conservatively attired. He wears glasses. He was cooperative throughout the assessment and appeared to put forth his best effort. He displayed adequate interpersonal skills with the examiner, but demonstrated limited spontaneity. His affect was flat, and he presented himself in a serious fashion. He was notably tense and did not appear to handle the pressure to perform very well (e.g., the anxiety aroused by certain tasks seemed to significantly reduce his ability to perform). The level of tension that he was experiencing might best be exemplified by the fact that he was twisting so hard on his pencil at one point the pencil broke.

S.D. was generally open with the examiner about his personal life, but did not appear to be in touch with his feelings. He stated that he likes school and that he has a number of girlfriends at school. He did admit to feeling sad when he thought of his family difficulties.

TEST RESULTS AND INTERPRETATION

A. Intellectual Factors

S.D. was administered the Wechsler Intelligence Scale For Children—Revised. He obtained a Verbal Deviation IQ Score in the Superior range (96th Percentile), a Performance Deviation IQ Score in the High Average range (87th Percentile), and a resultant Full Scale Deviation IQ Score in the Superior range. This overall of intellectual functioning places him at the 95th Percentile. Inter-subtest variability on the Verbal Scale reflects an exceptional strength in Verbal Concept-Formation and the ability to abstract. A relative weakness (Average range) was noted on a measure of short-term auditory recall, an area most likely affected by anxiety and tension. The remainder of verbal abilities are consistent with the High Average to

Figure 7.2. Continued.

to Superior ranges. Variability among the non-verbal subtests showed strengths (Superior range) in the areas of perceptual organization of both abstract and familiar stimuli. The remaining non-verbal abilities fall in the Average to High Average ranges. His ability to recognize visually the temporal recognition in a social context and to use foresight in planning his approach to a visual-motor task were noted to be the weakest areas.

B. Achievement Factors

In order to assess S.D.'s current levels of academic achievement, across the three basic areas of achievement (Reading, Spelling, and Arithmetic), he was administered the Wide Range Achievement Test—Revised and the Metropolitan Achievement Test, Advanced 1, Form JS. The results indicate that S.D.'s performance in the areas of Reading and Arithmetic are consistent with both intellectual and chronological expectancies. However, in the area of Spelling, he is performing at a level below both intellectual and chronological expectancies.

C. Visual—Motor Factors

S.D.'s performance on the Bender Visual Motor Gestalt Test reflected no significant visual-motor integration deficits. The reproductions were placed in an orderly fashion on the page suggesting fairly good planning ability. A sequential expansion in the size of the reproductions tends to suggest a low tolerance of frustration, in spite of initially overly constrictive controls. Overwork was observed in all of his drawings, suggesting the above noted levels of increased anxiety and tension with certain tasks.

Figure 7.2. Continued.

D. Social/Emotional Factors

Based upon the above test results, background information, and clinical interview, it appears that S.D. is a young man experiencing significant emotional difficulties. He is an extremely passive individual who tends to avoid the expression of negative feelings as well as possessing a strong desire to avoid environmental conflict. The test results suggest a fairly poor self-concept, a preoccupation with the values of others, and little awareness of his own needs. A significant level of depression is noted, as well as generalized anxiety. He lives with a tremendous amount of tension and a high level of stress from external sources. This would make him prone to various degrees of cognitive and behavioral decompensation, while under additional stress. This type of "decompensation" was evident on a number of the testing tasks, particularly on several of the timed tasks of the intelligence test. His tension level rose to the point on one particular task (Arithmetic subtest), that he broke his pencil. A high level of affective constriction was noted as well as the tendency to intellectualize his affective experience. The test results suggest that he is a young man who tends to put much affective distance between himself and those around him. He has exceptionally high aspirations and drive, particularly in intellectually-related areas. A major part of his identity appears to be with his self-perception as a high academic achiever as well as one who is very rule-bound and has a conventional orientation.

His reality testing, particularly during periods of stress and/or provocation, tends to be somewhat poor and would suggest that his judgment and decision-making capabilities may be poor. S.D. has not developed a consistent problem-solving style. Moreover, he tends to possess a mixed response style; sometimes engaging the environment in trial and error problem-solving while at

Figure 7.2. Continued.

other times attempting to "think things through." This appears to create a certain amount of disequilibrium. When a situation fits his problem-solving style he will do well, but when it does not, misdirected behavior will be noted.

The most significant finding is a suicide potential, with considerable underlying emotional pain and anger. This self-devaluation, poor judgment and decision-making difficulties under stress, propensity to get "caught up" in affective situations, and tendency to over-internalize and constrain his feelings, makes him at high risk, particularly when faced with unavoidable stress.

SUMMARY AND RECOMMENDATIONS

Psychological evaluation of young S.D., a thirteen-year-old Caucasion male, reveals that he is currently functioning in the Superior range of intellectual capacity. Academically, in the areas of Reading and Arithmetic, he is performing at levels consistent with both intellectual and chronological expectancies. In terms of personality, he is a young man who is found to be anxious, tense, depressed, and a significantly high risk. A tremendous amount of underlying emotional pain and anger, self-devaluation, poor judgment and decision-making capabilities, particularly under stress, and tendency to over-internalize and constrain his feelings, make him at risk, particularly during periods of unavoidable stress.

Based upon the above test results, background information, and clinical interview, the following recommendations seem appropriate:

1. A strong recommendation is for S.D. to be involved in individual psychotherapy on a long-term basis. The focus of such sessions should be upon: (a) expression of angry feelings; (b) expression of dysphoric feelings; (c) enhancement of self-image; (d) help in generalizing from previous learning situations to new, by role reversal, role-playing, etc., and (e) emphasis on age-

Figure 7.2. Continued.

appropriate socialization skills. An intensive psychotherapeutic venture is indicated.

2. Initially, the therapeutic efforts should be very gradual, so as to not minimize or re-orient S.D.'s defenses too drastically. He appears to be maintaining a rather "delicate balance" at this point, and an over-intrusive approach may result in decompensation.

3. Another recommendation is for school personnel to continue to monitor S.D.'s behavior for activities which may appear to be unusual, out of character, or self-destructive.

4. Social work services through the school appear warranted, in order to direct Mrs. L. to appropriate community resources.

5. S.D. should be encouraged to participate in extra-curricular activities, as indicated, particularly those involving relationships with peers. A school-based group, when his individual therapist feels that he is ready, may be of great benefit.

Charles D. Furman

Charles D. Furman, III, Psy.D.

Fred L. Alberts

Fred L. Alberts, Jr., Ph.D.
Licensed Psychologist

Figure 7.2. Continued.

CHAPTER **8**

"SIGNATURES" OF SUICIDE

Carol Tomlinson-Keasey, Ph.D.
and
Charles Blake Keasey, Ph.D.

The preparation of this chapter was facilitated by a research grant to the first author from the University of California-Riverside.

Carol Tomlinson-Keasey, Ph.D.

Professor of Psychology
University of California, Riverside
Riverside, CA 92521

Dr. Tomlinson-Keasey received her Ph.D. in developmental psychology at the University of California—Berkeley in 1970. Since then, she has taught at Rutgers University, the University of Nebraska, and the University of California—Riverside. Dr. Tomlinson-Keasey has published two books and dozens of chapters and articles concerned with the development of children and adolescents. Her research has focused on variables which influence optimal cognitive development. Dr. Tomlinson-Keasey's earlier research in the area of suicide examined the importance of seven factors in the suicides committed by gifted women. Her current research interests concentrate on the development of feelings of self-worth among gifted women. Dr. Tomlinson-Keasey is currently a professor of Psychology at the University of California—Riverside and Acting Dean of the College of Humanities and Social Sciences.

Charles Blake Keasey, Ph.D.

Associate Professor of Psychiatry
University of California, Riverside
Riverside, Ca 92521

Charles Blake Keasey received his bachelor's and master's degrees from Iowa State University. He completed his Ph.D. at the University of California—Berkeley in 1969, with a specialization in developmental psychology. Since then, he has taught at Rutgers University, the University of Nebraska—Lincoln and Loma Linda Medical Center. His responsibilities during the last 10 years have combined developmental and forensic psychology. The children he sees are having some developmental difficulties and the situation often has legal ramifications. Many of the children and adolescents he sees are depressed.

EDITORIAL ABSTRACT: *The purpose of this chapter is to provide the reader with a discussion of the "signatures" or causes of adolescent suicide. The chapter begins with a discussion of the developmental problems which occur during childhood and quite often, set the stage for an adolescent suicide. The second section of the chapter identifies situational signatures (e.g., peer relationships) common to adolescents. Events that trigger an adolescent suicide will be discussed in the third section. Also, behavioral indicators and case studies are presented.*

The reader should note that no single signature of adolescent suicide can predict an attempt or completion of the act of suicide. The important point is for the concerned helper, parent, or peer to become aware of the accumulation of warning signs that put adolescents at risk.

The newspaper headlines scream in oversize letters that four young people have taken their lives. In subsequent days, television cameras linger on the padlocked garage door where the teenagers committed suicide by inhaling poisonous fumes from an exhaust. On the evening news, reporters interview teachers and friends of the victims. Psychologists and psychiatrists are asked to offer their wisdom concerning the tragic event. Unfortunately, the knowledge of these mental health professionals has to be compressed into a 60 second interview between commercial spots. The present volume offers a more penetrating look at adolescents who commit suicide and considers the causes of suicide, as well as the detection and prevention of suicide among young people. Being able to prevent suicide is the end goal, but reaching that goal depends on several intermediate stesp. In this chapter, we will describe adolescents, who are at risk for suicide as well as those for whom risk is low. Being able to identify adolescents at risk is one of the first steps toward a successful prevention program.

Before proceeding to identify the "signatures" of suicide which might put adolescents at risk, an appropriate procedure is to indicate several caveats about the data to be reported. This volume focuses specifically on adolescent suicide, thus recognizing that adolescent suicide and adult suicide are motivated by different factors. Some of the differences are clear (see Maris, 1981). Adolescents who commit suicide are more likely than adults to be abusing alcohol or drugs. The contagion effect is more prominent among adolescent suicides. Adolescents are more likely to have experienced the loss of a loved one early in their lives and to have low levels of self-esteem (Maris, 1985). In addition, adolescents who commit are more likely to be female, to come from a dysfunctional family, to have attempted suicide previously, to be seeking revenge, and to have parents who are divorced (see Table 8.1 adapted from Maris, 1981). Of course, adolescent suicides are similar to adult suicides in that they both involved depression, isolation, chronic stress, and poor coping mechanisms.

TABLE 8.1
Differing Traits Between Adolescent and Adult Suicides

	Adolescent	Adult
1. Percent female	87%	45%
2. Low self-esteem	75%	53%
3. Dissatisfaction with life	73%	42%
4. Multiple suicide attempts	71%	32%
5. Death seen as revenge	50%	25%
6. Parents divorced	45%	13%
7. Suicide in family	38%	11%
8. Committed suicide while drinking	36%	19%

A second caveat to consider is the difficulty involved in studying suicide. Once a suicide occurs, the subject is no longer available to provide information. The suicide itself may color interviews with family, friends, and teachers. The grieving process and the guilt that families inevitably feel, mean that talking to interested researchers is not a high priority. One alternative to such subjective data gathered after the fact is to study individuals who attempt suicide. When they recover, they can provide data on their self-esteem, motivation, and so forth. Furthermore, the family is typically shocked into action by the suicide attempt and is in touch with mental health professionals. But the fact that the troubled individual is in therapy does not necessarily help research on suicide. The therapist's job is to work with the family and the adolescent to remedy the difficulty, not collect objective data for research purposes. Even if all therapists dutifully gathered objective information about the teenager, the family, and the peer group, the problem would remain because the sample of individuals who attempt suicide differs in significant ways from the sample of individuals who actually commit suicide (Wells, Deykin, & Klerman, 1985).

Another alternative is to follow a group of men and women on whom you already have a variety of information and wait until some of them commit suicide. This alternative is usually not viable because suicide is a comparatively rare event. If 100,000 adolescents were followed for a year, about 12 of them would commit suicide (Vital Statistics, 1986). For this reason only a handful of prospective studies of suicide are available (see Tomlinson-Keasey, Warren, & Elliott, 1986).

With the previous as background, one can easily see why information about suicide comes from the emergency rooms and psychiatric hospitals of our country. Here, investigators find a large sample of individuals who have tried to take their lives. In these crisis settings, researchers can collect detailed information on the "signatures" of suicide.

Shneidman (1971) was the first investigator to discuss "signatures" of suicide. The choice of the word signature was deliberate because suicide does not lend itself easily to a specific listing of causes. By talking about signatures, Shneidman conveyed the fact that many suicides have similar features, but he made it clear that predicting suicide for a single individual is very difficult. Just as risk factors for heart disease do not always predict a heart attack, signatures of suicide will not indicate an imminent suicide attempt. Any single risk factor has very weak predictive power. Nevertheless, a listing of signatures may well help psychologists, teachers, counselors, and parents identify the accumulation of warning signs and begin to take action that could remedy the problem.

In recent years, investigators have come to realize that adolescent suicide has a developmental component that is important. Prior to 1970, the personnel in suicide prevention centers thought of suicide as a temporary response to a personal crisis. Generally, suicidal adolescents were presumed to be people who were functioning reasonably well, but had encountered some severe stresses that precipitated a suicidal crisis. The severe stress of the crisis led to emotional arousal and the crisis was seen as limited to six weeks. In an important doctoral dissertation, Stein (1970) found that fewer than one-third of the subjects in the Los Angeles Suicide Prevention Center satisfied the criteria for crisis. His research was extended by Litman and Wold (1976) who pointed out that half of the individuals who ultimately committed suicide were chronically suicidal and had little acute situational stress. Psychological autopsies of eight of their subjects who committed suicide indicated that the suicides were independent of any crisis that existed at that time. Since these studies, accounts of adult suicides have been less focused on a specific crisis which triggers suicide and are more likely to examine lifestyles and life histories.

The situation with regard to adolescent suicide is perhaps more mixed. Many young people, at high-risk for suicide, demonstrate little or no precipitating stress prior to taking their lives. They do, however, have long developmental histories which indicate chronic emotional maladjustment (Peck, 1985). In the present chapter, we will begin by examining the developmental problems which occur during childhood. These problems often set the stage for adolescent suicide. During the teenage years, the problems of childhood intensify and the challenges which face an adolescent become evident. This period of escalating problems can be one in which situational signatures of suicide appear. Substance abuse, intensification of conflicts with parents, and isolation from peers are some examples. The second section of this chapter will identify situational signatures common to adolescents. A final triggering event usually precedes adolescent suicide. This trigger may be as innocuous as a television documentary on suicide or it may be as immediate as the dissolution of a meaningful relationship through suicide (Tishler, McKenry, & Morgan, 1981). The events that trigger suicide will be discussed in a third section. Finally, behavioral indicators and case studies will be presented.

THE MAGNITUDE OF THE PROBLEM

The problem of adolescent suicide, rather than abating under the flurry of recent media attention, has continued to grow. In 1984, the suicide rate for individuals 15 to 24 years of age had risen to 12.5 suicides per 100,000 (Vital Statistics, 1986). As recently as the 1950s, suicide among adolescents between fourteen and nineteen was a rarity. Only 3.5 adolescent males committed suicide for every 100,000. For females, it was even lower; only 1.8 girls per 100,000 committed suicide (Holinger, 1978). Now suicide among the young has become so commonplace that young people are habituating to it. Rather than evoking horror, the knowledge that a teenager in a local high school has committed suicide provokes only mild curiosity and transitory grief. The statistics verify a precipitous rise in adolescent suicides. Between 1950 and 1980, adolescent suicides increased 300% (Associated Press, 1986). In absolute numbers over 6,000 youths now murder themselves in the United States each year (Steele, 1985). Suicide is the second leading cause of death among adolescents 15 to 24 years of age in the United States (Vital Statistics, 1986). The Samaritans, a British suicide prevention group, reported that one-quarter of their phone calls come from teenagers (Young People, 1974). Further, the suicide rate of young men in the United States is among the highest in the world (Hendin, 1982). Suicide among this age group is now no different from the suicide rates of the adult population. In fact, while adolescent suicide has been skyrocketing, the suicides of adults over 40 have been decreasing (Pfeffer, 1986).

Another index of the magnitude of the problem is the number of suicide attempts among adolescents. Several studies indicate that 150 adolescents attempt suicide for every successful suicide (Jacobziner, 1965; McAnarney, 1975; Teicher, 1979). But these statistics are collected on adolescents who attempted suicide and came to the attention of the medical community. Smith and Crawford (1986) pointed out that 90% of the adolescents who attempt suicide will be missed if investigators rely only on medical contacts to determine who attempts suicide. The 350 midwestern adolescents in their study came from a typical high school, not from emergency rooms. Although the attempts these teenagers reported were not very serious, they still indicate that these youths felt a level of desperation that led to a suicide attempt. Extrapolating from their data, Smith and Crawford (1986) suggested that among a normal high school population, approximately 1 out of 10 students actually attempts suicide. In more troubled populations, the percentage of adolescents who attempt suicide is even higher. Robert Cairns (1987) reported that one-third of the troubled adolescents in his longitudinal sample have attempted suicide. Among delinquents, the incidence of suicide attempts is extraordinarily high. Alessi, McManus, Brickman, and Grapentine (1984) reported that 61% of their juvenile offenders have attempted suicide. No wonder then, why sociologists currently define adolescent suicide as the critical issue in suicide (Maris, 1985).

DEVELOPMENTAL HISTORY

The adolescent who attempts suicide does so within the setting of the family, and in response to stresses contained in the family (Kerfoot, 1980). Family conflict characterized by anger, ambivalence, rejection, and difficulties in communication are frequent among families in which adolescent suicide occurs. The majority of authors agree that most adolescent suicides are the culmination of years of maladaptive behavior growing out of a troubled childhood. Family dynamics have typically taken a negative turn when the child was very young and have persisted in that negative vein. For that reason, our discussion of the signatures of suicide, will explicate the developmental signatures that are often present when adolescents commit suicide.

Separations and Loss

Chronic and repeated separations between children and their parents figure prominently in adolescent suicides, whether the separation is through death, divorce, or desertion. The loss of a parent through death has been documented frequently as a correlate of suicide. In the study by Tomlinson-Keasey, et al. (1986), 50% of the gifted women who committed suicide had lost their fathers through death or desertion. Loss of a parent or other loved one probably stimulates suicidal activity in adolescents in different ways. Imitating the suicide is one way that adolescents have of responding to the loss. Suicidal behavior may also be the result of feelings of guilt and the desire for reunion (Petzel & Riddle, 1981).

Teicher (1979) investigated the lives of 50 suicidal adolescents. Seventy-two percent had lost one or both parents through divorce, desertion, or death. These teenagers had been raised by someone other than their parents twice as often as a control group of teenagers who were not suicidal. In addition, these adolescents had a model for suicide. Forty percent of the teenagers had a parent, relative, or close friend who had attempted suicide.

Divorce is a sign of family disruption and conflict and is often a signal that children are not getting the security and support that will help them negotiate adolescence successfully (McIntire & Angle, 1971; Teicher, 1979). As such, parental divorce has become a signature of adolescent suicide. Parental divorce, especially if it occurs during early childhood, often become the equivalent of parental loss, because many fathers are not able to maintain a relationship with their children. Parental loss, regardless of the cause, is a signature of childhood and adolescent depression and has negative implications for the development of a positive self-concept (Petzel & Riddle, 1981). Parents who divorce when their children are adolescents provoke a different chain of events in the emotional life of the teenagers (Petzel & Riddle, 1981). Feeling secure in the home environment and having adults who love and value you is essential when the challenges of adolescence feel overwhelming. In families that are divorced, adolescents have difficulty finding this security. As further evidence, Palas (1974) found that 85% of his sample of adolescent suicides occurred in divorced families. These results suggest that the presence of both parents throughout childhood helps protect the child from suicide (Petzel & Riddle, 1981).

Separation and loss, in the form of a relative who commits suicide, should also be considered a signature of suicide (Kallman & Anastasio, 1947). In some discussions, these suicides are viewed as evidence of genetic factors that might predispose a particular individual to suicide. To the extent that certain types of depression have a genetic component and hence could lead to suicide, this is a reasonable supposition (Black, 1986; Rainer, 1984). Among adolescents, however, we have to consider the equally likely explanation that the suicide of a relative serves as a model for the youth and has little to do with genetic predispositions. Such a contagion effect is discussed later in this chapter and occurs regardless of whether the suicide is a friend or a relative. Of course, the grief and guilt associated with the suicide of a relative can, by itself, propel an adolescent toward suicide. One adolescent male who attempted suicide indicated, in the weeks following his father's suicide, that he wanted to be with his father (Sturner, 1986).

In summary, the weight of the evidence indicates that family disruption, whether by death, separation, or divorce, is a common signature among adolescents who commit suicide (Hawton, 1986). The loss of or separation from one or both parents at crucial periods of development must be considered an important developmental signature of suicide (Kerfoot, 1980).

Family Interaction

Family conflict, characterized by anger, ambivalence, rejection, and difficulties in communication, is frequent among families in which adolescent suicide occurs. When compared to other adolescents, teenagers who commit suicide see their families as troubled and dysfunctional, far from the ideal family (Topol & Reznikoff, 1982). Suicidal adolescents report that they receive little affection from their families (Korella, 1972). Often, the family interaction is characterized by a punitive and restrictive atmosphere (Abraham, 1978). Suicidal adolescents have few fond memories of their families and the time spent together (McKenry, Tishler, & Kelly, 1982). Instead, conflict with the parents is seen as the most important extrinsic factor in adolescent suicide. Acute conflict is often the precipitating event for a suicide attempt (Mattsson, Seese, & Hawkins, 1969).

Rejection of the adolescent represents another dimension of family conflict that is common among suicidal adolescents (Petzel & Riddle, 1981). The suicidal adolescent feels expendable, and the suicide attempt complies with a parental wish, explicitly or tacitly conveyed, that the child is unwanted. These children are lonely, and feel emotionally detached, or dead, even though they are still alive (Herdin, 1982). The concept of the expendable child is even more pronounced when a stepmother or stepfather is present. One California boy expressed the feeling of being expendable, "I could drop dead and they (his parents) wouldn't know it until I started to stink" (Berkovitz, 1981).

This picture of an unpleasant family environment is confirmed by the parents of adolescents who attempt suicide (McKenry et al., 1982). The parents admit that their marriages are filled with conflict and as adults they derive little enjoyment from the time spent with their families. Interestingly, the fathers of these adolescents are depressed and seem to have low self-esteem while their mothers report being anxious. Each parent is likely to think that his/her spouse has poor parenting skills.

Families of adolescents who commit suicide are often centers of conflict. The conflict can lead to threats of a separation and culminate in a divorce. As indicated earlier, divorce is a common signature of suicide (Corder, Shorr, & Corder, 1974; Miller, Childes, & Barnes, 1982). In short, both suicidal adolescents and their parents describe a dysfunctional and unsatisfactory family environment. The adolescents feel hopeless about changing the pattern of their lives or their family situation (Topol & Reznikoff, 1982). They often express this hopelessness poignantly. "I felt helpless and like there was nothing I could do. And my life seemed at that time like a relatively cheap price for me to pay, because my life didn't seem to be worth that much at the time anyway" (Berkovitz, 1981).

Many of the characteristics of suicidal adolescents are found in their parents. The parents are often lacking in self-esteem (Tishler & McHenry, 1982). The parents of adolescents who attempt suicide are more likely to use alcohol and drugs than parents whose teenagers do not attempt suicide (Marks & Haller, 1977). Adolescents are often painfully aware of their parents' dependence on drugs. In two studies, 29% and 44% of the suicidal teenagers reported that at least one parent had a significant alcohol problem (McIntire, Angle, Wikoff, & Schlicht, 1977; Shaffer, 1974). An alcoholic parent is another factor contributing to the adolescent's feeling that they are already emotionally dead (Milcinski, 1974). Given the parents' history of drug and alcohol abuse, one is not surprised to find that 33% of the adolescents who used drugs in their suicide attempt went to their parents' supplies to obtain the drugs (McKenry, Tishler, & Kelley, 1983).

The picture of a dysfunctional family environment in which parents often model self-destructive coping patterns as a way of solving their problems is an important developmental signature when histories of adolescent suicides are recorded (McKenry et al., 1983). The result of such dysfunctional families resonates sadly through these adolescents' comments. "I want to escape the hell of living and find a better life in the next." "I am nothing but terrible" (Crumley, 1981).

Psychiatric Disorders

Emotional instability plays a major role in adolescent suicide (Black, 1986). In an increasing number of cases, the emotional instability appears to be chronic rather than situational. Cosand and his colleagues (1982) reported a history of emotional instability in over a third of the suicides among 15 to 19 year olds. The figure for 20 to 24 year olds is even higher. Approximately 50% of the suicides in this age group have some history of disturbance.

Although depression is by far the most common emotional disorder (Wells, Deykin, & Klerman, 1985), other forms of psychopathology can play a part in suicide ideation. McIntire et al. (1977) found that 10% of the adolescent attempters evidenced thought disorders. Furthermore, these teenagers were at high risk for suicide. Three of the four adolescents who had a thought disorder (75%) made a second suicide attempt within two years. The repeat rate for other high risk adolescents was 31%. None of the adolescents defined as low risk made a second attempt to kill themselves.

In addition to depression, Tishler and McKenry (1982) found that adolescents who attempted suicide had a wide variety of psychiatric disorders. Compared to other adolescents admitted to the emergency room, adolescents who attempted suicide had symptoms of anxiety, obsessive-compulsiveness, interpersonal sensitivity, hostility, and psychoticism. As a group, these troubled adolescents had less self-esteem. Based on these data, Tishler and McKenry argued that suicidal adolescents are in such a psychologically distressed state that they are unable to see alternatives to the stresses and problems in their environment. They overreact to their problems by turning anxious and hostile feelings inward. Psychiatric disorders, especially depression, must, therefore, be considered an important signature for adolescent suicide.

Prenatal Risk

In 1985, a surprising report concerning the correlation between prenatal events and adolescent suicide was published (Salk, Lipsitt, Sturner, Reilly, & Levat, 1985). Fifty-two adolescents who had committed suicide were matched with infants born just before and just after them. The birth records of the 52 suicides and the 104 controls were examined by researchers who were blind to the group membership of each infant. This blind, retrospective analysis indicated that the adolescents who committed suicide were far more likely to have experienced prenatal or perinatal distress. Respiratory distress occurred in 19.2% of the infants who later committed suicide. In the control groups, only 5.7% had similar problems. The mothers of infants who later committed suicide were also more likely to have chronic diseases during pregnancy and were less likely to seek prenatal care than the mothers of control infants. Taken together, 60% of the infants who committed suicide when they reached adolescence evidenced one or more of these risk factors. The same risk factors appeared among only 15% of the control infants.

How should these unexpected correlations be interpreted? One can argue that respiratory distress lays the foundation for some of the other signatures of suicide—impulsiveness, psychiatric disorder, and school failure. The exact neurological indicators involved in such a chain are not clear, but we know that the effects of moderate perinatal distress can still be seen at age eighteen (Werner & Smith, 1979). Chronic illness of the mother and the lack of prenatal care suggest another mechanism, a psychosocial one. Family stresses, financial pressures, and lack of knowledge about the need for prenatal care may reflect socioeconomic factors which will continue to operate as the child matures (Goldman, 1985). Perhaps these intervening variables, not the lack of prenatal care, govern the ultimate suicide (Goldenring, 1985).

Birth Order

The oldest child in the family is disproportionately represented among adolescents who commit suicide (Shaffer, 1974). The eldest male child is statistically more at risk than his younger brothers. Perhaps this is because the eldest child feels achievement pressure that seems to abate by the time the younger siblings reach adolescence. Perhaps it is because the eldest child must negotiate curfews, dress standards, and behavioral standards that differ greatly from the standards when his/her parents were young. The conflict over these matters might set the stage for suicide. As with all of the signatures of suicide, the important point to remember is what this finding means. The eldest child is more frequently represented than later children among adolescent suicides. By itself, this single fact is likely to predict little.

Intellectual Ability

Only a handful of investigators have looked at the intelligence of adolescents who committed suicide (Dudley, Mason, & Rhoton, 1973; Maxmen & Tucker, 1973). Surprisingly, Shaffer (1974) indicated that adolescents who committed suicide had above average IQs. Of the 28 children, aged 10 to 14 who committed suicide, 14 or 50% had IQs above 115. One explanation for this finding is that intelligent adolescents might well choose a method of suicide that was foolproof; hence they would succeed more often than other adolescents. This explanation is given some credence by Shaffer who reports that boys of superior intelligence often devised ingenious methods to commit suicide. One boy electrocuted himself with an elaborate apparatus he had built. Another devised an ingenious system of weights for drowning himself.

Signatures of suicide that can be extracted from the child's developmental history are plentiful. Beginning with the perinatal period, we see that respiratory distress of the infant may lead to neurological damage that forms the foundation for later psychiatric disorder. Such perinatal distress also may be an indicator of a dysfunctional family environment. During the childhood years, the loss of a parent or separation from either parent, whether due to death or divorce becomes an important signature of suicide. The childhood and adolescent years may see the child developing in a dysfunctional family, enveloped in conflict, rejected, or isolated. Such a family environment promotes the poor self-esteem and isolation that are so characteristic of suicidal adolescents. A psychiatric disorder, especially depression that is noticed in childhood or early adolescence, is another important developmental signature of suicide. These signatures indicate that the life path which ends with suicide is spotted with indicators well before the final milestone.

SITUATIONAL SIGNATURES

The signatures previously discussed have a continuing impact on the child. The loss of a parent, a conflict-ridden family, and depression continue to wield their power on a day-to-day basis. These developmental signatures tend to create a child who is insecure, and feels anxious for reasons that are difficult to pinpoint. The child's feelings of rejection and isolation are also very real. These early life events can set the stage for a troubled adolescence. As the child reaches puberty, he/she must begin to form a separate identity and armed with that fragile identity, make friends and create a circle of successes outside the home. When several signatures of suicide are present in the child's early years, the challenges of adolescence become steep peaks that cannot be scaled. These situational signatures can take the teenager one step closer to suicide.

Peers

Adolescents are very sensitive to feelings of rejection from the opposite sex. The loss of a girlfriend or boyfriend is frequently a precipitating situational signature. Crumley (1981) discovered that these severed relationships are often clinging attachments which represent an attempt on the part of the adolescent to make up for his/her feelings of emptiness.

Loneliness is another feeling that can precipitate suicide among adolescents. Teenagers who are lonely have more frequent and serious problems with peers, they are interpersonally sensitive and are less likely to have a close confidant (McKenry et al., 1982). "He was a loner" is often the first description that teachers and counselors offer concerning a teenager who has committed suicide. This impression is upheld in the majority of the studies of suicide (Peck, 1981). Loners are typically male and usually white (Peck, 1985). Their lack of friends emerges first in the early teens, and if it continues, can be translated into suicidal behaviors later in the adolescent years. Jan-Tausch (1965) looked at the friendships formed by 41 adolescents who committed suicide. He found that these teenagers had no close friends and no trusting or supporting relationships. They spent a great deal of time alone, had poor interpersonal relationships both with peers and adults, and reported feeling lonely and isolated much of the time.

Friendships were superficial and confidants were nonexistent. Female adolescents who attempt suicide report similar difficulties. Topol and Reznikoff (1982) indicated that suicidal females were the ones least likely to have a close confidant.

Peers are also an important factor in the contagious effect that is prominent among adolescent suicides. Suicidal adolescents are vulnerable to suggestion, probably because their family environment is not satisfying and their self-esteem is low. For this reason, a suicide in the local high school or among friends or relatives can serve as an impetus for adolescents to take their own lives.

Evaluating the effect of poor peer relationships requires that we step back and consider the developmental signatures of childhood in relation to the peer relationships of adolescence. Suppose a child lives in a tranquil home, with two parents who are interested and supportive. If he/she becomes a teenager without friends, he/she can find satisfaction in a host of solitary pursuits—stamp collecting, reading, writing, playing on the computer, or exploring nature. The satisfactory relationship with his/her parents will still allow for developing the necessary self-confidence and avoiding feeling isolated, anxious, and lonely. Similarly, a dysfunctional family can be partially offset by wholesome peer relationships. Freud and Dann (1951) were the first to notice that peers could substitute for parents. These investigators charted the development of children who lost their parents in the Holocaust. The peer relationships these children developed buffered the horror of their early lives and allowed them to become productive adults (Hartup, 1983). Peer relationships that are positive can often protect the adolescent who has been accumulating signatures of suicide. But rejection and isolation from peers can serve to trigger suicide among adolescents who have other signatures leading them toward suicide.

Cultural Risk Factors

Adolescent suicides are most frequent among Native Americans with 3.7 Native Americans committing suicide for every white adolescent (Wells, Deykin, & Klerman, 1985). Close examination of suicide among Native Americans indicates, however, that generalization across tribes is dangerous. The rate of suicide has remained low on reservations where the tribes practice traditional ways of living and where employment and educational opportunities within the tribal community enable youths to remain at home. On other reservations, the causes for suicide have been well documented. Seventy percent of the Native American adolescents who committed suicide had changed homes and caretakers several times before they were 15. Only 15% of the controls experienced this disruption in parenting. Fully one-half of the adolescents who committed suicide had experienced two or more losses by divorce or desertion. In addition, 40% of the parents of the adolescents who committed suicide had a history of frequent arrests. The young men on the reservation were following in the footsteps of these models; 80% of them had been arrested in the year preceding their suicide. These rather lifeless statistics paint a picture of the erosion of tribal and family tradition. With that erosion comes the loss of effective adult role models, an increase in the number of parents who are alcoholics, and a decrease in the role of the family. Unemployment and academic failure add to the low self-esteem that Native American adolescents feel who have grown up without tribal support or parental support. In essence, the child is thrown from home to home, has little or no chance to develop self-esteem, has minimal support, and then, as an adolescent is thrown into a world where unemployment and academic failure exaggerate feelings of despondency and hopelessness (Berlin, 1985).

A similar phenomenon was reported recently among Micronesian adolescents, where the suicide rate for males ages 15 and 19 is 66 per 100,000 and the suicide rate for males 20 to 24 is 101 per 100,000 (Rubinstein, 1983). Among adolescents on the Truk Islands, the suicide rate is even higher, 243 per 100,000 for 15 to 19 year olds and 255 per 100,000 for 20 to 24 year olds. Remember the comparison figure in the United States is 12.5 per 100,000 for the two age groups combined (Vital Statistics, 1986). Traditionally, adolescent socialization in Micronesia involved activities organized around communal linage houses. Each day, the men of the village would gather to make decisions and socialize. The adolescents in the village looked to these communal activities as a focus of their social identity. Within this group, the adolescents were valued for their ability to fish, sail, build houses, and garden. Feelings of competence and self-worth were, therefore, very high among the young men in the village. Since the second world war, the village level of organization has disintegrated, leaving male adolescents to be socialized by the family. At the same time, cultural imports for the West began to put Micronesian adolescents in conflict with the authority of the family. The result was a sense of anomie among the adolescents which fueled the epidemic of suicides (Rubinstein, 1983).

Black adolescents, as a group, have a lower suicide rate than any other racial group (Berman, 1986). White adolescents are three times as likely to commit suicide as Black adolescents (Wells, Deykin, & Klerman, 1985). The suicide rate for Black adolescents has remained remarkably stable since 1973 (Weed, 1985). In contrast, the suicide rate for white adolescents has continued to climb.

Japan's suicide rate always has been seen as high compared to Western cultures. The pressure among the youth of Japan is most noticeable among university students who have a suicide rate of 48.5 per 100,000 (Ishii, 1981). The pressures on university students are clearly unusual, because the suicide rate for all Japanese youth in their twenties is about 20 per 100,000. This compares to 12.5 in the 20 to 24 year olds in the United States. The unique stress that Japanese youth face is called *shiken jigoku* or Examination Hell. But blaming the high suicide rate on a single examination is inappropriate. Close examination indicates that, like American adolescents, Japanese adolescents who report suicidal fantasies have a number of difficulties with their families (Iga, 1981). The *skiken jigoku* is a situational signature that impels young men and women who are already in distress to chose suicide as an honorable way out of their difficulties (Iga, 1986).

The situational signatures described in this section revolve around the adolescent forming an identity. Whether in a tribal setting, a family setting, or any of several contemporary, industrialized countries, adolescents with a troubled childhood need to form friendships and belong to a culture in which they feel "at home." If they are successful in these settings, they can forge an identity despite their childhood difficulties. If these situational signatures are negative, and no supportive peers and no cultural "home" exist, the signatures for suicide continue to accumulate. In such individuals, a variety of seemingly small and innocuous events can trigger a suicide.

TRIGGERING FACTORS

A superficial examination of the literature might convince the reader that adolescent suicides are impulsive, misguided acts which were not really intended to end a life. But a thorough reading suggests that even though an impulse, haphazard event ends an adolescent's life, the decisions that led to the act were not capricious. An indication of the intent of adolescents is their repeated suicide attempts. Shaffer (1974) reported that 46% of the young suicides he studied had previously discussed, threatened, or attempted suicide. Cosand et al. (1982) reported a similar figure, but added that previous attempts were more common among females than males, perhaps because the methods females chose were more likely to fail. Adolescents who attempt suicide remain at risk in adulthood and 10% of those who attempt suicide will eventually die by suicide (Dorpat & Ripley, 1967). Those who don't die by suicide often continue to exhibit self-destructive behaviors, such as drug use and drug overdoses (Mehr, Zeltzer, & Robinson, 1982).

The adolescent years are generally a time when impulsive behavior is allowed to flourish. Heading to the beach at the last minute or deciding, on an impulse, to visit a friend who is at college 250 miles away, are accepted impulsive behaviors. Some investigators see suicide as similarly impulsive. Corder et al. (1974) found adolescents who attempted suicide to be more impulsive than a group of controls and to have a higher activity level than the controls. Similarly, suicide attempts among delinquent adolescents tended to be impulsive, rather than the result of thoughtful rumination (Miller, Chiles, & Barnes, 1982).

The other side of the coin, the side which says that adolescent suicide is a thoughtful decision, points to the planning that often accompanies a suicide, and the years of difficulty that preceded it. Going to the closet, grabbing a handgun in a moment of anger, and ending one's life in the next moment certainly occurs. But so does the suicide that is preceded by weeks of subtle goodbyes, in which the adolescent disposes of personal possessions, visits relatives, and then carries out a complex plan to end his/her life. In this section, the specific events which trigger suicide are discussed. Some of them seem mindless. Others continue a course toward suicide that has already been charted.

Impulsivity and Contagion

The contagion effect among adolescent suicides is very real. In just the last few years, we have witnessed an epidemic of suicides at an American Indian Reservation, several copy cat suicides when a particularly poignant suicide attracts the attention of the media, and suicide pacts among a group of teenage friends. All of these suggest that having a model who commits suicide is an important factor in providing adolescents to commit suicide (Sturner, 1986). Berman and Yufit (1983) argued that a model for suicide, in effect, gives the adolescent permission to act similarly. An example from Chappaqua, New York illustrates the contagion effect. In June of 1978, a 15 year old boy who was perceived as a social isolate hung himself. In September, an eleventh grade boy from the same community hung himself. In the next seven weeks, five more students, all from the same high school attempted suicide. During the same period one year earlier, none of the 1300 students at Chappaqua High had attempted or committed suicide (Robbins & Conroy, 1983). When investigators search for a link between suicides among teenagers, they often find one. In this case, four of the adolescents who attempted suicide had visited their friend while he was hospitalized after attempting suicide. One of these students later told the psychiatrist that she was caught up in the suicide gestures of her friends.

Suicides of friends and relatives have a profound impact on teenagers. Sturner (1986) reported that previous suicides by siblings, parents, friends, and schoolmates figured prominently among the 96 adolescent suicides he studied. He argued that the evidence of contagion is compelling enough to warrant therapeutic intervention by trained counselors immediately following a suicide in a relative or loved one. Similarly, he argued that counselors should descend on a high school if one of the students commits suicide. Counseling with close friends and classmates might well forestall further suicides.

Having a close friend or relative who commits suicide has an immediate impact on many adolescents. The effect of television presentations is not nearly as powerful. Yet television stories about suicide clearly trigger a significant rise in teenage suicides (Gould & Shaffer, 1986). Phillips and Carstensen (1986) identified 38 nationally televised news or feature stories about suicide and charted the fluctuation of the adolescent suicide rate before and after these stories were aired. During the week following the telecast, adolescent suicides increased by approximately seven percent. This increase was greatest among female adolescents. The fact that adult suicides fluctuated in only a minor way after the broadcasts indicates that adolescents are more suggestible than adults. Interestingly general information stories seemed to have a greater contagion effect than stories about specific individuals who committed suicide. Similar contagion effects were seen in New York City after three made-for-television movies dealing with suicide were broadcast (Gould & Shaffer, 1986). Six adolescents committed suicide in the two weeks before these movies. In the two weeks following these broadcasts, 26 adolescents committed suicide. The evidence from these two studies suggests that fictional presentations of suicide may have a lethal effect.

The contagion effect is difficult to pin down. How does media attention to a suicide trigger another suicide? Does it give tacit permission to an adolescent who has been contemplating suicide for years? Does it implant the idea for the first time? Perhaps contagion is not the only explanation for this increase. Maybe coroners are more likely to indicate that a death was due to suicide after such broadcasts. Perhaps parents are less likely to try to hide the cause of death. These and other alternative explanations are difficult to refute absolutely. Some critics have argued that media attention only facilitates suicide among those who would have committed suicide in the near future. If this were the case, suicides after a broadcast would initially increase and then decrease to a level lower than normal. No such decrease has been found. Here, then, is an example of a triggering effect which might be altered, and if so altered, might reduce the number of suicides.

If television broadcasts have a facilitative effect on suicide, does this effect generalize to other media, such as the music that teenagers prefer? Songs have received notoriety as suicide triggers, especially since a father of a boy who committed suicide, blamed the death of his son on the song "Suicide Solution" by Ozzy Osbourne. "Gloomy Sunday" by Javor and Seress has been banned from certain college campuses because well meaning administrators thought it might contribute to suicidal impulses (Peck, 1985). Despite these events, the evidence that such transient information might actually foster a suicidal impulse is rather weak.

Alcohol and Drug Abuse

The suicide rate for alcoholics is 270 per 100,000 and in the United States and between 7,000 and 13,000 alcoholic suicides occur each year (Roy & Linnoila, 1986). Depression is correlated with alcoholism. Whether the depression comes first, and leads to the alcoholism, or the reverse, is not clear. Certainly, depression is common among the relatives of alcoholics (Goodwin, 1982). But alcohol, by itself, can produce depressive symptoms (Vaillant, 1983).

Roy and Linnoila (1986) presented compelling documentation for the role that alcohol plays in suicide. They reported 21 follow-up studies of alcoholics, with data gathered from 10 countries. In all, they reported on a total of 27,956 alcoholics whose lives, and deaths, have been scrutinized. Seventeen percent of these individuals committed suicide. The five most carefully controlled studies, in which coroners' offices assigned psychiatric diagnoses to the suicide victims, indicate that alcoholism was the predisposing factor in 15% to 26.9% of the deaths. The average age of the alcoholics in these studies was, however, 46. What role does alcohol play in the lives of adolescents?

Drug and alcohol use are prevalent among suicidal adolescents (Garfinkel, Froese, & Hood, 1982). A look at 92 teenagers who attempted suicide used significantly more depressants, stimulants, marijuana, and alcohol (McKenry et al., 1983). Twenty of the 46 adolescents who attempted suicide had serious drug problems. Cocaine use is surfacing as a major factor in adolescent suicide. Daniel Lowenstein, a neurologist at UC—San Francisco reported on 133 cocaine users who came to San Francisco General Hospital with neurological complaints. Four of these patients had jumped from buildings and another nine developed a desire to commit suicide after using cocaine (Ritter, 1987). The effect, he argued, was not limited to chronic abusers. Among the first-time users, one became suicidal. Others became depressed and showed signs of personality change.

Denise Kandel (Kandel & Ravies, 1987) has done a systematic exploration of drug use among 1,158 adolescents. Her scale divided drug users into four groups. At one end were adolescents who used no drugs. Next were adolescents who only used alcohol and cigarettes. In a third group were teenagers who used marijuana. A fourth group used cocaine. Suicide attempts were positively related to the increased potency of the drugs used. Fifty-four percent of the cocaine users had attempted suicide. The correlation between drug use and suicide attempts was stronger for females than males. Kandel suggested that these young women are attempting to tranquilize themselves and that drug use is really self-medication designed to relieve tension. The females using the most potent drugs were functioning at lower levels on all dimensions—family interaction, peer relationships, and school success. These teenagers were at the outskirts of the school society and their family life was minimal. They were also likely to have eating disorders. If, in addition to the above problems, the girls had a history of trouble with the law, the likelihood of a suicide attempt was high.

Pregnancy

Women who are pregnant often feel depressed and take their own lives. Suicides among pregnant women are more likely during the first trimester and occur most often among unmarried women. In the more restrictive sexual atmosphere of previous decades, investigators found that 13% of pregnant females under seventeen years of age attempted or threatened suicide (Gabrielson, Klerman, Currie, Tyler, & Jekel, 1970). More recent data suggest that pregnancy among unmarried women is not the disaster that it used to be; in fact, some investigators feel that pregnancy confers some protection against suicide (Kleinert, 1979). Others have argued that adolescent females have sought pregnancies in the hope of alleviating their dissatisfactions with life. When these expectations are not fulfilled, suicides became more frequent (Toolan, 1980).

Failure

Occasionally, a suicidal crisis is triggered by a specific failure. Usually these failures involve a loss of identity (Rubinstein, 1986). Lucy an 18 year old high school senior had studied ballet for 9 of her 18 years. She had hoped to be awarded a scholarship to a major ballet academy after graduating from high school. Not only did she not receive the scholarship, she was not accepted at the prestigious academy. Her depression was immediate and suicidal fantasies filled her days. She lost interest in ballet, had a dramatic change in her self-image, and was blasé about all areas of her life. She was in great emotional pain. Crisis intervention helped her see that a variety of options existed. The suicidal crisis passed in about a month and Lucy began exploring ways she could continue to grow (Peck, 1985). Some suicidal crises are not as easily averted. A very successful male high school student in Rhode Island had lost an election for class president. His despondency over this small failure was a factor in his suicide three days later (Sturner, 1986). Perceived failure, then, is often the trigger for a suicidal crisis (Rubinstein, 1986).

Achievement Pressure

Whether or not suicidal adolescents are under greater pressure from their parents to achieve remains an unanswered question. The contradictions in the data probably reflect the differences in the way parents and teenagers perceive the situation. For example, McKenry et al. (1982) asked parents to fill out a questionnaire examining pressure to do well in school. This assessment revealed that the parents of suicidal teenagers did not differ in their expectations from the parents of teenagers who had not attempted suicide. However, when these investigators asked the adolescents, those who had attempted suicide perceived much greater parental pressure than those who had not.

Life's small affronts often assume mammoth proportions when viewed through the eyes of adolescents. Yet most adolescents negotiate these challenges successfully. In fact, adolescence is seen, generally, as a period of increasing self-esteem and competence (Petersen, 1987). Among suicidal adolescents, the reverse is true. Martin Seligman (1987) argued that adolescents get on a developmental track in early adolescence. Instead of following a positive track, suicidal adolescents seem consigned to a negative one. The trials of their childhood years have handicapped them so they deal less effectively with the intensification of life that is part of adolescence.

BEHAVIORAL INDICATORS

The signatures of suicide mentioned above are typically seen as predisposing factors that occur or not in the history of the adolescent. Behavioral indicators are much more likely to warn of immediate danger. In this section of the chapter, the literature concerning atypical behaviors that flash an immediate warning light for parents, counselors, psychologists, and friends will be examined.

Academic Failure

To adolescents contemplating suicide, school becomes superfluous. Many teenagers who commit suicide only attend school sporadically prior to their suicide (Shaffer, 1974). Other teenagers drop out altogether. A precipitous drop in school grades is a similar manifestation of the lack of interest which may presage suicide (Kandel & Ravies, 1987).

Atypical Eating or Sleeping Patterns

Sleep disturbances are one of the most common signs of adolescent difficulties (Bettes & Walker, 1986). Tishler, McKenry, and Morgan (1981) found that 81% of their sample of 108 adolescents had trouble sleeping prior to their suicide attempt. Eating patterns were also altered before the suicide. Almost two-thirds of the adolescents interviewed reported losing weight before their suicide attempt, most of them indicating that they had no taste for food.

Comments About Sense of Worthlessness

The myth that people who talk about suicide are the ones who sill do nothing about it has died slowly. This is particularly true with adolescents. Adults and teachers just cannot believe that an adolescent would take his/her life. Even males brandishing guns have been ignored or dismissed as "just being macho." Such actions should always be taken seriously. Even comments which indicate utter hopelessness should always elicit a response from parents, teachers, and counselors.

Dispersing Personal Possessions

One of the clearest signs of suicidal crisis is the dispersing of personal possessions. One high school student gave a friend his skis, his Walkman, and his tape collection. At the same time, he advised his girlfriend not to buy a dress for the prom. This clear cutting of lines to the future means that some action is imminent.

Obtaining Weapons or Barbituates

If weapons or drugs are readily available, the task of committing suicide is relatively easy. Typically, teenagers do not know enough about drugs to be sure of their actions. Hence, in the days or weeks immediately preceding the suicide attempt, subtle questions may be posed regarding the amount of a drug that one might safely take and what might be a lethal dose. These sorts of questions should serve as a warning to anyone working with adolescents. Similar questions about the type of ammunition used in a gun or where ammunition is kept should also raise an alarm for parents.

Use of Drugs or Alcohol

An increase in the use of drugs or alcohol may be the first indication that adolescents are trying to ease the difficulties they perceive in their lives. Parents who are alert to this sign can often arrange for their adolescent to talk to a counselor before a crisis is reached.

CASE STUDIES

Having outlined a variety of signatures for adolescent suicide, some case histories of adolescent suicide are present so that we might examine them to see whether one can locate signatures of suicide. Furthermore, look at the number of signatures present in each case and try to weigh the impact of those against any buffers that might exist in the child's environment.

> Chris, a 17 year old male hanged himself with his mother's stocking. He was not the first born, he had three older sisters. When Chris was two years old, his father left the home. The sisters soon left to start their own lives, leaving Chris with an overprotective mother who had a strict religious background.
>
> Chris' school years did not go well, he had variety of social problems and a slight speech impediment which contributed to his low self-esteem. He was a loner through junior high. By senior high he needed approval and support but found none. The day he killed himself seemed uneventful. (Litman & Diller, 1985)

Chris' suicide was not triggered by a particular event. Instead we see the signatures, present for many years, of father loss, peer isolation aggravated by a slight speech impediment, and estrangement from the only parent at home. All of these are powerful signatures of suicide. In Chris' life, we see no buffers to counteract the events that seemed to push him toward suicide.

Sally, a 15 year old girl was referred to a therapist after a suicide attempt. She began the therapy session by reading a 10 page handwritten letter in which she described her suicidal feelings, her sexual acting-out, her feeling that her parents hated her, and her excessive use of alcohol. She thought she was drinking to dull her feelings. Her mother admitted that she had never been close to Sally. Even during Sally's early years, they had battled over every conceivable issue—eating, toilet-training, discipline, and so forth. (Toolan, 1980)

In Sally's case, long-term conflict with her parents, alcohol abuse, and loneliness, despite her sexual adventures, were important signatures of suicide.

Recent studies, recognizing the importance of several signatures in one life, have compared the number of signatures in the lives of differing individuals. Detailed case histories obtained from friends and relatives who were interviewed after a teenager committed suicide indicated that these adolescents had an average of 8.3 signatures of suicide. A comparison group of peers had an average of 4.7 signatures of suicide (Litman & Diller, 1985). Tomlinson-Keasey et al. (1986) evaluated the signatures of suicide in the lives of women who committed suicide and a comparison group of women who did not. The women who committed suicide had an average of 3.87 signatures for suicide. The control women averaged 1.30 signatures of suicide. The point is not the presence or absence of any particular signature that predicts suicide, but the accumulation of the sorts of negative events that have earned the title "signature." The force of the signatures is especially powerful in lives with few positive events. Suicide results from a complex interplay of these signatures that have their most pernicious effect when they accumulate and interact over time, resulting in chronic despair, the loss of self-confidence, and a feeling of hopelessness.

CONCLUSION

Adolescence is a time of challenge, change, and adjustment. Because of the need to develop a unique identity, adolescence carries with it a considerable amount of anxiety. When the turbulence of adolescence is combined with a conflict ridden and dysfunctional home environment, adolescents lack the support and self-confidence to cope with the changes expected of them. Adolescence should be a time of exploring, of practicing newly found skills, of learning how to interact with friends of both sexes, and of finding the niches that spell success for each individual. When adolescence proceeds in a positive way, these milestones are managed readily, typically with a few major difficulties. For children who enter adolescence with a damaged sense of their own self-worth and who operate on the edges of the family, the school, and peer groups, the picture is much bleaker. Seemingly minor problems can precipitate a suicidal episode.

Interventions during adolescence must have as their goal the formation of a secure identity and sense of competence. During the early adolescent years, such interventions might ward off the isolation and lack of identity which are two signatures characteristic of suicidal adolescents. The actual triggers of suicidal crises sometimes seem paltry—a television show, a fight with a boyfriend/girlfriend. Yet, timely counseling might be appropriate at this stage. Through all of these stages, parents, teachers, and mental health professionals must be aware that depression, drug use, and suicide are increasing and they are interlocked problems that adolescents face. Recognizing the signatures of suicide, from childhood on, and taking action to keep the child on a positive developmental track could well save lives.

REFERENCES

Abraham, Y. (1978). Patterns of communication in families of suicidal adolescents. *Dissertation Abstracts International, 38,* 4669A

Alessi, N.E., McManus, M., Brickman, A., & Grapentine, L. (1984). Suicidal behavior among serious juvenile offenders. *American Journal of Psychiatry, 141,* 286-7.

Associated Press. (1986). Clues offered to spot teens planning suicide. *The Press Enterprise,* September 13, Section A—3.

Berkovitz, I.H. (1981). Feeling of powerlessness and the role of violent actions in adolescents. *Adolescent Psychiatry, 9,* 477-92.

Berlin, I.N. (1985). Prevention of adolescent suicide among some Native American tribes. *Adolescent Psychiatry, 12,* 77-93.

Berman, A.L., & Yufit, R. (1983). Suicide: Is it contagious? *Newsweek,* p. 3.

Berman, A.L. (1986). Helping suicidal adoelscents: Needs and responses. In C.A. Corr & J.N. McNeil (Eds.), *Adolescents and Death*, (pp. 151-64). New York: Springer.

Bettes, B.A., & Walker, E. (1986). Symptoms associated with suicidal behavior in childhood and adolescence. *Journal of Abnormal Child Psychology, 14*, 591-604.

Black, D. (1986). Adolescent suicide: Preventive considerations. *British Medical Journal, 292*, 1620-1.

Cairns, R.B. (1987). Incidence of suicide in delinquent adolescents. Personal communication.

Corder, B., Shorr, W., & Corder, R. (1974). A study of social and psychological characteristics of adolescent suicide attempters in an urban disadvantated area. *Adolescence, 9*, 1-6.

Cosand, B.J., Bourque, L.B., & Kraus, J.F. (1982). Suicide among adolescents in Sacramento County, California, 1950-1979. *Adolescence, 17*, 917-930.

Crumley, F.E. (1981). Adolescent suicide attempts and borderline personality disorder: Clinical features. *Southern Medical Journal, 74*, 546-9.

Dorpat, T., & Ripley, H. (1967). The relationship between attempted suicide and committed suicide. *Comprehensive Psychiatry, 2*, 74-9.

Dudley, H.K., Mason, M., & Rhoton, G. (1973). Relationship of beta IQ scores to young state hospital patients. *Journal of Clinical Psychology, 29*, 197-203.

Freud, A., & Dann, S. (1951). An experiment in group up-bringing. In R.S. Eisler, A. Freud, H. Hartmann, & E. Kris (Eds.), *The Psychoanalytic Study of the Child* (Vol. 6). New York: International Universities Press.

Gabrielson, I., Klerman, L., Currie, J., Tyler, N., & Jekel, J. (1970). Suicide attempts in a population pregnant as teenagers. *American Journal of Public Health, 60*, 2289-2301.

Garfinkel, B.D., Froese, A., & Hood, J. (1982). Suicide attempts in children and adolescents. *American Journal of Psychiatry, 85*, 324-9.

Goldenring, J. (1985, April 27). Perinatal events and adolescent suicide. *Lancet*, 986.

Goldman, D.W. (1985, April 27). Perinatal events and adolescent suicide. *Lancet*, 985-6.

Goodwin, D. (1982). Alcoholism and suicide: Associated factors. In E.M. Pattison & E. Kaufman (Eds.), *Encyclopedic Handbook of Alcoholism*. New York: Gardner Press.

Gould, M.S., & Shaffer, D. (1986). The impact of suicide in television movies. *The New England Journal of Medicine, 315*, 690-3.

Hartup, W.W. (1983). Peer relations. In E.M. Hetherington (Ed.), *Handbook of child psychology*, (Vol. 4). New York: John Wiley & Sons.

Hawton, K . (1986). Contributory factors in attempted suicide. In K. Hawton (Ed.), *Suicide and Attempted Suicide Among Children and Adolescents, (pp. 69-86). Beverly Hills: Sage Publications.*

Hendin, H. (1982). Suicide in America. New York: Norton.

Holinger, P.C. (1978). Adolescent suicide: An epidemiological study of recent trends. *American Journal of Psychiatry, 135,* 754-6.

Iga, M. (1986). *The Thorn in the Chrysanthemum.* Los Angeles: University of California Press.

Iga, M. (1981). Suicide of Japanese Youth. *Suicide and Life-Threatening Behavior, 11,* 17-30.

Ishii, K. (1981). Adolescent self-destructive behaivor and crisis intervention in Japan. *Suicide and Life-Threatening Behavior, 11,* 51-61.

Jacobziner, H. (1965). Attempted suicides in adolescence. *Journal of the American Medical Association, 191,* 101-5.

Jan-Tausch, J. (1964). *Studies of Children, 1960-1963, New Jersey Public School Studies.* Trenton, NJ: New Jersey Department of Education.

Kallman, F.J., & Anastasio, M.M. (1947). Twin studies on the psychopathology of suicide. *Journal of Nervous and Mental Disease, 105,* 40-55.

Kandel, D.B., & Raveis, V. (1987, April). Depression, suicidal ideation, and substance use in adolescence and young adulthood. Paper presented at Society for Research in Child Development. Baltimore, MD.

Kerfoot, M. (1980). The family context of adolescent suicidal behavior. *Journal of Adolescence, 3,* 335-46.

Kleinert, G.J. (1979, May). Suicide in pregnancy. Paper presented at annual meeting of American Psychiatric Association. Chicago, IL.

Korella, K. (1972). Teenage suicide gestures. A study of suicidal behavior among high school students. *Dissertation Abstracts International, 32,* 5039A.

Litman, R.E., & Wold, C.I. (1976). Beyond crisis intervention. In E. Shneidman (Ed.), *Suicide: Contemporary developments.* New York: Grune & Stratton.

Litman, R.E., & Diller, J. (1985). Case studies in youth suicide. In M.L. Peck, N.L. Farberow, & R.E. Litman (Eds.), *Youth Suicide,* (pp. 48-70). New York: Springer Publishing Company.

Maris, R. (1985). The adolescent suicide problem. *Suicide and Life-Threatening Behavior, 15,* 91-108.

Maris, R. (1981). *Pathways to suicide.* Baltimore, MD: Johns Hopkins University Press.

Marks, P.A., & Haller, D.L. (1977). Now I lay me down for keeps: A study of adolescent suicide attempts. *Journal of Clinical Psychology, 33,* 390-400.

Mattsson, A., Seese, L.R., & Hawkins, J.W. (1969). Suicidal behavior as a child psychiatric emergency. *Archives of General Psychiatry, 20,* 100-109.

Maxmen, J.S., & Tucker, G.J. (1973). No exit: The persistently suicidal patient. *Comprehensive Psychiatry, 14,* 71-9.

McAnarney, E.R. (1975). Suicidal behavior of children and youth. *Pediatric Clinics of North American, 22,* 595-614.

McIntire, M.S., & Angle, C.R. (1971). "Suicide" as seen in poison control centers. *Pediatrics, 48,* 914-22.

McIntire, M.S., Angle, C.R., Wikoff, R.L., & Schlicht, M .L. (1977). Recurrent adolescent suicidal behavior. *Pediatrics, 60,* 605-8.

McKenry, P.C., Tishler, C.L., & Kelley, C. (1982). Adolescent suicide: A comparison of attempters and nonattempters in an emergency room population. *Clinical Pediatrics, 21,* 266-70.

McKenry, P.C., Tishler, C.L., & Kelley, C. (1983). The role of drugs in adolescent suicide attempts. *Suicide and Life-Threatening Behavior, 13,* 167-75.

Mehr, M., Zeltzer, L.K., & Robinson, R. (1982). Continued self-destructive behaviors in adolescent suicide attempters, Part II. *Journal of Adolescent Health Care, 2,* 183-7.

Milcinski, L. (1974). Parents of the juvenile who committed suicide in Slovenia. In N. Speyer, R.F.W. Diekstra, & K. Van de Loo (Eds.), *Proceedings of the 7th International Congress on Suicide Prevention.* Amsterdam: Swet & Zeitlinger.

Miller, M.L., Chiles, J.A., & Barnes, V.E. (1982). Suicide attempters within a delinquent population. *Journal of consulting and Clinical Psychology, 50,* 491-8.

Palas, H. (1974). Suicide in young people. In N. Speyer, R.F.W. Kiekstra, & K. Van De Loo (Eds.), *Proceedings of the 7th International Congress on Suicide Prevention.* Amsterdam: Swet & Zeitlinger.

Peck, M.L. (1985). Crisis intervention treatment with chronically and acutely suicidal adolescents. In M.L. Peck, N.L. Farberow, & R.E. Litman (Eds.), *Youth Suicide,* (pp. 112-22). New York: Springer.

Peck, M.L. (1981). The loner: An exploration of a suicidal subtype in adolescence. In S.C. Feinstein, J.G., Looney, A.Z. Schwartzberg, & A.D. Sorosky (Eds.). *Adolescent Psychiatry*, (Vol. 9), pp. 461-7.

Petersen, A.C. (1987, April). Who expresses depressive affect in adolescence? Paper presented at the Society for Research in Child Development. Baltimore, MD.

Petzel, S.V., & Riddle, M. (1981). Adolescent suicide: Psychosocial and cognitive aspects, *Adolescent Psychiatry, 9*, 343-98.

Phillips, D.P, & Carstensen, L.L. (1986). Clustering of teenage suicides after television news stories about suicide. *The New England Journal of Medicine, 315*, 685-9.

Rainer, J.D. (1984). Genetic factors in depression and suicide. *American Journal of Psychotherapy, 38*, 329-40.

Ritter, M. (1987, April 12). Disabling results of cocaine use described. *The Press Enterprise*, Section A, page 3.

Robbins, D., & Conroy, R.C. (1983). A cluster of Adolescent suicide attempts. *Journal of Adolescent Health Care, 3*, 253-5.

Roy, A., & Linnoila, M. (1986). Alcoholism and Suicide. In R. Maris (Ed.), *Biology of Suicide*, (pp. 162-85. New York: Guilford Press.

Rubenstein, D.H. (1986). A stress-diathesis theory of suicide. In R. Maris (Ed.), *Biology of Suicide*, (pp. 162-85). New York: Guilford Press.

Rubinstein, D.H. (1983). Epidemic suicide among Micronesian adolescents. *Social Sciences Medicine, 17*, 657-65.

Salk, L., Lipsitt, L.P., Sturner, W.Q., Reilly, B.M., & & Levat, R.H. (1985, March 16). Relationship of maternal and perinatal conditions to eventual adolescent suicide. *Lancet*, 624-7.

Seligman, M. (1987, April). The development of depressive affect in adolescence: Biological, affective, and social factors. Symposium presented at Society for Research in Child Development. Baltimore, M.D.

Shaffer, D. (1974). Suicide in childhood and early adolescence. *Journal of Child Psychology, 15*, 275-91.

Shneidman, E. (1971). Suicide among the gifted. *Suicide and Life Threatening Behavior, 1*, 23-45.

Smith, K., & Crawford, S. (1986). Suicidal behavior among "normal" high school students. *Suicide and Life-Threatening Behavior, 16*, 313-24.

Steele, W. (1985, Novemer). Preventing the spread of suicide among adolescents. *USA Today*, 58-61.

Stein, K.M (1970). *A challenge to the role of the crisis concept in emergency psychotherapy.* Doctoral dissertation, University of Oregon, 1969.

Sturner, W.Q. (1986). Adolescent suicide fatalities. *Rhode Island Medical Journal, 69,* 471-4.

Teicher, J.D. (1979). Suicide and suicide attempts. In J. Noshpitz (Ed.), *Basic Handbook of Child Psychiatry,* Vol. II. (pp. 685-97). New York: Basic Books.

Tishler, C.L., McKenry, P.C., & Morgan, K.C. (1981). Adolescent suicide attempts: Some significant factors. *Suicide and Life-Threatening Behavior, 11,* 86-92.

Tishler, C.L., & McKenry, P.C. (1982). Parental Negative self and adolescent suicide attempts. *Journal of the American Academy of Child Psychiatry, 21,* 404-7.

Tomlimson-Keasey, C., Warren, L.W., & Elliott, J.E. (1986). Suicide among gifted women: A prospective study. *Journal of Abnormal Psychology, 95,* 123-9.

Toolan, J.M. (1980). Depression and suicidal behavior. In J.M. Toolan (Ed.), *Treatment of Emotional Disorders in Children and Adolescents.* (pp. 589-606). New York: Spectrum Publications.

Topol, P., & Reznikoff, M. (1982). Perceived peer and family relationships, hopelessness and locus of control as factors in adolescent suicide attempts. *Suicide and Life-Threatening Behavior, 12,* 141-50.

Vaillant, G. (1983). *The natural history of alcoholism.* Cambridge, MA: Harvard University Press.

Vital Statistics. (1986). Health and prevention profile, 1986. U.S. Department of Health and Human Services.

Vital Statistics. (1986). Advance report of final mortality statistics, 1984. *National Center for Health Statistics, 35,* No. 6.

Weed, J.A. (1985). Suicide in the United States: 1958-1982. In *Mental Health, United States, 1985.* U.S. Department of Health and Human Services.

Wells, V.E., Deykin, E.Y., & Klerman, G.L. (1985). Risk factors for depression in adolescence. *Psychiatric Developments, 3,* 83-108.

Werner, E.E., & Smith, R.S. (1979). An epidemiologic perspective on some antecedents and consequences of childhood mental health problems and learning disabilities. *Journal of the American Academy of Child Psychiatry, 18,* 292-306.

Young people, suicide and the need for attention. (1974, March). *Psychology Today,* p. 88.

PART IV PREVENTION AND INTERVENTION

CHAPTER **9**

OVERVIEW OF PREVENTION

Richard E. Nelson, Ph.D.

Richard E. Nelson, Ph.D.

Associate Professor, Dept of Counseling Psychology
Counselor, Counseling Center
University of Kansas, Lawrence

Dr. Richard E. Nelson received a B.S. and M.S. from Emporia State University, Emporia, Kansas and a Ph.D. from the University of Missouri-Columbia.

His past educational experiences include being a high school teacher, a high school and junior high counselor, a junior high principal, and a guidance specialist with the Kansas State Department of Education.

Since 1981 Dr. Nelson has conducted research in adolescent suicide, counseled with suicidal clients, and presented over 500 workshops and seminars throughout the midwest on the topic of adolescent suicide.

EDITORIAL ABSTRACT: *This chapter provides an excellent review of the literature related to adolescent suicide prevention programs, proposes content for school/ community based suicide prevention programs, and discusses recommendations for schools and communities interested in initiating a prevention program. The reader will find this chapter particularly concrete and constructive.*

The problem of adolescent suicide has been stated throughout this book. The rate of completed suicides among adolesents has doubled in the last 10 years and tripled in the past 20 years (Teenage Suicide, 1981). Today, suicide is second only to accidents as a cause of death in the 15 to 19 year old age group (Wellman, 1984). Yet in the 18 to 24 year old age group, suicide is the most common cause of death (Miller, 1981). Authorities believe that the actual number of youth suicides is considerably higher, claiming that many one-vehicle accidents and other fatal "mishaps" should be recorded as suicides.

The fact that suicide among adolescents is a probelm is not disputed. What kinds of educational programs, and what populations to reach with these programs, becomes the question.

Suicide is often refered to as "a permanent answer to a temporary problem." Is suicide prevention possible? Szasz (1986) felt the term prevention itself, especially when coupled with suicide, implies coercion. He further stated that coercion leads to institutionalization of the suicidal person.

This chapter will not deal with coercing suicidal adolescents to be institutionalized. It will deal with prevention of suicide from an educational standpoint—education of educators (administrators, teachers, and special services personnel), parents, and adolesents. Education of a variety of populations is the starting point for adolescent suicide prevention.

The literature is replete with examples of adolescent suicide attempts and completed suicides that could have been prevented if educators, parents, and/or adolescents had received basic information regarding suicide. In May of 1987, a 14 year old ninth grader in Laredo, Texas spent Friday evening, all day Saturday, and

Sunday morning talking with each of his 21 classmates. In each of the 21 conversations the 14 year old said either "I am going to kill myself" or "I am going to commit suicide". In each situation his peers, due to lack of basic information, either did not believe him, did not feel he was the "type," or felt he was not serious. At 4:00 p.m. on Sunday the 14 year old commited suicide.

Education is the key and initial focal point of preventing adolescent suicide (Shneidman, 1985). Suicide education must be developed for educators, parents, and adolescents.

This chapter includes the following sections: (1) review of the literature related to adolescent suicide prevention programs, (2) proposed content for school/community based prevention programs, and (3) implications of school/community based prevention programs.

REVIEW OF THE LITERATURE

Many schools, communities, organizations, and associations have responded to the problem of adolescent suicide by developing and implementing suicide awareness and prevention programs. The immediate problem for the developer of prevention programs is that many of the programs developed have not been reported in professional journals. Not a single reference source is available on the thousands of programs that have been developed throughout the country. Many of these programs have been developed as a result of multiple teenage suicides in a community.

Since schools are found in almost every community, they are in the best position to initiate, develop, and implement suicide prevention programs.

Aylward (1987) surveyed all high school counselors in Kansas. The survey investigated three areas: (1) the current incidence of attempted and completed suicides, (2) suicide prevention programs and services provided by schools, and (3) the perceived needs of high school counselors in the area of teenage suicide prevention programs. Sixty-seven percent of the high school counselors responded to the survey. Some of the alarming findings of this research project were (1) 70% of high school faculties had received no in-service training relative to suicide, (2) 95% of the schools had provided no suicide information for students.

In addition Aylward (1987) found that 36% of high school counselors had received no special training for working with adolescent suicide and that only 28% of the counselors had received suicide training from counselor education programs. Fifty-three per cent of the counselors felt their greatest need in suicide prevention was provisions for faculty in-service training. Forty-four per cent of the counselors desired additional suicide training for themselves.

Although the results of this research cannot be generalized to other states, it does suggest that much remains to be done in suicide awareness and prevention.

Educators

Educators play an important role in prevention of teenage suicide because they spend so much time with adolescents. An important step is to conduct in-service programs so as to help teachers understand causes, warning signs, myths, suggestions on what to do if they are concerned about one of their students. Optimally, this should be a regularly scheduled in-service and not an in-service in reaction to an attempted or completed suicide (Appel, 1984).

Educators must remember that discussing suicide does not promote suicidal behavor (Klagsbrun, 1976). For many teachers fear, not lack of concern, is what turns them away from a suicidal student (Peck, Farberow, & Litman, 1985). Ignorance of what to do, not an indifference toward doing something, leaves a teacher unwilling or unable to act effectively.

Although some teachers may become involved in intervention with suicidal adolescents, more often the guidance counselor, school psychologist, and/or social worker is(are) intervener(s). These special services personnel must be adequately trained in order to deal effectively with a suicidal adolescent. These personnel are in a unique position to act as liaison between the community and school, between mental health professionals and teachers, and between parents and students. One of the most important functions of the guidance counselor, school psychologist, and social worker is to construct a referral network of psychologists, psychiatrists, emergency telephone hotlines, and mental health agencies to contact in case of emergency.

Parents

Because nine out of ten suicide attempts take place at home, parents need to be aware of basic information relative to adolescent suicide. The most effective suicide prevention technique parents can exercise is to maintain open lines of communcation with their children. Parents also need to know the warning signs of suicide, what to do, and where to go for help (Henry & Morse, 1985).

Parents can lower the risk of teenage suicide by teaching their children some lessons about life during the child's developmental years. Elkind (1981, 1984) provided many insights in helping parents understand their children's stresses. He specifically emphasized stresses created by parents, schools, media, and society. Parents would be wise to teach their children: (1) bad times do not last forever, (2) showing your hurt helps you heal, (3) the child is an important member of the family, and (4) the child will be loved no matter what (Kline, 1986).

Adolescents

With the increasing incidence of adolescent suicide, schools are recognizing the importance of suicide prevention programs for adolescents. Research indicates that adolescents would first turn to a "friend" (91% of the time) to discuss suicidal thoughts. Friends were chosen as confidants over the choices of parents, other adults, teachers, school counselors, school nurses, or clergy (Peck Farberow, & Litman, 1985). With this in mind, it becomes apparent that although school staffs need to become well versed in suicide prevention, equally important is to teach students facts about suicide.

Sartore (1976) stated that suicide can be minimized through an educational program which emphasizes understanding rather than avoidance. He felt that students need information on causes, symptoms, and alternatives to suicide.

When adolescents who want to learn about suicide are not provided with reliable information they often seek out what they can as best they can. Often, their sources are rumor and speculation, and their experts are other adolescents (Peck et al., 1985).

School Prevention Programs

Positive evidence exists that well conceived suicide prevention programs are highly effective. In Fairfax County, Virginia, 20 adolescent suicides were reported in 1980-81. Following the implementation of a five-part suicide prevention program in 1982, the number of suicides dropped to four or five.

During the same school year, 1980-81, the Shawnee Mission, Kansas schools experienced 12 completed suicides among their five high schools. The school responded by appointing a district-wide suicide awareness/prevention committee. The committee, made up of school psychologists, counselors, administrators, teachers, and students, developed a four level program. The first level included providing suicide information programs for all special services personnel (counselors, psychologists, social workers, and nurses). The second level of the program provided suicide information for all secondary faculty. Level three provided extensive training for one high school counselor in each building. Level four developed printed information for teachers, parents, and students. This suicide prevention program dramatically reduced the number of suicides in the Shawnee Mission Schools.

Plano, Texas experienced eight teenage suicides in a sixteen month period between February, 1983 and May, 1984. The high school turned to community experts and students for help. The program developed by the high school in Plano, Texas is based on creating a one-to-one relationship to get problems solved. The most successful program in place in Plano is called Students Working All Together (SWAT). SWAT pairs high school students in a type of big brother or big sister arrangement. The targets of the SWAT team members are usually troubled students and transfer students. The basic rule for SWAT team members is to become sensitive to other students' problems and offer help. Students Thinking About Peers (STOP) and Believe It or Not I Care (BIONIC) are two other programs at the high school in Plano. The concerns of student volunteers in this program range from classmates who have been ill to groups focused on alcoholism and drug abuse. Since the beginning of this program, the school has received over 500 inquiries from 47 states and no suicides have occurred (Kline, 1986).

Jefferson County, Colorado had 18 teenage suicides between January, 1985 and June, 1986 (Tugend, 1986). Jefferson County used a community based program to provide information on adolescent suicide. Suicide Prevention Allied Regional Effort (SPARE) provided a coordinated outreach program for parents and professionals. The suicide prevention program provided workshops for schools, temples, churches and other places where young people gather.

The Los Angeles Unified School District (Barr, 1987) launched a suicide prevention program. The major focus of the program shows teachers and staff members a videotape on identifying warning signs.

In Florida, the Youth Emotional Development and Suicide Prevention Act of 1984 required each school district to develop suicide prevention programs in coordination with police, parents, and local youth agencies. Florida schools require students to take a life-management skills course, usually in 10th grade, which covers suicide.

The National Association of Secondary School Principals (1985) has published a pamphlet on "The Trauma of Adolescent Suicide." The pamphlet recommends the development of a *Crisis Resource Team.* This crisis team should be established to assist schools in any crisis situation, including suicide.

Phi Delta Kappa (Pfeifer, 1986) provides helpful information for schools relative to what schools can do about teenage suicide. Included in their recommendations are suggestions for a survival curriculum.

The American Association of Suicidology is an excellent source of information about adolescent suicide. It promotes research, public awareness and training for understanding and preventing suicide.

Davis (1982) provided an excellent review of adolescent suicide from 1940 through 1982. Hundreds of other resources are available to assist individuals in developing suicide prevention programs. Developers of prevention programs should

1. plan the program;
2. review the materials to be used;
3. co-sponsor the program with community agencies that work with adolescents;
4. provide opportunities for educators, parents, and adolescents to attend the program; and
5. evaluate the effect of the suicide prevention program.

SUICIDE PREVENTION PROGRAM CONTENT

This section will present suggested content (information to be presented) for suicide awareness and prevention programs. These recommendations are based on over eight years of experience in conducting over 400 workshops and seminars on suicide awareness and prevention. The majority of these workshops were provided for educators, parents, and adolescents. The content for the workshop (Nelson, 1985) was developed from a review of the literature on adolescent suicide and my experiences counseling with suicidal adolescents.

This suggested content provides a base for suicide awareness and prevention programs. Five content areas are recommended for prevention programs focused on educators, parents, and adolescents. The five areas are four components of prevention, general comments, myths, warning signs, and what to do.

Four Components of Prevention

The more people who understand and accept suicide for what it is—a needless and often preventable cause of death—the greater the chance that suicide will eventually be removed from the list of leading causes of death of adolescents.

The adolescent who is suicidal needs four components in their life. The four components are as follows:

A concerned friend. Over 80% of suicidal youth feel that their families do not understand them. Not being appreciated or understood by their families seems to be the most common factor in the continuing chaos and unhappiness in the young person's life. The concerned friend may be a peer, parent, teacher, counselor—the important point is that the adolescent feels that someone is in his/her life who will listen to him/her.

Accessable persons who know the warning signs. In over 80% of adolescent suicide attempts and completed suicides, warning signs exist (Peck et al., 1985). These warning signs often are not seen before the attempt, but after the attempts and/or suicide the warning signs become obvious. Those significant people in the lives of adolescents must become knowledgeable of these warning signs. These significant others include educators, parents, and peers—in essence, people who come in daily contact with youth.

People in their lives who are willing to talk with them openly and frankly about what they are feeling. Too often when a person is in crisis, Mrs. Lincoln (Collison, 1978) responses are used. Mrs. Lincoln responses are inappropriate responses to people in crisis , i.e. "other than that Mrs. Lincoln, how was the play". The suicidal adolescent is often told "you really shouldn't feel that way", "everyone thinks about suicide", "in a week you'll feel much better". If the individual really believed any of the above responses they would not be thinking of suicide as the answer to their problem(s). What the adolescent most needs is someone who will talk with them openly and frankly about what they are feeling and experiencing. They do not need judgment or criticism.

Someone who is willing to refer them to professional help. This may be one of the most difficult roles for educators, parents, and adolescents to fill. The adolescent is often reluctant to seek additional assistance. Remember that whatever is going on with the suicidal adolescent will not go away by itself. If concerned about making an error, remember that to err on the cautious side and lose a friendship is better than to err by not acting and lose a friend forever. Your first responsibility in any suicidal situation is to preserve life—not friendship (Klagsbrun, 1976).

General Comments About Adolescent Suicide

The following general comments about behavior and adolescent suicide are helpful in approaching suicide prevention.

To understand what a suicide is about, one must know the problem suicide is intended to solve. In almost all instances adolescent suicide is the response to a specific problem or series of problems (Klagsburn, 1976). In order to work with suicidal adolescents, problem identification and problem solving alternatives are key ingredients. Until the problem has been identified, no possible alternative solutions may be suggested.

Adolescents perception of their world is accurate to them, but may be perceived quite differently by adults. These perceptual discrepancies result in the adolescent looking at his/her situation and feeling that no answers exist, and the adult looking at the adolescent's situations and feeling things really are not serious. The adolescent has not had enough life experiences to allow him/her to realize problems can be solved, alternative solutions are possible. The adult, on the other hand, has had life experiences which reinforce the belief that people can survive difficult and traumatic experiences.

People behave according to how they feel about themselves at any given time (Dreikurs & Stolz, 1964). This basic principle of understanding human behavior is helpful in understanding suicidal adolescents. When the adolescent has an unsolvable problem, he/she feels that the situation is hopeless. As a result the behavior of the adolescent changes. This change in behavior is one of the major warning sign categories.

Suicide and depression are not synonymous (Shneidman, 1985). Depression has been experienced by everyone, however, the depression did not result in suicide. Even though suicide and depression are not synonymous, it should be noted that depression is evident in the majority of suicidal behaviors.

Suicide is most often done on impulse—but suicide is also premeditated. Suicidal behavior is thought about and planned. This premeditation provides clues for mental health professionals. The therapist working with suicidal adolescents needs to determine the specificity of the suidical plan. The greater the specificity, the higher the risk. Since suicide is most often done on impulse, at the height of a crisis, an important point to realize is that if the individual can be helped through the crisis, the urge to commit suicide will be diminished (Shneidman, 1985).

Over 25% of adolescent suicidal behavior occurs while the adolescent is under the influence of alcohol and/or drugs. The alcohol and drugs do not cause the suicide. The suicide ideations have been present before the ingestion of alcohol and drugs. The adolescent under the influence of a substance is not able to think and behave in a rational and logical manner. The adolescent has thought about suicide before, however the alcohol and/or drugs prohibits the rational and logical approach to problem solving.

Suicidal thoughts, threats, and actions are most often cries for help. Suicide prevention can only happen if it provides educators, parents, and adolescents with information that allows them to understand the thoughts, hear the threats, and see the suicidal behaviors. Repeated suicidal thoughts, threats, and actions often create a "cry wolf" syndrome. Suicidal thoughts, threats, and actions must be taken seriously. As stated earlier, to err on the cautious side is better than to not act at all.

Individuals interested in suicide prevention must be convinced that one concerned, caring person, can save the life of a suicidal adolescent. The suicidal adolescent feels alone and misunderstood. To have anyone, in any way, indicate he/she cares, is concerned, and is willing to help is extremely important.

Myths of Suicide

Myths of suicide, things believed to be true but are not, create many road blocks toward decreasing the rate of adolescent suicide attempts and completions. The myths of suicide must be dispelled in prevention programs. Some of the myths of suicide have been previously presented in Chapter 1 of this book.

Warning Signs

As stated earlier, warning signs always are present in suicidal behavior. Many times the warning signs are subtle. The warning signs of suicide are, in many respects, similar to adolescents experiencing substance abuse symptomology. The importance of recognizing warning signs is crucial. People under stress and in crisis/trauma situations do provide clues that indicate they are hurting and in trouble.

Researchers believe that most suicidal individuals convey their intentions to someone in their network of friends, family, or peers, either openly or covertly. These people are most intimately and extensively in contact with a particular suicidal adolescent. They are probably in the best position to recognize the signs and render help.

No one profile or checklist exists for identifying a suicidal adolescent. Suicide, like much of human behavior, is difficult to predict. Despite experts' best efforts, even they cannot say if or when a person will attempt suicide. But they have identified several warning signs which, particularly in combination, demand immediate concern and attention.

The following list of warning signs is not all inclusive, but they provide a base for what to look for in suicidal adolescents.

1. Suicidal threats. Suicidal threats can be classified into two categories: (a) veiled/disguised threats and (b) specific-desire-to-die threats. Veiled/disguised threats may include "sometimes I just want it to be over with", "I can't take it any more", "the world would be better off without me". These veiled/disguised threats are like little teasers—but they must be heard.

Specific desire to die statements leave no doubt about the adolescents intentions. "I'm going to kill myself", "I'm going to commit suicide." These direct threats require immediate attention. These direct threats require referral to competent mental health professionals. People who talk about suicide do attempt suicide and do commit suicide.

2. Sudden changes in behavior. This category of suicidal warning signs reflects the concept that people behave according to how they feel about themselves. When adolescents are experiencing stress, problems, and traumatic events in their lines, behaviors change.

Changes in eating behavior are common. Often the adolescent reduces the amount of food eaten. In some instances the adolescent binges on food.

Changes in sleeping behavior may be another warning sign. The adolescent may sleep an inordinate amount of time. Excessive sleeping allows the individual to avoid stress and conflicts. Insomnia is another warning sign of people in stress.

The adolescent considering suicide will often change dress and personal appearance. This change primarily results in an attitude of not caring what he/she looks like. Personal hygiene and grooming reflect their feeling of depression and low self-esteem. They quit caring about what they look like.

The suicidal adolescent's grades may drop and school attendance becomes sporadic. Educators, parents, and adolescents are in excellent position to observe these two changes.

The suicidal adolescent often demonstrates changes relative to activities that once were important to them. They become disinterested and drop out of these activities. This change is the adolescent's attempt to become isolated.

3. Depression and isolation. The suicidal adolescent will be depressed (Peck et al., 1985). This depression is often expressed by changes in behavior. The depression may be demonstrated by the adolescent's choosing isolation from friends and family. One of the difficulties in perceiving adolescent depression centers on the fact that adolescents often show their depression in ways that are different from how adults show their depression . The adolescent who is displaying acts of defiant, aggressive and rebellious behavior may be expressing their depression. Depressed people often have a negative view of themselves, they distort reality and they have a negative view of the future (Klagsbrun, 1976).

4. Giving away valued possessions. In some cases the suicidal adolescent will give valued possessions to their friends. The obvious process is that the young person has decided to commit suicide, but before they implement that decision they want their friends to have their most valued treasures.

5. Getting their house in order. Another warning sign revolves around "getting their house in order," taking care of unfinished business. The adolescent will often patch up old quarrels, make amends for past mistakes. They are taking steps to put their affairs in order. Such behavior is particularly alarming when other warning signs also are present.

6. Previous suicide attempts. People who have made serious suicide attempts are at the highest risk for actually killing themselves (National Institute of Mental Health, 1986). The suicide rate for repeat attempters is up to 643 times higher than the overall rate in the general population. Between 20 to 50% of the people who commit suicide had previously made attempts.

7. A loss in their life. A loss in an adolescent's life is often a contributing factor to suicidal behavior. The loss in their life may include break-up of a love relationship. This loss appears extremely difficult for many adolescents. Aylward (1987) found that a break-up in a love relationship was a contributing factor in 26% of suicide attempts and completed suicides.

Loss can be the death of a family member. Adolescents may have a concept of death that is different from the adult's concept of death. As people continue to have longer life expectancies many young people will not have experienced the death of grandparents and/or other family members. They don't comprehend the finality of death.

Loss of a parent through divorce also may be a factor in adolescent suicide.

Any significant loss should be recognized as a possible contributor to depresssive behavior and suicidal ideation.

The list of warning signs continues to be expanded. The seven warning sign categories previously presented provide a base for training educators, parents, and adolescents to recognize adolescents who may be at risk.

What To Do

When educators, parents, and adolescents have received the information on the Four Components of Prevention, General Comments, Myths of Suicide, and Warning Signs the next step is how may this information best be used.

The first step in helping a suicidal adolescent focuses on the individual who is willing to be the concerned friend. This person must be able to listen effectively (Peck et al., 1985). This begins with the process of *active listening. Active listening* is defined as (1) listening to what the person is saying, (2) listening to the words (vocabulary) the person is using, (3) listening to what the suicidal adolescent is not saying (reading between the lines and making assumptions), and (4) listening to what the person is feeling. In addition to these four parts of *active listening,* the listener does not judge and does not criticize. The role of the *active listener* may be fulfilled by educators, parents, peers, friends—anyone who is willing to become involved and refer the suicidal adolescent to appropriate counseling.

The second step in the helping process of adolescents in crisis is for the helper to possess the personal characteristics of empathy, warmth, and caring. Empathy is the ability to enter the world of the adolescent and experience what they are feeling. Empathy can greatly reduce the difference between the adolescent and adult perceptions of the crisis situaiton. Warmth and caring are more difficult to define. They are personal characteristics that convey to the adolescent that the helper is sincerely concerned about helping them. Warmth and caring, along with empathy, are most often communicated through non-verbal forms of communication. For suicidal adolescents to know they are with a person who is concerned and willing to get them the help they need is extremely important. Empathy, warmth, and caring communicates this concern and willingness to help.

The following are usefull suggestions for educators, parents, and adolescents.

1. **Educators.** Educators' key role in suicide prevention is to become suicide interventionists. Programs of suicide prevention are not developed to make educators counselors or therapists. Instead, prevention programs need educators who know the warning signs, can identify adolescents at risk, and make appropriate referrals. Many suicide prevention programs have identified specific steps for teachers to use in the referral process. The important issue is that the classroom teacher knows the suicide referral resources in the building and in the community.

2. Parents. Parents, assuming they have information on suicide, are in an excellent position to be able to observe warning signs. Parents' most important role in suicide prevention is seeking professional help when they observe behavioral changes and identify suicide warning signs. Too often parents see the behavioral changes and warning signs and do nothing. Often they don't know where to go for help or they feel their child is going through a phase in life.

Parents also are reluctant to seek help for their child because society often looks at suicide through the suicide myth syndrome. Too often suicide remains taboo.

The final suggestion for parents is to really look at the concept of active listenting. When listening begins between parents and children, each has a better understanding of the other. In a family setting listening opens many avenues of communication.

3. Adolescents. Over 90% (Peck et al., 1985) of the time adolescents who are thinking about suicide will confide in a friend. The suicidal adolescent may approach the friend with "whatever you do don't tell anyone, but I'm thinking about suicide." Confidentiality is important to the adolescent. The friend must understand the suicide threat is serious. The friend must understand that someone else is going to have to be told about the concern. Suicide prevention starts when the suicidal adolescent begins to talk to someone.

The adolescent who is thinking about suicide must learn that the first step is for him/her to talk to someone about what is being felt. Choose a friend, a teacher, a counselor, a parent—but choose someone who can be trusted.

Finally, the adolescent must know that suicidal feelings can happen to anyone. He/she must understand that verbal and behavioral clues, warning signs, always are present before a suicide. And the adolescent must hear the message from someone who cares that HELP IS AVAILABLE.

IMPLICATIONS

The scope of this Chapter has not allowed for a comprehensive coverage of all possible approaches to suicide prevention programs. It has concentrated on programs and suicide information for use with three audiences: educators (administrators, teachers, and special services personnel), parents, and adolescents. These three audiences were selected because they are major influences in the everyday life of adolescents. Suicide prevention programs for these audiences have been suggested since the middle of the 1950s. Shneidman and Farberow (1957) suggested "the greatest need of prevention of suicide is public education" (p. 93).

Recommendations

The following recommendations should be considered when establishing a suicide prevention program.

1. A proactive approach to suicide prevention should be considered. Many suicide prevention programs have been developed throughout the country after multiple suicides have occurred in a community. A proactive approach, before a problem exists, provides a climate that enhances thorough program development and implementation of comprehensive prevention programs.

2. Effective suicide prevention programs involve a broad base of community involvement and support. Too often schools are asked to respond to all of the concerns and problems of society. If a problem exists, turn to schools to solve the problem. Suicide prevention programs are most effective if they are developed by schools, in cooperation with community organizations and agencies that provide on-going services for adolescents. The broad based community developed programs take some of the stress off of schools. Community based programs allow adolescents more comprehensive servies. Some adolescents may prefer to use the services of a community organization and/or agency. Parent and adolescent representation must be a part of the suicide program planning team.

3. A school should have a Crisis Resource Team to help students, staff, and community deal with crisis situations (National Association of Secondary School Principals, 1985). The recommendation is that this team, often composed of a psychologist, nurse, social worker, teacher, administrator, counselor, and student, be responsible for dealing with the impact of a crisis in the school setting and for being of help to the family or student in crisis. The positive impact of the Crisis Team approach is that it is proactive and that it assists in dealing with the problem of adolescent suicide, plus the team is of assistance in other school/ student crisis situations.

4. **Many schools have approached suicide prevention by including information on suicide in school curriculums.** Suicide information in school curriculums provides an on-going program of prevention. The topic of suicide should be included in school curriculums, suggesting that discussions of suicide in the classroom can serve to help adolescents understand how their emotions influence their behavior and serve to lessen feelings of isolation when students learn their peers have similar problems. Yalom (1975) stated that universality (realizing other people have problems similar to your problems) is a strong curative factor in problem solving and therapy. Aylward (1987) found tha 35% of high schools had suicide information units in their curriculums. The majority of the suicide units were found in psychology, health, and family living classes.

Education is the key to suicide prevention. If just one adolescent is helped because an educator identified him/her as being at risk—if just one suicide attempt can be avoided because parents have picked up clues—if just one life can be saved because a friend has learned how to help—a beginning will have been made (Shneidman & Swenson, 1964).

REFERENCES

Appel, Y. H. (1984). *Adolescent suicide awareness training manual.* (Report No. PTM-400-18). Trenton, NJ: State Department of Education. (ERIC Document Reproduction Service No. ED 261 281).

Aylward, L. K. (1987). *Adolescent suicide in Kansas.* Unpublished master's thesis. University of Kansas, Lawrence

Barr, R. (1987, March 27). Many schools now prepared to prevent suicides. *The Lawrence, Kansas, Journal World,* p. 1.

Collison, B. B. (1978). The Mrs. Lincoln response. *Personnel and Guidance Journal, 57*(4), 180-182.

Davis, P. A. (1982). *A review of the literature on adolescent suicide from 1940 to present.* Unpublished master's thesis. University of Kansas, Lawrence.

Dreikurs, R. & Stolz, V. (1964). *Children: The challenge.* New York: Hawthorne Books.

Elkind, D. (1981). *The hurried child: Growing up too fast too soon.* Reading, MA: Addison-Wesley.

Elkind, D. (1984). *All grown up and no place to go.* Reading, MA: Addision-Wesley.

Henry, P. & Morse, M. (1985). *Teenage suicide: The final cry.* Raleigh, NC: Governor's Advocacy Council on Children and Youth. (ERIC Document Reproduction Service No. ED 261 314).

Klagsbrun, F. (1976). *Too young to die: Youth and suicide.* Boston: Houghton Mifflin.

Kline, P. (1986). How one school responded to a teen suicide epidemic. *Network for Public Schools, 12*(3).

Miller, D. (1981). Adolescent suicide: Etiology and treatment. In S. C. Feinstein, J.G. Looney, A. Z. Schwartberg, & A. D. Sorosky (Eds.), *Adolescent Psychiatry.* Chicago: University of Chicago Press.

National Associaiton for Secondary School Principals. (1985). *The trauma of adolescent suicide.* Reston, Va: National Association of Secondary School Principals.

National Institute of Mental Health. (1986). *Useful information on suicide.* Washington, DC: U. S. Department of Health and Human services, DHHS Publication No. (ADM) 86-1489.

Nelson, R. E. (1985). *Adolescent suicide: What can we do?* Unpublished manuscript, The University of Kansas, Lawrence.

Peck, M. L., Farberow, N. L, & Litman, R. E. (1985). *Youth suicide.* New York: Springer Publishing.

Pfeifer, J. K. (1986). *Teenage suicide: What can schools do?* Bloomington, IN: Phi Delta Kappa Educational Foundation.

Sartore, R. L. (1976). Students and suicide: An interpersonal tragedy. *Theory Into Practice, 15*(5), 336-339.

Shneidman, E.S. (1985). *Definition of suicide.* New York: John Wiley.

Shneidman, E.S., & Farberow, N.L. (1957). *Clues to suicide.* New York: McGraw-Hill.

Shneidman, E.S., & Swenson, D. M. (1964). Suicide among youth: Supplement to the Bulleton of Suicidology. Washington, DC: National Clearing House for Mental Health.

Szasz, T. (1986). The case against suicide prevention. *American Psychologist, 41*(7), 806-812.

Teenage suicide—A tragic impulse. (1981). *MD,* 49-52.

Tugend, A. (1986). Suicide's 'unanswerable logic'. *Education Week, V*(39).

Wellman, M. M. (1984). The school counselor's role in communication of suicidal ideation by adolescents. *School Counselor, 32*(2), 104-109.

Yalom, I. D. (1975). *The theory and practice of group psychoterapy.* New York: Basic Books, Publishers.

CHAPTER **10**

A MODEL PREVENTION PROGRAM

Beverly Celotta, Ph.D., Lic. Psych.
Golda Jacobs, M.A., N.C.C.
Susan G. Keys, Ph.D., N.C.C.
and
Geneva Cannon, M.Ed., N.C.C.

Beverly Celotta, Ph.D.

Consultant
Celotta, Jacobs, & Keys Associates, Inc.
Gaithersburg, MD 20878

Beverly Celotta is a licensed psychologist with over twenty years of experience in the mental health and educational fields. She received her B.A. in psychology from Queens Collge, her M.S. and Advanced Certificate in school psychology from Brooklyn College and her Ph.D. in Educational Psychology from the University of Colorado. Before becoming president of Celotta, Jacobs & Keys Associates, Inc., a program development firm, she served as a faculty member and assistant chairperson of the Counseling and Personnel Services Department at the University of Maryland. She also had served as a school psychologist and an educational research and evaluation specialist. Dr. Celotta has authored or co-authored over thirty articles, chapters, and manuals in the area of the application of systems theory to mental health program development. She is currently on the editorial board of *Measurement and Evaluation in Counseling and Development.* Recently she has assisted numerous counties and the State of Maryland in developing youth suicide prevention programs. She is a national trainer for the American Association for Counseling and Development and recently served as an expert witness on their behalf for a United States House Subcommittee conducting hearings on HR 457, a suicide prevention bill.

Golda Jacobs, M.A., N.C.C.

Consultant
Celotta, Jacobs & Keys Associates, Inc.
Gaithersburg, MD 20878

Golda Jacobs is a counselor with over fifteen years of experience in the mental health and educational fields. She received her B.A. in education from Roosevelt University and her M.A. in counseling from the University of Maryland. Before becoming a founding partner of Celotta, Jacobs & Keys Associates, Inc., Ms. Jacobs taught in the Counseling and Personnel Services Department at the University of Maryland. She had also served as a researcher, teacher, school counselor, field supervisor, and director of a system's based model guidance program. In addition, she has experience as a hotline crisis counselor. Ms. Jacobs has several publications in the area of program development and is an active presenter and trainer. She has worked on numerous consultation projects in a variety of areas such as needs assessment, computerized approaches to program development, and self management. In the area of suicide prevention she has served as a workshop leader and is a national trainer for the American Association for Counseling and Development. She has assisted numerous counties and the State of Maryland in their youth suicide prevention efforts.

Susan G. Keys, Ph.D., N.C.C.
Celotta, Jacobs & Keys Associates, Inc.
Gaithersburg, MD 20878

Susan Keys is a counselor with nearly ten years of experience in the mental health and educational fields. She received her B.A. from St. Mary's College and her M.Ed., A.G.S., and Ph.D. in counseling from the University of Maryland. Before becoming a founding partner of Celotta, Jacobs & Keys Associates, Inc., Dr. Keys taught in the Counseling and Personnel Services Department at the University of Maryland and had served as a school counselor. Dr. Keys has specialized in social problem solving training. She has several publications to her credit and has made numerous professional presentations at the state, regional, and national levels. She has worked on a variety of consultation projects including social problem-solving training, systematic case management, communication skills for the culturally different, and evaluating guidance and counseling programs. Recently she has assisted numerous counties and the State of Maryland in their youth suicide prevention efforts.

Geneva Cannon, M.Ed., N.C.C.

Supervisor of Guidance and Counseling
Worchester County, Maryland Public Schools
Newark, MD 21841

Geneva Cannon has been an educator for more than twenty years. She has been a classroom teacher, school counselor, and professional development coordinator. Currently, she is the Supervisor of Guidance and Counseling for Worchester County, Maryland Public Schools. She is also the Project Coordinator of *Lifelines: Helping Students Find Positive Alternatives*, a comprehensive school/community program designed to address the problems and concerns of youth suicide.

Ms. Cannon is a graduate of Salisbury State College and has begun doctoral studies through the University of Maryland. She is a National Certified Counselor (NCC). Ms. Cannon is a member of the Maryland State Department of Education Youth Suicide Prevention School Program Committee. She has served as a member of the Maryland Gubernatorial Task Force on Child, Teenage, and Young Adult Suicide and Other Associated Mental Health Problems. Ms. Cannon served on the Executive Committee of that Task Force and chaired the Committee on Program/Curriculum Design and Training.

During the past several years, Ms. Cannon has made presentations on youth suicide and related issues to civic and educational groups. In addition, she has provided direct assistance to school and community practitioners in their efforts to develop comprehensive and collaborative approaches to suicide prevention, intervention, and postvention.

EDITORIAL ABSTRACT: *This chapter begins with a discussion of the need for suicide prevention programs and the difficulties involved in their development. A description of some current programming practices follows. A set of requirements for suicide prevention programs is presented along with a programming model based on these requirements and a description of an actual program based upon the model. The chapter concludes with ideas for networking, program expansion and program evaluation.*

As we write this chapter two youths from Virginia committed suicide together, in what seems to be an unprecedented rash of group, cluster suicides by carbon monoxide poisoning. This is a tragic example of the rise in suicides in young people from five to twenty-four years of age. In response to this national tragedy many communities have developed or are in the process of developing suicide prevention programs. Feeling the urgency of the problem, many of these programs have been developed quickly without the benefit of carefully considered program development models.

This chapter presents a model for suicide prevention program development. It begins with a discussion of the need for suicide prevention programs and the difficulties involved in their development. This is followed by a description of some current programming practices. Next, a set of requirements for suicide prevention programs is presented along with a programming model based on these requirements and a description of an actual program based upon the model. The chapter concludes with a discussion of ways to network with others, expand the program, and ways to evaluate various program models.

THE PROGRAMMING CHALLENGE

Why should we develop youth suicide prevention programs? First, suicide impacts a large number of our youth. The number of reported youth suicides, over 5,000 a year (Department of Health and Human Services, 1984), have been estimated to be far fewer than the actual number (Freiberg, 1983). This underrepresentation is due to the fact that many attempts are often disguised as accidents or homicides (Freese, 1979); suicides committed by children under ten are often not counted as such (Eisenberg,

1984); coroners frequently will not label a death a suicide without the presence of a note (Freese, 1979); and many parents wish to disguise the fact of a suicide (Eisenberg, 1984).

Disturbingly, for each child who commits suicide, an estimated 50 to 100 more have attempted (Freese, 1979) and perhaps hundreds more who have given it serious thought. When one considers how many youngsters plan, attempt, or commit suicide and how many others interact daily with these troubled youngsters, or experience via the media the tragedies in other communities, we come to realize that suicide effects virtually all of our youth.

Secondly, a strong possibility exists that suicides can be prevented (Eisenberg, 1984). Professionals who have worked with suicidal youngsters agree that most either want to be saved, and give off signals to that effect, or at a minimum are ambivalent about taking their own lives.

And finally, as mental health professionals we are charged with the moral imperative of trying to keep youngsters mentally healthy, so that taking one's life is not viewed as a realistic option. We have no other choice but to make this our first priority.

Program Barriers

Having made the commitment to program for suicide prevention one may be faced by certain barriers that must be overcome in order to develop sound programs. The first barrier encountered is the mental health professional's unfamiliarity with developing programs that deal with life and death issues. We must learn to take more precautionary steps and use stricter program development standards.

A second barrier derives from the nature of suicide itself. All of the research evidence indicates that suicide is a multiply-caused phenomenon with causal factors ranging from the genetic to the societal levels (Celotta, 1985; Hawton, 1986). This poses a problem because programmers have to decide which one or more causal factors to target in their prevention efforts. Should one, for example, target the biochemical level, and work to increase serontonin (a brain chemical that is deficient in depressives who are suicidal)? Should one target the individual level and work to increase such factors as self esteem and stress management skills? Should one target the group level and work to decrease parental and peer pressure for example, good grades? Or finally, should one target the societal level and work to eliminate drugs or shape media coverage of suicide?

A third barrier is the difficulty mental health professionals may have when working with various segments of the general population and with other professionals. In much of our recent programming efforts we have worked with a variety of mental health and other professionals, including representatives from the judicial system, the media, the religious and business communities, as well as representatives from the community at large. Each group has its own ideas, values, and feelings related to the problem of suicide and its remediation. Yet, consensus is critical for a program's success.

Some segments of the community may believe that suicide is not a significant problem, while others may acknowledge the existence of the problem but feel that it is best to ignore it in an attempt to avoid its exaserbation. Some feel that the church and home are the only places where life and death issues should be addressed, while still others find the topic simply too painful to address at all.

Mental health professionals find that turf issues may arise when they are working with allied professionals. Some services may be regarded as sacred for a particular specialization (i.e., "only psychologists should do risk assessments"). For a program to be successful, however, the various groups will have to agree on the importance of using or developing identical and/or similar skills in order to provide prompt, effective service in times of crisis.

Some mental health professionals do not want to work with suicidal youngsters. For some, time is an issue, for others, their job descriptions or training, and for still others, personal discomfort.

A fourth barrier arises from unresolved legal and ethical issues. At present many states do not have any laws that deal with youth suicide. The following questions are often left unanswered. Is a suicide attempt illegal? Does (or should) an adult have to report an attempt? Is an agency or institution that has a suicide prevention program liable if youngsters commit suicide? If a family wishes to disguise an attempt or completion, can or should one expose it?

A fifth barrier concerns the fact that distressed youth often do not come to the attention of a mental health professional. Many youngsters will not turn to adults for help but, instead, to peers. Compounding this problem is the fact that most untrained peers will not tell an appropriate adult about the problem as they feel they are violating a sacred trust of friendship. If the peer attempts to involve an adult, frequently that adult does not know how to intervene, does not feel comfortable intervening and/or may feel that doing so is not appropriate.

A sixth barrier concerns the lack of relevant information available to program developers. Sound information is needed to develop effective programs; yet we lack timely and accurate information about the number of youngsters who actually attempt and commit suicide, the characteristics of these youngsters and the most effective interventions for them. A recent series of conferences on suicide prevention sponsored by the Task Force on Youth Suicide of the U.S. Department of Health and Human Services addressed these issues and, after careful consideration by experts in various fields, left a large number of questions unanswered.

Most mental health professionals are not usually working with such a serious, complex, and disturbing phenomenon, where they need to work with others who may have different ideas, values and feelings, where many unanswered legal and ethical questions exist, where those needing the most help are often not brought to their attention, and where the information is so limited. Herein lies the programming challenge.

CURRENT PROGRAMMING EFFORTS

Obtaining information about the more than one hundred suicide prevention programs believed to be in existence is at present a difficult task. Inundated with the task of implementation, many programmers do not have the time and/or inclination to publish information about their programs. Often programmers must learn about prevention efforts by word of mouth, or by happening upon information scattered throughout various journals, newsletters, and newspapers. These are highly unsatisfactory methods for those of us who need timely, accurate information.

A recent national report, however, has shed some light on general state-wide efforts in suicide prevention (Office of the Inspector General, 1986), but more information about specific programs and their effectiveness is greatly needed. In response to this problem the American Association for Suicidology has begun to study and evaluate model programs nation-wide.

Some current programming efforts that have come to our attention are summarized in the following paragraphs. Because an exhaustive account of all programs is neither possible at this time, nor appropriate to the scope of this chapter, we have selected certain programs as illustrative of features we believe to be representative of programming efforts nation-wide. The following features are explored: the use of a community base in programming efforts, the incorporation of specific program components, and the use of a systematic programming procedure.

Community Base

Some programmers feel the importance of having community involvement in program development and a number of suicide prevention programs have included representation from various sectors of the community. For example, in the Arkansas Lifesavers program, the advisory committee included teachers, school administrators, survivors, and the media (Office of the Inspector General, 1986). The advisory committee for the program in the Fairfax County, Virginia Public Schools included school representatives, parents, representatives from public and private mental health agencies, hospitals, universities, the medical association, and the police (Fairfax County Public Schools, 1985). In other programs, such as those in Washington and California, the schools and community mental health agencies have formed a partnership for helping suicidal youngsters (Office of the Inspector General, 1986).

Most programs that we have reviewed, however, do not have a comprehensive community base. Often one finds that community mental health agencies and school systems are operating separate, noncoordinated programs.

Specific Program Components

Some programs have incorporated components that are intended to help youngsters avoid serious mental health problems. For example, in one Michigan county a pilot program was initiated to teach coping, problem solving, and survival skills as part of the eighth grade curriculum (Office of the Inspector General, 1986). Fairfax County, Virginia has a student stress program for all high school youngsters (Department of Health and Human Services, 1986). In Montgomery County, Maryland a group of high school students perform in a traveling road show that deals with the problems of youngsters and how to solve them (G. Jacobs, personnel communication, March 30, 1987). In Delaware a brochure on youth suicide was distributed to all high school students (Office of the Inspector General, 1986).

Other programs, also intended to help youngsters avoid serious mental health problems, involve the community at large. In Plano, Texas, for example, the local churches have made an effort to strengthen family activities (US News and World Report, 1984). The Dallas Suicide and Crisis Center provides community education in the form of a speakers' bureau (Department of Health and Human Services, 1986). In Fairfax County, Virginia films are available for parental viewing (Fairfax County Public Schools, 1985). The Cherry Creek program in Colorado has a parent training component (Barrett, 1981).

Some program components focus on a narrow segment of the youth population, such as those youngsters who are undergoing considerable stress. For example, in the Cherry Creek program (Barrett, 1981) both individual and group counseling is available for students under stress, and groups exist for students whose parents are undergoing divorce.

Some program components were designed to provide an early detection and intervention function. In the state of Washington, the mental health agency is implementing an early intervention project. Here teachers screen elementary aged children (kindergarten through third grade) for risk of mental health problems, including suicide (Office of the Inspector General, 1986). In Mesa County, Colorado school officials interviewed all students at a junior high school to identify, refer, and treat youngsters who might be at risk (US News and World Report, 1984). The Maternal and Child Health Program in Connecticut has a program located in school based health clinics and young parents' classes for screening youth at risk (Office of the Inspector General, 1986).

Some program components are designed to help youngsters who are currently in a crisis. Many communities like Plano, Texas, have established hotlines (US News and World Report, 1984). The Arkansas Lifesavers program has established Caring Committees, which include a student, counselor, parent, and nurse (Office of the Inspector General, 1986). At each junior and senior high, this group serves as a referral resource for troubled youngsters.

Still other program components are designed to assist after a suicide has occurred. In Delaware several support groups exist for survivors of suicide (Office of the Inspector General, 1986). Nationwide support groups are available for survivors such as Ray of Hope and Seasons (Department of Health and Human Services, 1986).

Most programs have focused on youngsters in crisis; several have developed a component to help youth avoid problems; fewer still provide services for the community in the aftermath of a suicidal tragedy.

Systematic Procedures

Few programs appear to have used a systematic programming procedure. One exception is the program in the Cherry Creek Public Schools in Denver, Colorado (Barrett, 1981). A needs assessment was conducted, objectives were specified, a comprehensive set of program manuals was developed, and an objective based evaluation was conducted. The Maryland State Department of Education is presently facilitating the development of systematic programming efforts state-wide (G. Cannon, Personal Communications, February 10, 1987).

Programs vary considerably in the major features and specific strategies utilized. Some communities have only a crisis hotline, for example, while others like the Cherry Creek program use a systematic procedure and has program components that assist youngsters in avoiding problems as well as helping those in crisis. Most programs, however, have serious gaps in their coverage. The following model was designed to help systems provide the comprehensive program necessary to address the problem of youth suicide.

REQUIREMENTS FOR YOUTH SUICIDE PREVENTION PROGRAMS

In order to build any prevention model, a necessary procedure is to synthesize in some meaningful and concrete fashion, all of the current information about suicide. Our extensive research and that of others on stress in children and adolescents (Celotta & Jacobs, 1981; Cohen-Sandler, Berman, & King, 1982; Celotta & Sobol, 1983; Celotta, Jacobs, & Keys, 1987) has led us to believe that youngsters today, as young as five or six, are living highly stressful lives. The foundation of our model is built upon the premise that the majority of youngsters have too much stress in their lives, too few coping skills, and insufficient adult support. Those who are most "at risk" have enormous stress, totally inadequate coping skills, and little or no adult support. In fact, many high-risk youngsters consider suicide as the only way they can cope with their problems.

Using stress as a focus we feel the following program requirements are necessary in order to develop an effective prevention program. The first requirement is that the program have a community base. This is important for two major reasons. First, suicide prevention is too complex, costly, and demanding a problem for any one group in the community to address alone. Second, because our youth are members of home, school, work, religious, and other community groups, responsive, caring adults and peers need to be in all of these settings so that youngsters can get the education and support they need when and where they need it.

The next requirement is the incorporation of three basic, interrelated subprograms or program components: inoculation, crisis intervention, and postvention. Each of these components addresses different facets of stress prevention. *Inoculation* assists all youngsters by reducing stress factors, teaching stress coping skills, and providing help with overwhelming stress. Crisis intervention assists those youngsters who are in an immediate crisis by providing appropriate intervention. Postvention assists all youngsters in the community by quickly reducing the stress that occurs after a suicide.

The final requirement is the use of a systematic program development procedure. This helps to assure that programs are responsive to the community's needs, that resources are used efficiently and effectively, that problems can be detected and corrected quickly, that success is measurable, and that there exists a sense of purpose and direction. All of these attributes help increase the chances for a successful program.

The following model was designed to meet the three aforementioned requirements: the use of a community base, the inclusion of the three basic components, inoculation, crisis intervention, and postvention, and the use of a systematic program development procedure.

THE LIFELINES MODEL FOR DEVELOPING SUICIDE PREVENTION PROGRAMS

The Lifelines Model was designed to help various communities in Maryland develop suicide prevention programs. Although any one of the three program features can be used independently, our model requires the simultaneous use of a community base, the inclusion of the three components, and the use of a systematic procedure for program development. These features are the "who," "what," and "how" of the model. The community base describes "who" should be involved in the programming efforts, the three components describes "what" the program should include in its basic structure, and the systematic program development procedures describes "how" the community should put the program together. The model combines all of the best features of current programs and is based upon both our research and experience.

The Community Base

Various segments of the community must be involved in the program to assure success. Representatives should be selected from schools (i.e., Board members, pupil service professionals, teachers, students, aides, administrators, and parents), mental health, social services and youth agencies, hotlines, hospitals, business and industry (especially employers of youth), police, the court system, local and state governments, religious groups and the media. Various socio-economic levels in the community also should be represented. To include community members who might disagree with the need for the program also is important. If these members are not included in the early planning stages, they may sabotage the program at a later stage.

Having the broadest possible representation is critical. In a recent program development effort the authors realized they had excluded one critical community segment, the school bus drivers. We realized our omission when we learned of a youngster who told a bus driver that he was feeling down and that he intended to hurt himself in auto-shop class by kicking a jack out from under him. When the supervisor of transportation discovered the youth had actually done this (the youth was slightly injured), he requested involvement in the program and training for all bus drivers.

The Three Components: Inoculation, Crisis Intervention and Postvention

A prevention program that is not supported by the three critical components of inoculation, crisis intervention, and postvention will not be balanced and as such will allow too many youngsters to turn up at the higher end of a suicide continuum. The suggestion is that three advisory committee subgroups be selected to manage the activities of each component. The three program components and their goals are discussed next. Both the components and goals have been derived by a logical analysis of research on various correlates of suicide (Hawton, 1986; Celotta, Jacobs, & Keys, 1987) and by a review of programs practices nationwide. For each component suggestions are made concerning various types of appropriate goal related activities and community members who might implement these activities.

Inoculation. The purpose of an inoculation component is to assist in the development of mentally healthy youngsters. This is a harder task today than previously because more environmental stressors, less parental attention, less influence from extended families, and less rootedness in the community exist. In order for our children to develop adequately we need help from the entire adult community. Teachers, religious and community groups leaders, the media, and others must help parents promote mental health. The three main inoculation goals are to help youngsters avoid unnecessary stress, to teach youngsters ways to deal with reasonable stress, and to support youngsters who are overwhelmed by stress.

The community can work together to help youngsters avoid unnecessary stress by creating a safer environment. Parents can be taught the importance of removing toxic substances and lethal weapons from the home and of providing supervised places to play. Strong family units can be promoted by developing a family life curriculum or helping families under stress get assistance. Also essential is fostering health enhancing values, attitudes and behaviors. Parents and teachers can work to enhance self-esteem and problem solving skills, for example. Parents and religious leaders can help youngsters develop appropriate concepts about death, dying, and suicide.

School counselors and other school mental health professionals can teach youngsters to recognize stress in themselves and others, to communicate about it, and to manage it. Stress management skills can be taught in the guidance curriculum starting at the elementary level.

To support youngsters who are overwhelmed by stress, all adults and peers in the community can serve as "gatekeepers." These gatekeepers must be able to identify those youngsters who are overwhelmed by stress and/or are presenting suicidal signals. These youngsters must then be seen by mental health professionals who can determine an appropriate course of action. Gatekeepers must remain in contact with the youngsters and monitor the effectiveness of any intervention for several months after termination and during times of increased stress (i.e., SATS, a suicide in the community).

Crisis Intervention. The purpose of a crisis intervention component is to assist youngsters in the midst of a crisis. To do this the community must form a "round-the-clock and calendar" safety net so that protection is available for youngsters in crisis at all times.

This safety net is formed by numerous members of the health and mental health professions. A youngster in crisis may interact with a member of a crisis team, a member of the rescue squad, an emergency room nurse, an admitting doctor, and/or a psychiatrist. Too often these professionals do not operate in cooperation with each other leaving gaping holes in the net. We know of cases where the school sent for the police and the police decided no problem existed, where the rescue squad driver told an admitting nurse that a youngster wasn't serious about killing himself, and where a youngster who slashed her wrists was sewn up and sent home from the hospital without any follow-up procedures. A critical procedure is to have a set of written procedures that is agreed upon and implemented by the entire network of health and mental health service providers.

A crisis intervention team is very important; no single individual should have to make critical, and perhaps life and death, decisions alone. In addition, the use of a team assures that qualified professional help is immediately available for a youngster in need.

The five main crisis intervention goals are to determine the risk/lethality level of a youngster who seems to be overwhelmed by stress and/or presents suicidal signals, to select an appropriate intervention plan, to counsel youngsters at "low risk," to provide psychotherapy to youngsters at "high risk," and to handle suicidal emergencies.

Once the youngster comes to the attention of a member of the crisis intervention team a risk/lethality assessment must be done immediately. Then based upon the assessment findings an appropriate intervention is selected by the team and explained to the youngster and his/her parents by a member of that team.

Youngsters judged to be at "low risk" are then provided with counseling. Here the important action is to reduce the immediate stress by selecting short term, achievable counseling objectives. Strategies are then implemented, monitored, and evaluated. Counseling is usually carried out by a mental health professional on a school or agency crisis intervention team.

Youngsters judged to be at "high risk" are provided with psychotherapy. The risk will be reassessed, a diagnosis made, and a treatment plan initiated, monitored, and evaluated. Follow-up information is given to the school and/or other referral agency. Treatment is typically conducted by psychiatrists and/or clinical psychologists in hospitals, mental health agencies, or in private practice.

All adults in the community must be prepared to handle a suicidal emergency. They must know how to provide immediate, emergency care, transfer a suicidal youngster to an emergency facility, monitor treatment at the emergency facility, and move the youngster if the treatment does not appear to be appropriate. In addition, they must provide follow-up care.

Youngsters in crisis need immediate and effective intervention. If insufficient effort is given to these youngsters in crisis, a greater number will attempt or commit suicide.

Postvention. The purpose of a postvention component is to help the community to get back to normal after a suicide has occurred. A postvention team, prepared with agreed upon procedures, springs into action when a tragedy strikes. The two main goals in postvention are to facilitate the healing process and to prevent cluster suicides.

Community members can support the family and close friends of the victim in order to help them deal with the loss. The community members must be nonjudgmental, and must listen to the bereaved but also respect their right to privacy. They might also suggest grief counseling or support groups to families needing additional help.

In order to prevent cluster suicides, the community members must help put the death in the proper perspective context. This can be done by not making a "hero" out of the victim or by not sensationalizing the story in the media. The behavior of all youth must be monitored and youngsters who seem especially distressed during a three month period of time following the suicide should be reassessed for risk/lethality. The community must try to understand the factors involved in the suicide and to use this understanding in future prevention efforts.

All three program components—inoculation, crisis intervention, and postvention—are critical to a program's success. If the task of designing the three components seems too great a drain on current resources, then develop one at a time, starting with the crisis intervention component so that youngsters who are in dire need can be assisted first. One must make sure, however, that all three are in place as soon as possible.

A Systematic Program Development Procedure

Having described the "who" (community base) and the "what" (three components) of the model we turn our attention to the "how" of the model, or the programming process. This procedure has a Getting Ready phase followed by seven basic steps (Celotta, 1979; Celotta, Lang, & Jacobs, 1981; Celotta, Jacobs, & Keys, 1985) all of which are fully described in paragraphs that follow. These steps are a logical progression from assessing needs to evaluating and revising the program, although occasionally some retracing of steps may be needed when the program bogs down. The procedure is also cyclical in nature; when on cycle is completed, another is initiated until all program goals have been met.

Getting Ready. The first step in programming begins with the selection of a program coordinator. This coordinator can be based in any community organization, but is typically located in a school system because the school has contact with virtually all of the youngsters in the community. This coordinator then obtains some hard data about the need for such a program, and armed with these data goes to the appropriate levels of administration for support. Upper levels of administration needs to be continually updated on program progress so that when final approval is needed the unexpected problems can be avoided.

Once this support is achieved the coordinator finds a few community sponsors who will help with some initial decisions such as how to get start up resources and which community leaders to approach for support and advice. Once identified, these leaders are asked to serve on an advisory committee.

The program coordinator meets with the advisory committee and discusses the need for a suicide prevention program and ways they can be involved in program development.

The advisory committee decides upon a program mission, philosophy, structure, program goals, and a program name. Next they examine projected resources of time, personnel, physical space, and materials and make plans to acquire these resources. Over time they also will determine how they will communicate with their respective groups and how they will retrain community members. Three subgroups are established to deal with the three program components. Finally, specific member roles and timelines are identified.

Assessing Needs. The inoculation, crisis intervention, and postvention subgroups meet and list and discuss those factors or need areas that appear to be contributing to the suicide problem in their community. The factors are analyzed to see if significant relationships exist among them. Each factor is then converted into a needs statement. As an example, assume that when considering an inoculation goal, a community finds that many parents in dual career families are not able to provide adequate discipline. The written needs statement might be "Parents need to find effective ways to discipline their youngsters in a minimum amount of time." These need statements are put in priority order and selected for targeting.

If more information about a need area is desired, the component subgroup can conduct a focused assessment. Here, members of one or more groups are surveyed and asked more specific questions about the particular need. In our example, the parents might be surveyed to discover the types of discipline techniques they are presently using and which ones appear to be effective.

Specifying Objectives. Once the needs assessment process is complete, the advisory committee specifies objectives. Decisions are made about what will be accomplished, how change will be measured, what criteria will be used to measure success, and by what date results are expected. In the example given previously the following objective might be written: "Parents will be using more appropriate discipline methods at home, as measured by a brief, written survey of methods used. To meet the criteria at least 80% of the parents will list two or more appropriate methods. This shall be accomplished by the need of the first program year."

Generating Alternative Strategies. Once objectives have been specified, the advisory committee finds a number of ways the objectives can be met. This can be done using brainstorming techniques with the suggested strategies recorded for later use, if necessary. In our example, the advisory committee came up with the following strategies for the objective dealing with appropriate discipline methods: devote a PTA meeting to discipline methods, run small groups for parens, hire a counselor to work with all parents who request help with discipline, use the community newspaper to inform parents about effective discipline methods, start a hotline for parents who feel they are losing control or need some guidance, and have the religious community focus on the need for proper discipline.

Selecting Strategies. The list of strategies is now pared down to the few that seem ethical and feasible. Strategies are designed in detail and a written procedure manual is prepared. In our example, running parenting groups was selected as one of several strategies that would be used to meet the particular objective. An eight-week discussion series was planned which would be lead by mental health volunteers from the community. The group format and procedures were detailed in the procedure manual along with additional strategies related to this and the other program objectives.

Implementing Strategies. At this step the program staff are selected and trained and other administrative details are considered. The larger community is informed about the implementation plans and how they might be involved. The strategies are implemented, monitored, and revised if necessary. In our example, the mental health volunteers were screened and trained, and decisions were made as to meeting times and places and ways to advertise the groups. The group sessions began and were monitored periodically by a member of the inoculation team. As a result of the monitoring, notation was made of some parents not regularly attending meetings. The inoculation committee decided that this was due to the fact that the meeting time was too early in the evening for dual career families. The time was changed and attendance improved.

Evaluating. Upon completion of each strategy or set of strategies, each objective is evaluated according to the plan in the specifying objectives step. The results are analyzed along with any additional data that may exist. The advisory committee decides how well the objective was met and whether any gain noted was worth the cost. If any objective was not fully met, the committee tries to understand why. The findings for each objective are then written and shared with the community. In our example, for the one objective focused on, the parents were surveyed at the end of the program year. Eighty-seven percent said that they used three or more discipline methods that were judged to be appropriate. In addition, the groups were becoming so popular that more groups had to be set up. The committee examined these results and decided that the objective had been met and that it was worth the expended resources. A letter was sent to community members telling of the program's success, mentioning these findings as well as findings related to the other objectives.

Revising. In this step programmatic changes are made in response to the evaluation findings or new needs arising in the community. Changes can occur in one or more program steps. In our example, the particular objective had been met at a reasonable cost. Numerous suggestions were made by community members, however, that the focus of the groups go beyond discipline, and deal with all facets of parenting. A focused assessment was planned to identify topics that would be of most interest to the parents.

Having discussed all three program features, the use of a community base, the incorporation of the program components of inoculation, crisis intervention and postvention, and the use of a systematic programming procedure, we will now describe an actual program based upon the model. Discussion of the program will be organized according to these program features.

THE LIFELINE PROGRAM

The idea for the suicide prevention program called Lifeline: Helping Students Find Positive Alternatives was conceived in Worcester County, Maryland in 1983-4 school year when information became available that at least 37 students out of a school population of approximately 5,000, had seriously contemplated suicide. By the end of 1986, a Board approved program was in place (Worcester County Public Schools, 1986). Space does not permit a detailed description of the program, but interested readers can write to the authors for information on how to obtain a copy of the program manual.

The Community Base

Worcester county is a small school district on the Eastern shore of Maryland. Youngsters come from diverse socioeconomic and cultural backgrounds. One highly positive feature of this community is that members interact frequently with each other in numerous capacities in response to community needs.

An initial meeting to discuss the program was held and more than fifty community leaders attended. Included were representatives from the school board, upper levels of administration, pupil personal services, school health services, teaching staff, PTA, student body, clergy, police department, local radio, television, and newspapers, community mental health, social service agencies, the life crisis center, and local colleges. In addition, several parents who had lost youngsters to suicide were present at the meeting. From this group, 41 participants served as advisory committee members.

The Three Components

From the beginning, the program was organized around three basic components: awareness (this is the same as the model's inoculation), crisis intervention and postvention. Each component has major goals; for example, one awareness (inoculation) goal is "to assist students in developing effective problem-solving and communication skills for dealing with emotional situations" (Worcester County Public Schools, 1986, p. 1); one crisis intervention goal is "to provide school counselors a recommended course of action which addresses the needs of at-risk students, attempters, and vulnerables" (Worcester County Public Schools, 1986, p. 3); and one postvention goal is "to provide support to the school in the event of an attempted or completed suicide" (Worcester County Public Schools, 1986, p. 3).

The Systematic Program Development Procedure

Getting Ready. When the superintendent and Board learned that 37 students had seriously considered suicide as an option, the Board members gave support to the development of a prevention program. Program co-coordinators were chosen and they selected community leaders to attend an initial three day working meeting.

At this meeting, experts talked about suicide in general and about ways the community might work to prevent it. This was followed by a general discussion during which time ideas about program mission, philosophy, and structure were discussed. Although not precisely articulated at the time, the program mission was "to gain a greater understanding of youth suicide and to develop a plan of action designed to deter Worcester County youth from this self-destructive behavior" (Worcester County Public Schools, 1986, p. i). A guiding philosophy with the following assumptions was established at that first meeting: (1) youth suicide is a tragic but preventable problem; (2) it will take the coordinated effort of all community members to remedy; (3) intervention should begin in the elementary schools or sooner; and (4) the making of positive life choices would be emphasized rather than suicide or death education.

The group decided that the program would be named Lifelines: Helping Students Find Positive Alternatives. They also decided to include the three components: awareness, crisis intervention, and postvention. Resources would come from both the Board of Education as well as from the community group representatives who would volunteer their time and expertise.

For the remaining two days, participants met in one of four subgroups: awareness, crisis intervention, postvention, and the media.

Assessing Needs. As each of the subgroups met they determined some of the major need areas for their component. For example, the postvention group decided that it was very important for a school to get back to "business as usual" in a very short time after a suicidal attempt or completion.

Each area tried to make sense of their component needs. For example, many of the needs discussed in the crisis intervention area, such as the difficulties involved in informing parents or having "round the clock" crisis assistance, seemed to be related to the larger need to have available, written procedures for every contingency in a crisis. Formal needs statements were not written, as suggested by the model. This particular group tended to be less formal about procedures.

The subgroups had reached consensus on the need areas by the third day and presented these to the entire group.

Specifying Objectives. At a subsequent working meeting, several months later, the three subgroups began to work on establishing component objectives. One of several awareness objectives selected was: "Students will continue to develop an awareness of feelings and of positive ways to deal with them" (Worcester County Public Schools, 1986, p. 1). This was to be measured by the results of teacher observation, informal feedback from counselors and peers. The criteria for this and the other objectives were not spelled out at this point, as the model suggests, but in most likelihood will be before the evaluation period begins. One of several crisis intervention objectives selected was "Students will be able to demonstrate that they are less depressed, less helpless, less hopeless" (Worcester County Public Schools,

1986, p. 31). This will be measured by the results of counselor and teacher observations, and by reports by the postvention and crisis intervention team managers.

Generating Alternative Strategies. As each subgroup worked together they thought of various ways they might meet each objective. For example, the crisis intervention group considered a variety of different ways the could assess risk and lethality.

Selecting Strategies. The subgroups considered each suggested strategy and selected those that would meet the objective efficiently. The awareness (inoculation) strategies (Kindergarten through eighth grade) were based on the use of the stories that would normally be read to or by the students. The awareness (inoculation) subgroup studied the Ginn Reading Program and looked for stories that would emphasize certain identified Lifeskills, such as developing a positive self concept and seeking help. They then did a curriculum match for these Lifeskills. Teachers would be asked to use certain additional discussion questions and follow-up activities that related to the awareness objectives. In the ninth grade the Family Life and Human Development curriculum would use a variety of suggested activities to reach the component objectives. The school counselors would supplement the program by working with youngsters who seemed under stress.

The crisis intervention subgroup designed a comprehensive procedure for handling crises on a 24 hour basis. The procedure called for the use of a trained crisis intervention team, led by the school counselor, at each school. Details, such as phone numbers of professionals who could be reached in a crisis, how to work with parents, and how to get an emergency petition at odd hours, were included, as were risk/lethality assessment and life contracts forms.

The postvention group decided that an Aftercare team was needed that would respond to any school in crisis. Emergency procedures were specified and included in a postvention packet to be kept in each school. In this packet would be, among other things, a set of instructions for using a phone tree and for conducting an early morning staff meeting, a partially filled in document that would form the basis for a press release, and a list of suggestions for dealing with the family of the victim.

At this point in the procedure the program had to receive the approval of the Worcester County Board of Education. A program framework was prepared and was then reviewed by the Board. The program was approved without a great deal of revision.

Once the program was approved a final program manual was produced and distributed to the appropriate school personnel and community members.

Implementing Strategies. At this writing counselors have received training in crisis management, parents have received training in awareness and crisis intervention skills, and plans have been made to train other groups in the community. Some teachers have begun to work with the Ginn series. The program is being monitored by the program coordinators.

Evaluating/Revising. The steps of evaluating and revising have not yet been reached. But at the appropriate time, each objective will be evaluated according to the plans previously described and decisions will be made about the costs and benefits of the program to date. The community will be informed about the evaluation findings. Revisions will be made if needed.

The program seems to be working smoothly; it continues to have community involvement and cooperation; and it has been shared with other systems in Maryland. As far as we know it is the only program nation-wide that satisfies all three suicide prevention programming requirements.

Now that we have considered the development of a specific program, an important step is to take a look at broader issues such as how we can network with other programmers, how we can expand our programs to respond to other youth issues, and how we can evaluate the effectiveness of program models.

PROGRAM NETWORKING

We feel that those involved in suicide prevention program development can make a contribution to others by sharing their ideas and resources. Those at the regional level systems can share strategies and perhaps assist in time of crisis. In one recent example a system reached out to another that was experiencing a unique tragedy and offered to send mental health personnel to assist.

Sharing needs to occur at the state level as well. A resource center at this level could provide information and materials to communities that requested them. A statewide newsletter could be distributed which reported on upcoming conferences and recommended materials. Because programmers often do not have the time to write about their programs, state based reporters can interview various programmers and can write about local prevention programs in the newsletter.

At the national level a central, suicide prevention programming clearinghouse might be established. Such a clearinghouse could be responsible for providing technical and financial assistance to model programs, conducting programmatic research, and collecting and disseminating information. In addition to its regular staff, it could have experts in suicide prevention serving terms as researchers/consultants who would be available to counties and states. The clearing house could maintain a data base that would store publications, materials, lists of speakers and consultants, as well as data kept on model programs. The database would allow researchers and program developers to have access to summary data that could be used to answer an almost unlimited number of questions such as the following: (1) What are the various systems doing in regard to prevention programming? (2) How successful is each system, or a group of systems, using their internal evaluation findings (i.e., meeting program objectives)? (3) How successful are they using external evaluation findings (i.e., actual attempt and completion rates)? (4) Is there a relationship between internal and external evaluation finding? (5) Are different regions of the country having differential success rates? (6) Do certain programs work best with certain cultural groups? In addition to using summary data, whole cases can be read by those requiring greater detail about one or more programs.

PROGRAM EXPANSION

Because much effort and many resources go into the development of suicide prevention programs, and because the hope is that the crisis intervention and postvention components will not be needed too often, the desire would be to have the programs serve more than one purpose. Once the community is working as a team and solving its suicide problems in a systematic way, other types of problems may be processed by the team. Problems such as drug and alcohol abuse, a high dropout rate, and teen pregnancies all require a systematic, community approach for adequate resolution.

A new subgroup could be selected to work on one of these or other pressing concerns. The subgroup can explore ways the existing prevention program can be used for a new purpose. Most new problems can probably be subsumed under the existing program, particularly if stress has been a program focus, because almost all major problems experienced by our youngsters have been correlated with increased stress and increased suicide risk.

If the new problem is to be incorporated into the existing program structure, some slight modifications may be needed to the program goals. The advisory committee then would proceed as they normally do with the seven steps of program development previously described.

COMPARING PROGRAM MODELS

We must learn about what program models produce the best results for what types of communities. We feel that the federal government and/or national suicide organizations should evaluate program models by sponsoring a nationwide, suicide prevention program development and evaluation effort.

To find out what types of models are most effective, the clearinghouse previously described, could sponsor a number of programs using a variety of program models, and see which are most effective from an internal and external evaluation perspective. Systems selected for sponsorship would be required to specify the program model and record program progress in a standard way (to be used in the database discussed). Internal data to be recorded would include, at a minimum, a statement of need and the underlying problems in the system, a statement of program objectives, a description of program strategies and materials, a statement of the evaluation findings, and a description of problems faced. External data to be recorded would include records of the number of suicides, attempted suicides, and accidents in the system.

Until we systematically evaluate our program models we are in a most precarious position.

CONCLUSION

Much needs to be done at all levels—individual, community, regional, state and national—if we are to help our young choose life. If developing a comprehensive program seems overwhelming, it can be. If it seems to require an enormous commitment and sacrifice, it does. If you are wondering if your community should develop such a program, it should, it must, for all of our youngsters are awaiting your help.

REFERENCES

Barrett, T. (1981). *The self-destructive behavior of adolescents seeking solutions.* Denver, CO: Cherry Creek Schools.

Celotta, B. (1979). The systems approach: A technique for establishing counseling and guidance programs. *American Personnel and Guidance Journal, 57,* 412-4.

Celotta, B. (1985). Preventing suicide and depression: Starting early. St. Mary's County, MD: Paper presented at Eight Annual Child Welfare Day.

Celotta, B., & Jacobs,G. (1982). Children's needs: Implications for guidance programs in the 80s. *The School Counselor, 30,* 50-6.

Celotta, B., Jacobs, G., & Keys, S.G. (1985). *Designing accountable mental health programs,* Workbook. 14904 Piney Grove Court, Gaithersburg, MD: Celotta, Jacobs, & Keys Associates, Inc.

Celotta, B., Jacobs, G., & Keys, S. (1987). Searching for suicidal precursors in the elementary school child. *American Mental Health Counselors Journal, 9,* 1, 38-50.

Celotta, B., Lang, J., & Jacobs, G. (1981). A systems-oriented social development program. *The School Counselor, 28,* 285-90.

Celotta, B., & Sobol, E. (1983). Needs assessment: Reconciliation of children's, parents', and teachers' views. *Education, 104, 2,* 176-9.

Cohen-Sandler, R., Berman, A., & King, R. (1982). Life stress and symptomatology: Determinants of suicidal behavior in children. *Journal of the American Academy of Child Psychiatry, 21,* 178-86.

Department of Health and Human Services, National Center for Health Statistics (1984). *Advance report of final mortality statistics, 1982. Monthly Vital Statistics Report, 33,* 9. Supplement. U.S. Department of Health and Human Services.

Department of Health and Human Services, Project Share. (1986). Left behind. *Sharing, 9,* 2, p. 2.

Department of Health and Human Services, Project Share. (1986a). A lesson in prevention. *Sharing, 9,* 2.

Department of Health and Human Services, Project Share (1986b). Dallas action against suicide. *Sharing, 9,* 2, pp. 4-8.

Eisenberg, L. (1984). The epidemiology of suicide in adolescents. *Pediatric Annals, 13,* 1, 47-53.

Fairfax County Public Schools, Department of Student Services and Special Education. (1985). *The adolescent suicide prevention program.* Fairfax, VA.

Freese, A. (1979). Adolescent suicide: Mental health challenge. Public Affairs Pamphlet No. 569, New York.

Freiberg, K. (1983). *Human development: A life-span approach* (2nd ed.). Monterey, CA: Wadsworth.

Hawton, K. (1986). *Suicide and attempted suicide among children and adolescents.* Beverly Hills, CA: Sage.

Office of the Inspector General, Office of Analysis and Inspections. (1986). *Inventory of state initiatives in addressing youth suicide: National program inspection,* control #p-09-86-00099.

U.S. News and World Report. (Nov. 12, 1984), pp. 49-50.

Worcester County Board of Education. (1986). *Lifelines: Helping students find positive alternatives.* Worcester County, MD.

CHAPTER **11**

INTERVENTIONS WITH NATIVE AMERICANS

James B. Jordan, M.S.

James B.Jordan, M.S.

National Center for American Indian &
Alaska Native Mental Health Research
Dept. of Psychiatry
University of Colorado Health Sciences Center
Denver, CO 80262

James B. Jordan, M.S. is currently a Doctoral Candidate at the University of Denver Counseling Psychology Department. He is working on research at the National Center for American Indian and Alaska Native Mental Health Center in Denver, Colorado, the only NIMH funded center for American Indians in the country. He is Choctaw Indian and was reared in several cultures in the United States and abroad. Current research interests are in cross-cultural psychology, minority mental health concerns, suicide prevention, and training non-Indian therapists working with American Indian clients. His other interests are in oil paining and kayaking.

EDITORIAL ABSTRACT: *Native American adolescents are at high risk for suicide attempts and completions. This chapter discusses Native American suicide trends; treatment issues such as intentionality, self-report measures, diagnostic protocols and the use of the DSM-III; treatment approaches such as client roles, psychoanalytical and existential foundations, family and systems therapy, cognitive-behavioral therapy and group therapy; and, implications for future investigation. Practitioners who work with Native American adolescents will find the contents of this chapter pertinent and useful.*

Psychotherapy with Native American clients offers a challenge to the culturally aware therapist. At issue are the underlying premises of western psychology and value orientations within psychotherapy. The core issue is the generalizability of therapeutic processes that have been developed within a European (or "western" cultural context). Do western oriented psychotherapies work well with non-western or traditional peoples? The purposes of this chapter are to critically examine western therapies in the cultural context of Native Americans and to examine methods to modify existing therapy approaches to fit Native American cultural perspectives. Although traditional Native American healing approaches to depression are viewed as being important, the scope of the present chapter focuses only on western therapies. Psychotherapy is based upon several clinician conceptual tools that most be examined: psychological processes, diagnostic self-reports and protocols, and the DSM-III (APA, 1980). The term Native American will be used throughout this chapter to refer to all indigenous people of the continental United States, Canada, and Alaska.

The recent (1985) epidemic of suicide by nine adolescent and young adult men on the Wind River Reservation in Wyoming has again reminded the Unites States of the mental health problems of Native Americans on reservations. The initial response by the national media has framed these problems in terms of the hopelessness that prevails on the reservations (Rocky Mountain News, Denver, 1985). Tribal leaders and counselors have described the repeated method by hanging as a sickness of some kind and a domino effect. Consulting psychiatrists and psychologists from regional mental health facilities have described these young Native American men as not being sure of what their cultural identity is.

They expressed concerns that they can't treat the depression if they don't know who the individuals in need are. The common themes are the issues of poverty, cultural adaptation versus cultural identity, and the unique relationship that Native Americans have with the United States government.

An overview of the incidence of Native American suicide reveals a disproportionate rate for this population (Bynum, 1972; Havighurst, 1971; McIntosh & Santos, 1981). However, the image of a "suicidal Indian" in despair is not accurate. Shore (1975) has disputed this stereotype and cites tribal specific suicide rates to demonstrate this inaccurate portrayal. Suicide rates vary greatly among different tribes; the annual rate ranges from 8 to 100 per 100,000.

Mental health professionals have reported on Native American suicide since the 1930s (Devereaux, 1942, 1961). Devereaux's early work in this area explored Mohave suicide from a psychoanalytic perspective. Pine (1981) investigated ethnographic reports to determine what role suicide has played in Native American tradition. He noted that suicide was traditionally infrequent and not an esteemed social value. Many of the tribes believed a person who committed suicide could not enter the afterworld. The range of attitudes in traditional settings was wide. Sanctions ranged from for suicide to strong sanctions against suicide. For example, the Delaware did not condemn suicide but viewed it as a form of insanity to be pitied (Heckwelder, 1819). Whereas, the Choctaw viewed suicide very negatively, not only denying the suicide a proper burial, but also considering the person an enemy (Swanton, 1928, 1931). Pine (1981) found that some traditions contrast with modern demographics such as the historically higher rate of suicide among Native American women than men.

Native American Suicide Trends

The generally accepted concept is that this population as a group shows suicide rates higher than those for the general population, although the estimate rates vary from twice to slightly higher than the national average (McIntosh & Santos, 1981; Swenson, 1969; Webb & Williard, 1975). In the Native American suicide literature is indicated the similar phenomena to the general population of females having more attempts at suicide; and males having more successful suicide attempts (Havighurst, 1971; McIntosh & Santos, 1981; NIMH, 1975). The most disturbing fact, however, is the average age of suicide among this population. Among many of the Native American tribes, the risk of suicide peaks during the adolescent and young adult development stages (Clarke, in press; May, 1987; McIntosh & Santos, 1981). The critical time of incidence of suicide for Native Americans is between the ages of 15 and 24 with a consistent decline thereafter. This statistic is contrary to the national average of a peak in old age (McIntosh & Santos, 1981). Therefore, suicide prevention should begin in early adolescence.

Several authors have summarized the suicide rates by regions: the Arctic coast and Canada (Balicki, 1960, 1961; Butler, 1965; Forbes & Van Der Hyde, in press; Fox & Ward, 1977; Frausm, 1974; Kraus, 1971, 1974; Kraus & Buffler, 1975; MacLean, 1979; Parkin, 1974; Seyer, 1979; Travis, 1983; Ward & Fox 1977; Ward, Fox, & Evans, 1977; Ward, 1979); the Northwest (Cutler & Morrison, 1971; Shore, 1972; Termansen & Peters, 1979); and the plains (Barter & Weist, 1970; Bynum, 1972). Not all the regions have been summarized.

Many tribal specific patterns of suicide have been documented: the Navajo with a very low rate of suicide (Levy, 1965; Levy, Kunitz & Everett, 1969; Miller & Schoenfeld, 1971, 1973; Miller, 1979; Wyman & Thorne, 1945); the Shoshone-Bannock with a very high rate (Dizmang, 1968); the Cheyenne (Barter & Weist, 1970; Curlee, 1969; Dizmang, 1967); the Papago (Conrad, 1972; Conrad & Kahn, 1973); the Shoshone-Paiute (Duck Valley, 1970); the Apache (Everett, 1970; Levy & Kunitz, 1962); the Iroquois (Fenton, 1941); the Cherokee and Lumbee (Humphrey & Kupferer, 1982); the Eskimo (Leighton & Hughes, 1955; Maynard & Twiss, 1970; Mindell & Stuart, 1968); the Blackfeet (Pambrun, 1979); the Quinault (Patterson, 1969); the Ojibwa or Chippewa (Spaulding, (1985); and summarily by McIntosh, & Santos, (1981) and McIntosh, (1984).

PSYCHOLOGICAL PROCESSES AND TREATMENT ISSUES

Intentionality

Suicidal death is not a clear concept when viewed as a psychological process. Death may be classified as intentional, unintentional, and subintentional (Shneidman, 1967). A definition of *intentional death* is self explanatory—suicide. *Unintentional death* refers to death as an accident, no intention—consciously or otherwise. *Subintentional* death is the psychological construct of suicide by unconscious motivations. This latter category takes into account all kinds of deaths about which the degree of intentionality is unknown. Subintentional death probably accounts for a large number of Native American deaths, although they are not reported as such. Examples of subintentional death with Native Americans would be the act of suicide by drinking oneself to death, ignoring the warning labels of spray paint cans and "huffing" the poisonous fumes, and binge drinking and then driving.

The National Institute of Mental Health (NIMH, 1975) suggested that subintentional death and intentional death can be viewed as a continuum of self-destructive behaviors—from self-assaultive to self-destructive to suicidal. When an individual abuses himself/herself without full awareness of its life-threatening aspects, the term used for such behavior is self-assaultive. Indian binge drinking would be an example of this behavior. When individuals have known about physical problems and take no corrective measures to care for themselves, the term for this behavior is self-destructive. Suicidal behavior is a clear plan with intentionality. The Wind River reservation adolescents that committed suicide by hanging is a sad, but clear example.

A brief summary of treatment issues most common with this population and the literature which summarizes the topic include alcohol (Binton, Miller, Beauvais, & Oetting, in press; Loretto, Beauvais, & Oetting, in press, Mail & McDonald, 1980, NIMH, 1975) Snake, Hawkins, & LaBoueff, 1976); alienation (Holmgren, Fitzgerald, & Carman, 1983; Oetting, Beauvais, & Edwards, in press); drug abuse (Beauvais & Oetting, in press; Beauvais, Oetting, & Edwards, 1985; Binion et al., in press); family dynamics (Berlin, 1985); acculturation and assimilation (Barnouw, 1950; Berry, Wintorb, Sindell, & Mawhinney, 1981; Hippler, 1969; Kahn, 1982); cross-cultural depression (Miller & Schoenfeld, 1973; Shore, 1979; Shore & Manson, 1981); and reservation vs. urban issues (Borunda & Shore, 1978).

DIAGNOSTIC PROBLEMS

Self-Report Measures

Several problems accompany assessment of depressed and suicidal Native American adolescents. Psychiatric assessment has long been questioned with this population. Manson, Walker, and Kivlahan (1987) summarized some of the inherent validity, reliability, and specificity problems of the assessment self-rating scales—*Cornell Medical Index, Health Opinion Survey (HOS), Alcohol Use Inventory,* and *Minnesota Multiphasic Personality Inventory (MMPI).* These authors summarized that the *Cornell Medical Index* proved to be invalid with 38 items with Eskimo populations. However, another review with Oklahoma Indians had far less problems (Martin, Sutker, Leon, et al., 1968). Some items were problematic but overall the instrument seemed to be reliable with the Oklahoma population. The HOS appears to have had acceptable validity when compared to the independent clinical assessments with certain Eskimo populations and Pacific Northwest coast Indians. But with some Eskimo populations, the HOS scores bore little relation to clinical judgment in the moderate to mild impairment categories.

The MMPI is the most common psychological measure used in assessment in the U.S., including Native American populations. An important aspect to remember in assessment of adolescents is that this instrument has a bottom age reliability of 15 or 16 years of age. Pollack and Shore (1980) reported significant elevations on the subscales F (Validity), Pd, and Sc, for Northwest Coast, Plateau, and Plains tribes. Plains Indians were found to have the highest F and Hy scores. The researchers stated that "there is significant cultural influence on the results of the MMPI in this population...It appears that cultural influence overrides individual pathology and personality differences in influencing the pattern of the MMPI" (p. 948). These elevated scores may be misinterpreted by therapists as a more bizarre or deviant personality structure than is present. Pollack and Shore (1980) pointed out the differential diagnostic problems between nonpsychotic depression and schizophrenia using the MMPI with this population. They suggested that Native Americans appear to describe their symptomatology of nonpsychotic depression and schizophrenia in an identical manner. Dana (1986) stated that because the MMPI is a criteria-based test, an imposed etic (assumed universal trait) is often inappropriately placed on Native American responses. The Pollack and Shore study and others (Dana, 1983; Hoffman, Dana, & Bolton, 1985) demonstrated the inherent problems of the MMPI and the underlying assumptions of these imposed ethics with clinical diagnosis.

Other diagnostic problems using assessment devices with Native American populations were summarized by Dana (1986), including the Rorschach and Thematic Apperception Test.

Diagnostic Protocols

In contrast to the self-report measures as listed above, diagnostic protocols appear to have more reliability in the diagnosing of Native American depression. However, the worldview of Native Americans regarding depressive features do not fit neatly into classic DSM-III criteria. Manson, Shore, and Bloom (1985) demonstrated differences in the reporting of depressive features by the Hopi—using a structured diagnostic interview (*The Schedule for Affective Disorders and Schizophrenia—Lifetime Version* or SADS-L), the *Diagnostic Interview Schedule (DIS)*, and the *American Indian Depression Schedule* (AIDS)—Hopi version. They pointed out that the Hopi appear to differentiate depressive symptoms into eight categories of problems having to do with (1) appetite change, (2) abnormal sleeping patterns, (3) fatigue, (4) psychomotor retardation or agitation, (5) marked disinterest in sex, (6) a low sense of self-worth, (7) disoriented thought processes, and (8) suicidal ideation. The therapist must decide upon which categories are cultural specific and (non-DSM-III clinical diagnosis) and which are major depressive disorder criteria. The diagnosis is contingent in part on the presence of one or more symptoms in five of the eight Hopi categories of depressive symptoms. From the Manson et al. (1985) study the indications are that more reliability is with diagnostic protocols in assessing depression, but caution is still advised with culture specific indices of grieving.

Diagnostic and Statistical Manual of Mental Disorders (DSM-III)

Diagnosis of major depression and dysthymic disorder using the DSM-III is contingent upon criteria involving length of time of symptoms. A cultural bias exists in the DSM-III regarding concepts of time in regard to Native American patients. One particular DSM-III bias concerns temporal concepts of grieving. For the diagnosis of major depressive episode, the DSM-III specifies the presence of four of eight depressive symptoms nearly every day for at least two weeks; in children under six, at least three of the first four symptoms. For the diagnosis of dysthymic disorder a two year time duration of symptoms is required for adults—for adolescents and children, one year is sufficient (American Psychiatric Association, 1980). For some tribes of Native Americans such as the Hopi, the socially expected time of grieving for a death is a year. This may mean depressive features when in fact they are acting according to culture specific expectations. If another death occurs in the extended family during this grieving time, the time is extended. Other examples of culture specific grieving process were summarized by Lewis (1975), Manson and Shore (1981), and Peniston (1978).

For the diagnostician using the DSM-III with Native American patients, the clinical judgment should include considerations of the patient's framework of time and grieving in differentiating major depressive episode, dysthymic disorder, uncomplicated bereavement, and other conditions with depressive features.

To summarize the diagnostic problems inherent in working with Native Americans, the therapist should be informed of the shortcomings of self-assessment measures, diagnostic protocols and diagnostic manuals such as the DSM-III. One danger is that of over pathologizing.

TREATMENT APPROACHES

Client Roles

Therapy in the western sense has the client's expectation of a high value placed on vocabulary, self-disclosure, introspective-analysis, a desire for self-conscious change, and the assumption of active client behavior change. To the western therapist, traditional Native American people quite often appear passive, both in their demeanor and in their thinking processes. What is actually occurring in initial client sessions is that the therapist is being observed in a slow deliberate fashion—time is of no consequence.

introduction, observing, and initiating polite, formal conversation are all a traditional process of interaction.

Dinges, Trimble, Manson, and Pasquale (1981) discussed the traditional Navaho role expectations of the client. They noted that one of the reservation therapist's goals is to get the client more actively involved with their own treatment. This western therapist action-orientation is at odds with the traditional Navaho's disvaluation of preoccupation with self, introspection, and self-disclosure. In addition, this cultural conflict will result in the therapist labeling the client "resistant."

Therapy with adolescent suicide prevention has to take traditional values into consideration as a part of the patient/therapist dyad. The time allotted to patients may need to be redefined. With the immediacy of potential suicide, the cross-cultural therapist is placed in a bind—a bind that the therapist must resolve. At present, no dependable clinical methods are reported in the literature that can help resolve this ethical bind of patient welfare versus professional competence. However, cultural sensitivity and training in cross-cultural psychology can prepare the therapist not to blunder through the client crisis. By not assuming the client's passivity as yet another depressive indicator, the therapist may be able to enter the client's world and begin an understanding of the dynamics.

Psychoanalytical and Existential Foundations

The premises of Psychoanalytic and Exitential psychotherapy are that these concepts are universal to all people. By accepting this western viewpoint the therapist is able to organize his/her thoughts in to a working construct from which to operate. An important aspect as this point is to draw attention to the Cartesian concept of mind/body duality upon which Psychoanalysis and Existential psychotherapy is based. To the therapist, the turmoil of the client is an interaction of the mind as a separate entity—with the physical body and its biological urges. In fact, all western psychotherapists are based upon this Cartesian premise. The one exception is not a psychotherapy per se, that of Behaviorism. Some Native American worldviews do not differentiate between the mind as a separate entity from the physical body.

The general characteristics of the dynamic structure of psychoanalysis (Yalom, 1980) is the formula:

DRIVE —> ANXIETY —> DEFENSE MECHANISM

The dynamic structure of existential psychotherapy is the formula:

AWARENESS OF CONCERN —> ANXIETY —> DEFENSE MECHANISM

Both formulas make the assumptions that conscious and unconscious psychic operations evolve to deal with anxiety—these defense mechanisms constitute psychopathology; and humans are driven by anxiety to psychopathology such as depression.

To some Native American tribes such as the traditional Seminole, disease (depression) was caused by spirits entering the body. This is a common belief across tribes and Alaskan natives. The difference is the western and traditional native worldviews may be seen in the light of Rotter's internal/external locus of control (albeit, this neat dichotomy does not always work well). The psychoanalysis and existentialists have a bias of interpretation toward internal locus of control. That is psychopathologies derive from internal sources; whether they are biological in nature (psychoanalytic drive) or mental (existential awareness). Traditional Native American belief systems quite often attribute human behavior in response to external (environmental) spirits and forces. With these worldview assumptions in mind, the following therapies are given a Native American perspective in their content.

Existential Psychotherapy

Existential crises are an integral part of the suicidal Native American adolescent. The following existential concepts, death, isolation, meaninglessness, and freedom are used as a format to discuss the therapeutic issues of Native American adolescents. The assumption of this therapy is that these are ultimate concerns of all humans.

Death. The author's opinion is that existential crises occur at earlier ages for Native Americans—in contrast to Anglos. Based on statistics the Native American suicide peaking in adolescence and early adulthood, there appears to be an early understanding by Native Americans of the larger context of being Indian. The speculation is that a realization of their race's political and cultural history with the majority Anglo culture is a predecessor to existential crises. Not only has this history been with the Anglo people, but especially with the United States government. In the Native American group memory is the perception of a dying of a tribal way of life and culture. This may even be perceived as a death of a race. This perception is not literally true, but the perceived theme may be. The strong basis of reality to this perception is that the United States government has indeed broken every treaty that has been signed for the preservation of the Native American way of life (Deloria, 1969). For the Native American adolescent, this realization of death is a precipitator for the formulation of a lowered self esteem, self image, and (presumed) existential crisis. This crisis occurring at a younger age, when less ego strength, more impulsiveness, and less acquired social interaction skills would precipitate a higher suicide rate with this age group.

Isolation. Native American youth may become aware that their people are isolated from the majority culture. This realization and experience of isolation probably are at both a conscious and an unconscious level. Similar to Frankl's (1959) experience of isolation at a personal level and as a Jew in the Nazi concentration camps, Native Americans may experience a total isolation that is the American policy history of reservations and Indian Territory (i.e., Oklahoma). For Native Americans, their history has been a predominate theme of separation and physical isolation of their people. Native Americans have been isolated physically, emotionally, and mentally from their White neighbors. They have been mentally isolated from the dominate culture's WASP worldview. This has been an especially important issue as acculturation/ assimilation issues are widely quoted as central to understanding the Native American despair. In addition, isolation is anathema to the Native American worldview—a harmony of tribal group and nature.

Meaninglessness. For the Native American adolescent growing up in a dual world of traditional and majority culture, the difficulty is to create meaning in their existence. Acculturation and assimilation play a key role in this struggle of "being."

For the purpose of clarity, the terms acculturation and assimilation need to be defined. These terms are often used indiscriminately in the anthropological and cross-cultural *psychology* literature. For our purposes, *acculturation* is when the individual indicates the majority cultural values; the reference point of being is to the Anglo culture—away from the individual's Native culture. *Assimilation* is the universal process of adaptation to another culture—while keeping one's own culture in context. The point of reference is the Native culture in relationship to the foreign culture.

For the Native American adolescent, the process of acculturation can be an extremely negative experience. The sense of being can be made meaningless if traditional values are not handed down. This is further complicated by what language is taught first. The worldview of Native Americans are formed from the concepts inherent in the tribal language. If English is taught first, the worldview is acculturated to western meaning.

In addition, Indian adolescents have to deal with their "Indianness." Indianness is the self-conscious identity that may or may not be stereotypical and has the aspect of expectations of being Indian that is assigned by the media, the American mythology, and also by genuine traditional Indian values. For some adolescents living in traditional settings such as the Navaho or Hopi reservation, Indianness may not be as big a consideration as it is to urban Indians. However, the reservation adolescent interacting with Anglo adolescents is reminded of their difference. Many stereotypical images are of being a "real Indian" with which adolescent has to come to grips. The process of "becoming" during adolescence is a sensitive self-awareness. The traditional coming of age ceremonies marked a clear identity and placed the adolescent in the expected role of his/her sex, tribal position, and family presence in relationship to the larger group. With the erosion of these ceremonies, the Native American adolescent does not have that clear identity. Adolescent development has been made meaningless with the erosion of these ceremonies and subsequent acculturation.

The treatment issue for the existential therapist is to help the adolescent find meaning in context to their being Native American without forcing the stereotypes of "Indianness." In addition a sensitivity toward cultural identity by the therapist is necessary to help the client keep their Native American culture as the point of reference in their being—and to help the (inevitable) assimilation process of interaction with the Anglo culture.

Freedom. For the Native American adolescent who is struggling with the existential crises of meaninglessness, the issue may be one of control. The perception may be made that the Anglo culture has all the control over the individual's live. The adolescent may seek ways to regain that sense of control. Out of despair the Native American adolescent may consider the idea of suicide as an act of regaining that perceived lost control. Maybe suicide is an act of regaining meaningfulness—by seeking freedom in death. However, this may be complicated by a distorted learning/modeling process. An example of a distorted learning process can be seen in the Wind River example. One hanging immediately followed another; during the funeral, yet another hanging occurred. These individuals were also probably acting under the muddled thinking process of depressive thought disorder. Without healthy thinking processes occurring, suicide was an easy alternative. This final act to regain freedom may be a part of an overall sequential existential crises for Native Americans in this state of crises.

The therapist and community mental health planners should concentrate preventive measures around this existential phenomenon. The mental health community should consider providing culture-specific methods to offer alternatives to this distorted view of loss of freedom. The act of suicide may become a viable alternative to the existential pain of loss of meaning in life and loss of freedom. The therapist's goal is to instill alternatives to interpretation of freedom.

Family and Systems Therapy

For the Native American adolescent, the sense of "being" is in relation to the family, the group, the tribe. This group dynamic is not true of all Native American adolescents. When it is not, it may be an indicator of a possible negative acculturation issue. This sense of "being" in a group context implies working within the individual's worldview and value system. For the urban Indian youth or the Indian youth residing in a non-Indian environment, there usually is a very real sense of identity with being a part of this ethnic group, but at a sublimated level. Sometimes this takes on the cultural phenomenon of "Pan-Indianness"—that is, the youth identifies with a blend of many tribal beliefs. Whatever the case may be, the therapist should look for the Native context of group-belongingness as a part of the family/system.

Family therapy focuses on the familial worldview of the client(s). The family's value system is the immediate context for the identified adolescent client. By working in this context, the therapist is able to more closely align with the client's value system and dynamics of being—and to facilitate change.

Attneave (1982) suggested that the source of Native American family disturbances and symptoms is not too different from those of other families: "enmeshment and lack of generational boundaries, well-meant but misdirected efforts to forge working relationships, misunderstandings of self and others, reenactment of the results of cutoff relationships, effects associated with unfinished grief work, and the need to cope without being overwhelmed by anxiety" (p. 61).

However, importance should be placed upon the adolescent's suicidal behavior in the context of the family's value system. Questions to consider with Native American adolescents should include the following: Is the suicidal ideation a result of an enmeshed family and a possible acting-out? Are generational boundaries culturally prescribed, or are they true enmeshment? Does acculturation and the blurring of cultural generational roles play a part in this perceived lack of boundaries? Does the adolescent follow culturally specific expressions of grieving—when a friend or relative has died? If so, what are the family's cultural expectations of mourning?

Systems theory would incorporate the broader dynamics of the individual in relation to tribe or tribal group (e.g., confederated tribes). The individual's self concept could be made more tangible by relating to the relationships of family honor, tribal position, and value relationship to peers. Systems based theory also may imply an activist role for the therapist. This might include community mental health lectures, home visits to significant others, consultation with tribal leaders and elders, and generally being a working part of the system. This may prove difficult for the outside-the-system organized crisis team.

Cognitive-Behavioral Therapy

As Beck (1967; 1977) has articulated about suicide, it is most closely related to the depressive triad of negative self-conception, negative interpretations of one's experiences, and a negative view of the future. To the Native American adolescent, these cognitive distortions may be made up of such self—statements as, "I can't live (perfect) traditional values, therefore I must die"; or "I can't control my life, I must regain control by freeing myself through death"; or "There's no future in being 'Indian'." In addition, the individual can assume a dichotomous cognitive distortion of either a perfect traditional way of life—or of becoming "white." The cognitive-behavior therapist works to change these cognitive distortions by seeking alternative belief systems with the client and client integration of positive cognitions. In utilizing a specific treatment approach like Beck's cognitive-behavioral therapy, therapists are able to articulate suicide counseling in explicit, meaningful terms; the therapists is able to be concrete and more action oriented than in the philosophical existential and psychological therapies.

Group Therapy

Several authors have written anecdotal descriptions of successful group work with Native Americans (Edwards & Edwards, 1974, 1980, 1984; Edwards, Edwards, Daines, & Eddy, 1978; McDonald, 1975). Kahn, Lewis, and Galvez (1974) ran an evaluation study of a group therapy procedure with Papagos but did not design the group therapy for psychological outcome or process. Instead, their evaluation of outcome was based upon a correlation of arrest and school absence to success of group therapy. In the literature controlled studies concerning efficacy, outcome, or process with this population using group therapy do not appear. However, a logical conclusion would be that this form of therapy would be a worthwhile method considering the high value Native Americans place on group interaction and matriarchial group consensus. Several issues are involved in group work with Native Americans that should be noted. Respect for the privacy of others may be a particular concern in group dynamics.

Traditionally, Native Americans do not speak for others out of a respect for their autonomy and independence. Edwards and Edwards (1984) suggested that for Native Americans to assess the feelings of their significant others may be inappropriate. An important aspect for many Native Americans is not to embarrass or dishonor themselves, their family, or friends. By seeking professional help, adolescents may be bringing discredit to their families. Once again, the assumptions of a western therapy may be at odds with traditional Native American values. The presumption in this form of therapy is that one can ask open questions of an intimate nature to all of the group members. An ethical dilemma for the therapist in this situation is whether to impose western values of inquiry or not. The welfare of clients and their age level of non-autonomy are issues to be considered in group suicide prevention. Apparently a necessary procedure is to impose western values of inquiry to help facilitate group dynamics (and therefore maintain appropriate client welfare ethics), but equally important is to modify group techniques to accommodate the needed respect for the client's cultural norms so that the group dynamics work. Research and more study in this area of therapy would appear to be of high value.

Several of the more popular therapies have been examined and with modification, their efficacy could remain intact. By implementing cultural specific values to existing therapy approaches, synthesizing a viable therapeutic environment is possible. Each of the therapies discussed have inherent cultural conflicts. The suggestion is that traditional Native American therapies such as the talking circle, sweat lodges with healing ceremonies, medicine ceremonies by traditional healers be examined for potential use in suicide prevention. But just as western therapies must be scrutinized for their efficacy, so should traditional Native American therapies. This topic is beyond the scope of the present chapter but should be given much importance in future research.

REFERENCES

American Psychiatric Association. (1980). *Diagnostic and statistical manual of mental disorders*, (third edition). Washington, D.C.: APA.

Attneave, C. (1982). American Indians and Alaska Native families: Emigrants in their own homeland. In M. McGoldrick, J.K. Pearce, & J. Giordano (Eds.), *Ethnicity & family therapy* (pp. 55-83). New York: Guilford.

Balikci, A. (1960). Research on Arvilikjuarmiut suicide patterns. *Transcultural Research in Mental Health, 8*, 35-6.

Balikci, A. (1961). Suicidal behavior among the Netsilik Eskimos. *North, 8*(4), 12-9.

Barnouw, V. (1950). Acculturation and personality among the Wisconsin Chippewa. American Anthropological Association. *Memoirs, 52*(4), Series No. 72.

Barter, J.T., & Weist, K.M. (1970). *Historical and contemporary patterns of Northern Cheyenne suicide.* Paper presented at the Meeting of the American Psychiatric Association, San Francisco.

Beauvais, F., & Oetting, E.R. (In press). Indian youth and inhalants: An update. *Epidemiology of inhalant use.* NIDA Monograph. Rockville, MD: NIDA.

Beauvais, F., Oetting, E.R., & Edwards, R.W. (1985). Trends in the use of inhalants among American Indian adolescents. *White Cloud Journal, 3*(4), 3-11.

Beck, A.T. (1967). *Depression: Clinical, experimental, and theoretical aspects.* New York: Harper & Row.

Beck, A., Rush, A.J., & Kovacs, M. (1977). *Individual treatment manual for cognitive-behavioral psychotherapy of depression.* Unpublished manuscript, Philadelphia General Hospital, Philadelphia, PA.

Berlin, I.N. (1985). *Suicide among American Indian adolescents.* Washington, D.C.: National American Indian Court Judges Association.

Berry, J.W., Wintorb, R.M., Sindell, P.S., & Mawhinney, T.A. (1981). *Psychological adaptation to culture change among the James Bay Cree.* Paper presented at the 5th International Circumpolar Health Symposium, Copenhagen.

Binion,, A., Miller, D.C., Beauvais, F., & Oetting, E.R (In press). Rationales for the use of alcohol, marijuana, and other drugs by Indian youth. *International Journal of the Addictions.*

Borunda, P., & Shore, J.H. (1978). Neglected minority—urban Indians and mental health. *International Journal of Social Psychiatry, 24*(3), 220-4.

Butler, G.C. (1965). Incidence of suicide among the ethnic groups of the northwest territories and Yukon territory. *Medical Services Journal, 21*, 252-6.

Bynum, J. (1972). Suicide and the American Indian: An analysis of recent trends. In H.M. Bahr, B.A. Chadwick, & R.C. Day (Eds.), *Native Americans today: Sociological perspectives,* (pp. 367-77). New York: Harper & Row.

Clarke, G.N. (In press). Treatment of depression and suicide among American Indian youth. *American Indian and Alaska Native Mental Health Research: Journal of the National Center.*

Conrad, R.D., & Kahn, M.W. (1973). An epidemiological study of suicide and suicide attempts among the Papago Indians. *Proceedings, 81st Annual Convention, American Psychological Association, 8, part 1*, pp. 449-50.

Conrad, R.D. (1972). *Suicide among the Papago Indians.* Master's Thesis, University of Arizona, Dept. of Psychiatry.

Curlee, W.V. (1969). Suicide and self-destructive behavior on the Cheyenne River reservation. In *Suicide Among the American Indians, 34-6.* (USPHS Publication No. 1903). Washington, D.C.: Government Printing Office.

Cutler, R., & Morrison, N. (1971). *Sudden death: A study of characteristics of victims and events leading to sudden death in British Columbia with primary emphasis on apparent alcohol involvement and Indian Sudden deaths.* Vancouver, B.C.: Alcoholism Foundation of British Columbia.

Dana, R.H. (1983, March). Assessment of Native Americans: Guidelines and a format for test interpretation. In R.H. Dana (Chair), *Psychological assessment of Native Americans.* Symposium conducted at the meeting of the Society for Personality Assessment, San Diego, CA.

Dana, R.H. (1986). Personality assessment of Native Americans. *Journal of Personality Assessment, 50*(3), 480-500.

Deloria, Jr, V. (1969). *Custer died for your sins.* New York: Avon.

Devereaux, G. (1942). Primitive psychiatry II: Funeral suicide and the Mohave social structure. *Bulletin of the History of Medicine, 11*(5), 522-42.

Devereaux, G. (1961). Mohave ethnopsychiatry and suicide: The psychiatric knowledge and psychic disturbances of an Indian tribe. *Smithsonian Institution Bureau of American Ethnology Bulletin 175.* Washington, D.C.: U.S. Government Printing Office. (Part 7, pp. 286-484).

Dinges, N.G., Trimble, J.E., Manson, S.M., & Pasquale, F.L. (1981). Counseling and psychotherapy with American Indians and Alaska Natives. In A.J. Marsella & P.B. Pedersen (Eds.), *Cross-cultural counseling & psychotherapy,* (pp. 243-78). New York: Pergamon.

Dizmang, L.H. (1967). Suicide among the Cheyenne Indians. *Bulletin of Suicidology, 1,* 8-11.

Dizmang, L.H. (1968). *Observations on suicidal behavior among the Shoshone Bannock Indians.* Paper presented at the First Annual National Conference on Suicidology, Chicago, IL (12P).

Duck Valley Indian Reservation Tribal Mental Health Committee. (1970). *Suicide among the Shoshone-Paiute on the Duck Valley Indian Reservation: A survey report.* Public Health Service No. HSM 73-70-235.

Edwards, E.D., & Edwards, M.E. (1974). Social group work with young American Indians. *Monograph #9, Faculty Development—Minority content in mental health.* Boulder, CO: Western Interstate Commission for Higher Education.

Edwards, E.D., & Edwards, M.E. (1980). American Indians: Working with individuals and groups. *Social Casework: The Journal of Contemporary Social Work, Oct.,* 498-506.

Edwards, E.D., & Edwards, M.E. (1984). Group work practice with American Indians. *Social Work with Groups, 7*(3), 7-21

Edwards, E.D., & Edwards, M.E., Daines, G.M., & Eddy, F. (1978). Enhancing self-concept and identification with "Indianness" of American Indian girls. *Social Work with Groups, 1*(3), 309-18.

Everett, M.W. (1970). Pathology in White Mountain Apache culture: A preliminary analysis. *Western Canadian Journal of Anthropology, 2*(1), 180-203.

Fenton, W.N. (1941). *Iroquois suicide: A study in the stability of a culture pattern.* Anthropological Papers, No. 14 (Smithsonian Institution, Bureau of American Ethnology Bulletin, No. 128), 79-139.

Forbes, N., & Van Der Hyde, V. (In press). Suicide in Alaska 1978-1984: Updated data from state files. *American Indian & Alaska Native Mental Health Research: The Journal of the National Center.*

Fox, J., & Ward, J.A. (1977). *Indian suicide in Northern Ontario.* Paper presented to the Annual Meeting of the Canadian Psychiatric Association, Saskatoon, Saskatchewan, September 1977.

Frankl, V.E. (1959). *Man's search for meaning: An introduction to logotherapy.* New York: Pocket Books.

Frausm, R.F. (1974). Suicide behavior in Alaskan Natives. *Alaska Medicine,* 2-6.

Havighurst, R.J. (1971). The extent and significance of suicide among American Indians today. *Mental Hygiene, 55,* 174-7.

Heckwelder, J. (1819). *Transactions of the historical and literary committee of the American Philosophical Society.* Philadelphia: Abraham Small.

Hippler, A.E. (1969). Fusion and frustration: Dimensions in the cross-cultural ethnopsychology of suicide. *American Anthropologist, 71,* 1074-87.

Hoffman, T., Dana, R.H., & Bolton, B. (1985). Measured acculturation and MMPI-168 performace of Native American adults. *Journal of Cross-Cultural Psychology, 16,* 243-56.

Holmgren, C., Fitzgerald, B.J., & Carman, R.S. (1983). Alienation and alcohol use by American Indian and Caucasian high school students. *Journal of Social Psychology, 120*(1), 139-40.

Humphrey, J.A., & Kupferer, H.J (1982). Homicide and suicide among the Cherokee and Lumbee Indians of North Carolina. *International Journal of Social Psychiatry, 28*(2), 121-8.

Kahn, M.W. (1982). Cultural clash and psychopathology in three aboriginal cultures. *Academic Psychology Bulletin, 4*(3), 553-61.

Kahn, M.W., Lewis, J., & Galvez, E. (1974). An evaluation of a group therapy procedure with reservation adolescent Indians. *Psychotherapy, Theory, Research, & Practice, 11*(3), 239-42.

Kraus, R.F. (1971). *Changing patterns of suicidal behavior in North Alaskan Eskimos.* Paper presented at the 2nd International Symposium on Circumpolar Health, Nordic Council for Artic Medical Research, Oulu, Finland.

Kraus, R. (1974). Suicidal behavior in Alaska Natives. *Alaska Medicine, 16*(1), 2-6.

Kraus, R., & Buffler, P.A. (1975). Suicide in Alaska Natives: A preliminary report. *Proceedings of third International Symposium on Circumpolar Health, University of Toronto,* pp. 556-7.

Leighton, A.H., & Hughes, C.C. (1955). Notes on Eskimo patterns of suicide. *Southwestern Journal of Anthropology, 11,* 327-38.

Levy, J.E. (1965). Navajo suicide. *Human Organization, 24,* 308.

Levy, J.E., & Kunitz, S.J. (1962). Notes on some White Mountain Apache social pathologies. *Plateau, 42,* 11-9.

Levy, J.E., Kunitz, S.J., & Everett, M. (1969). Navajo criminal homicide. *Southwestern Journal of Anthropology, 25,* 124-52.

Lewis, T.H. (1975). A syndrome of depression and mutism in the Ogala Sioux. *American Journal of Psychiatry, 132,* 753-5.

Loretto, J., Beauvais, F., & Oetting, E.R. (In press). The primary cost of drug abuse: What Indian youth pay for drugs. *National Center for American Indian & Alaska Native Mental Health Research: The Journal of the National Center.*

MacLean, B. (1979). *Deaths by violence among Canadian Native peoples.* Unpublished government report, August 1979, Mental Health Division, Health Services & Promotion Branch, Health & Welfare Canada, Ottawa, Ontario.

Mail, P., & McDonald, D. (1980). *Talapai to Tokay: Bibliography of alcohol use and abuse among Native Americans of North America.* New Haven, CT: HRAF Press.

Manson, S., & Shores, J.H. (1981). *Relationship between ethnopsychiatric data and Research Diagnostic Criteria in the identification of depression within a Southwestern American Indian tribe.* Paper presented at the American Anthropological Association Annual Meeting, Los Angeles, California, December, 1981.

Manson, S.M., Shore, J.H., & Bloom, J.D. (1985). The depressive experience in American Indian communities: A challenge for psychiatric theory and diagnosis. In A. Kleinman & B. Good (Eds.), *Culture and depression*, pp. 331-68.

Manson, S.M., Walker, R.D., & Kivlahan, D.R. (1987). Psychiatric assessment and treatment of American Indians and Alaska Natives. *Hospital and Community Psychiatry, 38*(2), 165-73.

Martin, H.W., Sutker, S.S., Leon, R.L., et al. (1968). Mental health of eastern Oklahoman Indians: An exploration. *Human Organization, 27*, 308-15.

May, P.A. (1987). Suicide and self-destruction among American Indian youths. *American Indian & Alaska Native Mental Health Research, 1*(1), 52-69.

Maynard, E., & Twiss, G. (1970). *Hechel lena oyate kin nipi kte, that these people may live: Conditions among the Oglala Sioux of the Pine Ridge reservation.* Washington, D.C.: U.S. Department of H.E.W. Public Health Service (DHEW Publication Number HSM 72-508).

McDonald, T. (1975). Group psychotherapy with Native American women. *International Journal of Group Psychotherapy, 25*(4), 410-20.

McIntosh, J.L., & Santos, J.F. (1981). Suicide among Native Americans: A compilation of findings. *Omega: Journal of Death and Dying, 11*(4), 303-16.

McIntosh, J.L. (1984). Suicide among Native Americans: Further tribal data and considerations. *Omega: Journal of Death and Dying, 14*(3), 215-229.

Miller, S.I., & Shoenfeld, L.S. (1971). Suicide attempt patterns among the Navajo Indians. *International Journal of Social Psychiatry, 17*, 189-93.

Miller, S.I., & Schoenfeld, L.S. (1973). Grief in the Navajo: Psychodynamics and culture. *International Journal of Social Psychiatry, 19*, 187-91.

Miller, M. (1979). Suicides on a southwestern American Indian reservation. *White Cloud Journal, 1*(3), 14-8.

Mindell, C., & Stuart, P. (1968). Suicide and self destructive behavior in the Oglala Sioux. In *Pine Ridge Research Bulletin, No 1*, 14-23. (Indian Health Service) Washington, D.C.: Government Printing Office.

National Institute of Mental Health (NIMH). (1975). *Suicide, homicide, and alcoholism among American Indians: Guidelines for help.* Washington, D.C.: DHEW Publications No. (ADM) 76-42.

Oetting, E.R., Beauvais, R., & Edwards, R. (In press). Alcohol and Indian youth: Social and psychological correlates and prevention. *Journal of Drug Issues.*

Pambrun, A. (1979). Suicide among the Blackfoot Indians. *Bulletin of Suicidology, 7*, 42-3.

Parkin, M. (1974). Suicide and culture in Fairbanks: A comparison of three cultural groups in a small city of interior Alaska. *Psychiatry, 37,* 60-7.

Patterson, H.L. (1969). Suicide among the youth on the Quinault Indian reservation. U.S. Senate Committee on Labor and Public Welfare, Part 5, Special Subcommittee on Indian Education. Washington, D.C.: U.S. Government Printing Office, pp. 2016-21.

Peniston, E. (1978). The ego strength scale as a predictor of the Ute Indian suicide risk. White Cloud Journal, 1(2), 15-8.

Pine, C.J. (1981). Suicide in American Indian and Alaska Native Tradition. *White Cloud Journal, 2*(3), 3-8.

Pollack, D., & Shore, J.H. (1980). Validity of the MMPI with Native Americans. American Journal of Psychiatry, 137, 946-50.

Rocky Mountain News. (1985). October 6, pp. 22-3. Indian leaders struggle to cope with epidemic of suicides. (John Ensslin, Staff writer).

Seyer, D. (1979). Suicide in the Native Indians of Canada. *Proceedings of 10th International Congress of Suicide Prevention, 1,* 344-55.

Shneidman, E.S. (1967). Some current developments in suicide prevention. *Bulletin of Suicidology, 1,* 31-4.

Shore, J.H. (1972). Suicide and suicide attempts among American Indians of the Pacific northwest. *International Journal of Social Psychiatry, 18,* 91-6.

Shore, J.H. (1975). American Indian suicide—fact and fantasy. *Psychiatry, 38,* 86-91.

Shore, J.H. (1979). Epidemiology of depression among American Indians. *Memo University of Oregon Medical School,* Portland, NEED REST OF ENTRY.

Shore, J.H., & Manson, S.M. (1981). Cross-cultural studies of depression among American Indians and Alaska Natives. *White Cloud Journal, 2*(2), 5-12.

Snake, R., Hawkins, G., & Laboueff, S. (1976). *Report on alcohol and drug abuse, Task Force Eleven: Alcohol and drug abuse.* Final Report to the American Indian Policy Review Commission. Washington, D.C.: U.S. Government Printing Office.

Spaulding, J.M. (1985). Recent suicide rates among ten Ojibwa Indian bands in Northwestern Ontario. *Omega: Journal of Death and Dying, 16*(4), 347-54.

Swanton, J.R. (1928). Social organizations and social usages of the Indians of the Creek Confederacy. *U.S. Bureau of American Ethnology Annual Report, 42,* 23-472.

Swanton, J.R. (1931). Source material for the social and ceremonial life of the Choctaw Indians. *U.S. Bureau of American Ethnology Bulletin, 103,* 282.

Swenson, D.D. (1969). Suicide in the United States. In *Suicide Among the American Indians*, 1-6, (USPHS Publication No. 1903). Washington, D.C.: Government Printing Office.

Termansen, P.E., & Peters, R.W. (1979). *Suicide and attempted suicide among status Indians in British Columbia.* Paper presented to the World Federation of Mental Health Conference, Salzburg, Austria.

Travis, R. (1983). Suicide in Northwest Alaska. *White Cloud Journal, 3*(1), 23-30.

Ward, J.A., & Fox, J. (1977). A suicide epidemic on an Indian reserve. *Canadian Psychiatric Association Journal, 22*(8), 423-6.

Ward, J.A., Fox, J., & Evans, A.L. (1977). *Suicide and the Canadian Indian.* Paper presented to the 9th International Congress for Suicide Prevention and Crisis Intervention, Helsinki, Finland, June, 1977. Proceedings, pp. 389-406.

Ward, J.A. (1979). *The response of an Indian community to a suicide epidemic: A follow-up report.* Paper presented to the Tenth International Congress for Suicide Prevention and Crisis Intervention, Ottawa, Ontario, 17-20, June 1979. Proceedings (Vol. 2), pp. 147-50.

Webb, J.P., & Williard, W. (1975). Six American Indian patterns of suicide. In N.L. Farberow (Ed.), *Suicide in different cultures*, pp. 17-33. Baltimore, MD: University Park Press.

Wyman, L.C., & Thorne, B. (1945). Notes on Navajo suicide. *American Anthropologist, 47*, 278-87.

Yalom, I. (1980). *Existential psychotherapy.* New York: Basic Books.

CHAPTER **12**

INTERVENTIONS WITH COLLEGE CAMPUS POPULATIONS

Allen J. Ottens, Ph.D.
Lynn Fisher McCanne, Ph.D.
and
Alan J. Farber, Ph.D.

Allen J. Ottens, Ph.D.

Staff Psychologist
Counseling and Student Development Center
Northern Illinois University
DeKalb, Illinois 60115

Allen J. Ottens received his doctorate in counseling psychology from the University of Illinois. He was formerly assistant professor in the Department of Social and Preventive Medicine, University of Maryland School of Medicine, and staff psychologist in the Psychological Services Clinic, Cornell University. He also served as assistant director of the Counseling Center at Villanova University. Presently he is coordinator of student development programming at the Counseling and Student Development Center, Northern Illinois University. Dr. Ottens is a licensed psychologist and a member of the American Psychological Association. He is the author of numerous papers that have appeared in such publications as the *Journal of Behavior Therapy and Experimental Psychiatry* and the *Personnel and Guidance Journal.* He has written two books for adolescents and young adults, *Coping with Academic Anxiety* and *Coping with Romantic Breakup.* The latter book was recently recommended by the Committee on Books for Young Adults of the New York Public Library as having special appeal for this age group. Dr. Ottens' areas of professional interest include crisis intervention, cognitive therapy, research on academic anxiety, and student development.

Lynn P. Fisher McCanne, Ph.D.

Associate Director and Training Director
Counseling and Student Development Center
Northern Illinois University
Dekalb, IL 60115

Dr. McCanne has been at Northern Illinois University for twelve years, most recently as the associate director and training director of the Counseling and Student Development Center (1984-87, acting director June-December 1986). From 1975 to 1984, she was a psychologist at the Health Service Mental Health Clinic. Her Ph.D. (1974) and M.A. degrees in clinical psychology are from Ohio State University and her B.A. (1970) is from Occidental College in Los Angeles. She was born and reared in southern California and has retained an affection for that part of the country. Since her migration to the Midwest, she has developed professional clinical and research interests in counseling, training, group processes, adult survivors of incest, and eating disorders. Other, less professional interests include family (husband Thomas R. McCanne, professor, NIU Department of Psychology, and son Bobby), music performance, reading, and sports.

A member of several national and regional associations of psychologists, counselors, and college personnel, Dr. McCanne has been recognized in Who's Who of Emerging Leaders of America, Who's Who Among Human Services Professionals, and Who's Who in the Midwest. In her recent presentations and publications, she has co-authored "Suicidal Behavior on the College Campus: Student Affairs Responds" (ACPA-NASPA convention, March 1987, Chicago), and "Crisis Intervention on the College Campus" (in *Assessment and Crisis Intervention with Speical Students*, in press). Other published and presented works have been in the areas of eating disorders; group processes and treatment; and women's academic, professional, and personal issues.

Alan J. Farber, Ph.D.

Staff Psychologist
Counseling and Student Development Center
Northern Illinois University
DeKalb, IL 60115

Dr. Farber received his doctoral degree in Counseling Psychology from Michigan State University in 1986. Since completing his pre-doctoral internship at Colorado State University's Counseling Center, he has served as staff psychologist and coordinator of career services at the Counseling and student Development Center at Northern Illinois University in DeKalb. A member of the American College Personnel Association, Dr. Farber is a directorate member of Commission VI (Career Counseling and Placement). He co-presented: "Suicidal Behavior on the College Campus: Student Affairs Responds" at the 1987 ACPA convention in Chicago.

Dr. Farber's professional interests include college student development and adjustment, peer counseling, and the effect of divorce on adolescent identity. He is presently undertaking an investigation of the relationship between college students' relations with parents and career indecision. He and his wife of eight years, Mary Theresa Gawrys, a psychiatric nursing instructor at Northern Illinois University, are presently basking in the excitement of the recent birth of their first child, David Joseph.

EDITORIAL ABSTRACT: *This chapter views the suicide problem from the perspective of university counseling center staff. Epidemiology is reviewed—How prevalent is suicidal behavior among college students? Contributing familial, academic, social, and psychological variables are presented in all their complexity. Legal, ethical, and practical concerns which college administrators must face when dealing with a suicidal crisis are discussed. The authors explore prevention and postvention and present a case study that illustrates the management of a campus suicidal crisis.*

"I have at various times regarded suicide as the one most active gesture in an otherwise apparently passive existence; in other words, life seemed proscribed by death, and, if any individual feels he can effect no substantial change in his life, then suicide seems an active and logical alternative." (Anonymous, in Shneidman & Farnsworth, 1972, p. 131).

So wrote a Harvard student as he chronicled the sequence of events around his contemplated self-destruction; the attempt, rescue, hospitalization, confrontation with university officials, call to parents, therapy sessions, and worry about others' reactions.

Evident in this student's essay is the complexity of his psychological state prior to the suicide attempt. What is also noteworthy is the complexity of the sequence of responses after the attempt. Unraveling the complexity of the suicide act and structuring the complex manner of responding to it are the two main foci of the college student suicide literature.

Serious psychological discussion of student suicide can be traced back to the 1910 meeting of the Vienna Psychoanalytical Society (Friedman, 1967). The Society's panel, consisting of such seminal thinkers as Freud, Adler, and Stekel, convened over concerns about suicides among the students of the *Gymnasium* and speculated about possible causes.

Since that meeting, dozens of articles and reports have been devoted to the topic of student suicide, including a public television documentary, "College Can Be Killing" (1978). Even as this book goes to press, a national student affairs conference, "The Problem of Suicide On Campus" is scheduled at Louisville, Kentucky; and a special issue is being planned of the *Journal of College Student Psychotherapy* on preventing college student suicide.

This seven-section chapter reflects the complexity of this multi-faceted topic. In the first section, college student suicidal behavior is viewed from an epidemiological perspective. Next, we examine some variables—family, academic, social, and psychological—that have been associated with our topic. Third, we present legal, ethical, and practical concerns which higher education administrators face when dealing with campus suicidal crises. Fourth, we describe a model for interviewing students in suicidal crises. Fifth, we detail some preventive environmental interventions. Sixth, we consider the issue of postvention. Finally, a case study is presented in which we raise questions which need to be addressed when managing a campus suicidal crisis.

EPIDEMIOLOGY

In 1937 Raphael, Power, and Berridge estimated that 10% of the students seen at the University of Michigan's mental hygiene unit presented with suicide attempts or suicide threats. Since that time numerous efforts have been made to determine the prevalence of suicide and suicidal behavior among college students. Parnell (1951) reported that suicide rates for men enrolled at Oxford University were 11 times that of same-age, non-student males. Ross (1969), drawing from 38 studies and reports, cited disproportionately high rates of suicide among male students at universities in Britain and the United States. Ross reported an overall annual suicide rate of 19.3 per 100,000 British male students during the period 1948-1958, and 10.5 per 100,000 U.S. male students from 1920-1967. Referring to the latter findings, the author concluded that the rate of suicide among American male students is 50% higher than for comparable-aged American male non-students. Such findings have resulted in the assumption "...that the incidence of suicide among college students is relatively high compared to same age peers..." (Mishara, 1982, p. 142).

However, a sophisticated reinterpretation of American college student suicide research by Schwartz and Reifler (1980) casts doubt on such conclusions. Survey data obtained from 53

American universities and colleges between 1971 and 1976 revealed an annual rate of seven suicides per 100,000 students. This suicide-per-student ratio is significantly less than previously reported and contrary to previous studies, is significantly lower than the incidence in a sex-matched comparison group based on a 20- to 24-year-old, non-student, U.S. white population. Sims and Ball (1973) at the University of Alberta and Kraft (1980) at the University of Massachusetts (Amherst) also have reported comparatively low per annum suicide rates among students at their universities (5.4 and 5.6 per 100,000, respectively).

Several authors (Schwartz, 1980; Schwartz & Reifler, 1980; Seiden, 1971) have cited possible explanations for the early reports of high suicide rates among college students. First, studies may have been prompted by the occurrence of several campus suicides, resulting in spuriously high incidence rates. Second, these data were often derived from campuses unrepresentative of the general college population. Third, as Schwartz (1980) noted, only a small number of suicides were reported so that an overreporting of only one or two dramatically altered the data. Fourth, the criteria for classification as "students-at-risk" differed substantially among the various studies. Fifth, compared to non-students, college students tend to be a medically healthier group with access to excellent health facilities. This might decrease their comparative mortality rate by means other than suicide. Finally, the earlier studies used different and often questionable data for the determination of non-student comparison groups. For example, Schwartz and Reifler (1980) reported that, "In one study (Parrish, 1957) a comparison rate was derived using annual, national data for the United States white population in the 15-24 year age range matched on sex with the student sample, while another (Bruyn & Seiden, 1965) used cumulated data for a state population with a different age and racial composition but not matched for sex ratio" (p. 206). These issues are not meant to downplay the importance of suicide as a mental health problem on college campuses, but rather to warn against unsubstantiated generalizations regarding its absolute and comparative incidence.

Authors have questioned the accuracy of college suicide-related record-keeping (Schwartz, 1980; Schwartz & Reifler, 1980; Westefeld & Pattillo, 1987). Westefeld and Pattillo surveyed 147 college counseling center directors and found that few kept records of suicide attempts and completions. They recommended establishing a national clearinghouse for compiling such data. Schwartz (1980) has argued for future studies to employ consistent methodology and reporting practices.

Numerous surveys have attempted to determine the extent of suicidal ideation and suicide attempts among American college students. Wright, Snodgrass and Emmons (1984) reported that among 1,812 college student survey respondents, 5.7% of the males and 6.1% of the females indicated that they had seriously considered attempting suicide during the past six months. Craig and Senter (1972) found that 30% of 792 underclasspersons had considered suicide during an academic year. Mishara, Baker, and Mishara (1976), using lifelong prevalence rates, found that 65% of 293 university students had thought about suicide, and that 15% had attempted suicide at some time in their lives. Murray (1973) reported that 41% of 80 beginning psychology students had at some time in their lives thought about killing themselves. Mishara (1982) found that among 140 student respondents, 13.6% were suicide attempters, and 59% knew someone who had attempted suicide. These survey data support the claim that past and present suicidal ideation and attempts are relatively common phenomena among college students.

As greater percentages of Americans attend college and as the number of older students increases, the comparative suicide incidence between students and non-students may be a moot issue. Epidemiological studies will remain flawed until reporting procedures are consistent and until the definition of "student" is standardized. However, conflicting findings notwithstanding, the aforementioned studies confirm the common sense notion that suicidal behavior is a serious problem on college campuses, as it is everywhere in our society.

VARIABLES RELATED TO SUICIDAL BEHAVIOR IN STUDENTS

Over forty years ago, Raphael et al. (1937) provided a personality profile of the suicidal college student:

> ...he appears primarily rather on the over-sensitive, shy and self-conscious order, inclined to over-react, to worry, and emotionally rather delicately

balanced...(H)e seems...timid, fearful and insecure in the face of the enveloping life situation, and acutely concerned respecting that part...of life now confronting him, i.e. the academic test and responsibility.

...we find him to be poorly socialized and not fusing readily into the societal mass...(H)e has developed marked feelings of inferiority...He is anxious as to the future and at sea as to occupational or vocational procedure... Further, he is very likely not to have achieved effective sex adaptation and has been handicapped and malconditioned by negative influences in the family process...(p 9)

In this section we explore variables related to suicidal behavior in students—family, academic, social, and psychological—that researchers and clinicians have considered salient since the days of Raphael and his associates.

Family Variables

When Bernard and Bernard (1982) asked students why they considered suicide or made an attempt, the second most common reason was "family problems," endorsed by 21% of the sample. Family background is thought to play a significant role in students' suicidal behavior, because many students are at a developmental crossroads *vis-a-vis* the family, struggling to achieve autonomy and separation but still to some degree dependent on the family for financial and/or emotional support. Yet, Knauth (1981) has argued that college therapists often underrecognize the importance of the family-student relationship as a factor in students' psychiatric problems.

Knauth (1981) cited the case of a 19-year-old student who made a serious suicide attempt during her second pregnancy. A previously aborted pregnancy had resulted in severe conflict between the student and her parents, and she feared rejection if she chose a second abortion. This case reflects the more general finding that parental conflict and lack of support are associated with adolescent suicidal behavior (Schrut, 1968). Relatedly, conflict can contribute to the adolescent's alienation from the family, which increases suicide risk (Wenz, 1979). A family's intolerance of its members' efforts to separate and change also can precipitate suicidal behavior (Richman, 1979). These themes appear relevant as well for the college student as revealed in a study by Wright et al. (1984). Wright et al. identified 105 students who indicated that during the previous six months they had seriously considered attempting suicide. These students were differentiated from a control group of non-suicidal students on a number of childhood variables, including parental anger, physical abuse by parents, many conflicts with parents, parental depression, lack of parental support, and maternal emotional problems.

Loss of a parent through death, separation, desertion, or divorce can be a strong determinant of adolescent suicide behavior (Dorpat, Jackson, & Ripley, 1966; Miller, 1975; Schrut, 1968). However, parent loss alone does not necessarily lead to suicide; other factors (e.g. ego strength, support of remaining family members) must be taken into account (Glaser, 1978). The child's age at the time of the death of a parent may also be a consideration (Stanley & Barter, 1970). As with adolescents in general, parental loss appears to be a factor in college student suicide. In a classic study, Paffenbarger and Asnes (1966) reviewed the records of over 40,000 students from Harvard University and the University of Pennsylvania. They found that compared to a control group, students who suicided were over half again as likely to have come from families where the father was ill or deceased or where parents had separated; moreover, twice as many suicidal students were from homes where the father had died. Interestingly, there was no difference between groups as far as death of mother was concerned. These data have limited generalizability because all subjects were males. Later, Blaine and Carmen (1968) in a retrospective survey at Harvard and Radcliffe Universities found that 52% of their sample of attempters had suffered the death or separation of a significant other. More recently, Adam, Lohrenz, Harper, and Streiner (1982) found that college students who had lost a parent before age 16 were more likely to report suicidal ideation and attempts that students from intact families.

A crucial point is to understand the meaning of a suicide attempt from a family systems perspective (Held & Bellows, 1983). An attempt may be a student's method of reversing a parent-child role reversal. Held and Bellows noted that in some families the adolescent or young adult is placed in the role of parent or nurturer to dependent or inadequate parents. Here the child has been designated the "hope" of the family, responsible for satisfying some ungratified family needs as, for example, when parents have achievement needs that have been unfulfilled. To escape this burden, the student may attempt suicide, thereby becoming more in need of nurturing that the parents.

In summary, family conflict, loss, and lack of support appear to be significant factors in college student suicidal behavior as well as in the broader adolescent population. Also, students who subintentionally become overly responsible for meeting family dependency needs may be at higher suicide risk; however, further research is needed to establish such a connection.

Academic Variables

In a review of the college suicide literature, Knott (1973) listed the "intense, competitive atmosphere" of higher education as a tentative covariable of suicidal gestures. Academic failure, competitiveness, and test anxiety are often cited by the public and counseling professionals as important precipitants of student suicide, but the research appears equivocal. In fact, Ross (1969) speculated that academic failure *per se* is not so much a precipitant of suicide as is the loss of parental love engendered by failure.

Based on results from a study at the University of California (Berkeley), Seiden (1966) came down squarely on academics as a significant risk factor in student suicide. He found that students who suicided were concerned about schoolwork (and about physical health and relationships, as well). Moreover, in retrospective reports from friends and families, these students were characterized as chronically dissatisfied with their performance and doubtful of their academic adequacy. In reality, they had achieved satisfactorily. Grimly, Seiden predicted an increasing incidence of student suicide due, in part, to the growing competitiveness of school environments. Another finding of Seiden's study was that suicides at Cal-Berkeley occurred most frequently during the first six weeks of a semester. One might speculate that if academics were a strong factor, more suicides would occur during the final examination period. In fact, Rook (1959) found more suicidal activity around examination time at England's Cambridge University.

Schwartz and Reifler (1980) discussed a probable difference in suicide rates at different universities. Their statistical analysis pointed to a possible higher rate of suicide at very selective American institutions compared to more representative ones. However, to determine if the differences are due to greater academic pressure, selection criteria, socioeconomic variables, or availability of campus support services is possible.

Two recent studies shed light on the impact of academic concerns on student suicidal behavior. Bernard and Bernard (1982) found that academic pressures accounted for only 7% of the reasons given by a group of students who had thought about or attempted suicide. Carson and Johnson (1985) found that students with low grade point averages were somewhat more likely to have considered suicide compared to a non-suicidal control group. However, students cited "personal problems" (e.g., loss of relationship or illness) rather than grades or tests as precipitating events for the suicidal ideation. Hence, Carson and Johnson felt that their results corroborated Bernard and Bernard's findings. We caution that both studies surveyed students from public universities in the southeast and that the results, therefore, may have limited generalizability.

Academic competitiveness and pressures may be a suicide risk factor for some college students, but others apparently minimize their impact upon suicidal ideation and/or behaviors. Perhaps this is due to the degree of *behavioral freedom* a student perceives in his/her academic situation; in other words, does the student perceive the academic situation to be controllable (Dowd & Milne, 1986)? Some students operate from a relatively freer behavioral framework with regard to academics. They refuse to play the competition "games" and they feel free to transfer, change majors, quit school, or appeal. Presumably, these students feel their academic problems are under some control and thus are less inclined to resort to life-threatening behavior over academic themes. On the other hand, some students perceive few options in an academic crisis and regard their problem as insoluble, uncontrollable, and irreversible. For example, a student may attribute failure to insufficient aptitude, a condition not easily rectified. Other students may feel trapped in a system where self-acceptance depends on academic success. One author (A.O.) recalls a graduate student who made a serious suicide attempt after failing a "last chance" foreign language proficiency exam. She perceived herself as not free to abandon her quest for an advanced degree after having invested so much effort in it.

Social Variables

Several years ago, the first author of this chapter reviewed reports and statements made as part of the investigation of the suicide death of a student. A recurring theme made by those who had shared his living environment was, "I didn't know him well." His virtual anonymity was pathetically underscored by the fact that in the various reports, his name was spelled several different ways.

The student suicide literature is replete with remarks and observations about social isolation and/or unsatisfactory social relationships. For example, Knott (1973) listed impoverished interpersonal relationships as a possible covariable of student suicide gestures and Hersh (1985) and Ross (1969) cautioned that social isolation is a major risk factor. Bernard and Bernard (1982) found that students chose "social problems" (e.g., love relationships, dating, friends) as the most common reason for their suicidal attempts/ideation. In this section, we review findings regarding social variables and student suicidal behaviors.

Paffenbarger and Asnes (1966) found that those students who suicided had a lower rate (47%) of participation in extra-curricular activities compared to control subjects (58%). This finding, they noted, is "...consistent with classical hypotheses that associate suicidal tendency with lack of sociability" (p. 1031). Summarizing results from his study at the University of California (Berkeley), Seiden (1971) observed that the typical suicide victim was essentially asocial, withdrawn, and virtually friendless. In this regard, Wright et al. (1984) found that compared to control subjects, student suicide ideators were more likely to rate themselves on the negative end of bipolar adjective continua, choosing adjectives such as "hated," "unpopular," "unrecognized," "unfriendly," and "follower." Wolfe and Cotler (1973) found that attempters were less likely than "psychiatric" or "normal" controls to have religious affiliation, and an unspecified "large percentage" had no social (e.g., fraternity or sorority) affiliation.

Dashef (1984) made the important clinical observation that suicidal students often form close, dependent relationships with a single peer, and that suicidal behavior may result when that relationship fails. Indeed, as Mishara (1982) pointed out, suicidal college students could be trapped in a vicious cycle, for when they do verbalize their distress to peers, they may often receive "closed responses" (e.g., changing of topic, a joke, advice to get professional help, or inattention), thereby exacerbating the impoverishment of their social situation.

Psychological Variables

The earlier excerpt of Raphael et al. (1937) alluded to two psychological variables connected with suicidal tendencies among college students: anxiety and depression. Anxiety and depression, however, are not necessarily useful predictors of suicide, and their roles in suicidal behavior may be further complicated depending upon the type of suicidal behavior being investigated.

Braaten and Darling (1962) classified suicidal student patients at Cornell University's Mental Health Clinic along a three-point severity continuum: thinking about, threatening, or attempting suicide. Less than 20% of the sample consisted of suicide attempters. This sample was compared to a non-suicidal patient control group. Braaten and Darling found that for males, scores on MMPI scales 2, 7, and 8 were significantly higher for suicidal students than for male controls; for women, scales 2 and 8 were similarly significantly elevated. The symptom picture suggested by a 2-7-8 profile reflects self-doubt, lack of self-esteem, anxiety, feelings of hopelessness, and proneness to suicidal ideation; the 2-8 profile is indicative of depression with anxiety and agitation and some preoccupation with suicidal thoughts (Stelmachers, in Lachar, 1974). Clopton (1974) pointed out that in a number of studies patients who threaten suicide score higher on scale 2 than those who commit or attempt suicide. However, Braaten and Darling found no significant differences on the MMPI scales among thinkers, threateners, or attempters.

Later, Wolfe and Cotler (1973) compared a group of student suicide attempters with a group of non-suicidal "psychiatric" controls and a non-patient group. On measures of interpersonal anxiety and depression, the attempters and "psychiatric" controls scored significantly higher than the non-patient group. However, no significant differences were found on these measures between attempters and "psychiatric" controls. Wolfe and Cotler noted that their results were consistent with the difficulties encountered by other researchers in trying to discriminate between suicidal and non-suicidal patients. Rather than measuring emotional levels, perhaps college student suicide research endeavors might take a more fruitful direction by investigating the cognitive correlates of suicidal behavior. Suicidal individuals may often exhibit a thinking style that diminishes their ability to cope flexibly with stressors (Levenson, 1974). Cognitive rigidity, dichotomous thinking, and "tunnel vision" yield few functional behavioral alternatives, and as a result one may resort to poorly thought out or impulsive actions—a suicide attempt being one such action.

Kraft (1980) studied the records of the 19 students who committed suicide during the 20-year period, 1959-1979, at the University of Massachusetts (Amherst). He recommended that as a part of preventive efforts, college counseling and mental health facilities should target efforts toward depressed and extremely anxious students. He also noted that these features do not discriminate the suicidal from the non-suicidal student. However, one of Kraft's findings was that of the 19 suicides, 11 students had received assistance at the university's mental health service prior to the suicide; moreover, seven had contact within one week of the suicide.

The concept of suicide as an act of aggression turned inward has generated an immense theoretical and research literature. To survey that literature is far beyond the scope of this chapter. However, two studies by Lester will be mentioned. Using a paper-and-pencil measure of aggression, Lester (1967a) found no difference in the manner and direction of expressing aggression between subjects who had attempted or threatened suicide compared to a non-suicidal control group. Lester (1967b) matched 20 attempters (students at the University of Rochester School of Medicine and Dentistry) against 20 non-suicidal controls. He compared Rorschach responses (barrier and penetration scores) and found no significant differences between groups. These studies failed to support the notion that suicide can be interpreted as a tendency to turn aggression onto self.

Of course, suicidal behavior is associated with disorders of personality and development as well as affective and anxiety disorders. College mental health workers are familiar with the impulsive, self-injurious behavior of the borderline client. Also, bulimic clients (some of whom may be diagnosed as borderline) may have suicidal tendencies. In a recent survey, Robbins, May, and Corazzini (1985) found that college counseling center staff perceive students as presenting with more serious emotional and/or behavioral problems than in the past. Hence, identifying and responding to suicidal students will continue to be a major challenge for professionals in this field.

ADMINISTRATIVE CONSIDERATIONS

During suicidal crises, administrators in higher education are confronted with complex legal, ethical, and practical concerns. The administrator constantly weighs the individual's welfare against responsibilities to others (e.g., parents, the university community). Given the complexity of these issues, surprisingly little professional literature is available to guide the administrator and other concerned professionals in developing policies and procedures (Moorman, Urbach, & Ross, 1984; Ponterotto, 1987; Rockwell, 1983). Perhaps due in part to this lack of guidance, Hendrickson and Cameron (1975) discovered that California administrators consistently underrated their campuses' suicide rate; saw the problem as more national than local in scope; and had implemented few of their own creative preventive suggestions on their campuses. Bernard and Bernard (1980) reported that institutions varied widely in their responses to suicidal students, from inaction to dismissal. Also, unclear was which administrators were responsible for deciding how to deal with the student. While acknowledging administrators' concerns about potential disruption of the educational mission, protection of the institution's image, and avoidance of liability for failure to act to prevent suicide, Bernard and Bernard (1982) found that the administrators' overriding concern was protecting the student's welfare rather than the institution's.

How are higher education administrators to view student suicidal behavior? What are the legal, ethical, and practical administrative concerns that should govern decisions? What information should be considered? In this section we speak to several administrative issues: dismissal of the suicidal student; malpractice liability; hospitalization; and confidentiality.

Dismissal

Section 504 of the Rehabilitation Act of 1973 (amended 1974) prohibits discrimination against any handicapped person (29 V.X.C. S 794). Section 45 of the *Code of Federal Regulations* (45 C.F.R. 84) defines the term "handicapped" broadly to include emotional and psychological handicaps. Those regulations prohibit exclusion from educational institutions if the handicapped person is otherwise qualified. In addition, regulations prohibit pre-admission inquiry as to whether someone is handicapped. Once enrolled, due process notice and opportunity for a hearing are required if the institution withdraws a handicapped student for any reason other than academic incapacity. Bernard and Bernard (1980) argued that suicidal students are protected by these laws, and that institutions may be in violation if they summarily dismiss a student for suicidal threats or behavior or require pre-admission psychiatric screenings.

Among actions taken for "the good of the student" dismissal from the academic institution is perhaps the most questionable. Traditionally, acutely suicidal students were removed from campus to protect the individual and to avoid disruption of the learning environment (Slimak & Berkowitz, 1983). Bernard and Bernard (1980) surveyed all International Association of Counseling Services-accredited college counseling centers during the academic year 1975-1976. They found that in response to suicide attempts, nearly half the centers required the student to withdraw from school. In apparent defiance or ignorance of existing laws and regulations, many made no provision for hearings, even when requested. More recently, Bernard and Bernard (1982) found that academic pressures accounted for a minor proportion of student suicidal behavior. They also noted that students seldom manifest disruptive suicidal behavior in class. Dismissal suggests that the educational environment is a major cause of the suicidal behavior and that dismissal would protect the academic environment from disruption. If the former is shown not to be the case and if anticipated disruption is unlikely, and given that social isolation is cited as a risk factor for suicidal behavior, then perhaps banishing the student from the academic environment has been an ill-founded practice.

Malpractice Liability

Slimak and Berkowitz (1983) outlined six major types of malpractice suits brought against mental health practitioners: faulty diagnosis; improper certification in a commitment proceeding; failure to exercise adequate precautions for a suicidal patient; breach of confidentiality; faulty applications of therapy; and promise of a cure. Sexual abuse of clients and counselor failure to warn third parties of potential danger from a client also have become legal issues. Slimak and Berkowitz made several suggestions which might reduce liability in these areas, among them: having forensic experts train campus mental health staff regarding current techniques for predicting dangerousness; allowing staff rapid access to additional professional opinion when dangerous behavior is possible; maintaining accurate, detailed records; communicating warning if dangerous behavior is determined; and developing strong ties between the counseling center and legal counsels of the university and psychological associations.

Hospitalization

Counselors' professional literature and academic training offer sparse guidance regarding hospitalization of clients, despite the fact that counselors are almost inevitably confronted with such decisions (Moorman et al., 1984; Ponterotto, 1987). In a review of recent literature on crisis intervention and hospitalization, Ponterotto suggested that hospitalization, and especially involuntary commitment, be avoided if possible, due to such iatrogenic effects as potential lifelong stigma, loss of self-control, and lowered self-esteem. However, Ponterotto emphasized that clients' physical well-being always must be paramount, so that hospitalization is an option when a potential exits for suicide or assault, bizarre behavior, and/or agitation leading to panic or loss of impulse control. Hospitalization could be avoided if the student does not present clear, imminent danger to self or others, seems to have capacity for self-care, has a social support network, can be relied on to use outpatient services, and displays adequate reality-testing. If these conditions are not met, according to Ponterotto's review, hospitalization affords some assets: safety, diagnostic procedures, and a therapeutic milieu.

Ponterotto (1987) presented procedures to follow once hospitalization is indicated. procedures depend on local, state, and/or federal legal processes. Procedures also vary with respect to the counselor's work setting and the communication network between university administrators, university medical staff, and local hospital personnel. Following Ponterotto's advice, we urge college counseling and administrative staffs to understand local statutes, court policies, and attitudes on matters of hospitalization, especially involuntary commitment proceedings.

Confidentiality

The professional is guided by ethical standards and legal requirements. The *Ethical Standards* of the American Association for Counseling and Development (1981) and the *Ethical Standards of Psychologists* (American Psychological Association, 1977) focus on respecting the individual's integrity and rights. In Section B.4 of the *Ethical Standards* is stated that when instances of "clear and imminent danger" occur the counselor must "inform responsible authorities" and assume "responsibility for the client's behavior." Ethical questions concerning suicidal college students revolve around issues of confidentiality, the university as substitute parent (*in loco parentis*), and potential conflict of interest when involved professionals are responsible to both student clients and the university community (Moorman et al, 1984).

Moorman et al. found that few college mental health services had written policies with respect to confidentiality practices. Most of the surveyed services only notified administrators of a student's mental health contacts if she/he required hospitalization or had attempted suicide. Moorman et al., after reviewing practical issues when dealing with suicidal students, leaned toward occasional limited disclosure to appropriate campus personnel on the basis of weighing risks and benefits of withholding or disclosing information.

In considering when to notify others (e.g., administrators, family) that a student is suicidal, Moorman and her colleagues recommended no notification in the clear-cut case where a student is distressed but not in danger. The other clear-cut case is when a student's distress and/or suicidal potential is so evident that hospitalization is indicated; at this time campus personnel and usually parents would be notified.

However, a "gray" area exists when concerns exist about a student's judgment, emotional stability, self-care, and safety but when no overtly dangerous behavior or suicidal intent is found. In such cases, Moorman et al. believed that the examiner might require and should discreetly seek information or consultation from university personnel. Such personnel might include the staff of the college mental health service, the dean of students and/or residence hall director. Prior to contacting these individuals, the examiner should discuss the implications with the student, obtain his/her consent, and explain the limits of the disclosure.

As to what information should be revealed from the campus mental health worker to other campus administrators, Moorman et al. recommended limiting disclosure to what the other person may need to know to protect the well-being of the student and immediate community. This might include the general nature of the problem, the student's psychological state, threats from or to the student, and the feasibility of the student returning to his/her residence.

With regard to notifying parents, Rockwell (1983) encouraged their involvement in the decision to hospitalize unmarried students. Steenland (1973) recommended routine parent involvement only if a campus had no psychiatric, medical or clinically-skilled non-medical personnel available, in which case he urged notification and insisted that parents take immediate custody. However, when qualified staff were available on campus, Steenland encourage examination and treatment with the option of informing parents even, if necessary, against the student's wishes, although he noted the desirability of the student's calling his/her parents.

CRISIS INTERVIEWING

In this section, we address the issue of crisis interviewing and explicate a model for clinical practice. The model is based on the work of Jeffrey Hersh (1985) who has identified key stages of the crisis interviewing process as it applies to the special needs of the college student. Hersh proposed five essential steps of crisis interviewing: approaching the situation; making contact; making an assessment; making interventions; and making a disposition. These steps are designed to achieve two main goals: to help the student re-establish psychological equilibrium and to ascertain that the student is no danger to self or others. Hersh acknowledged that these steps overlap; however we present crisis interviewing in discrete steps to illustrate more clearly how the process unfolds.

Approaching the Situation

When approaching the student in crisis or before initiating the crisis interview, the therapist can act in several ways to help the student regain some emotional equilibrium. The recommendation is for the therapist to display a sense of confidence: his/her composure is a facilitative counterpoint to the student's agitation. Second, reassurance can be communicated by expressing optimism that the crisis is likely to be short-lived and has a favorable prognosis. Third, the student in crisis should be provided with a stress-reducing milieu: a safe, distraction-free office and sufficient therapy time so that the situation can be discussed without rush. Finally, before initiating the interview, a review of case notes and/or collateral information will help the therapist gain composure and begin planning how to proceed.

Making Contact

This second step is Hersh's model involves establishing a connection between the therapist and student so as to reduce panic and feelings of isolation. The therapist should actively communicate empathy toward the student. This can be achieved by therapist nonverbal behaviors (eye contact, encouraging nods, a brief touch on the arm) and by minimal prompts to facilitate problem articulation (e.g., "what happened today?", "How are you feeling?", "When did things start to get worse?"). If the student is unable to explain why he/she feels so distressed, the therapist can review recent experiences in the areas of schoolwork, social and sexual relationships, living situation and/or family. Attending behavior and careful probing provide needed structure. Also, by his/her suicidal ideation or behavior, the student may be saying, "Take care of me." Therefore, the therapist must sometimes take temporary responsibility in terms of setting limits, choosing therapeutic interventions, and involving significant others in the crisis intervention process.

Making an Assessment

Careful assessment is essential during the crisis interview. Assessment is necessary to determine the student's functioning, life situation, and potential for self-harm. The therapist should first consider the student's accessibility to evaluation. Serious interfering factors (e.g., intoxication, sedation, or marked agitation) may necessitate detoxification and/or brief hospitalization. Some basic demographic data should be obtained (e.g. age, marital/family status, address, year in school). The therapist should take a brief treatment history (e.g., past hospitalization, help sought for physical or health problems, use of prescription and/or over-the-counter medications). With regard to psychological functioning, the therapist should note the student's appearance and behavior. For example, is the student's affect congruent with his or her experience? Does the student relate in a comfortable, strained, detached, or aggressive manner? Does he/she speak openly and coherently? The therapist must informally assess intellectual capacity and note any formal thought disorder delusions, hallucinations, or marked affect.

Where assessing suicide potential, the therapist should be alert for several important risk factors: (1) when a plan is formulated; (2) when a history of previous attempts exists; (3) when the student is psychotic; (4) when a history of drug and alcohol use exists; (5) when the student is seriously depressed; (6) when the student has a history of unsuccessful medical treatment or recent physical trauma; (7) when the student experiences an important loss or anniversary of a loss; (8) when the student is living alone or has cut off contact with others; and (9) when the student is coming out of a depression or after hospitalization for depression (Hersh, 1985, p. 288).

During the assessment step, the therapist should take seriously any mention of suicide or any suicidal behaviors or "gestures" engaged in by the student. If a student has formulated a suicide plan, the therapist will need to determine its specificity and the methods by which the student would carry it out.

Because of the need for rapid treatment and assessment of distraught and/or suicidal students, practitioners may find it inconvenient to use screening instruments. Nevertheless, brief measures should be available for evaluating depression and suicide potential. We describe several examples of brief measures that may be useful to the campus crisis therapist.

Barrow, Talley, Miller, and Zung (1985) report the the 20-item *Zung Self-Rating Depression Scale* is quickly and reliably scored and easy to complete, even for individuals in distress. Barrow et al. suggested, "...that an accurate assessment of the degree and nature of depression during the intake process may increase the probability of suicide prevention" (p. 53).

The *Scale for Suicide Ideation* (Beck, Kovacs, & Weissman, 1979) is a 21-item measure of the extent of the wish to die, the desire to make an active suicide attempt, details of any plan, internal deterrants, subjective feelings of control, and courage to make an attempt. The clinician completes the scale based on a semi-structured interview. Although developed as a research tool, its brevity, correlation with clinical ratings, sensitivity to changes over time, and measures of the validity recommend the scale for evaluating suicide potential.

The suggestion is that high risk suicidal individuals have restricted future time perspectives. The *Time Questionnaire* (Yufit & Benzies, 1972), a semi-projective instrument, has been shown to be of some use for differentiating high risk suicidal patients from non-suicidal and low risk patients.

Making Interventions

Interventions should be chosen which assist the student to regain pre-crisis functioning and to ensure his/her safety. Hersh emphasized that helping the student to an understanding of the crisis is a major therapeutic intervention. Not only should the student have identified the crisis precipitant, but he/she also should understand the particular psychological meaning of the event.

Besides achieving this insight into the problem, additional interventions may include (1) listening, an effective intervention for building rapport, gleaning information, and permitting catharsis; (2) utilizing interpersonal resources, such as encouraging the student to connect with friends, parents, or helpful significant others; (3) utilizing institutional resources, such as enlisting campus health services or residence hall staff to assist the student;

(4) advocacy, when students need the support of campus professionals to deal with institutional red tape; (5) giving information, often pertaining to sexuality, drugs, appetite disorders, or myths about mental illness; and (6) exploring alternative coping mechanisms, such as relaxation, exercise, social outreach, and healthful diet.

Making a Disposition

In this last step of the Hersh model, the student's situation is reviewed so that a prudent disposition can be made. Often the decision is made to terminate the crisis interview and allow the student to return to his/her place of residence. In that event, the therapist has ascertained that the student is at a low risk of committing self-injurious behaviors. The therapist may have determined that the student's agitation has been sufficiently reduced during the crisis interview; that the student has expressed hope for the future and described appropriate planful or coping activities; and that he/she will have available interpersonal support (sibling, residence hall staff, roommates). Before terminating the interview the therapist may have scheduled a follow-up appointment with the student, given information about after-hours emergency contact, and/or obtained the student's signed consent allowing for contact with individuals in the student's support network.

On the other hand, the therapist may have determined from the interview that the student is in such emotional disequilibrium that judgment is impaired or that the student is making suicidal threats and/or efforts. In this case, medication and/or hospitalization are usually indicated. The therapist will need to consult with mental health colleagues and perhaps appropriate university administrators regarding this more serious disposition. A determination will need to be made regarding parental notification. In instances where a suicide-prone student threatens to leave the office or tries to do so before a disposition can be made, the therapist should enlist the aid of university security personnel to guard office exits. As Hersh emphasized an important procedure is to keep the student informed about the process of medication and/or hospitalization and why such is being recommended.

ENVIRONMENTAL INTERVENTIONS

Besides providing crisis intervention and individual psychotherapy, colleges have developed many programs and outreach efforts that play a primary preventive function, reduce stress, and/or provide immediate personal assistance. In this section we discuss several of these programs/efforts and provide a few examples of each.

Environmental Restructuring and Design

Conyne, Banning, Clack, Corazzini, Huebner, Keating, and Wrenn (1979) noted that environmental design combines an environmental focus with preventive purpose. Examples of such environmental design include scheduling midsemester breaks to relieve student stress; housing student services in prominent campus locations; and arranging the architecture and landscaping to facilitate student affiliation. With respect to suicidal behavior, Hoffer (1972) and Knott (1973) stressed the importance of environmental restructuring of educational and living environments to promote student-student and student-staff contact. For example, Hoffer noted a program at the University of Rochester to intentionally house freshmen with upperclass students to facilitate contact with older peers. Phillips, Pitcher, Worsham, and Miller (1980) recommended "memory support procedures" (notes, open books) for reducing examination stress.

Telephone Assistance

In a recent survey of college counseling center directors, 46% of the respondents reported that 24-hour emergency coverage was available on their campuses (Roney, Wiley, Croteau, & Gelwick, 1986). After-hour telephone requests for assistance are typically forwarded from the infirmary, security office, or residence hall to an on-call therapist. In response to a shortage of trained therapists on campuses, many innovative after-hour phone services have been developed. Tucker, Megenity, and Vigil (1970) trained students, staff, and faculty volunteers to staff phones to provide support, information, and referral. Hill and Harmon (1976) and Thurman, Baron, and Klein (1979) described a University of Texas program that makes available around-the-clock recorded telephone tapes providing information about mental and physical health.

Peer Counseling

Often students prefer turning to their peer group for help during a personal crisis (Dana, Heynen, & Burdette, 1974). Many colleges sponsor peer counseling training to supplement campus helping resources and to capitalize on the "front-line" position peers occupy when crisis occur. In a recent survey of college counseling center directors, 78% of the respondents indicated that their center provided peer counseling programs, and a third of the programs used peers in suicide and crisis intervention (Salovey & D'Andrea, 1984). At American University, a student-operated hotline received 7,000 calls each semester, handling problems related to drugs, sex, loneliness, and depression (Leventhal, Berman, McCarthy, & Wasserman, 1976). Fondacaro, Heller, and Reilly (1984) developed "friendship networks" in an effort to reduce adjustment problems and feelings of isolation among graduate students living in a high-rise dormitory where several suicides had occurred.

Faculty/Staff Involvement

Pascarella and Terenzini (1976) found that the frequency of contact between freshmen and faculty was related positively to students' academic, intellectual, and personal growth. In a subsequent study, Terenzini and Pascarella (1980) found that discussing problems with faculty members may help freshmen to alleviate some of their stress. Albert, Forman, and Masih (1973) recommended assigning students to faculty members or older students who would act as concerned mentors. These authors also stressed the need for readily available tutoring services, as well as an office of ombudsman to assist students with institutional grievances. Jones and Najera (1976) have described the formation of a "helping network" at Brown University consisting of students, administrators, staff, and faculty. This network facilitated the provision of care for the student in crisis as well as those affected by the crisis. Sprinkle and Mattheus (1984) described the formation of an Emergency Intervention Team (EIT) at the University of Wyoming. The EIT was comprised of 10 two-member teams. When alerted to an emergency a team contacted the student, assessed the situation, and took action such as referring the student to the appropriate campus service or escorting him/her to the hospital emergency room.

Suicide Education/Crisis Intervention Training

Phillips (1983) has described a suicide education program conducted by college counseling center personnel aimed at training residence hall staff in the evaluation, intervention, and referral of potentially suicidal students. In response to a rash of campus suicides at Cornell University, Ottens (1983) developed a non-credit course for students, faculty, and staff, entitled "Life-threatening Emotional Crisis: Assessment and Response." Ottens found that the pre-post test responses of course participants indicated increases in the willingness to intervene in a suicidal crisis in a more directive yet empathic manner.

Physical Barriers to Suicide

Other environmentally oriented interventions involve the imposition of physical barriers to suicide. Examples include shatterproof windows, windows with security screens, and inaccessibility to rooftops. At the University of Illinois, a protective "cage" was built around the stairwell of the multi-story Psychology Building. Spiked metal fences flank the bridges across Cornell's campus gorges. Whether these barriers are more likely to reduce the incidence of deaths resulting from drunkenness or "horseplay" than from suicide attempts is debatable.

POSTVENTION

Considerable attention has been paid to the issues that arise following a suicide attempt or completion in the non-college population (e.g., Cain, 1972; Hatton, Valente, & Rink, 1977; Hewitt, 1980; Rosenfeld & Prupas, 1984; Wallace, 1973). In general, however, the literature on college student suicide has not thoroughly addressed such follow-up issues as the potential for reoccurrence, the emotional impact on significant others, and the student's post-attempt social and academic adjustment. Literature has typically focused on how the counseling center or college responds to the student's suicidal behavior.

Hipple, Cimbolic, and Peterson (1980) recommended systematic follow-up including support services for the suicidal student, and an evaluation of the institutional response to the incident. Halberg (1986) advocated the use of a crisis situation flow sheet in the event of a student death. Halberg's step-wise response to this event includes (1) investigation at the scene of the accident; (2) notification of appropriate persons on campus; (3) notification of next-of-kin; (4) development of a press release; (5) determination of how to deal with close friends and significant others; (6) communication with legal counsel; and (7) treatment of grief after the funeral.

Wright et al. (1984) recommended that the counseling center continue to follow up each student who has made suicidal gestures for as long as he/she remains enrolled in school. However, such a practice may prove to be an unreasonable burden for the counseling center staff of a large university, and calls into question the suicidal student's subsequent rights of confidentiality and privacy.

Seiden (1971) recommended the use of psychological autopsy procedures which involve interviews with friends, family, and associates of suicide completers and attempters. In addition to increasing the professional's understanding of suicidal behavior, this procedure "...serves to relieve the stigmatizing guilt and anxiety which frequently accrue to the survivors" (p. 248).

Hospitalization has previously been discussed as serving both preventive and therapeutic functions with suicidal students. Regarding postvention, Ross (1969) state that, "The danger of discharging a person to an empty dormitory room without provision for social support cannot be overstated" (p. 110). He claimed that many suicides occur during the period following the onset of improvement and discharge from the hospital. The first author (A.O.) is aware that Cornell University has initiated a policy through its Residence Life Committee to allow students returning from medical leave to have priority for being assigned on-campus housing.

According to Steenland (1973) one of the options following a suicide attempt includes the temporary withdrawal of the student. He claims that often the appropriate procedure is to hold a meeting between the student, a counselor, parents or next of kin, and the director of the counseling services or college physician, to jointly determine whether or not to retain the student. If withdrawal is deemed appropriate, the student's fitness to return to college must be appraised at a later date. This decision may be based upon data derived from a clinical interview, psychological testing, recommendations from the therapist the student may have been seeing subsequent to withdrawal, as well as other evidence of stability."

In regard to this issue, Bernard and Bernard (1980) claimed that institutions that dismiss the suicidal student "...would seem to assume that causation is somehow related to academia" (p. 111). However, as mentioned in the administrative section of this chapter, little evidence exists to suggest such a cause-effect relationship. Instead, the authors claim that dismissal may intensify the student's distress by providing more of that which contributed to the student's original problems: social isolation and the experience of personal failure. In addition to such therapeutic issues, the authors addressed the ethical and legal issues regarding dismissal (i.e., denying an education to an "emotionally handicapped" individual). The reader is directed to the Bernard and Bernard (1980) article for a discussion of the legalities regarding academic dismissal of the suicidal student. Wright et at., (1984) noted that dismissal is justifiable only when hospitalization is required, or when the student's continued presence will significantly interfere with the needs and rights of other students.

CASE STUDY

In this section, we present a case study to detail issues, procedures, and processes concerning the management of campus suicidal crises. During these crises, on-campus professionals in such areas as counseling, residence hall living, health services, security, ministry, and administration may become involved. They may provide services within their specialties, but they also may interact with each other, with off-campus professionals, and with the student's family. In these interactions, questions may arise as to the extent of appropriate intervention, standard procedures, coordination of efforts, and role clarification. The case study addresses confidentiality and trust, legal and ethical consideration, parental involvement/notification, coordination with other campus professionals, client aftercare, insurance coverage, postvention with the campus community, consultation with colleagues, and clarification of rules.

Part 1

You are a university counseling center psychologist. At 2:00 a.m. on a Saturday during the school year, you are alerted by the on-call system. A residence hall advisor (R.A.) informs you that a student (Susan) is in her room threatening to kill herself. Susan's roommate told the R.A. that Susan had written a suicide note and now demanded to be left alone. The R.A. exclaims that "The word is out and the whole floor is in an uproar."

At this point in the crisis knowing what questions to ask often is considerably more important than knowing all the answers. A key question is how will susan's immediate safety be assured. Is she alone? If so, what should be done? If not, who is with her? What does the suicide note say? What other relevant information is known about Susan: substance use; previous suicide threats/attempts; previous contact with an R.A.; other recent crises; therapy anywhere? Who else has been apprised of this situation (e.g., residence hall director, family, campus security, other staff)? Is Susan an active counseling center client? If so, should you contact her primary therapist? Does any treatment/intervention plan already exist for her?

The above questions are therapeutic considerations, but there may also be administrative concerns. Does the university have written policies or procedures for such an occurrence? If others are to be contacted, who are they and who should do the contacting? Should the residence hall director or subordinates by notified? Should campus security be alerted and if so, when? Have they been trained for mental health emergencies?

General issues raised in Part 1 include the availability, accessibility, and extent of after-hour services. Also relevant are accurate assessment and rapid, effective intervention. If residence hall staff and campus security get involved during crises, their prior training is essential. In such a crisis the most pressing need is not providing counseling but maintaining the student's life (Steenland, 1973).

Part 2

Susan's saga continues. You determine that your presence is necessary and arrive on the scene 30 minutes later. Susan's roommate and the R.A. are with Susan in her room. Students crowd about in the hallway and lobby. Entering the room, you ask Susan if you can speak with her, but she responds in a belligerent tone: "Why don't you all just leave me alone and mind your own business!" What do you do now?

At this point, you need to consider a number of therapeutic questions. Do you have enough information to assess Susan's suicide potential? If not, how will you obtain it? Does she have the right to be left alone, or is setting limits the "correct" therapeutic move? As Steenland (1973) suggested, suicidal behavior can be understood as requesting help in managing one's life, but often the suicidal student angrily resists that help. However, the student's anger is less important than helping him/her stay alive. At present, assuming that Susan is suicidal, does she possess means to harm herself or others? What will you do if Susan attempts to leave the premises?

Whether Susan's behavior disturbs the hall's living environment is another administrative question. If she is being disruptive, options to consider include calling campus security, encouraging residence hall staff to take disciplinary action, or dealing with the behavior therapeutically. Do the other students exacerbate the situation? What are their needs? Can you find someone else to attend to the curiosity and well-meaning concern of the bystanders?

You made the decision that face-to-face contact was necessary to deal effectively with this emergency. Under what circumstances do you make that decision? Are mandated policies or procedures available to help you make that decision? Who is your "client" in this situation? Is it Susan, the residence hall staff, other residents, the university? How do you decide what is therapeutic for Susan as opposed to the rights of other students who become involved in an emergency? A critical issue in this crisis is assessing suicide risk and intervening when the individual is uncooperative.

Part 3

With some coaxing, she agrees to speak with you in the presence of her roommate. After an hour's interview, you determine that Susan is a very high suicide risk. After explaining voluntary and involuntary hospitalization procedures, Susan reluctantly agrees to admit herself voluntarily into the local hospital's inpatient psychiatric unit.

What is left undone? Again, you will need to consider the needs of the hall residents. Are close friends, roommates, and others being affected adversely by the morning's events, and if so, how do you address their needs? Hipple et al. (1980) addressed these questions in a case study of cooperative responses by housing and counseling staff to a suicide. The housing staff took such actions as arranging emergency medical aid, meeting with residents of the victim's floor, and providing follow-up. The counseling center arranged for notification of the student's family, trained housing staff in postvention techniques, and was available for consultation. Hipple et al. (1980) demonstrated the advantages of good relationships between counseling center and residence hall staffs. However, as the counseling professional involved in this case, you need to consider limits of your ability to respond to all who are part of the crisis. Among those limits are Susan's right to confidentiality and your legal and ethical responsibilities.

Your responsibility for the therapeutic management of this emergency may extend beyond Susan herself. How can you prepare the residence hall personnel for her return from the hospital? Will the counseling center and/or residence hall personnel be notified of her return? When and by whom? Should someone notify Susan's parents, and if so, who? Steenland (1973) pointed out that although parents may naturally want to be made aware of the crisis, they also may react by feeling and acting helpless, angry, or punitive. He stated that the societal consensus is that 18-year-olds have reached the age of majority and have the right of privileged communication. On the other hand, Rockwell (1983) urged allying with parents and involving them whenever possible in the decision to hospitalize.

Is there a protocol for counseling center follow-up in this type of case? What are the policies and procedures for communicating with hospital and residence hall personnel? Once Susan is discharged from the hospital, can you arrange for an expeditious appointment at the counseling center? What is the university's/ counseling center's policy regarding mandatory counseling? What if Susan refuses treatment or is inappropriate for treatment at the university facility? In cases of refusal of treatment, many schools would call the parents; a few would call the police and/or initiate involuntary commitment (Bernard & Bernard, 1980; Steenland, 1973). However, as discussed earlier in this chapter, such drastic actions may have been applied selectively. For example, not all suicide attempts come to the attention of institution personnel. In a recent survey (Bernard & Bernard, 1982), of the 75 students who had been suicidal while in college, only one reported institutional involvement in the incident. Drastic action also may not be in the student's best interest. In Bernard and Bernard's survey (1982), 80% of those students who made a suicide attempt in college stayed in school and felt later that it had been the right decision. Overall, how do you simultaneously address Susan's issues, residence hall and university concerns, and counseling center issues and responsibilities?

In hospitalizing Susan, you and she must have considered her insurance coverage and her parents' possible financial obligation. (You should already have considered your own liability coverage.) Once the decision has been made to hospitalize, you are faced with practical details. What legal documents are required? What is the policy concerning transportation and how is that to be arranged? Who, if anyone, becomes responsible for case management now? What are the follow-up concerns for Susan, the residence hall, and others?

As a counseling center staff member, you have just taken on multiple roles of evaluator, therapist, consultant, case manager, and/or administrator. How do you clearly delineate and juggle these roles? How do others perceive you?

In this case study, we presented an emergency requiring a psychologist to provide rapid assessment and intervention to prevent suicide. Questions are raised with respect to confidentiality, psychologist roles, coordination with other campus professionals, parent notification, client aftercare, postvention, and insurance coverage. No easy answers exit, but the questions are key to guiding professional behavior in such an emergency.

REFERENCES

Adam, K.S., Lohrenz, J.G., Harper, D., & Streiner, D. (1982). Early parental loss and suicidal ideation in university students. *Canadian Journal of Psychiatry, 27,* 275-281

Albert, G., Forman, N., & Masih, L. (1973). Attacking the college suicide problem. *Journal of Contemporary Psychotherapy, 6,* 70-78.

American Association for Counseling and Development (1981). *Ethical standards.* Alexandria, VA: Author. (Originally published by American Personnel and Guidance Association).

American Psychological Association (1981). Ethical principles of psychologists. *American Psychologist, 36,* 633-638.

Barrow, J.C., Talley, J.E., Miller, K.H., & Zung, W.W.K. (1985). The Zung Self-Rating Depression Scale as an intake screening instrument. In J.E. Talley & W.J.K. Rockwell (Eds.), *Counseling and psychotherapy services for university students,* (pp. 50-61). Springfield, IL: Charles C. Thomas.

Beck, A.T., Kovacs, M., & Weissman, A. (1979). Assessment of suicidal ideation: The Scale for Suicidal Ideation. *Journal of Consulting and Clinical Psychology, 47,* 343-352.

Bernard, J.L., & Bernard, M.L. (1980). Institutional responses to the suicidal student: Ethical and legal considerations. *Journal of College Student Personnel, 21,* 109-113.

Bernard, J.L., & Bernard, M.L. (1982). Factors related to suicidal behavior among college students and the impact of institutional response. *Journal of College Student Personnel, 23,* 409-413.

Blaine, G.B., & Carmen, L.R. (1968). Causative factors in suicidal attempt by male and female college students. *American Journal of Psychiatry, 125,* 834-837.

Braaten, L.J., & Darling, C.D. (1962). Suicidal tendencies among college students. *Psychiatric Quarterly, 36,* 665-692.

Bruyn, H.B., & Seiden, R.H. (1965). Student suicide: Fact or fancy? Journal of the American College Health Association, 14, 69-77.

Cain, A.C. (1972). *Survivors of suicide.* Springfield, IL: Charles C. Thomas.

Carson, N.D., & Johnson, R.E. (1985). Suicidal thoughts and problem-solving preparation among college students. *Journal of College Student Personnel, 26,* 484-487.

Clopton, J.R. (1974). Suicidal risk assessment via the Minnesota Multiphasic Personality Inventory (MMPI). In C. Neuringer (Ed.), *Psychological assessment of suicidal risk* (pp.118-133). Springfield, IL: Charles C. Thomas.

College Can Be Killing [Film]. (1978). Chicago: WTTW.

Conyne, R.K., Banning, J.H., Clack, R.J., Corazzini, J.G., Huebner, L.A., Keating, L.A., & Wrenn, R.L. (1979). The campus environment as client: A new direction for college counselors. *Journal of College Student Personnel, 20,* 437-442.

Craig, L.E., & Senter, R.J. (1972). Student thoughts about suicide. *Psychological Record, 22,* 355-358.

Dana, R.H., Heynen, F., & Burdette, R. (1974). Crisis intervention by peers. *Journal of College Student Personnel, 15,* 58-61.

Dashef, S.S. (1984). Active suicide intervention by a campus mental health service: Operation and rationale. *Journal of the American College Health Association, 33,* 118-122.

Dorpat, T.L., Jackson, J.K., & Ripley, H.S. (1966). Broken homes in attempted and completed suicide. *Archives of General Psychiatry, 12,* 213-216.

Dowd, E.T., & Milne, C.R. (1986). Paradoxical interventions in counseling psychology. The Counseling Psychologist, 14, 237-282.

Fondacaro, M.R., Heller, K., & Reilly, M.J. (1984). Development of friendship networks as a prevention strategy in a university megadorm. *Personnel and Guidance Journal, 62,* 520-523.

Friedman, P. (Ed.). (1967). *On Suicide.* New York: International Universities Press.

Glaser, D. (1978). The treatment of depressed and suicidal adolescents. *American Journal of Psychotherapy, 23,* 252-269,

Halberg, L.J. (1986). Death of a college student: Response by student services professionals on one campus. *Journal of Counseling and Development, 64,* 411-412.

Hatton, C.L., Valente, S.M., & Rink, A. (1977). *Suicide: Assessment and intervention.* New York: Appleton-Century Crofts.

Held, B.S., & Bellows, D.C. (1983). A family systems approach to crisis reactions in college students. *Journal of Marital and Family Therapy, 9,* 365-373.

Hendrickson, S., & Cameron, C.A. (1975). Student suicide and college administrators: A perceptual gap. *Journal of Higher Education, 46,* 349-354.

Hersh, J.B. (1985). Interviewing college students in crisis. *Journal of Counseling and Development, 61,* 286-289.

Hewitt, J. (1980). *After suicide.* Philadelphia: Westminster Publishing.

Hill, F.E., & Harmon, F.M. (1976). The use of telephone tapes in a telephone counseling program. *Crisis Intervention, 7,* 88-96.

Hipple, J.L., Cimbolic, P., & Peterson, J. (1980). Student services response to a suicide. *Journal of College Student Personnel, 21,* 457-458.

Hoffer, W. (1972). What's being done about campus suicide. *College Management, 7,* 8-11.

Jones, F., & Najera, G.A. (1976). The helping network: Reactions and actions stimulated by students' acute mental illness in a university community. *Journal of the American College Health Association, 24,* 198-202.

Knauth, E.C. (1981). Importance of family assessments in the evaluation of psychiatric problems of college students. *Journal of the American College Health Association, 30,* 131-133.

Knott, J.E. (1973). Campus suicide in America. *OMEGA: Journal of Death and Dying, 4,* 65-71.

Kraft, D.P. (1980). Student suicides during a twenty-year period at a state university campus. *Journal of the American College Health Association, 28,* 258-262.

Lachar, D. (1974). *The M.M.P.I.: Clinical assessment and automated interpretation.* Los Angeles: Western Psychological Services.

Lester, D. (1967a). Suicide as an aggressive act. *Journal of Psychology, 66,* 47-50.

Lester, D. 1967b). Attempted suicide and body image. *Journal of Psychology, 66,* 287-290.

Levenson, M. (1974). Cognitive correlates of suicidal risk. In C. Neuringer (Ed.), Psychological assessment of suicidal risk (pp.150-163). Springfield, IL: Charles C. Thomas.

Leventhal, A.M., Berman, A.L., McCarthy, B.W., & Wasserman, C.W. (1976). Peer counseling on the university campus. *Journal of College Student Personnel, 17,* 504-509.

Miller, J. (1975). Suicide and adolescence. *Adolescence, 10,* 13-23.

Mishara, B.L. (1982). College students' experiences with suicide and reactions to suicidal verbalizations: A model for prevention. *Journal of Community Psychology, 10,* 142-150.

Mishara, B.L., Baker, A.H., & Mishara, T.T. (1976). Frequency of suicide attempts: A retrospective approach applied to college students. American *Journal of Psychiatry, 133,* 841-844.

Moorman, J.C., Urbach, J.R., & Ross, D.R. (1984). Guidelines for consultation with university personnel in student psychiatric emergencies. *Journal of the American College Health Association, 33,* 91-94.

Murray, D.C. (1973). Suicidal and depressive feelings among college students. *Psychological Reports, 33,* 175-181.

Ottens, A.J. (1983). Evaluation of a crisis training program in suicide prevention for the campus community. *Crisis Intervention, 13,* 25-40.

Paffenbarger, R.S., & Asnes, D.P. (1966). Chronic disease in former college students. III. Precursors of suicide in early and middle life. *American Journal of Public Health, 56,* 1026-1036.

Parnell, R.W. (1951). Mortality and prolonged illness among Oxford undergraduates, *Lancet, 1,* 731-733.

Parrish, H.M. (1957). Epidemiology of suicide among college students. *Yale Journal of Biology and Medicine, 29,* 585-595.

Pascarella, E.T., & Terenzini, P.T. (1976). Informal interaction with faculty and freshman ratings of the academic and non-academic experience of college. *Journal of Educational Research, 70,* 35-41.

Phillips, B.N., Pitcher, G.D., Worsham, M.E., & Miller, S.C. (1980). Test anxiety and the school environment. In I.G. Sarason (Ed.), *Test anxiety: Theory, research and applications* (pp.327-346). Hillsdale, NJ: Erlbaum.

Phillips, W.C. (1983). Suicide education for residence staff: Identification, intervention, and referral. *Journal of College Student Personnel, 24,* 376-378.

Ponterotto, J.G. (1987). Client hospitalization: Issues and considerations for the counselor. *Journal of Counseling and Development, 65,* 542-546.

Raphael, T. Power, S.H., & Berridge, W.L. (1937). The question of suicide as a problem in college mental hygiene. *American Journal of Orthopsychiatry, 7,* 1-14.

Richman, J. (1979). The family therapy of attempted suicide. *Family Process, 18,* 131-142.

Robbins, S.B., May, T.M., & Corazzini, J.G. (1985). Perceptions of client needs and counsleing center staff roles and functions. *Journal of Counseling Psychology, 32,* 641-4.

Rockwell, W.J.K. (1983). Initial communication with the parents of emotionally disturbed university students. *Journal of the American College Health Association, 28,* 205-210.

Roney, L.K., Wiley, M.O., Croteau, J.M., & Gelwick, B.P. (1986, April). *Psychological emergencies on campus: Standard of care issues.* Paper presented at the meeting of the American College Personnel Association, New Orleans, LA.

Rook, A. (1959). Student suicides. *British Medical Journal, 1,* 599-603.

Rosenfeld, L., & Prupas, M. (1984). *Left alive: After a suicide death in the family.* Springfield, IL: Charles C. Thomas

Ross, M.R. (1969). Suicide among college students. *American Journal of Psychiatry, 126,* 106-111.

Salovey, P., & D'Andrea, V.J. (1984). A survey of campus peer counseling activities. *Journal of the American College Health Association, 32,* 262-265.

Schrut, A. (1968). Some typical patterns in the behavior and background of adolescent girls who attempt suicide. *American Journal of Psychiatry, 125,* 107-112.

Schwartz, A.J. (1980). Inaccuracy and uncertainty in estimates of college student suicide rates. *Journal of the American College Health Association, 28,* 201-204.

Schwartz, A.J., & Reifler, C.B. (1980). Suicide among American college and university students from 1970-71 through 1975-76. *Journal of the American College Health Association. 28,* 205-210.

Seiden, R.H. (1966). Campus tragedy: A study of student suicide. *Journal of Abnormal Psychology, 71,* 389-99.

Seiden, R.H. (1971). The problem of suicide on college campuses. *Journal of the American College Health Association, 41,* 243-248.

Shneidman, E.S., & Farnsworth, D.L. (1972). *Death and the College student.* New York: Behavioral Publications.

Sims, L., & Ball, M.J. (1973). Suicide among university students. *Journal of the American College Health Association, 21,* 336-338.

Slimak, R.E., & Berkowitz, S.R. (1983). The university and college counseling center and malpractice suits. *Personnel and Guidance Journal, 61,* 291-294.

Sprinkle, R.L., & Mattheus, T.E. (1984). A model and a program for emergency student services. *Journal of College Student Personnel, 25,* 476-477.

Stanley, E.J., & Barter, J.T. (1970). Adolescent suicidal behavior. *American Journal of Orthopsychiatry. 40,* 87-96.

Steenland, R. (1973). Options in suicidal crisis. *NASPA Journal, 10,* 328-332.

Terenzini, P.T., & Pascarella, E.T. (1980). Student/faculty relationships and freshmen year educational outcomes: A further investigation. *Journal of College Student Personnel, 21,* 521-528.

Thurman, C.W., Baron, A., & Klein, R.L. (1979). Self-help tapes in a telephone counseling service: A three-year analysis. *Journal of College Student Personnel, 20,* 546-550.

Tucker, B.J., Megenity, D., & Vigil, L. (1970). Anatomy of a campus crisis center. *Personnel and Guidance Journal, 48,* 343-348.

U.S. Government. *Code of Federal Regulations.* Title 45: Section 84.

U.S. Government. (1976). Office of Federal Register. 29 U.S.C. Para. 794 (Supp., 1977).

Wallace, S. (1973). *After suicide.* New York: John Wiley and Sons.

Wenz, F. (1979). Self-injury behavior, economic status, and the family anomie syndrome among adolescents. *Adolescence, 14,* 387-397.

Westefeld, J.S., & Pattillo, C.M. (1987). College students' suicide: The case for a national clearinghouse. *Journal of College Student Personnel, 28,* 34-38.

Wolfe, R., & Cotler, S. (1973). Undergraduates who attempt suicide compared with normal and psychiatric controls. *OMEGA: Journal of Death and Dying, 4,* 305-312.

Wright, L.S., Snodgrass, G., & Emmons, J. (1984). Variables related to serious suicidal thoughts among college students. *NASPA Journal, 22,* 57-64.

Yufit, R.I., & Benzies, B. (1973). Assessing suicidal potential by time perspective. *Life-Threatening Behavior, 3,* 270-282.

CHAPTER **13**

CRISIS INTERVENTION

Rosemary A. Thompson, Ed.D.

Rosemary A. Thompson, Ed.D.

Drug Education/Crisis Intervention Specialist
Chesapeake Public Schools
Chesapeake, VA 23320

Rosemary A. Thompson, Ed.D., LPC, is Drug Education/Crisis Intervention Specialist for Cheaspeake Public Schools, Chesapeake, Virginia, and Adjunct Assistant Professor in Counselor Education at Old Dominion University, Norfolk, Virginia. During her fifteen years in the public school sector, she has been a psychology teacher, school counselor, school guidance director, and assistant principal for instruction. From a practitioner's perspective, she offers a formidable basis for her expertise in intervention programs for at-risk adolescents. Dr. Thompson has published widely in national counseling and educational journals on topics dealing with critical needs of adolescents and conducts seminars at local, state, and national conferences.

A native of Virginia, Dr. Thompson earned a B.S. degree in English and psychology from Radford University; a M.Ed. from The College of William and Mary in counseling; a C.A.G.S. from Old Dominion University in counseling; and an Ed.D. in counseling and administration from The College of William and Mary. She is a Licensed Professional Counselor, a National Certified Counselor, and maintains a private practice in educational consultation.

Dr. Thompson has served on the editorial board of *The School Counselor*, the editorial board of the *Journal of Counseling and Development*, and is currently editor of *The Virginia Counselor's Journal*. She was named Hampton Roads Counselor of the Year in 1985. Dr. Thompson currently resides in Virginia Beach, Virginia with her husband Charles R. Thompson, an engineer, and their two children Ryan and Jessica.

A Silent Scream

"Cell and bell" marks the structure of the school;
A six hour logic is the rigid "golden rule".
A silent scream echoes from impersonal, sterile walls;
Illusion, bleak despair lurk in estranged halls.

"Time-on-task" evolves as the teacher's arduous chore;
Promoting content over feeling is the fundamental class core.
A silent scream reluctantly sits alone there;
Haunting a young troubled mind, and yearning to share.

"Clocking-in and dropping-out" marks a parent's rushed demeanor;
I'll get to know him better, when he becomes a senior!"
A silent scream desperately lives disillusioned here;
New defenses, repression and obsession mask unshed tears.

A caring nature and welcomed shelter is the counselor's role;
But schedule changes, clerical tasks consume the daily toll.
A silent scream becomes a critical therapeutic source;
Perchance, I'll see him discussing the new elective course.

Content, task and structure punctuate our institutional forms;
Depression and alienation succumb as interpersonal norms.
What if...the silent scream decided it was time to quit,

called an unsuspecting friend,

then slit his fragile wrist?

Rosemary A. Thompson

EDITORIAL ABSTRACT: *In this chapter is presented school-based intervention strategies for preventing adolescent suicide. Extensive information on the roles of teachers, administrators, students, counselors and the district-wide crisis intervention team is included.*

Within the context of the school-as-community, the self-destructive potential of young people is a travesty of ambiguous proportion. Classmates, parents, teachers, and relatives experience both the direct implications of a student's death and the residual long-term effects of a significant loss. Personal loss or threat of loss increases a person's suicide risk. This is a very significant suicide indicator among adolescents. Invariably, all people affected must ultimately cope with confusion, blame, anger, fear, guilt, and various stages of the grieving process. What also continues to be clear is that when one suicide death occurs within a school, other students are immediately put at high risk.

Balk (1983) identified acute emotional responses of students after the death of a peer. He revealed that while peer support and chances to talk with friends about the death at such a time of loss were important aids to effective coping with death, many peers feel uncomfortable talking about it. They frequently avoid the survivors to decrease the discomfort of not knowing what to say or how to say it. Balk maintains that young people sometimes hide their feelings of grief because they are not considered acceptable in public; and as a result, adolescents are often confused about the source of their reoccurring grief reactions.

The survey by Tishler et al. (1981) of 108 adolescents revealed 20% had experienced a recent death of a friend or relative; 22% were exposed to a recent suicidal episode of a family member. The young people surveyed also stated that their inability to come with the loss led them to begin having suicidal thoughts themselves. Rappeport (1978), commenting on counseling intervention with survivors of a sudden death experience, stressed that young people need structured opportunities to talk about the death as a means to test and retest reality. Validation of feelings as a perceptual check is particularly important to adolescents. Talking about the death and related anxieties in a secure environment provides a means to "work through" the experience and serves to prevent destructive fantasy building when young people cannot test their ideas in a secure environment against the real world.

Stanford (1978) further suggested the need for direct intervention in schools with survivors. Teachers need help in understanding and handling young people's normal yet often inappropriate reactions to death. Glasser (1978) stated that young people often take cues as to how to react from the adults around them more than from the event itself. A paramount need is for counselors, educators, and other support personnel to address the emotional needs of survivors and intervene to enhance coping skills and ultimately to prevent future suicides, and related self-destructive behavior.

School personnel need to understand and respond to adolescent anxiety related to asking for help. Powell et al. (1985) found that "The risk a student must take to talk to a significant adult is to be considered a problem case." In addition adolescents may manifest resistance to seeking help related to feelings of loss of control and fear of dependency, "being found out." having to "tell everything," or submission to a powerful authority such as a school administrator.

School-as-Community Crisis Intervention Strategies

The school-as-community crisis intervention strategies for preventing adolescent suicide includes the following components: (1) the school community link; (2) the evolution and training of the district-wide crisis intervention team: partnerships with other helping professionals; (3) staff development in-service education of teachers, administrators, and other support personnel; (4) developing a crisis communication contingency plan: demonstrating responsibility and responsiveness; (5) student awareness, education, and morale: enhancing school climate; (6) structured intervention procedures for individual school crisis team members; and (7) identifying procedures for the day after a student suicide: mobilizing the crisis team after a suicide has occurred and assisting at-risk adolescents.

SCHOOL COMMUNITY LINK

A comprehensive, district-wide suicide intervention and prevention program provides a commitment to policy and structured procedures for decreasing the personal and the institutional liabilities for self-destructive behaviors. Such a program involves the effective mobilization of current resources, and the collective commitment of administrators, teachers, parents, students, and other support personnel. The underlying premise is a belief in human potential and the value of life. Specifically, program goals should outline (1) procedures the individual school and respective community can develop to initiate a prevention program, (2) strategies to follow in developing a plan to deal with the suicide crisis, (3) activities and steps to follow at the time of an actual suicide crisis, (4) the education of all groups that interface with the school community (P.T.A., advisory boards, clubs, and community service organizations), (5) the identification of skilled helping professionals, and (6) educational media resources that the school and special interests groups could utilize at either the prevention or intervention stage of a school/community suicide prevention intervention program. School/community objectives could include to (1) develop parental participation in the development of school programs and to provide ongoing continuing education for parents in areas of concern (e.g., teenage stress, depression, or related self-defeating behaviors, etc.), (2) develop a sense of a united commitment to assume responsibility for problems that affect the entire community (e.g. alcohol/drug abuse, suicide prevention, peer pressure, child abuse, and the effects of violence on children), (3) encourage support and reestablish open communication between parents and their children, and (4) provide community education for parents and other concerned constituents.

External Articulation: The Advisory Committee

Fundamentally, an assessment needs to be made of community resources and an identification of human resource personnel in the community that could become barriers (because of lack of training, education, or limited perspectives of the school environment) to program facilitation and implementation. The appointment of an advisory committee made up of local school and community resource personnel can provide a collective perspective when making recommendations for the design of a prevention effort, as well as identify existing resources needed to effectively implement a suicide intervention and prevention program. The committee should include members of the school staff with different roles and responsibilities, representatives from local community agencies identified through the community resources assessment, helping professionals in private practice, and concerned parents. Furthermore, the organization of an advisory committee fosters networks between institutions and community agencies with a common vision to provide services and programs for education, awareness, and growth. The committee could be composed of

school principal(s),
central office administrative staff,
medical professional(s),
social worker(s),
school psychologist(s),
school counselor(s),
police officer(s),
parent(s),
school nurse(s),
community mental health counselor(s),
local PTA/PTO board member(s),
and local minister (s).

The primary role of the advisory committee would be to recommend a series of awareness and prevention activities designed to reach counselors, teachers, parents, students, and administrators. The committee can also provide a network of available community resources such as a twenty-four hour crisis line, referral services, speakers bureau, and educational media resources such as pamphlet and brochures. The committee could identify various community support groups such as survivors of suicide, alateen, narcotics anonymous, and various local support systems for adolescents and adults.

EVOLUTION AND TRAINING

Internal Training

School personnel vary widely in their formal training and their clinical experiences with depressed and/or suicidal adolescents. Consequently, not all school counselors or school psychologists can provide counseling or therapy. However, caregivers in schools need not be trained as therapists in order to contribute in a highly significant way to suicide prevention efforts or to assist an adolescent through healthy crisis resolution.

School-based Action Plan

A critical component of a suicide prevention plan is a school-based action plan. A well planned prevention program may make unnecessary a suicide intervention with an adolescent. Yet, to have an effective prevention program a systematic intervention action plan is most important. The recommendation is for the local school principal as instructional leader to appoint staff members to serve on a School Crisis Intervention team (SCIT). The team members may include but are not limited to the following personnel:

- The principal or designee who clarifies local school policy and procedures pertinent to suicide prevention and intervention plans (i.e. documentation, intervention, referral and follow-up procedures).

- The school guidance director, designated counselor, assistant principal, or other school personnel who assumes the responsibility for organizing activities involving staff, students, and local community.

- The Designated Crisis Intervention Team Leader who organizes activities and resource personnel in the event that the Crisis Intervention Action Plan (CIAP) must be implemented.

An example of a School Crisis Team and Intervention Plan is provided in Figure 13.1.

Team members also should understand that their duties are long-term because they will have key responsibilities in both the prevention stage and the intervention stage, should the latter ever require implementation. Suggested activities of the team include the following:

- Determine local faculty, student, and community needs related to suicide education and prevention activities (school divisions and communities will vary in their knowledge, expertise, and sophistication).
- Arrange for and provide appropriate training for school personnel within their particular school.

(Continued on p. 372)

School Crisis Team And Intervention Plan

Each school has identified a school crisis team which includes members of the administration, guidance, and identified teachers. When a student threatens to commit suicide or a staff member believes a student plans to attempt suicide, the following steps are to be taken:

1. The staff member should immediately refer the student to the appropriate counselor or principal.

2. The counselor or principal should interview the student to determine the accuracy of the suicide threat. If the threat seems real, the counselor or principal will immediately call the parent or guardian to discuss the situation and explain that intervention is necessary.

3. Documentation of the suicide threat and intervention procedures should be maintained by counselor or principal in the student's category II record.

4. The counsleor or principal should provide the names of professional resources to the parents. If parents fail to respond to the suicide threat of their child or fail to contact a professional resource for the student, the counselor or principal should contact the coordinator of Chesapeake Public School's Psychological Services for professional support. Psychological Services in conjunction with the counselor or principal of the school, will evaluate the situation and determine whether court services and/or child protective services should be contacted.

5. If the counselor or principal during the interview determines that the student is not in imminent danger or has not threatened suicide, the counselor or principal will provide appropriate monitoring or follow-up as necessary.

Figure 13.1. An example of a School Crisis Team and Intervention Plan used in Chesapeake Public Schools, Chesapeake, VA.

- Develop and provide a student awareness and education program.

- Coordinate and provide opportunities for parents and other persons in the local community to learn about suicide prevention.

- Identify volunteer faculty members willing to receive more specialized training in communication and group facilitation skills to work in groups with adolescents.

- Facilitate the development of a resource list of school and community resource personnel willing to provide inservice training, to make P.T.A. presentations, to accept referrals for intervention at the time of a suicide threat, and to work with the school in the event of a suicide crisis. Suggested resources include district pupil personnel services and public and private mental health professionals.
- Process for content and understanding The Crisis Intervention Action Plan (CIAP) which will be implemented in the event of a suicide crisis.

With appropriate training, most school counselors and school psychologists can conduct and facilitate crisis intervention procedures. However, staff development and training could be provided in the following areas for members of the crisis team:

1. A profile of the contemporary adolescent
    - definition of high risk population
    - life stages and adjustment difficulties
    - identifying characteristics of students at risk
    - recognition and differentiation of suicide states on a continuum of acute to chronically depressed
    - recognition of family dynamics and dysfunction
    - etiology of adolescent depression
2. Suicide and other self-destructive behaviors among adolescents
    - adolescent coping strategies
    - attitudes and ethical responsibilities regarding suicide
    - utilization of the Suicide Assessment and Intervention Form (SAIF) (See Figure 13.2 for an example.)

(Continued on p. 374)

CHESAPEAKE PUBLIC SCHOOLS

Crisis Assessment and Intervention Form
(Confidential Information) Referral Date ______ Time ______

Student's Name ____________________ BD___ Age___ Sex: M F

School ____________________ Grade ____ Teacher ________

Parent's ____________________ Phone (H) ________ (W)______

Address ____

Student Referred By ______________ Relationship ____________

Reason for Referral ________________________________

____

____

____

Stressors (current disposition)	Symptoms: (How Long)
☐ Loss of significant other by death, divorce, separation (who, when) ____________	☐ Disturbance in sleep ☐ Disturbance in appetite ☐ Weight loss/gain ☐ Isolation/withdrawal
☐ Loss of important peer relationships break-up of boyfriend/girlfriend relationship	☐ Lethargic ☐ Accident prone
☐ Apparent alienation/rejection of parent(s)	☐ Truancy/running away ☐ Aggression/agitation ☐ Impaired ability to concentrate
☐ Recent failure at school—relationships, sports, academic standing, etc.	☐ Thinking/talking about wish to be dead
☐ Recent involvement with the law	☐ Sexual problems (promiscuity, identity, pregnancy)
☐ Does not belong to an identified peer group	☐ Frequent clinic visitor ☐ Change in personal appearance
☐ Other stressors ____________	☐ Somatic complaints (headaches, etc.) ☐ Drug/alcohol abuse ☐ Lacks interest ☐ Has given away prized possessions
Emotional State: ☐ Guilt ☐ Anxiety ☐ Hopelessness ☐ Feelings of being bad ☐ Feels should be punished	

Figure 13.2. Example of a Crisis Assessment and Intervention Form

Self-destructive Plan

Method: ______________ Is implement available? ☐ Yes ☐ No
How lethal is the method? ☐ High ☐ Low

Place: ______________

Time: ______________

Has the student made a public declaration of his intent? ☐ Yes ☐ No

Prior thoughts of suicide? ☐ Yes ☐ No When did they first occur? ______

How frequently does the student think about suicide? ______________

Prior threat? ☐ Yes ☐ No When? ______________

Prior attempt? ☐ Yes ☐ No When? __________ Method? __________

Hospitalized for depression or suicidal behavior? ☐ Yes ☐No When? ______

Received outpatient treatment? ☐ Yes ☐ No When? ______________

Student is willing to sign a life line contract? ☐ Yes ☐ No

Figure 13.2. Continued.

3. The school Crisis Intervention Team
   - methods of crisis intervention
   - roles and responsibilities
   - mobilization of the crisis intervention team
   - intervention with the student at-risk
   - activating and completing the action plan
   - information about resources such as suicide crisis lines, emergency services, local helping professionals

STAFF DEVELOPMENT

Administrators

The success of any program within a school is seriously dependent upon the involvement of the principal. Teachers and other support personnel often take their cues for their own responsibility from the leadership in the school. When principals take an active part and interest in prevention and intervention activities, so do respective faculties.

Teachers and Other Support Personnel

Fundamentally, long-term approaches such as psychological education and concurrent prevention strategies can be taught to teachers, paraprofessionals, and other support personnel. Many deliberate psychological skills training programs currently exist for children and adolescents (Bash & Camp, 1980; Goldstein et al., 1979). Other models to stimulate thinking and to help students to recognize, identify, and express their feeling about living provide both education and systematic delivery (Joan, 1986; and Quest National Center, 1982).

Short-term in-service education for people who work directly with adolescents involves creating an awareness that (1) the problem is serious and of epidemic proportion, (2)faculty and staff do have skills to help, and (3) a referral and support system is available to assist them. Essentially, the school principal is perhaps the best judge of the type of in-service training needed, the personnel to use, and the issues to be discussed. Suggested strategies could include conducting two short workshops sessions to discuss and disseminate information relating to adolescent suicide.

Session I. Provide general educational information about adolescent suicide vis-a-vie one of the many educational media presentations on the market, followed by a discussion of the signs, symptoms, and profile of the at-risk student.

Session II. Provide a discussion by trained helping professionals in the identification and referral process of a student who appears suicidal. Provide the instructional staff with specific guidelines and procedures for referring students. Small in-service sessions by teacher planning well is more conducive to discussion and interaction, rather than large faculty meetings at the end of the day.

In-service Information for Teachers

Public awareness and concern have grown as the number of children lost to suicide has increased, and citizens in communities throughout the country have looked to public agencies and institutions for assistance. The risk that a student will commit or attempt a suicide is greater today than ever before. School staff members are in a unique position to recognize the possibility of self-destructive behavior and to take action to save a life, particularly for students who cannot or will not turn for help to their families and friends. To do so, however, teachers and other school personnel must be able to recognize symptoms and know how to react to a student in such a crisis situation.

Significant Indicators of Crisis In Students

Crisis can occur in all students regardless of age. "A crisis" is a state of acute emotional distress that includes a temporary inability to cope by means of one's usual resources of problem-solving and coping strategies. Any event can be a hazard for an individual if he/she does not have adequate coping mechanisms for the situation or if the person is vulnerable to the particular event. The crisis is usually brief in duration. The positive resolution of a crisis depends on crisis intervention, that aspect of crisis management carried out by human resource people in or outside of school, such as the school's crisis team leader, nurse, teacher, principal, counselor, minister, or mental health professional. Essentially, "crisis intervention" is a short-term helping process. It focuses on resolution of the immediate problem through the use of the student's personal, social, and environmental resources. Some significant factors and predictors of a student in crisis may include one or more of the following indicators.

Jacobs (1971) has identified factors that contribute to an adolescent attempting suicide:

- longstanding history of problems, which are escalated in adolescence;
- failure in coping techniques, which leads to a loss of hope; and
- progressive isolation from meaningful social relationships.

Farber (1968) further outlined three predictors of adolescent suicide:

- a low state of hope,
- a low sense of competence, and
- a history of prior suicide attempts.

In assessing the degree of risk, one also must pay attention to several other indicators:

- the level of depression,
- the level of impulse control,
- the degree of hopefulness,
- the coping techniques the adolescent usually employs,
- the history of past attempts, and
- the significant others in the adolescent's life.

An adequate support system is critical to suicidal adolescents. There is a fundamental need to know that someone cares.

Jacobs (1980) further identifies the following verbal or behavioral messages which may be considered at risk for suicide:

- prevailing sadness, lack of energy, difficulty in concentrating, loss of interest or pleasure in regular activities, or atypical acting-out behaviors, anger, belligerence to authority figures, alcohol/drug abuse, sexual promiscuity, and running away from home;
- academic failure in school, often accompanied by the adolescent's feelings of disinterest or helplessness;
- social isolation-lack of close friends or confidants-even though the adolescent may have superficial contact with a group of peers;

- disharmony or disruption in the family, divorce, separation, alcoholism, and physical or sexual abuse;

- recent loss of or suicide attempt by a loved one or family member and/or break-up with boyfriend or girlfriend;

- atypical eating/sleeping patterns;

- verbal remarks about sense of failure, worthlessness, isolation, absence, or death and written stories, essays or projects displaying the same themes;

- collecting pills, razor blades, knives, ropes or firearms;

- giving away personal possessions and writing a suicide note; previous suicide attempt. (p.108)

Teacher's Responsibility

If a student threatens suicide or manifests other self-destructive behaviors your reaction and responsiveness could make a difference in a positive crisis resolution. Crisis intervention techniques involves establishing a supportive relationship with the student. Intervention can be technically easy, but emotionally difficult.

What To Do. If a student makes a suicidal statement,

- show concern and avoid being consumed by the students emotional distortions of what is occurring;

- listen with genuine interest;

- ask questions in a calm, straight forward manner;

- accept and encourage appropriate expression of affect such as grief or anger;

- help clarify the issues;

- do not leave the student; and

- refer the student to a member of the school crisis team.

Note: A school employee is not held liable for a breach of confidence when action is taken on behalf of a student whose behavior may be harmful to himself/herself or others. Very often, teachers are "first finders" of students in distress.

What To Ask.

- Ask questions to ascertain the seriousness of the student
- ask what feelings have prompted the desire to commit suicide,
- ask questions about the student's home situation and relationships with friends,
- ask if the student has talked with anyone else about suicide, and
- ask if consideration has been given to the means of suicide and the steps taken to secure those means.

What Not To Do. If a student tells you that he/she is thinking about suicide:

- do not refuse to talk about it;
- do not lecture;
- do not offer platitudes or simple answers;
- do not analyze the person's motives, try to impose your own value system regarding suicide and death;
- do not argue or try to reason;
- do not try to challenge the student or use scare tactics;
- do not be sworn to secrecy; and
- do not involve yourself in therapy; leave that to a professionally trained person.

DEVELOPING THE CRISIS COMMUNICATION CONTINGENCY PLAN

Community awareness programs are the areas over which the school has the least control, especially at the secondary level where parents become less involved in their child's activities. The school personnel, however, must try to communicate and educate their constituents about issues such as teen stress, suicide, substance abuse, and other self-destructive behaviors. This approach is important for two fundamental reasons: (1) parents made aware of the problem in a non-threatening environment may be more responsive to school personnel should their child ever be involved in a suicidal crisis; and (2) community support may be more easily obtained in the event of a crisis if the community perceives the school as having done all it could to prevent a crisis situation.

Demonstrating Responsibility and Responsiveness

When confronted with a crisis situation, one person, preferably the principal, must assume responsibility for developing a Crisis Communication Contingency Plan (3CP). A 3CP provides a systematic procedure to disseminate information more efficiently, and to foster school/community stability. A 3CP also anticipates events that could occur with specific procedures to manage rumor and misinformation, as well as foster stability and congruency of information. Fundamentally effective public relations in the school should encompass much more than merely reacting to reporters and media personnel. The following investment procedures could be implemented systematically to provide objective, accurate, and timely information:

- write a comprehensive crisis communication contingency plan (3CP) that details who to contract, designates human resources, and utilizes a communication tree (who calls whom) to facilitate the flow of information;
- routinely distribute copies of the 3CP to all school personnel annually during back-to-school orientation activities;
- develop a fact sheet about school programs, resources, and services for students and their families as a handout at

regularly scheduled meetings for groups and organizations that interface with the school (P.T.A. boards, advisory committees, feeder schools, etc.), and in the event of an emergency;

- designate a central office area (clinic, attendance office, etc.) to coordinate information gathering and dissemination; and

- take initiative with the media.

A statement should be made as soon as the crisis occurs to show that school officials are perceptive and responsible to community and school needs. Remind faculty and staff that only designated spokespeople are authorized to talk with news media. Perhaps, one of the most subtle defenses against the occurrence of future suicides is for a school official to be firm and assertive with information given to the media. The excitement, the lurid, and the romantic depiction of a student's suicide seems to attract troubled adolescents, and promote the act as a viable alternative. Displaying a student's death on the front page of the local newspaper (complete with picture and quotes from grieving classmates) gives the victim a fame in death that he/she may not have achieved in life. Perceived as a hero or martyr, many adolescents may personalize the act and see themselves in place of the victim.

Leeann Lane-Malbon, (personal communication, July 11, 1987) director of the Survivor of Suicide program at Tidewater Psychiatric Institute in Virginia Beach, Virginia suggests that reporters take extra effort to show that alternatives to suicide do exist. Lane-Malbon maintained, "it's inappropriate to glamorize the person who died." "It's important that we teach people about suicide and how to prevent it" "Newspaper stories which are done sensitively help with the education process." A number of things should be avoided:

- Don't put suicide stories on the front page of the newspaper. Placing the story on the inside page, or near the bottom may reduce the "copycat" phenomena.

- Don't use the word suicide in the headline.

- Don't use photographs or intimate descriptions of the victims life. This promotes over-identification with the victim.

- Don't fail to mention alternatives to suicide. If suicide is the only alternative mentioned, it serves to advertise the method.

- When communicating information to faculty, staff, students, or parents, maintain a "unified position and a uniform message."

Keep messages concise, clear, consistent, and tailored to each targeted group with accuracy and sensitivity. Hannaford (1987) maintained that one important procedure is to develop a "SOCO"—a "single overriding communication objective" when dealing with the media. The role of the designated contact person and a SOCO is to focus upon a communication objective, bringing the topic back to the objective and reinforcing it with accurate information as much as possible. Essentially, the more a topic is framed and the objective discussed, the more it is likely to appear as part of a reporter's focus in the story.

In addition, the principal or designee may wish to appoint a community steering committee composed of clergy, health professionals, community leaders, or P.T.A. representatives. This group can assist in arranging programs on the subject of preventing self-destructive behaviors at churches, synagogue, clubs, and organizations. Community support systems also can assist in providing the same uniform message, and reinforce information about programs and services the school can provide for families and their children.

To foster additional continuity, the parent-teacher associations (and other community groups that agree to sponsor programs on adolescent stress and related self-destructive concerns for parents) also could be encouraged to hold their program about the same time that in-school educational programs for teachers and students are scheduled so that families who wish to discuss the topic further would be equally informed. School personnel can be supportive and resourceful to groups organizing parent programs, especially in the selection of appropriate speakers.

Reciprocal attendance of teachers and school administrators at the programs sponsored by parents also can help reinforce the importance of the subject and provide continuity and an opportunity for parents to ask questions about the in-school programs for teachers and students. In some instances, members of the advisory or steering committee can serve as speakers at community programs. This can serve as an evaluation of the effectiveness of a program and for planning in the future.

Other questions to consider for evaluation purposes are the following:

- How effective are educational and awareness programs giving information, raising consciousness or changing attitudes?

- Are the goals of the community education approaches realistic and related to consumer needs?

- Is the material up to date and related to specific populations?

STUDENT AWARENESS, EDUCATION, AND MORALE

Students need to be made aware of the facts about suicide in an honest, objective, non-emotional setting. They need to be informed of

- factors related to suicide such as drug and alcohol abuse, family problems, and relationships with girlfriends and boyfriends;

- ways they can help their peers who may be experiencing problems of stress or adjustment;

- how to deal with daily frustrations and stress; and

- where and to whom to go for help for themselves and their friends.

Educational information may be appropriately incorporated into units of study in existing health and social science curricula, or the school may want to develop programs in which school counseling personnel visit scheduled "core subject" classes throughout the year to teach units of study that pertain to managing stress, life crises, and how to help a friend. Whatever approach is used, all students should be systematically exposed to accurate information, and be provided with an opportunity to share an open dialog in a secure environment with a significant adult.

Information for Students

A suicidal peer may feel that they can no longer cope with problems and that suicide may be the only way out. Most people think about suicide at some point in their lives. Most people find that these thoughts are temporary and that things do get better. Suicide is a needless and permanent solution to short-term problems.

Major Life Crises for Students. The following is a list of major life crises for students which often trigger a suicide or suicide attempt. Helping students to know these and where to obtain assistance may prevent the suicide or the attempt:

- death of a family member,
- the divorce or separation of parents,
- the adolescent's own pregnancy/or father of a child of an unwed mother,
- a change in residence,
- romantic breakup,
- loss of social or financial status of the family,
- severe disappointment,
- severe physical illness, and
- precipitating psychological illness such as depression.

Help students to recognize that when the feel like ending their lives, or know someone who wishes to end his/her life, they need to remember that help is available; problems can be solved; suicide can be prevented. To aid students in identifying significant indicators of crisis situations "Help Cards" or "Crisis Cards" could be distributed. Illustration of information to include is shown in Figure 13.3.

What To Do. When you suspect that a friend or family member may be suicidal, you may become nervous and anxious. This is a normal feeling. A helpful procedure is to remember the following:

- Believe and trust your intuition that the person may be self-destructive or want to hurt himself/herself.

- Communicate your concern for the well-being of the person. If a friend says "I'm so bummed out I could kill myself"...say, "I don't want you to" thus affirming that you care for him/her and that your relationship is important. Be an active listener and show your support.

- Be direct. Talk openly and freely and ask direct questions about the person's intentions. Try to determine if the person has a plan for suicide, i.e., the how, the when, and the where.

- Get professional help. Encourage the friend to seek help from a school counselor, teacher, minister, or someone who can help solve the problem. If the person resists, you may need to get the necessary help for him/her.

What Not To Do. Help the student learn what not to do as well as what to do. They, as well as you, need to remember the following things.

- Do not allow yourself to be sworn to secrecy by the suicidal friend. You may lose a friendship for the moment, but you can save a life forever.

- Do not leave the person alone if you believe the risk of suicide is immediate.

SOME SIGNIFICANT INDICATORS OF CRISIS IN STUDENTS

Crisis can occur in all students regardless of age. Most frequently the student in crisis may attempt or commit suicide. Some significant indicators of a student in crisis may include one or more of the following.

Significant Indicators

Suicide threat
Verbal hints indicating self-destructive behavior or that life would be better if student did not exist
Preoccupation with thoughts of suicide or death.
Previous suicide attempt.
Family member or close friend has attempted or completed suicide.
Making final arrangements, giving away possessions.
Sudden unexplained cheerfulness after prolonged depression.
Keeping guns, knives, or lethal medicines in student's possession.
Breakup with boyfriend or girlfriend and withdrawal from other friendships

School Indicators

Failing or drop in grades
Difficulty concentrating on school work
Loss of interest in extra-curricular activities
Social isolation
New to school
Frequent referrals to office because of behavior, tardiness, truancy
Academic learning difficulties

Physical Indicators

Changes in eating or sleeping patterns
Weight gain or loss
Neglect of personal appearance
Lethargy, listlessness
Frequent physical complaints
Pregnancy
Prolonged or terminal illness
Drug or alcohol abuse

Family Indicators

Loss of family member (or anniversary of loss) through death, separation, or divorce
Rejection by family members
Financial change, job loss
Recent household move
Family discord
Change in immediate family or household membership
Alcoholism or drug use in the family
Student is a victim of physical, sexual, and/or emotional abuse
Running away from home
Family history of emotional disturbance

Social and Emotional Indicators

Noted personality change
Depression, feelings of sadness
Withdrawal, does not interact with others
Agitation, aggression, rebellion
Sexual problems (promiscuity, identity, pregnancy)
Feelings of despair, hopelessness, helplessness
Feelings of being bad or the need to be punished
Unexplained accidents, reckless behavior
Recent legal involvement

Significant Times of Danger
Rites of Passage

Graduation
Completion of parental divorce
Anniversaries of unhappy events (parental deaths, severe losses)
Holidays, particularly family holidays
Vacation times, especially if child is isolated
Change of season
Custody disagreements

NOTE: Help cards or crisis cards are a highly visible information that serves to provide a measure of security for young people and adults. School divisions might consider investing in printing and circulating help cards as a prevention alternative.

Figure 13.3. Help Card or Crisis Card.

- Do not act shocked at what the person tells you.

- Do not counsel the person yourself, find a responsible adult.

- Do not debate whether suicide is right or wrong. This may make the person feel more guilty and depressed.

School Resources To Seek. Students need to know who within the school is willing and able to be of assistance at a time of crisis or approaching crisis. Identify those persons, the list may include

- counselors,

- teachers,

- school psychologist or social worker,

- nurse,

- principal,

- student activities director,

- club sponsor, and

- coach.

Improving School Climate and Student Morale

In addition to student education and awareness programs, perhaps there is a need for school personnel to identify and implement programs and activities within the school-as-community that foster a positive school climate; promoting the self-worth of the adolescent. The need for such a program is emphasized by such proponents as Sprinthall (1984) and Dinkmeyer (1971): "The lack of a required sequentially developmental program in self-understanding and human behavior testifies to an educational paradox: we have taught children almost everything in school except to understand and accept themselves and to function more effectively in human relationships" (p.62).

Rogers (1980) further asserted, "If we are truly aware, we can hear the silent screams of denied feelings echoing off every classroom wall" (p.251). He added, "I deplore the manner in which, from early years, the child's education splits him or her: the mind can come to school, and the body is permitted peripherally to tag along, but the feelings and emotions can live freely and expressively only outside the school" (p.263). Powell et al. (1985) in their observations of the high school-as-community further revealed that "the price of a conversation with a caring adult was that a student would have to risk being considered a problem case" (p.46). Consequently, the perrenial dominance of cognitive endeavors over affective domains serves to obscure the adolescents search for meaning and relatedness to larger society.

Collective efforts invested around structured activities to discuss adjustment anxieties in a secure environment could enhance the self-worth of the struggling at-risk adolescent. Ongoing programs in the schools are crucial to provide opportunities for all adolescents to express feelings and to know that significant adults care about their well-being, emotionally as well as intellectually. The following activities (not all inclusive) are offered with the understanding that variations will be needed to (1) meet the various maturity and developmental life adjustment needs of student populations, and (2) meet the various responsive needs and commitment goals of schools and their respective communities. These activities however could be a viable catalyst to open communication and the validation of perceptions and feelings of both adults and adolescents.

- Set up a monthly program in which teachers recommend students who do not usually receive recognition to eat lunch with the principal, assistant principal, coach, or other significant adult in the adolescent's life.

- Have a "student of the week" or "student of the month" program in which each instructional discipline selects a student to be recognized. Achievement need not be the only criteria for selection; the dependable average student, the student who exhibits good citizenship also could be recognized.

- Set up a routine system in which each teacher telephones the homes of four or five students a week to relate some positive aspect of the student's role in class.

- Develop a "student adoption program" where each member of the instructional staff adopt an at-risk student (with behavioral adjustment problems, attendance problems, or family problems, etc.) to meet with them on a daily basis to discuss problems, progress or barriers to success and develop short-term strategies to enhance success rather than failure.

- In school newsletters or newspapers, recognize as many students as possible for contributions to the school. Try to find students who are seldom identified and find a significant contribution. Identify and recognize other areas in which students excel such as vocational/technical areas; student volunteers in local activities such as a hospital auxiliary, fire department; and student employees of the month, through school work programs.

- Promote clubs and service organizations that are altruistic and other-centered. Students often rediscover their self-importance by learning that they are valued by others. To do so gives students an opportunity to feel they have meaning and can effect change, or enhance the quality of life. Organizations or participation in such activities as Students Against Drunk Drivers (SADD), Rock Against Drugs (RAD), the Special Olympics, Sub Teens Recreational Activities to Educate (STATE), and Responsible Educated Adolescents Can Help America (REACH America) are selected examples.

- Implement an on-going student support group as part of the student services of the school counseling program. Provide the opportunity to share anxieties in a secure environment and to achieve validation from a significant adult in a helping capacity provides significant support for adolescents. Topics could include

  dealing with life-transitions and change,
  academic pressure,

parental separation and divorce,
competition and the meaning of excellence,
death, loss, or separation: Necessary losses to personal growth, and
maintaining interpersonal relationships.

- Develop a student stress program which can be preventive and circumvent the direct discussion of suicide with students focusing on many of the factors found to precipitate self-destructive behaviors. Classes on suicide are often not as successful as student classes and programs about stress, followed by small group discussion and other group activities. Emphasis could be placed on the social, emotional, and curative factors that adolescents possess as a group to manage personal, social, or academic disappointments or frustrations.

- Train volunteer teachers to serve as positive role models and to lead group discussions on subjects of time-management, stress, and academic problem-solving strategies. Mental health professionals can serve as resource people to the schools to present 4 to 6 week units in targeted classes.

- Institute a peer counseling program. Development of a peer counseling program is based on the premise that adolescents invariably turn to their peers for needed support and understanding, as well as a validation of their perceptions and feelings. In addition students as products of a structured training program have been found to be less dogmatic, more open to new ideas, and felt more adequate as a person upon completion of the training experience (Thompson, 1986). By learning new skills such as listening, paraphrasing, and expressing empathy, the peer helper develops a stronger sense of self as well as a belief in the efficacy of the process of helping. The primary focus is on prevention and the enhancement of personal worth among self and peers.

Fundamentally, adolescents are trained to help others as effective leaders, group listeners, and positive role models. A peer counseling program also extends the school counselor's reach to the school population as skillful listeners and special friends. Peer roles and responsibilities may include:

academic high school planning options and information,

career information and dissemination,

discussion of social and emotional concerns in groups,

new student to school orientation responsibilities,

feeder school orientation of incoming students,

information about community resources and hotlines,

information and distribution of school guidance and counseling materials,

information and resources regarding referral processes for individual student concerns, and

articulation agents for programs and services of the school counseling department.

- Structure training experiences for student volunteers. The following goals could be included:

  developing increased awareness of self and others,

  developing facilitative communication skills,

  developing problem-solving and decision-making skills,

  self-knowledge and exploration including clearly defining one's own value system,

  developing small group counseling skills and facilitative techniques,

  recognizing and referring at-risk students to responsible adults.

- Design a curriculum for school counselors to team teach with selected curricula such as health education in order to present pertinent information to students during the study of a mental health unit. A team approach can provide a secure environment in which to discuss controversial issues; this approach also increases the visibility and accessibility of counselors on the secondary level. Objectives and structured lessons could be developed to allow students to discover and express their own attitudes and beliefs about suicide,

present the facts of suicidal behavior and to dispel the myth around the subject,

provide students with information that will help them better understand depression and suicide ideation,

teach strategies for dealing with stressors and/or disappointments,

teach students to use the resources within their school and community,

make students aware of their roles as potential "first finders" of suicidal peers,

provide students with appropriate courses of action to take if they encounter potentially suicidal peers, and

formally integrate suicide prevention into the secondary curriculum.

A student curriculum which focuses on suicide prevention is an important component of a school-based intervention effort. However, it is also one of the most controversial. Competing philosophies seem to exist: one consists of the inoculation model which says that a few are killed but more are helped; and the other is the "loss of stigma" that results from extensive coverage of a student suicide. The controversy is based on the apprehension that teaching such a unit will stimulate thoughts of suicide among classmates. A recurring anxious question among educators, researchers and mental health professional is "does a frank discussion of suicide in the schools actually prompt more young people to kill themselves?" Grant (1987) who has led numerous teen suicide prevention and therapy techniques workshops believed "that suicide prevention program definitely do not trigger more suicides, but actually help young people to open up about their feelings of depression, loneliness, and isolation and find support from their teacher, peers and family" (p. 3)

Ideally, the development and implementation of a comprehensive services curriculum could be designed for the "mastery of daily problem-solving skills such as self-competency, enhancement of interpersonal relationships, communications, values, and the awareness of roles, attitudes and motivation" (Worrell & Stilwell, 1981). Personal development could become an integral part of the secondary school curriculum and evolve as a required carnegie unit which is integrated into the student's program of studies much like computer literacy, driver's education, or fine arts. Powell et al. (1985) lended credence to this potential maintaining that along with the horizontal, vertical, and extracurricular, the "service curriculum" is the fastest-growing component with the comprehensive high school. Programs within the services curriculum directly address social or psychological problems such as grief, child abuse, depression, and alienation or emotional and social problems deemed educationally valid. Some schools provide special programs depending on their populations such as daycare for children of students; rehabilitation for delinquent teens; services for special needs or handicapped students, and remedial services such as tutorials, laboratories, and resource rooms for students in academic trouble (Powell et al. 1985, p. 33).

STRUCTURED INTERVENTION PROCEDURES

Each school in a district should organize it's own school crisis intervention team which could include members of the local administration, school counselor(s) identified teacher(s), and other significant adults. All local teams will be collectively assembled routinely for training in suicide intervention and crisis management skills. The school crisis team's primary responsibility would be to mobilize local resources and to follow specific procedures in the event a student manifests suicidal ideation or reveals a plan. These procedures are strengthened by administrative directives or local school board policy. For example, when a student verbalizes suicide ideation, the following steps may be outlined by administrative policy:

- The staff member or student should immediately refer the student to the appropriate counselor or administrator.

- The counselor or administrator should interview the student to determine the accuracy of the suicide threat. If the threat is confirmed, the counselor or administrator immediately should involve the parent or guardian to discuss the situation and explain that intervention is an alternative.

- Documentation of the suicide threat and intervention procedures should be maintained by the counselor or administrator in the student's confidential file.

- The counselor or administrator should provide the names of professional resources to the parent or guardian. If the parents fail to respond to the suicide potential of their child or fails to contact a professional resource for the student, the counselor or administrator should contact the coordinator of pupil personnel or psychological services of the school district for professional advisement and support. Psychological services in cooperation with the counselor or administrator of the school will evaluate the situation and determine whether court or child protective services should be contacted.

- If during the interview the student, the counselor, or the principal determine that the student is not in imminent danger or at high risk for a potential suicide, appropriate monitoring, follow-up, and documentation should be provided.

Interviewing a Student in Crisis

Assisting, interviewing, and counseling a suicidal youth ultimately involves utilizing the principles of crisis intervention. Nondirective approaches to therapy should be avoided during the initial stages of intervention. Essentially, nondirective approaches lack the control that school personnel (counselors, school psychologist, etc.) will need to guide the young person through the crisis. A high degree of perceptiveness on the part of the interviewer is necessary to sense the state of the student's crisis and to intervene adequately. The interviewer's approach should focus on resolution of the immediate problem with the mobilization of personal, educational, social, and environmental resources. The primary outcome is to explore more concrete and positive alternatives to help the student re-establish a sense of control over his/her life.

The positive resolution of a crisis depends on crisis intervention, that aspect of crisis management carried out by resource people in or outside of school such as the school's crisis team leader, nurse, teacher, principal, counselor, minister, or mental health professional. Essentially, crisis intervention is a short-term helping process. It focuses on resolution of the immediate problem through the use of the student's personal, social, and environmental (school and home) resources. Unfortunately, many students choose suicide as a resolution to their own personal distress as a means to gain control or to communicate to others.

When a student contacts a significant adult, the following seven step procedure (Sue, Sue, & Sue, 1981) can be useful:

- maintain contact, rapport, and establish a therapeutic relationship with the student;
- obtain necessary information and documentation (see Crisis Assessment and Intervention Form Figure 13.2);
- evaluate suicidal potential;
- clarify the nature of the stress and focal problem;
- assess the student's present strengths and resources;
- recommend and initiate an action plan (see Figure 13.1); and
- notify the parent or guardian as well as identify referral resources.

Assessing the Student's Suicide Plan and Risk Potential

Knowledge which is not shared is information that could serve to decrease the risk of self-destructive behavior. The assessment of the suicidal plan is the process of determining the likelihood of a suicide (Hoff, 1984). Assessing the suicidal plan and method should be viewed from the perspective of intrinsic lethality (potential physiological damage: gun versus pills, cutting versus gas, etc.), availability of lethal resources, timing, and planning of details (see Figure 13.4). Inherently, educators, parents, peers, and helping professionals frequently ask how does one gauge the seriousness of a suicide attempt? For example, is a person who takes a fatal overdose in close proximity to others more lethal to self than a person who takes less of the drug, but in an isolated setting? Fundamentally, the intent of the individual often needs to be inferred from his/her actions which may be ambiguous at best. Hoff and Resing (1982) maintained that distinguishing between immediate and long-range risk for potential suicide is not only a critical life-saving measure; it is also important for preventing or interrupting a vicious cycle of repeated self-injury. If immediate risk is high and it is not uncovered in assessment, a suicide attempt can result. Conversely, if immediate risk is low (e.g., cutting a wrist, swallowing a parent's tranquilizers) and the response is high (i.e., the same as though life were at stake) coupled with indifference among caregivers to the meaning or motivation of the physical, self-destructive act, the self-destructive behavior is unintentionally reinforced to the dismay of the helper. Fundamentally, what is communicated to the person in effect is demonstrated by the helpers inferred behavior: "Do something more severe (medically) and they will pay attention to me." If the cry for help is repeated and the response message the same, a completed suicide may have obtained greater potential. Several direct questions should be asked sensitively, in a secure environment regarding ideation, lethality of methods, availability of destructive means, and specificity of the suicidal plan. An example of a School Counselor Action Plan is provided in Figure 13.5.

Suicidal Ideation. Ask directly, "Are you thinking about hurting yourself?" "Are you in so much pain that ending your life seems to be the only thing left for you to do to change how you feel?"

Short Term Treatment Plan. Counseling intervention strategies should focus on an active approach that produces immediate relief for the student. For example, attempt to calm the adolescent by mutually developing a short-term treatment plan with the student. Such a plan serves to reduce the feelings of hopelessness

Manifestations	Intensity of Risk	Individual Rating
Academic Progress Attendance	1 Low—maintains attendance and academic progress concurrent with past performance 2 Moderate—occassionally fails a class; some concern for school 3 High—chronic absenteeism; drop in school performance; hostile toward school and administration	________
Anxiety	1 Low 2 Moderate 3 Severe	________
Depression	1 Low 2 Moderate 2 Severe	________
Physical Isolation	1 Low—vague feeling of depression; no withdrawal 2 Moderate—feelings of helplessness, hopelessness and withdrawal 3 High—hopeless, helpless, withdrawn and self-deprecating . . .	________
Available Resources	1 Low—either intact or able to restore them easily 2 Moderate—some turmoil regarding trust; strained relationships attainable 3 High—very limited or nonexistent; student sees himself without resources	________
Communication	1 Low—able to communicate directly and nondestructively 2 Moderate—ambiquous; may use self-injury to communicate and gain attention. 3 High—feels cut off from resources and unable to communicate effectively	________
Routine Interaction	1 Low—fairly good in most activities 2 Moderate—moderately good in selected activities 3 High—not good in most activities	________

Figure 13.4. Behavioral manifestations or overt symptoms to help predict a potential suicide.

Manifestations	Intensity of Risk	Individual Rating
Coping Strategies	1 Low—generally constructive 2 Moderate—some strategies are self-defeating 3 High—predominately destructive	______
Significant Others	1 Low—several are available 2 Moderate—few or only one available 3 High—only one or none available	______
Previous Suicide Attempts	1 Low—none, or of low lethality 2 Moderate—none, to one or more of moderate lethality 3 High—none to multiple attempts of high lethality	______
Recent Loss	1 Low—none or 1 more than one year ago 2 Moderate—one less than 12 months ago 3 High—recent loss of significant other	______
Drug abuse	1 Low—infrequent to excess 2 Moderate—frequently to excess 3 High—continual abuse	______
Suicidal Plan	1 Low—vague, fleeting ideation but no plan 2 Moderate—frequent thoughts, occasional plan 3 High—frequent or constant thoughts with a deliberate plan	______

Figure 13.4. Continued.

SCHOOL COUNSELOR ACTION PLAN

Support Resources (identified by student)	Support Resources (identified by counselor)
__________	__________
__________	__________

Lethality of Method	____ High	____ Medium	____ Low
Availabity of Means	____ High	____ Medium	____ Low
Specificity of Plan	____ High	____ Medium	____ Low
Suicidal Risk	____ High	____ Medium	____ Low

ACTION TO BE TAKEN

Date: __________ Time: __________

Crisis Team Member:

	YES	**NO**	**N/A**	**PERSON RESPONSIBLE**	**DATE COMPLETED**
Contact Parents					
Notify Principal					
Notify Community Mental Health					
Consult with local school/ community mental health liaison					
Notify Social Service					
Notify police or youth service officer					
Is it safe to let student go home?					
Is the student in need of 24 hour supervision?					
Is student provided with contact person and phone number?					
Is student scheduled for contact with school counselor for the following day?					
Other (specify)					
__________					

Figure 13.5. An example of School Counselor Action Plan.

and lack of control over circumstances that the student may be experiencing.

Lethality of Method. "Ask specifically, what have you been thinking of doing?" The counselor should also determine the student's knowledge about the lethality of the chosen method. For example, ask "Do you have any pills; do you know how many would be an overdose?"

High Lethal Methods

- firearm
- hanging
- carbon monoxide poisoning
- intravenous injection
- barbiturate or antidepressant overdose
- car accident

Lower Lethal Methods

- cutting wrist
- nonprescription drug overdose (with the exception of aspirin and tylenol)
- tranquilizers (such as valium & dalmane)

Availability of Self-destructive Means. Direct intervention with the abrupt removal of very lethal methods such as firearms or prescription drugs can often save a life until the crisis is over. Specifically, direct significant others such as friends or family to remove lethal methods from the home. If trust, empathy, and rapport have been established between the counselor and the student at-risk, then consider engaging the at-risk student actively in the process of disposing of the lethal weapons or substances.

Specificity of Plan. Ask the student directly, "Do you have a detailed plan worked out for ending your life?" Asses whether or not a specific time, place, and circumstance has been developed and whether or not significant adults are available who could assist in intervention. If availability, plan, and lethal method are in place, the student is an immediate high risk for a potential suicide. Immediate intervention and possible hospitalization becomes the most logical course of action (Waltzer, 1980). School personnel (counselors, school psychologist, nurse, etc.) must be knowledgeable about reliable, expedient referral sources and have available a network of various helping professionals in the mental health community. The course of action the counselor takes includes conferring with one's immediate supervisor, contacting the parent(s) or guardian, and facilitating proceedings toward hospitalization of the adolescent. Finally, the student should not be allowed to leave the school without the close supervision of a responsible adult (see Figure 13.4 and 13.5, School Counselor Action Plan).

Contact. If, however, a student who manifests suicidal ideation is already under psychiatric care and is not going to consent to being hospitalized, the school personnel (counselor, school psychologist) could help the student make it through to the next appointment by the means of a written contract. An example of a suicide prevention contract according to Getz et al. (1983, p. 269) is as follows:

> (1) I, ______________________, agree not to kill myself, or cause any harm to myself during the period from _____ to _______________ the time of my next appointment with
> ____
>
> (2) I agree to get enough sleep and to eat well.
>
> (3) I agree to get rid of things I could use to kill myself.
>
> (4) I agree that if I have a bad time and feel that I might hurt myself, I will call ____________________________, my counselor, immediately at # ________________ or the Crisis Center at # ____________________________.
>
> (5) I agree that these conditions are part of my counseling contract ______________________________
> with ____
> signed ____
> witnessed _______________________________________
> date ____

Such a suicide contract can be modified according to the individual needs of the person. The contract is one means of involving the individual and produces a good deterrent for the person to not attempt suicide prior to contracting or talking with someone. The contract is a tool which should be used in conjunction with protective measures and never in isolation. Conferring with the student's therapist and relaying pertinent information also would be a preventive measure in the pursuit of professional support and consultation.

PROCEDURES FOR THE DAY AFTER A STUDENT SUICIDE

In order to prepare adequately for a crisis situation, the School Crisis Intervention Team (SCIT) should have made the necessary anticipated logistical arrangements before a crisis occurs. These arrangements include, but are not limited to the following eight subheadings that follow.

Identification of Personnel Needs

Identify members of the faculty who are willing to talk to students in small groups. These groups are intended for students who are not experiencing intense problems, but who do need to obtain congruent information and understanding about the death of a classmate from a significant, responsive, and caring adult. Teachers should provide general information and answer questions and facilitate concerns. They also could assist in identifying students who are experiencing more intense adjustsment problems or student who have fewer support resources. Other school personnel resources could include the administrative staff, school nurse, school psychologist, and community counseling personnel.

- Identify personnel who can provide more indepth, one-to-one counseling.
- Designate a contact person to facilitate communication with central office personnel.
- Activate the Crisis Communication Contingency Plan (3CP) and the contact person who is designated to work with the media.
- Designate a person to serve as case manager or team leader (depending on professional orientation) of the SCIT to schedule departmental meetings or individual and group meetings for students.

- Designate a person to work with and organize community resources and clubs or organizations.

Fundamentally, the number of persons needed to accomplish the first two items will depend on the size of the student population and the number of students in crisis. Facilitating the last four items do not necessarily have to be filled by different individuals.

In-school Building and Educational Resource Needs

Specific resources within the school must be made available.

- Designate specific rooms to hold small group sessions or consultation with staff, students, and parents.

- Designate specific rooms that can be available for community consultation and information.

- Free a telephone line in order to contact parents, central office personnel, or community mental health resources.

- Identify appropriate literature, films, and other educational materials for students, parents, faculty, and community groups.

- Provide guidelines, structure, and resources for teachers to use in small educational groups.

Prepare Teachers

Teachers need to have preparation ahead of time so as to have structured procedures to deal with students on the first day after a student suicide crisis. The procedure may be as follows:

- Conduct a faculty meeting before school on the first day after a suicide.

- Discuss the situation and explain specific procedures for the day.

  Introduce school and other personnel who will be involved in counseling students.

Explain the role and function of the School Crisis Intervention Team and provide teachers with a schedule of counseling sessions which may occur.

- Handout procedures to be discussed with students at the beginning of the school day. Thoroughly discuss procedures to be sure all teachers understand their role in communicating and processing information for students. The first hour of the school day should be spent providing students with accurate information as well as processing the death in small groups.

- Encourage teachers who may feel uncomfortable discussing the situation with students by providing those teachers with the option to request a member of the SCIT to be present in their rooms with them to answer student questions.

- Ascertain that teachers and members of the SCIT know to whom to report, and to whom to refer students or families in crisis.

- Establish support groups for the deceased's present and previous teachers who may need assistance in coping with their own feelings and arrange for their classes to be covered while they are in the group sessions. Confidentially inform teachers involved of the plans or provisions that have been made available for them.

Teachers' or SCIT Members' Duties

The suggested procedures on the first day of school after a suicide is for teachers or SCIT members to conduct the first hour session as follows:

- Announce the death of the student using accurate facts.

- Let students know they will be (1) informed of funeral arrangements; (2) excused from classes to attend the funeral with written permission from parent or guardian.

- Maintain the traditional ethnic or differing cultural mores regarding procedures and protocol of students from different cultural or ethnic backgrounds. The cultural diversity in many school settings cannot be ignored. Education and responsiveness to different roles and rituals will help diffuse rigidity and expectations of their ethnic groups for the deceased.

- Announce that friends of the deceased will be allowed to meet in a group at __________ a.m. in room __________. Excuse friends of the deceased to go to the meeting.

- Open the discussion with remaining students. Let them know it is normal to be upset. Try to maintain a calm climate. Direct the discussion toward identifying ways the class members might do something positive in the absence of their peer. Caution must be taken to prevent any collective activities that would glamorize the suicidal act or make it appear as a heroic alternative on the part of the adolescent. Types of innocuous activities may include writing a poem to be read at the funeral of the deceased, or other choose-life or living alternative activities (Joan, 1986).

- Announce that adults will be available to students for counseling, talking, and listening. Record the names of students who express interest in counseling or further processing and submit them to the SCIT leader or case manager.

- Inform students that they will be called to the office and escorted to the appropriate counseling area throughout the course of the day

- Inform students that for the remainder of the day, they should follow their routine schedule of classes

- All members of the SCIT should determine student needs, personnel and resources needed and outline procedures to follow.

Principal's Duties

At the time of an actual suicide crisis, the SCIT should be assembled immediately and the principal should do the following:

- Contact the central office liason in order that they can adjust their schedules to meet at the local school if necessary.

- Contact the individual designated to work with the media in order that statements can be prepared before being contacted by the media.

- Meet with the family of the deceased to offer assistance.

- Arrange for a morning faculty meeting for the first day of school after the suicide.

- Finalize procedures for the first day of school after crisis.

- Make arrangements for substitutes or parent volunteers who may be needed for teachers who are to facilitate discussions and to process feelings for students.

Short-Term Arrangements

Make short-term arrangements for the first day that include the following:

- Allow students with questions to talk in small groups with selected teachers, members of the SCIT, and mental health professionals in the community.

- Provide for the most severely affected students to be seen individually by the school counseling staff, SCIT, and/or mental health professionals.

- Divide student population into the following categories as soon as possible:

  (1) Those students who need to be seen by a counselor immediately.

  (2) Those students with less severe problems, but who need follow-up work such as a referral to community agencies or parental conferences. (Very often, when a student commits suicide, many

students become identified as high risk because of reoccurring suicide ideation or some other underlying personal dysfunction or self-defeating behavior.)

(3) Those students who are experiencing mild or moderate coping problems whose progress needs monitoring.

(4) Those students who are adjusting adequately and do not need further monitoring.

- Meet daily for staffing meetings with the SCIT to discuss student needs and to assign responsibilities for counseling, consulting, referral, or monitoring of students.

Case Manager's or Team Leader's Duties

The case manager or team leader of the SCIT should do the following things:

- Contact teachers and other staff members who volunteered and were trained to work as group facilitators before school begins so they can be prepared. The focus would stress the communication of feelings, the recognition that others have faced similar anguish and have survived; and the realization that our reactions to loss and stress are normal.

- Make arrangements to notify community leaders, agencies, churches, and parents of the actions being taken by the school or the programs provided.

- Schedule if necessary, meetings for parents and community resource people.

- Contact other member of the city-wide SCIT if necessary to assist in activities.

- Contact other resources within the district such as psychological services, and private counseling agencies with whom the school has already made arrangements for assistance.

Essential Components

Finally, during the crisis period the following components must be considered:

- a calm, organized atmosphere be maintained;
- all involved be kept informed of the status of plans, events, actions, and schedules;
- daily staffing meetings be held to review and modify plans with schedules developed and communicated to promote accountability;
- sufficient helping professionals be involved so that a few people are not overworked;
- staff members should routinely be reminded to take time for themselves and engage in stress reduction activities during the course of their day;
- counseling services be made available for faculty and staff members who may need to share their anxieties and frustrations in an environment that is nonjudgmental;
- all students and faculty members expressing difficulty in maintaining adequate coping skills during and after the suicide crisis be taken serious and appropriate assistance be made available to help them; and
- a normal schedule of extracurricular and instructional periods be maintained for the majority of the student body to provide routine and structure and to promote interpersonal stability.

SUMMARY

Suicide intervention and prevention in the school-as-community does not end with a student's death. Public awareness and concern has grown as the number of youth lost to suicide has increased. Educators and citizens in communities throughout the nation have looked to public institutions including the school for intervention, prevention, and assistance. School counselors, administrators, and mental health professionals need to develop systematic strategies to intervene with survivors, as well as potentially at-risk students.

Young people continue to communicate and demonstrate through self-destructive behaviors that they need help with understanding their feelings of confusion, loss, alienation, loneliness, depression, anger, sadness, and possibly guilt. Students future coping strategies with their uncomfortable but normal feelings, their ability to adjust, maintain control, and mastery over their everyday life experiences, will ultimately be dependent on the assistance they obtain and the resources they identify. Counselors, administrators and other school personnel can provide the climate that fosters prevention and intervention with at-risk students. Collective efforts to provide structured programs and secure environments to "work through" significant losses are necessary to arrest the present cycle of self-destructive behaviors of contemporary adolescents.

REFERENCES

Balk, D. (1983). How teenagers cope with sibling death: Some implications for school counselors. *The School Counselor, 31*, 2, 150-158.

Bash, M.A., & Camp, B.W. (1980). Teacher training in the think aloud classroom program. In G. Cartledge & J.F. Milburn (Eds.), *Teaching social skills to children* (pp.143-179). New York: Pergamon Press.

Dinkmeyer, D. (1971). Top priority: Understanding self and others. *Elementary School Journal, 72*, 62-71.

Farber, M. (1968). *Theory of suicide.* New York: Funk & Wagnalle

Getz, W.L., Allen, D.B., Myers, R.K., & Linder, K.C. (1983). *Brief counseling with suicidal persons.* Lexington, MA: D.C. Heath.

Glasser, W. (1978). Parent anxiety adds to fears. *The School Counselor, 26*, 2, 90-91.

Goldstein, A.P., Sprafkin, R.P., Gershaw, N.J., & Klein, P. (1979). *Skillstreaming the adolescent: A structured learning approach to teaching prosocial behavior.* Champaign, IL: Research Press.

Grant, A. (1987). Accelerating teen suicide rate spurs prevention programs. *Guidepost 29,* 15m, p.3-9.

Hannaford, P. (1987). Consultant offers tips for dealing with the media. *NASSP Newsleader, 34,* 8, p.4.

Hoff, L.A. (1984). *People in crisis.* Reading, ME: Addison-Wesley.

Hoff, L.A. & Resing, M. (1982). Was this suicide preventable? *American Journal of Nursing. 80,* 1106-1111.

Jacobs, J. (1971). *Adolescent suicide.* New York: Wiley & Sons.

Jacobs, J. (1980). *Adolescent suicide.* New York: Irvington.

Joan, P. (1986). *Preventing teenage suicide: The living alternative handbook.* New York: Human Science Press.

Powell, A.G., Farrer, E., & Cohen, D.K. (1985). *The shopping mall high school.* Boston: Houghton Mifflin.

Rappeport, J.R. (1978). *Death education in the school. The School Counselor, 26,* 2, 93-4.

Rogers, C.R. (1980). *A way of being.* Boston: Houghton Mifflin.

Skills for adolescents (1982). Columbus, OH: Quest National Center.

Sprinthall, N.A. (1984). Primary prevention: A road paved with a plethora of promises and procrastinations. *Personnel and Guidance Journal,* Apr., 491-95.

Sue, D., Sue, D.W., & Sue, S. (1981). *Understanding Abnormal Behavior.* Boston: Houghton Mifflin.

Stanford, G. (1978). An opportunity missed. *The School Counselor, 26,* 2, 96-98.

Thompson, R.A. (1986). Developing a peer group facilitation program on the secondary school level: An investment with multiple returns. *Small Group Behavior, 17,* 1, 105-12.

Tishler, C., McKenry, P., & Morgan, K. (1981). Adolescent suicide attempts some significant factors. *Suicide and life threatening behavior, 11,* 86-92.

Waltzer, H. (1980). Malpractice liability in a patients suicide. *American Journal of Psychotherapy, 31,* 1, 89-98.

Worrell, J., & Stilwell, W.E. (1981). *Psychology for teachers and students.* New York: McGraw-Hill.

CHAPTER **14**

FAMILY THERAPY AND NETWORKING

Artis J. Palmo, Ed.D.
and
Linda A. Palmo, Ph.D.

Artis J. Palmo, Ed.D.

Professor of Counseling Psychology
Department of Counseling Psychology,
School Psychology, and Special Education
College of Education
Lehigh University
Bethlehem, PA 18015

Dr. Artis J. Palmo has been teaching in the Counseling Psychology Program at Lehigh University since 1971, the same year that he received his doctorate in counseling from West Virginia University. His major areas of research and teaching include marriage and family counseling, group processes, and adolescent suicide. Throughout his career, Dr. Palmo has been actively involved in various professional groups, including serving as the chair of the North Atlantic Region of the American Association for Counseling and Development and representing the region on the AACD Board. In addition, he is a past-president of the Pennsylvania Counseling Association. Dr. Palmo has published numerous journals and recently co-authored a text on group counseling.

Dr. Palmo is a licensed psychologist in Bethlehem, Pennsylvania where along with his wife, they operate a private practice in counseling. The Palmo's have two children, Peter and Michael, and reside in Bethlehem.

Linda A. Palmo, Ph.D.

Associate and Licensed Psychologist
Bethlehem Counseling Associates
Bethlehem, PA 18017

Dr. Linda A. Palmo is a licensed psychologist in private practice specializing in marriage and family counseling, with special emphasis on counseling children and adolescents. Before receiving her doctorate in counseling from Lehigh University, Dr. Palmo was an elementary teacher, elementary school counselor, and a college counselor. She has been active in serving the Lutheran Ministries as a therapist, consultant, and trainer. In addition, she has published articles for journals and co-authored chapters for two books. Presently, in addition to her private practice, Dr. Palmo serves as the consulting psychologist to the rehabilitation unit of the Easton Hospital.

Along with her husband and co-author, Dr. Palmo resides in Bethlehem with her family, including two boys, Michael and Peter.

EDITORIAL ABSTRACT: *The focus of this chapter is on the use of family therapy and professional networking in the therapeutic treatment of suicidal adolescents. There are three major sections presented in this chapter: (1) the variety of self-destructive behaviors demonstrated by adolescents; (2) family therapy as a treatment modality with suicidal adolescents; and (3) consultation and networking in the treatment of the suicidal adolescent and the family.*

This chapter will focus on the use of family therapy and networking among mental health professionals as productive methods for the treatment of adolescents exhibiting self-destructive behaviors. While previous chapters have presented information on the prevalence and extent of the problem of teenage suicide, this chapter will detail the specific therapeutic interventions with families of suicidal adolescents and the necessity for mental health professionals to network and consolidate their efforts to deter these problems. The problem cannot be overstated that teenage suicide is epidemic, severe, and difficult to treat.

At the time of the preparation of this chapter, the nearby community of Bergenfield, New Jersey, was receiving notoriety because of the multiple suicides of four adolescents. The effects of their deaths produced unsuccessful attempts by two other teenagers and the successful suicide of another. In addition, reports have been of copycat attempts throughout the country that can be directly attributed to the tragedy in Bergenfield (Viadero, 1987). These incidents demonstrate the inadequacy felt by communities, schools, mental health professionals, and parents as they face the tremendous problem of teenage suicide.

The Bergenfield tragedy provides examples of the three major concerns presented in the chapter—the diversity of self-destructive behavior, the role of the family in the problems of the suicidal adolescent, and the necessity for total community involvement in the resolution of the problems. The first section of the chapter presents the broad variety of self-destructive behaviors and tendencies demonstrated by adolescents, the interpersonal dynamics of the teenager, followed by a segment discussing the role of the adolescent as a family member and complex human being. Second, the use of family therapy as an effective mode of treatment is presented. The discussion presents the many nuances of family therapy with a suicidal adolescent as the identified client. In addition, the discussion includes the presentation of case examples.

Finally, the chapter discusses the importance of professional consultation and networking throughout the treatment process for the suicidal teenager. Considering the extent of the problem of suicide and the numerous factors and influences that contribute to the problem, the effective psychotherapeutic treatment of the adolescent sometimes becomes a very complex process involving therapeutic, ethical, and legal concerns. Therefore, if the treatment of the self-destructive youth is to be productive, the mental health professional must be able to utilize the multiplicity of services and professionals in the surrounding community. The most frequent professional error that has been observed is the professional who attempts to take care of the problem alone without involving other professionals. School counselors, private practitioners, and hospital personnel are all guilty of attempting to treat the suicidal teenager without involving other professionals.

SELF-DESTRUCTIVE TENDENCIES IN ADOLESCENTS

The wide range of self-destructive behaviors exhibited by teenagers can sometimes be overwhelming to parents, school personnel, and mental health professionals. Typically, the adult interacting with the suicidal youth feels very inadequate and unable to help in any effective manner. The primary goal of the adolescent's suicidal behavior is to make those around him/her feel as inadequate and helpless as they themselves feel.

Self-destructive behaviors can vary from taking a bottle of aspirin to slashing of wrists to dare-devil antics with the automobile. The tremendous need for a "thrill" can lead adolescents to situations that are very dangerous and suicidal. At times, treatment is easier for the teenager who has verbally and/or behaviorally demonstrated his/her suicidal tendencies and admits to the desire to commit suicide than for the more subtle self-destructive teenager. Those adolescents who have not made an overt, identifiable attempt at taking their life, but continually act out in ways that are very risky, can be difficult to effectively identify and treat therapeutically (Farberow, (1980).

For those teenagers who have made overt attempts at suicide, the professionals involved can readily provide services for the youth and the family. However, for the teenager who does dare-devil tricks on a motorcycle, frequently skips school, and appears uninvolved in school, what can professionals do? Even the motorcycle dare-devil is less of an enigma and problem when compared to the teenager who is president of the class, well-liked by his peers, and achieving in school, but leaves the house one day to take a walk and shoots himself. Or the anorexic girl who proceeds to destroy herself by ignoring her physical well-being.

The point being made is this: NO CLEAR, SIMPLE PROFILE EXISTS OF THE TYPICAL TEENAGE SUICIDE VICTIM OR THE AT-RISK TEENAGER! Teenage suicide victims and at-risk teenagers come in many varieties (Husain & Vandiver, 1984), which means professionals involved in the education and treatment of teenagers must be flexible in diagnosis, conceptualization, and treatment planning. Also, those involved with teenagers cannot continue to deny the magnitude of the problem. What may be true of one teenager, may not be true of another. While one teenager will give rather obvious clues another will be more secretive and indirect. Every professional involved with teenagers must be sensitive to signs of suicidal ideation, both the obvious and the subtle.

Interpersonal Dynamics of the Adolescent

Typically, several maladaptive interpersonal dynamics are exhibited by suicidal teenagers in their interaction with the family, friends, and school personnel. Frequently, in an attempt to deal with the people around them, the suicidal teenager resorts to some very powerful behaviors to gain the attention he/she desires. The four prevalent behaviors are psychological blackmail, anger, manipulation, and control.

The first, *psychological blackmail*, is a very powerful and dynamic method used by the teenager to assure attention, power, and pity. Psychological blackmail is best exemplified as the teenager saying, "You can't make me do anything, but if you try, I'll kill myself!" The suicidal teenager may use this approach with his/her parents, other teenagers, or school personnel. It is an extremely powerful tool that is used by the teenager to control others.

Psychological blackmail is a very difficult problem to treat, because known cases of teenagers threatening to kill themselves have actually followed through and have done it. So the blackmail cannot be ignored, because the chance is always present that the teenager might act on this threat.

In addition to psychological blackmail, a second interpersonal dynamic is the *anger* being displayed by the suicidal adolescent. To commit suicide is one of the most angry actions that one person can do, and to threaten suicide is the second most angry act. The mental health professional must assist the teenager in understanding the origin of the anger, while explaining the dynamics of the anger to the adults associated with teenagers.

One case example can demonstrate the nature of the power associated both with anger and psychological blackmail. A 17 year old boy was referred for private therapy by the school psychologist for failing grades and what appeared to be severe depression. During the initial interview with the parents, what was very apparent was that their son was using his depressed mood and anger to keep the parents away from him. The power of the son over the parents also was evident by his absence at the initial session. When queried about their son's absence at the session, both parents stated they "...did not want to upset him." When asked to explain "upset," the parents related being frightened by his anger/temper, as well as his withdrawn behaviors afterward. Basically the boy had learned to use his anger/temper as a blackmail technique, while saving the depressive behaviors for the pity he wanted from the parents.

This example leads to a discussion of the final two maladaptive interpersonal dynamics, *manipulation* and *control*. By using blackmail or anger, the suicidal teenager can very effectively manipulate and control almost any situation. For example, the depressed high school senior who has been identified as an at-risk student asks her English teacher to be excused from an assignment because she had a "bad night at home." The teacher, fully aware of the girl's at-risk status releases her from the assignment. The girl succeeded in manipulating the teacher and gaining control of the situation.

Therapeutically, times do occur when the adolescent with suicidal ideation should be granted some exceptions in order to make it through some difficult times. However, once the teenager has been stabilized, the adults closely associated with the teenager must be given help and direction in handling the attempts at blackmail and control. The mental health professional, in consultation with the other professionals involved with the teenager, must be able to effectively determine the inappropriate interpersonal dynamics that are incorporated within the behaviors of the suicidal teenager.

The Complexity of Adolescent Behavior

In detailing the interpersonal dynamics of the suicidal adolescent, an important procedure is to note that self-destructive tendencies, as well as other behavioral and emotional tendencies, must be viewed within the context of the adolescent's total development. The characteristic behaviors and personality dynamics of the teenager must be diagnosed with an understanding of the roller-coaster nature of the traits, behaviors, and day-to-day variations of this stage of human development. The assessment of self-destructive tendencies in adolescents must be determined with the context of other demonstrated interpersonal dynamics. The effective therapeutic intervention is determined from the conceptualization of the total picture of the adolescent, not simply the suicidal tendencies.

Three basic patterns of behavior are included in the presenting problem of suicidal ideation. The first pattern is the adolescent who leaves a trail of increasingly self-destructive behaviors. Each step demonstrates a greater magnitude and more overt level of maladaptive behaviors. The behaviors are not only self-destructive but are also non-compliant and typically rebellious. As time goes by, professionals involved with this pattern of behavior know that something is significantly wrong in the adolescent's life.

The second pattern involves behaviors of an adolescent that see-saw between self-destruction and typical every day functioning. The self-destructive behaviors are acted out in reaction to a specific person, circumstance, or physical location. The presented behaviors are inconsistent and extremely confusing for the involved professionals to understand and create chaos in the life of the adolescents. For example, on Monday the adolescent is fine, on Tuesday the same adolescent is deeply depressed. The operative dynamic is the inconsistency and reactionary nature of the maladaptive behaviors.

The final pattern is the most difficult to diagnose previous to a suicidal attempt. In this sequence of events, the adolescent is compliant, conforming, and a perfectionist with no self-destructive or acting out behaviors visible. On a chosen day, the adolescent commits a suicidal act or completes a successful suicide. The only clues to the final event are the rigid adherence to perfectionism and a high level of self-expectation.

Therapeutic Interventions

In any of the patterns presented, the first professional to recognize the self-destructive tendencies of the adolescent must follow through on the duty to warn parents or guardians of the clear and present danger exhibited by the adolescent (Everstine, Everstine, Heymann, True, Frey, Johnson, & Seiden, 1980). Therefore, as soon as the self-destructive tendency is identified, the family becomes extremely pertinent to the development of a treatment plan for the adolescent.

As an example, Nancy, a 17 year old junior in high school, was referred for a vocational assessment to assist her in choosing a college and a major. At the very first counseling session, what became readily apparent was that Nancy was not simply confused about her educational future, but also very depressed about her general status in life. She reported various physical problems, eating problems, lack of sleep, and general nervousness. Socially, she reported feeling out of place with her friends and all alone. Within her family, Nancy felt unsuccessful, withdrawn, and unimportant. Nancy confided to her therapist that she was contemplating cutting her wrists rather than face choosing a college. The immediate responsibility was for the therapist to inform Nancy's parents of the clear and present danger issue within Nancy's life.

The parents' assessment of Nancy was much different. They saw her as achieving in school, happy with her friends, and having normal relations with her siblings at home. Having raised three older children, Nancy's parents felt that she was simply traversing the typical hurdles from adolescence through early adulthood. The parents never saw the depression or suicidal ideation. The thrust of the vocational assessment came in assisting the family to understand and give credibility to the self-destructive tendencies Nancy was experiencing.

Denial by the Family

The preceding example demonstrates a common concern faced by mental health professionals. After the identification of the suicidal adolescent, the typical reaction of the parents is to deny the serious nature of the problems expressed by the adolescent. The denial system of the parents and family can occur in various areas.

First, and most obvious, the parents and family will frequently deny the problem's severity. Parents often respond that their child is just seeking attention, avoiding responsibilities, or wanting a new stereo, car, or clothes. Frequently, the parents are accurate in their assessment of the teenager's need for attention and avoidance of responsibilities; however, they frequently deny the reality of the problem and the life-threatening nature of the teenager's suicidal ideation. The parents do not want to hear that their child is having severe problems or adjustment difficulties.

Second, the parents are reluctant to admit to their child's difficulties because they would have to admit to their own problems, mistakes, and avoidances. Not only does a denial by the parents of the teenager's problems exist but also present is a denial of their role in the development of the problems. Before the teenager can begin to take "ownership" for his/her problems, the parents and family must take responsibility for their part in the problem development.

Finally, the suicidal teenager is often denied mental health services because parents feel their child will "outgrow" the difficulties. Denying that the child and family have problems means that the mental health professional is almost helpless to demonstrate the need for therapy, unless the teenager exhibits some direct behaviors that cannot be denied as problems, e.g., a suicide attempt, drugs or alcohol, pregnancy, anorexia, or another severe problem.

Denial is a major part of the treatment process with suicidal adolescents. Because the parents or the teenager deny the severity of the problem does not mean they are "wrong," "bad," or "inadequate"; but rather indicates the first stages of trying to accept the problem. The mental health professional needs to understand that the denial system of the family is usually very strong at first, and that the major goal of initial therapy is having the parents and the family accept the problem. To argue the severity of the problem or to become embroiled in a power struggle with the parents is an error. The professional needs to understand and accept the denial, and work with the family toward dealing with the problem before any understanding will take place. The primary goal is the protection and safety of the adolescent.

FAMILY THERAPY WITH THE SUICIDAL ADOLESCENT

Once the suicidal adolescent has been identified by a professional and the parents have been notified of the self-destructive tendencies of their child, the process of therapeutic inventions has begun. The mental health professional or school official who contacts the parents is essentially conducting the initial interview in the therapeutic interventions with the family. The quality and substance of that first contact will provide the initial framework through which all subsequent interventions will be viewed. Often the professional who identifies the self-destructive tendencies of the adolescent is not in a position to provide continuing therapy to the family. The most common example of this dilemma is the school counselor who identifies the problem within the school setting and contacts the parents to refer them to another mental health professional. This referral process is germane to professional networking and the subsequent therapeutic intervention of family therapy.

Duty to Warn and Professional Networking

Prior to the first contact with the parents, a need exists to assess the lethality (Wekstein, 1979) of the suicidal adolescent.

This assessment of lethality is pertinent for two reasons. First, the law requires mental health professionals to fulfill a duty to warn (Everstein et al., 1980) the next of kin or the county crisis intervention unit if a person poses a clear and present danger to self or others. As discussed in the first section of this chapter, self-destructive tendencies of adolescents come in varying patterns and varying levels of lethality. Therefore, the strength of the warning to parents must be consistent with the strength of the self-destructive tendencies of the teenager. Previous chapters in this book identify the factors involved in determining lethality. The warning to parents must reflect a cognizance and detailing of the factors that identify their child as a suicidal adolescent. The specifications of the warning are particularly pertinent within the context of the common denial systems of the family.

Second, the assessment of the lethality of the suicidal adolescent is pertinent to the determination of where the family is being referred for therapeutic services. The decision for the mental health professional is whether the family should be directed immediately to an in-patient hospital setting for the adolescent or whether the family should be referred to an out-patient mental health professional for therapeutic services. This decision is complicated by two factors: the resistance often encountered in having the family follow through with treatment at all and the tremendous burden of responsibility on the professional providing the warning in this life-threatening situation.

The professional networking between the identification of the suicidal adolescent and the subsequent mental health services, whether in-patient or out-patient, must be in place prior to the eruption of the crisis. For example, school counselors must develop relationships with private practitioners or agencies who will provide immediate services to families when contacted during a crisis. Community mental health professionals need to establish relationships with hospital personnel who will facilitate in-patient care, if necessary. If these professional relationships have not been in place prior to identification of the suicidal adolescent, it is possible to have the resistance and denial of the family supercede the necessity for mental health services.

Beginning Family Therapy

In the majority of cases, the family will be a part of the treatment plan in continuing mental health services after the identification of a suicidal adolescent. Beginning family therapy should be used to discuss several important issues. First, the parents must be enlightened and made aware of the significance of the problem of teenage suicide. Although the parents may see their child as having problems, the therapist must impress upon the parents that the problems expressed by teenagers often end in a suicide attempt or suicide. Although the problems expressed by the teenager may seem minor to the adults, the problems are not minor to the teenager. Therefore the first responsibility for the professional is *awareness.* Make the parents aware of the problem, enlist their cooperation in resolving the problem, and establish that a suicidal adolescent constitutes a family problem.

Second, as discussed earlier, the parents and the child must begin to understand the *patterns of denial.* The teenager must understand the underlying motivations for his/her behavior and not deny the bizarre nature of using suicide as a way of handling difficulties. Likewise, the parents must begin to accept their role in the teenager's suicidal patterns. The parents cannot claim "innocence," but must begin to work towards a mutual understanding, with the teenager, of the problems being exhibited in the family. In order to effectively assist the family, the therapist must be able to help individuals understand their own denial systems as well as systems used by the family. Successful resolution of the denial by the family will almost assure successful treatment of the teenager.

Third, the mental health professional should begin to explain the *developmental nature of the problems* expressed and exhibited by the teenager. The parents and child need to understand that the expressed problems developed over an extended period of time and can only be helped through a consistent effort over an extended period of time. Once the family develops new methods of problem resolution, the difficulties of the teenager should begin to decrease and ultimately disappear.

One final point needs to be mentioned. The authors use a three session assessment model with families and individuals. We utilize the three sessions to conceptualize the problem(s), determine the severity of the problem, assess the individuals involved, assess the family as a unit, and make a determination of the types of therapeutic modalities to be used over the course of treatment. Following the initial three sessions, the treatment plan is discussed with the parents and child, and a commitment is made for treatment. In the development of a therapeutic treatment plan, the mental health professional must understand all the dynamics in the family and not focus solely on the suicidal adolescent.

Parental Role in the Suicidal Adolescent's Behavior

The most difficult aspect of family therapy involving a suicidal adolescent is attempting to have the parents understand their role in the development of the pathological behavior. Parents typically exhibit the same types of behavior as the suicidal child, except the behaviors are usually exhibited in more socially acceptable ways. The parents typically refuse or deny the behaviors of the child because they do not want to admit their own inadequacies, weaknesses, or problems.

For example, a 17 year old boy was referred to the therapist for failing grades, "bad" attitude, and depression. After meeting the parents and the child, it was quite obvious that the mother was very depressed and the relationship between mother and father was very strained. The parents individually, and as a couple, represented everything that was described as a difficulty with their son. Looking closely at the parents, the following could be determined:

1. Mother, at the very least, could have used therapy for her own depression.

2. Mother and father needed to learn to communicate effectively between each other.

3. Mother and father needed to learn to communicate with their son.

4. Mother and father had high expectations for themselves and their son, but felt very inadequate in their role as parents and workers.

5. Mother and father avoided issues until they became a crisis.

In this case, the son's difficulties were being openly demonstrated by the parents' behavior with the son and within their relationships with friends, associates, and co-workers. The parents were concerned about the son being lonely, while both parents spent a large portion of their life alone. They wanted their child to talk more, but both did not take time to speak to each other or with their children. Crisis issues for the parents were avoided until the very last minute.

The intent of this example was to demonstrate that disturbed behavior being exhibited by the suicidal child is most often a reflection of the issues being faced by the parents individually and as a couple. If therapy with the teenager is to make satisfactory progress, the parents must come to realize their contribution to the pathological nature of their child's behavior. Therefore, the most effective treatment modality for assisting the suicidal teenager is through long-term therapy. The child's problems are the family's problems, and must be handled through a family treatment modality.

Understanding the Family Dynamics

With the numerous changes that have occurred in society over the past twenty years, the pressure on adolescents to assume adult behaviors earlier and earlier has created some severe difficulties for parents and adolescents alike (Elkind, 1981). The authors refer to those children who have equal status with the adults in the household as "parentified" children. Typically, the suicidal adolescent is parentified, or in other words, has been given the primary responsibility for directing his/her own life. The parentified teenager has more freedom to choose his/her own activities; fewer responsibilities and chores in the home when compared to privileges; and been given equality with the parents during disagreements, discussions, and decision-making.

An example of the power of parentified children is the 16 year old girl who was hospitalized for an attempted suicide by a drug overdose. The parents were quite happy to have their daughter under protective care during the height of the emergency. However, their support for hospital care changed when the daughter requested to go home on the second day because she now felt fine and decided the hospital had some real "strange" people staying there. Rather than follow the hospital's recommendation, the parents removed the child from care, even though their daughter was exhibiting obvious at-risk behaviors.

The family dynamics of a suicidal adolescent typically include a parentified child who has decided that they are alone in the world without reliable support systems. Often the biggest disappointment for the adolescent has been the loss of appropriate parental support and subsequent trust. No matter what the origin of the parentified child, both the parents and child must be encouraged to assume their age appropriate roles. The parents must become true parents and not the child's companion, friend or playmate. On the other side, the adolescents must assume their role as a child and be taken out of the control position of the household.

Treatment Plans

When developing a treatment plan for the family of a suicidal adolescent, the particulars of exactly who should attend each counseling session is one of the components of the plan. Depending on the family, various plans can be developed. A treatment plan can include individual counseling for the suicidal adolescent, family counseling with the entire family, marital counseling, individual counseling with various family members, or a combination of any of these options. What is absolutely imperative is that the mental health professional provide services for the suicidal adolescent that include the family as a component of the treatment plan. Individual sessions with the adolescent must be utilized to bridge the gap toward inclusion of the family in the services.

An example serves to demonstrate the importance of this point. Joan, a 17 year old high school senior, was referred to counseling for poor school attendance and an abrupt fall in academic grades. Joan felt confused about her reluctance to continue to attend school and expressed a desire to die. She felt her life was in shambles. Her counselor decided to conduct two individual sessions with Joan to evaluate the suicidal ideation and then meet with Joan and her parents. Between the first and second appointments, Joan and her mother had an intense argument about Joan's boyfriend. After the argument, while Joan was in her room, Joan's mother took an overdoes of sleeping pills and was subsequently hospitalized for in-patient care for depression.

As demonstrated by the example, a treatment plan must be developed with a full understanding of the interpersonal dynamics of the suicidal adolescent, the reactions of the parent's role in the problem, and the family dynamics. The mental health professional involved in determining the treatment plan must be confident and knowledgeable about all the nuances and variations that can be idiosyncratic to each family of a suicidal adolescent and be ready to handle any crisis situations that arise.

NETWORKING AND PROFESSIONAL CONSULTATION AMONG MENTAL HEALTH PROFESSIONALS

As presented throughout the initial sections of this chapter, the tremendous responsibility and challenge for assisting the suicidal adolescent and his/her family is at times overwhelming. The effective mental health professional must have a sophisticated and complete network of helping professionals and organizations in order to satisfactorily treat the problem. The following sections will examine the various networks needed by the mental health professional in the treatment of suicidal adolescents.

Networking with Professional Colleagues

For mental health professionals providing family therapy, they must maintain contact with other professionals for additional sources of advice as well as personal support. The authors' experience has been that treating families having severe difficulties can be very emotionally and physically draining. Therefore, an extremely important procedure is to have other professionals available to assist in case analysis, treatment planning, crisis management, and general support.

Professionals associated with agencies need to share the burdens of treating suicidal adolescents with their colleagues so that the weight and responsibility for the case are dispersed among the staff. Although the treatment is the primary responsibility of the assigned therapist, having others aware of the problems involved with the case is a real benefit. In addition, the ethical responsibility of the professional is to inform other professionals of the serious nature of the problem in case the therapist is not readily available for emergencies.

For the private practitioner, professional networking and consultation can be more difficult. However, the private practitioner must develop a network of consultants and advisors in order to provide satisfactory services for the suicidal adolescent and his/her family. At the very minimum, the private practitioner needs ready access to a clinical psychologist, psychiatrist, and a psychiatric hospital. In addition, the practitioner needs some professional peers who can be consulted for advice, possibly doing co-therapy, or being available for emergencies. The private practitioner cannot be a "lone ranger" in the treatment of suicidal adolescents, but must have close ties to other professionals, professional groups, agencies, and hospitals.

Networking and Consultation with the Schools

The practitioner contracted to provide the treatment for the family must have close contacts with the school. In presentations to school personnel, the authors advise school counselors, teachers, and administrators to demand specific feedback from the mental health professional regarding suicidal students. If the school personnel do not receive the appropriate feedback, we suggest that the school refer their students and families to those practitioners who will return calls, provide reports, and visit the school for consultations.

Networking between the practitioner in the field and the school is very important. The communications between the family therapist and the school and vice versa can promote the successful treatment of the adolescent, parent crises, and provide support for those interacting with the adolescent. Effective networking can provide the school personnel with the necessary directions for treating the child in school while providing the practitioner with the necessary feedback for effectively treating the adolescent in family therapy.

In summary, the responsibility of the family therapist is to consult with school personnel and assist the school counselor and teachers in handling the suicidal teen. On the other hand, the school personnel are responsible for informing the therapist of the teenager's activities and behavior at school. This two-way responsibility is critical in the treatment of suicidal ideation. The following example will demonstrate this point.

Mary, a 16 year old junior, made a suicide attempt by taking a number of Tylenol tablets at home. She was taken to a local hospital for emergency medical treatment and referred for a psychiatric evaluation. Mary's family was in therapy at the time of the attempt and immediately informed their own therapist. After talking with the psychological staff at the hospital, the therapist suggested to the parents that Mary be hospitalized. In addition, the therapist suggested to the hospital staff that Mary be tested for possible pregnancy. As suggested, Mary was pregnant, in addition to the faint-hearted attempt at suicide.

After a short stay in the psychiatric unit of the hospital, Mary was released to her parents and returned to school. Both of these events, release to the parents and a return to school, were difficult situations. Once Mary, was in school, she complained of physical ailments and feeling depressed. School personnel, assuming she was a blatant suicidal youngster, would contact her parents and send her home. After two days of the same behavior, the therapist was contacted. The therapist was able to explain to the principal, counselor, and nurse that Mary was an "acting out" adolescent who was only minimally suicidal. Because Mary was manipulating school personnel, she was able to disrupt the home environment, because both parents had to leave their jobs to be at home with her.

Through an extended consultation with the school staff and the parents, the therapist was able to convince everyone that Mary's behaviors were not self-destructive. Previous to the consult, the school was considering placing Mary on home-bound instruction, which was exactly what she wanted. However, through the efforts of the school staff, with professional support from the therapist, Mary was maintained in school.

Hospitalization and the Returning Adolescent

Once the teenager has been diagnosed as a danger to himself/herself, no other choice exists but hospitalization. The hospitalization can be either voluntary or involuntary, depending upon the resistance exhibited by the adolescent or the level of denial presented by the family. Either way, the adolescent is protected from harm in the hospital, which is the critical issue.

After the crisis at the time of the hospitalization, the professional serving the family must prepare both the parents and the school for the return of the teenager. Networking with the professional staff of the hospital, the therapist will be able to prepare the family for the integration of their child into the day-to-day life of the family.

Two important aspects of the treatment process can occur while the adolescent is in the hospital. First, the therapist can assist the family with critical issues related to the hospitalized child; but also, the family can use the time to examine issues not related to the hospitalized child. Frequently, the hospitalized child has created such a disruption in the house, that the parents and other children have not had the opportunity to work on their problems and relationships. Therefore, therapy without the problem child can create some changes in the family by adjusting the relationships among the parents and the parents and the children.

Second, while the child is hospitalized, the practitioner, in conjunction with the hospital staff, can conduct one or more sessions with the parents and the second child in the protective confines of the hospital. The authors use the period of hospitalization to push the parents to present difficult issues that they may have been reluctant to raise with their child. In this way, if the child is going to react in a negative or self-destructive fashion, he/she is in the protective confines of the hospital.

For example, Sue's parents had kept a secret of the fact that she was her mother's daughter by another man, and not the man she assumed to be her father. The parents decided that Sue should know this fact. Therefore, the therapist had the couple present this information while Sue was hospitalized. Sue was able to talk about this revelation in individual and group therapy as well as act out her problems in psycho-drama sessions. Any acting out behaviors could be handled in the hospital, rather than have Sue be a "terror" with her family without any support.

The other group to be given assistance following the hospitalization of a teenager is the school. Counselors, administrators, and teachers need to be given whatever information is critical for their involvement with the teenager. Too often, the adolescent is hospitalized, gone for two weeks, and then returned to the school. In the meantime, the school personnel know very little about what has happened or what to do now that the student has returned.

The community professional's responsibility is to network with the family, the hospital, the school, and the teenager to assist all involved in the satisfactory adjustment of the teenager. Since the teenager ultimately returns to the school, the school personnel also need to be effectively networked with the hospital. The authors, while conducting in-service programs for schools, suggest that the schools, demand the involvement of the hospital staff with the school. In this way, the schools have direct contact with the professionals serving their student.

Through the advice and directions of the practitioner and the hospital staff, the entire school staff will be better able to serve the adolescent having difficulty. All of the school staff, including custodians, need to be trained in the identification and treatment of adolescents with suicidal ideation. In the case of students returning from hospitals, the staff need to be consulted and given adequate information to assist the teenager. Networking among community services, the school, and the hospital will make this occur.

ETHICAL CONCERNS

Although numerous ethical and legal concerns exist for professionals involved with the suicidal adolescent, we would like to center on five primary concerns. First, as mentioned earlier in the chapter, the professional has the *duty to warn* the parents of the serious nature of their child's difficulties. Because of the unstable nature of the adolescent, we recommend that teachers, counselors, administrators, and therapists react to the suicidal ideation quickly. An over-reaction to the problems presented by the adolescent is better than an under-reaction.

Second, the professional has the responsibility to maintain the appropriate professional contacts for providing the most effective *referrals* for the adolescent and his/her family. Because problems exhibited by the adolescent can change from moment to moment and day to day, the professionals involved in the treatment of the suicidal adolescent must have easy access to the most appropriate mental health services. Also, the professional treating the adolescent must know when to refer the case if the problems go beyond his/her abilities and training.

Third, mentioned in the previous section, the professional providing services must establish a network of other professionals to assist in the treatment of the suicidal adolescent. In addition, as the crisis decreases, the professionals must be able to consult and exchange information related to the case. The therapist providing family therapy must maintain contact with the school and vice versa. *Networking, consultation, and communication* are responsibilities of each professional involved in the treatment of the suicidal adolescent.

Fourth, the ultimate care and nurturance of the suicidal adolescent rests with the parents and family. Frequently, we have observed well-meaning school counselors attempting to care for the adolescent as if the parents did not exist. As harsh or uncaring as it may seem, the professional cannot supplant the parents regardless of the lack of concern expressed by the parents. The risk for the adolescent, the school counselor, and the school is much too great. For example, school counselors will often give their home phone numbers to the suicidal adolescent in an attempt to offer the adolescent assistance during this difficult time. However, this is a real error in judgment. What happens if the teenager calls the counselor, but nobody is at home? The teenager is in need of help, but the one person who said he/she would always be there for them is out for the night. The point is this, each professional must share the responsibility for the treatment of the adolescent. *The family is ultimately responsible for the care and safety of the adolescent, with the assistance of the professionals from the community.*

Finally, each school district must be *active in their treatment* of suicidal adolescents and their families. As noted recently (Splitt, 1987), parents have filed suits against the school, blaming the school for the suicidal death of their child. Whether or not the parents were successful in their suit, the schools and other organizations involved in the education and treatment of teenagers must be active in the care of those teenagers having problems. Also, each school district must develop stated policies and procedures for the handling of students in crisis.

Also, as all school personnel know, not every parent is willing to accept that their child is having difficulties and is need of therapeutic assistance. For those parents who reject mental health services for the suicidal adolescent, the school must continue to be active in attempting to get help for the adolescent. If all attempts fail, the chief school administrator must notify, in writing, the parents of the suicidal adolescent of the school's continued concern for their child's welfare. Copies of the letter also should be sent to the appropriate mental health agencies informing them of the serious nature of the adolescent's problems and the parent's reluctance to be involved in treatment.

IMPLICATIONS

The therapeutic treatment process for suicidal adolescents is a very challenging endeavor for all of the involved professionals. The necessity for networking among all professionals involved in the treatment process cannot be overstated. If the mental health professional is to promote the successful treatment of the teenager with suicidal ideation, he/she must be skilled as a family therapist, be comfortable in a consulting relationship with the schools, and maintain a working relationship with hospitals treating suicidal teenagers. Family therapy and networking are necessities in treating such a critical problem as teen suicide.

REFERENCES

Elkind, D. (1981). *The hurried child.* Reading, MA: Brunner/Mazel.

Everstine, L., Everstine, D.S., Heymann, G.M., True, R.H., Frey, D.H., Johnson, H.G., & Seiden, R.H. (1980). Privacy and confidentiality in psychotherapy. *American Psychologist, 35,* 828-40.

Farberow, N.L. (1980). Indirect self-destructive behavior: Classification and characteristics. In N.L. Farberow (Ed.), *The many faces of suicide: Indirect self-destructive behavior* (15-27). New York: McGraw-Hill.

Husain, S.A., & Vandiver, T. (1984). *Suicide in children and adolescents.* New York: Spectrum Publications.

Splitt, D.A. (1987, April). School law. *The Executive Educator,* p. 12.

Viadero, D. (1987). Apparent link between media coverage and 'copycat' suicides worries experts. *Education Week,* VI(28), 1-20.

Wekstein, L. (1979). *Handbook of suicidology: Principles, problems, and practice.* New York: Brunner/Mazel.

PART V
LEGAL ISSUES

CHAPTER **15**

LEGAL CONSIDERATIONS FOR THE PRACTITIONER

J. Jeffries McWhirter, Ph.D.
and
Robert J. McWhirter, B.A., J.D. Candidate

J. Jeffries McWhirter, Ph.D.

Professor
Division of Psychology in Education
Arizona State University
Tempe, AZ 85281

J. Jeffries McWhirter is a Professor in the Counseling Psychology program in the Division of Psychology in Education at Arizona State University. He received his Ph.D. in counseling psychology in 1969 from the University of Oregon. Prior to receiving his doctorate, he was graduated from St. Martin's College (Olympia, Washington) and holds masters degrees from Oregon State University and the University of Oregon.

Dr. McWhirter is the author of 16 books, monographs, and training manuals and over 50 articles which have been published in such journals as *The Counseling Psychologist, Small Group Behavior, Journal of Counseling Psychology, The School Counselor, Journal of Clinical Psychology, Counselor Education and Supervision, Journal of Learning Disabilities, Journal of Family Counseling* and the *Personnel and Guidance Journal.* He is a member of the American Association for Counseling and Development and the American Psychological Association.

He has been a visiting (summer) professor to eighteen universities including the University of Toronto, The University of Navarra (Spain), The University of Maine, the University of Victoria, and the University of Vermont. In 1977-78 he was a Senior Fulbright-Hays Scholar to Hacettepe University, Ankara, Turkey, and in 1984-85 a Fullbright Senior Scholar to Catholic College of Education-Sydney and Western Australia College of Advanced Education.

In addition to his work in suicide prevention, his areas of special interest include small group research, family counseling and parent education, counseling theory and practice, learning disabilities, and international aspects of counseling.

Robert J. McWhirter, B.A., J.D. Candidate

Arizona State University
Judicial Clerk for Vice Chief Justice Stanley G. Feldman
Supreme Court of Arizona

Robert McWhirter attended Arizona State University and received an honors degree in history in 1983. As an undergraduate, Mr. McWhirter was active in student government and interned with the Arizona State Legislature (Spring, 1983).

After graduation Mr. McWhirter worked in South America. Specifically, he taught learning disabled and mentally retarded children (mostly caused by malnutrition and scarcity) in a Peruvian shanty-town on the outskirts of Lima. This experience increased his desire to contribute to a more equitable world.

During law school, Mr. McWhirter externed at *The Arizona Center for Law in the Public Interest* and was active in the Arizona chapter of the American Civil Liberties Union. In addition, he has clerked for two Phoenix law firms between school semesters.

After law school Mr. McWhirter will embark on a prestigious judicial clerkship for Vice Chief Justice Stanley G. Feldman of the Supreme Court of Arizona. After this experience with Justice Feldman, Mr. McWhirter plans to begin legal practice and continue legal and academic research.

EDITORIAL ABSTRACT: *The literature on the legal ramifications of suicide for the health care practitioner, school or mental health counselor is limited. Given the fact that suicide touches the roles of practitioners in the health care professions, the mental health profession, and the legal profession, this dearth of information constitutes a rather unusual situation. This chapter discusses issues relating to whether or when the law will hold a health care practitioner, school or mental health counselor responsible for an adolescent suicide attempt or completion. In addition, suggestions for what practitioners can do during the process of treatment or counseling therapy to avoid law suits are provided.*

Great trauma is connected with the death of a loved one, especially when the death is an adolescent suicide. After such an event, family and friends display a range of emotions—sadness, anger, guilt, self-recrimination. They ultimately need to find an outlet for these negative feelings. That outlet often includes casting the blame elsewhere (Drukteinis, 1985). After an adolescent suicide, the health care practitioner, the counselor, or the institution that was working with the victim before the death may receive the blame. Klein and Grover (1983) reported that 15% of all reported psychiatrist malpractice cases involve suicide or attempted suicide (1983). These law suits not only relieve guilt-ridden family members, they also protect the image of the victim.

At the outset we must make one point. Being *sued* for the suicidal death of a client or patient is different than being *liable* for that death. Anyone with a reasonable claim in our society can sue anyone else. In most states, a person can file suit for only a fifty dollar court fee. A health care practitioner or school counselor can take steps to minimize the possibility of a law suit but no guarantees can be given that a surviving family member will not initiate a suit. Thus, a health care practitioner or counselor should check the status of his/her own insurance and the insurance of his/her employer. A health care practitioner or counselor should find out the extent of the coverage and whether the employer's insurance covers malpractice cases against employee health care practitioners and counselors.

Even though family members can easily file suits, this does not mean that these law suits will be successful. Without legal grounds, a court will not hold a health care practitioner or school counselor liable. However, family members may file suit without much thought to this fact. Thus, after a suicide or suicide attempt, the psychiatrist, counselor, or therapist may find himself/herself face to face with the American legal system.

The legal system has never really known what to do with suicide. Historically, the English made suicide illegal. Punishments included refusal to bury the victim's body on church grounds, mutilation of the victim's body, burial of the victim within a crossroad, and driving a stake in the heart of the victim's body (Drukteinis, 1985; Wright, 1975; Litman, 1967). Although these sanctions were not transplanted to America, suicide was originally illegal in most parts of this country as well (Marzen, et al., 1985). This raised problems. How does one "punish" suicide? The victim, of course, is immune from punishment. Sanctions, therefore, tended to punish the surviving friends and family rather than the person who committed the "crime." Partly because of this inherent inconsistency, state legislatures changed the legal status of suicide so that today it is no longer illegal to commit suicide (Litman, 1967; Marzen, 1985). However, even though suicide is no longer illegal, in most states to aid a person committing suicide is illegal [e.g., Model Penal Code 210.5(2)].

Thus, a health care practitioner, psychologist, or school counselor need not fear criminal sanctions unless they have aided in a suicide. In an exceptional situation should a counselor or therapist help in planning an adolescent's suicide, provide the means to accomplish the act, or in some other way actively help in the person's self behavior, the counselor or therapist may indeed be subject to criminal sanctions. However, since aiding suicide is not part of even the most avant-garde therapy, this will probably not be a legal issue.

In the civil law (i.e., where people sue each other rather than criminal law where the government prosecutes persons for crimes), an ambiguity exists as to the legal standards in cases involving suicide. For example, most malpractice law suits are based on the allegation that someone did something wrong (e.g., a medical doctor leaves a scalpel in a patient). Because the physician behaved wrongly, the law holds him/her responsible for his/her acts (i.e., the physician must pay the injured party or family). Suicide, however, results from a deliberate act of self-destruction (Kjervik, 1984). How then can someone else, besides the victim, be responsible? In what situations will the law hold a health care practitioner or school counselor responsible for the suicidal death of a patient? In short, what are the legal ramifications, for the health care practitioner or school counselor, of adolescent suicide? The major portion of this chapter will attempt to answer these complicated questions.

In addition to liability, other legal problems are connected with the subject of adolescent suicide. Adolescent suicide is recognized as a major American health problem (Kjervik, 1984) and the legal system has responded to this fact. State legislatures and courts have developed mechanisms to deal with suicide. Usually, state health care agencies attempt to identify and help adolescents at risk of committing suicide. For example, possibly a court will commit an adolescent to a state mental hospital after a suicide attempt. In certain situations, a conscientious health care practitioner or school counselor may even encourage this commitment. Many states do not adequately fund mental health programs or state hospitals. One of the jobs of a good health care practitioner or school counselor may be to get resources for the adolescent client. A portion of this chapter will alert health care practitioners about what may be available in the legal environment to help their patients after a suicide attempt.

REVIEW OF RELATED LITERATURE

Only limited literature exists on the legal ramifications of suicide for the health care practitioner or school counselor. This is rather odd because it is a subject that touches two distinct and divergent fields: the health care profession and the legal profession. Perhaps the reason for this is that only recently have courts held third parties responsible for a suicidal death (Howell, 1978). Thus only a limited number of law suits and consequently only limited literature are available.

The existing literature usually only explains the law, with one exception. Berman and Cohen-Sandler (1983) started with the question of what constitutes "reasonable professional judgement." Because of the subjective nature of this field, the question of what constitutes "reasonable professional judgment" may be difficult to answer. However, as will be explained in the next section, this is very important in malpractice cases. A deviation from it can mean liability for the health care practitioner, school counselor, or institution. Berman and Cohen-Sandler (1983) sent a hypothetical case study to health care practitioners and received reactions on how the treatment of a high risk suicide patient should have been conducted. Their conclusion was that possibly mental health associations (e.g., the American Psychological Association, or the American Association for Counseling and Development) could and need to establish guidelines defining the minimum standard of care. They further concluded that it could benefit the profession as a whole to establish standards for practitioners to follow. Even though published standards may give grounds for individuals to sue health care practitioners and institutions in certain cases, if the profession does not establish guidelines, the courts may.

The rest of the literature on this subject tends to focus on "the law." Literature from the legal field is mostly devoted to discussing legal doctrine (e.g., Schwartz, 1971; Howell, 1978; Knuth, 1979). For the most part these articles explain the law using recent cases and court decisions. The authors of these articles usually intend to give judges and legal practitioners some idea of how to deal with cases in which people sue after a suicidal death or injury. We have used basically the same methodology in the next section of this chapter. However, we are more specific in our use of cases and practical situations than most of the legal studies. We intend to give health care practitioners and school counselors an idea of what to expect from the legal system; not, necessarily, to guide the legal system.

The literature on the subject of suicide written by health care practitioners tends to be similar to that in the legal field. Case studies ar used to explain the legal aspects of suicide (Klein & Glover, 1983). These authors, as one might expect, write for health care practitioners and focus on practical hints to guide their actions (e.g., Litman, 1967; Berman & Cohen-Sandler, 1983). We use a similar approach in the last section of this chapter and have generated a list of "dos and don'ts" for health care practitioners. We intend that this list will protect health care practitioners and counselors from liability.

Interestingly, the two sets of literature diverge on a key point. The literature from the health care field is generally much more preoccupied with the danger of law suits than the literature from the legal field. For example, Slawson and Flynn (1977) reported that hospitals have a 25% to 33% chance of being sued after patient suicides. Articles from the legal field, however, recognize that courts generally view suicide as an individual act. Therefore, the law does not affix blame on third parties, like health care practitioners and school counselors, because a third party has no liability for the independent act of the suicide victim (Schwartz, 1971; Howell, 1978). The literature from the legal profession reports that, at the present time, practicing psychiatrists have a relatively low rate of harassment from malpractice law suits (Berman & Cohen-Sandler, 1983). Thus, legal articles tend to theorize on questions of legal doctrine (Schwartz, 1971; Knuth, 1979; Howell, 1978) instead of reporting any impending danger that the legal system will impose on the health care profession (Slawson & Flynn, 1977).

APPLICATION AND CASE STUDIES

The legal ramifications of adolescent suicide are the focus of this chapter. However, the number of cases in which the families of adolescent suicide victims have sued the health care practitioner, institution, or school counselor is limited. In addition, the few court cases that do exist which involve adolescent suicide generally do not involve the family survivors suing a school counselor or psychologist. Consequently, we focus on cases generally involving adult suicide or attempted suicide to explain the legal standards. We assume that these standards will be the same, regardless of whether the victim is an adolescent or adult, and regardless of whether the therapist is a psychiatrist, psychologist, or counselor. As of yet, the courts have not held school counselors liable for the suicidal death of their students. The courts have reasoned that schools, and counselors working in schools, have the primary responsibility of educating students, not treating their mental problems. In other words, schools do not assume a duty to care for the psychological health of students and to prevent their suicide.

Case Study

A young woman saw a counselor at the university counseling center. Her therapist, "an educator by profession," administered the center. He had counseled the girl and administered her personality and aptitude tests. After a time, the therapist terminated the interviews and six weeks later, the young woman committed suicide. Her parents sued, claiming that the counselor failed to secure emergency treatment for the girl, and also, failed in not informing them of their daughter's emotional state.

The court, in *Bogust v. Iverson* (1960), held that the parents did not have grounds to sue the school. The school only had a responsibility to educate and not to provide mental health services. In addition, the court held that an educator cannot be held to the same standard as someone trained in medicine/psychiatry. Any duty to inform parents of their daughter's medical/psychological condition could only be based on special knowledge in psychiatry. The court reasoned that an educator does not have that special knowledge.

Even though the court exonerated the university/school counselor, several notable issues are in the previous case. First, the case is nearly thirty years old. A court today may recognize that universities and colleges now often have large, well-staffed counseling centers and have assumed responsibility for their student's mental health. Second, the court partly based its decision on the fact the counselor was not trained in medicine or psychiatry. A court today may be much more inclined to find that "an educator" may indeed have the special training necessary to make informed professional health care decisions, especially when educators have degrees in counseling or psychology and purport to be experts in mental health issues.

Indeed, the insurance industry today recognizes that non-psychiatrists are valid health care providers (*Blue Shield of Virginia v. McCready, 1982*). Thus, with the advent of third party payments, now available in some states to counselors and psychologists, the courts may begin to hold non-medical health care practitioners and school counselors liable for the suicidal deaths of the student clients. In other words, they too may soon be subject to malpractice law-suits. Because many counselors and psychologists now have malpractice insurance, more law suits may occur in the future. Because they now have insurance, counselors and psychologists now have assets that make law suits against them more attractive. For the first time, psychologists and counselors have "deep pockets." Because of these anticipated changes in the law, the next section examines the legal standard to which courts have held other health care practitioners (like psychiatrists). If and when school counselors begin to be sued, the standards will probably be similar to the ones currently guiding health care practitioners and institutions.

Standard of Care of Health Care Practitioners and Institutions

As previously stated, only recently have the courts held third parties responsible for suicidal death. Courts traditionally have viewed suicide as an individual's intentional, willful act without third party blame (Kjervik, 1984; Schwartz, 1971). Typically, courts have allowed relatives and heirs of the victim compensation in only exceptional circumstances (Howell, 1978; Mutual Life *Insurance Company v. Terry,* 1973). In fact, Howell, reported that even though courts are today more willing to hear relatives' claims against third parties, these cases are statistically infrequent (1978). This is surprising since suicide is the tenth leading cause of death in the United States and the second leading cause of adolescent death (Kolb, 1977).

Third-party liability for suicide began with workers' compensation cases. In fact, civil liability for suicide often arises in cases after an injury in the work place (Drukteinis, 1985; Howell, 1978). If the injury emotionally affected the worker and led him/her to suicide, the courts have allowed the relatives compensation under workers' compensation laws. The legal field has labeled this the "chain of causation rule" (Batt, 1983). The work-related injury was the first link in the chain that "caused" the worker to commit suicide. This is the same basic legal theory as in most malpractice cases. If a surgeon leaves a scalpel in a patient, a law court can hold the doctor responsible and may require him/her, then, to pay the patient for any injury. This is because the doctor "caused" the injury to the patient (Prosser, et al., 1984).

Cases against health care practitioners and other counselors, however, are usually based on a different legal footing than the workers' compensation cases. The issue is not causation. Families of suicide victims do not sue claiming that the hospital, psychiatrist, or counselor "caused" the death of their loved one (Knuth, 1979). Rather, the family members claim that the health care practitioner or institution had a duty to prevent the suicide and that the practitioner or institution did not meet that duty (Drukteinis, 1985).

A legal duty arises in several ways. For instance, we all have a "duty" not to break the law (Prosser et al., 1984). If a person drives over the speed limit, and an injury occurs to a third party, the courts may hold that person responsible for the injury. This is true even if the injury would have happened regardless of the speeding, because the person "breached a statutory duty" (Prosser et al., 1984). Also, everyone has a duty to show "due care" in their daily actions. If a person does something that is not illegal but, given the circumstances, is reckless, a court may hold that person partly responsible for any resulting injury because the person "breached a duty of due care" (Prosser et al., 1984).

The duty to prevent suicide is a "special duty." The health care practitioner or institution assumed a duty to provide health care services. They, therefore, know about the patient's potential for suicide and (supposedly) have the power to prevent it (Knuth, 1979). This duty makes the "cause" of the suicide (i.e., the patients' act) irrelevant. In certain circumstances, the voluntary act of the victim does not relieve the health care practitioner or institution of the duty to prevent the suicide (Drukteinis, 1985).

Because health care practitioners and institutions assume a duty to prevent suicide, courts hold them to a "standard of care." Health care practitioners must act out on their superior knowledge. They cannot merely do what would be reasonable for the untrained lay person. This is like the situation of medical doctors. They must conform to the "standard of care" of the medical profession rather than the standards of a person not trained in medicine. For instance, the doctor who left the scalpel in the patient did not provide the national standard of care expected of doctors (Prosser et al., 1984). When this is combined with "causation" (i.e., the injury the scalpel caused), a court will hold the doctor liable. Like medical doctors, health care practitioners and institutions must meet the standard of care of the profession. The professional must exercise "reasonable professional judgment" (Berman & Cohen-Sandler, 1983).

"Reasonable professional judgment," however, is not an objective standard (Berman & Cohen-Sandler, 1983). For example, a therapist in a particular case may not think that a past history of assaults and homicidal tendencies necessarily signifies that this patient has suicidal tendencies. However, another therapist may think the opposite. Thus the standard is undefined, without clear rules and guidelines for the therapist.

Case Study

A man made an unprovoked attack on a friend and also physically assaulted and bit two bystanders who attempted to subdue him. The police arrested him and took him to a hospital where the admitting psychiatrist determined that the man was mentally ill and possessed "violent and homicidal tendencies." The psychiatrist and his colleagues further determined that the man needed extensive treatment in a mental institution. The hospital, however, did not have the facilities to conduct treatment for more than 18 days. Because the police had requested the man's detention, the hospital turned him over to the police after the 18 days. At the time the man appeared calm and displayed no symptoms of violence. However, after four days in police custody, the man hanged himself with his elastic socks.

After the suicide, the man's wife sued the doctors. She claimed that they were negligent in not recognizing that the man's homicidal tendencies also displayed suicidal potential. An expert witness that the wife's lawyer obtained, stated that, in his opinion, a patient who displays homicidal tendencies also possesses a drive to destroy himself. Is this the standard or not?

The court in *Fernandez v. Baruch* (1968) held that it was not. The wife only had one expert witness who testified "according to his personal opinion." He did not testify that his view represented the "generally accepted view in the profession." Thus, the court found no connection between homicidal and suicidal drives. The court relieved the defendant psychiatrists from liability.

The above case illustrates an important point about the standard of care that the courts may impose on counselors in the future. The reasonableness of counselors' actions will be judged only after the court has determined that there are grounds to believe that they deviated from the "generally accepted view in the profession." In other words, persons suing must have "experts" testify that the counselor deviated from accepted practice (Klein, 1983). Berman and Cohen-Sandler (1983) reported that in the case of health care practitioners, they will not be liable for errors in subjective judgment.

Case Study

A Phi Beta Kappa college graduate frequented George Washington Bridge on the Hudson River. Subsequently, the young man became a patient in the psychiatric ward of a hospital. After three months in the hospital, a resident physician authorized a release pass for the young man. A month later his body was found floating in the Hudson River near the bridge. The young man's mother brought a law suit against the hospital and doctors, claiming that they were negligent in granting the pass.

The court in *Fiederlein v. City of New York Health, Etc.* (1981), held that the mother did not have a valid claim against the hospital and psychiatrist, even though an expert witness testified that he would not have granted the young man's pass. The court stated that with every medical judgment exists a risk of error, "but that mere error in medical judgment does not give rise to a viable claim of medical malpractice." The mother's expert witness did not prove that the psychiatrist's decision deviated from professional standards.

If a question exists as to whether a health care practitioner or institution deviated from professional standards, a jury will decide the case. A key factor in the jury's decision as to whether a health care practitioner or institution used "reasonable professional judgment" is the degree to which the victim's suicide attempt was "foreseeable." Health care practitioners and institutions have a duty to prevent the suicidal death of their patients and clients when it is "reasonably foreseeable" that the event will occur (Knuth, 1979). On this point, however, a divergent view is held between legal theory and psychotherapy. Although research continues and knowledge increases, a conspicuous lack of predictive indicators exist upon which health care practitioners and institutions can rely (Kjervik, 1984). In other words, often to tell whether a specific patient or client will commit suicide is impossible. Thus, for courts to hold health care practitioners and institutions responsible for not preventing "foreseeable" suicides would be arbitrary when suicides may indeed not be foreseeable. In the future, counselors and psychologists may have to deal with this same problem.

The word "foreseeability," however, has a technical meaning in the law (Prosser et al., 1984). Health care practitioners do not necessarily need to predict the future in every case. As stated before, the lack of predictive indicators in this field would preclude such a standard. Rather the requirement is that health care practitioners and institutions act "reasonably." To put the standard as plainly as possible, the health care practitioner must not violate a *future juror's* notion of common sense. If a "reasonable hospital staff" should have predicted the suicide (i.e., that it was "foreseeable") and should have done something different than what they did to prevent it (i.e., that they were negligent), then liability will follow (Kjervik, 1984). The fact that the juror is deciding what is reasonable from a position of hindsight may indeed cut against the practitioner, hospital staff, or, in the future, the school counselor and psychologist.

Case Study

A man attempted suicide by cutting his wrists. After being treated for his physical injuries, his family brought him to a mental hospital. The hospital had an "open door" therapy approach where treatment de-emphasizes physical restraint of the patient and attempts to foster a "homelike" environment. No locks were on the doors, nor bars on the windows; patients freely moved about the hospital and even left if they so chose. The therapists argued that this freedom expedited the process of rehabilitation. They recognized, however, that the suicidal patient was at greater risk in this situation. The staff placed the man in a second-story room with a window. The window had no bars on it and it could be opened by a crank. The man jumped out the window and killed himself. His wife sued the hospital, claiming malpractice.

The court, in *Meier V. Ross General Hospital* (1968), held that the wife had a valid law suit and sent the case to a jury. Placing a man, who had just attempted suicide, in a second story room with an openable window created a presumption of negligence on the part of the defendants. Under these circumstances, the psychiatrist should have concluded that "the patient would be likely to harm himself in the absence of preclusive measures."

Foreseeability, then, is judged from the juror's perspective. The influence on the jury of a past suicide attempt illustrates this point. A past suicide attempt is generally considered important in predicting a future suicide. In a trial, of course, the plaintiffs (e.g., the victim's family) will use this to show the jury that the suicide was (or should have been) "foreseeable" to the hospital defendants and that they, therefore, should have prevented it (Kjervik, 1984).

Case Study

A teacher attempted suicide one morning in her bedroom and her son found her. Upon admission in the hospital, the diagnosis entered on the woman's charts was "attempted suicide." The hospital staff placed her alone in a room and began intravenous feeding. Although her family made repeated requests to see her, the hospital staff refused. They assured the family that she would be closely watched. The woman remained unattended but was observed from time to time by a nurse who looked through a peep-hole in the door. That night, the staff found the woman dead, having strangled herself with plastic tubing from her feeding apparatus.

The court, in *Kent v. Whitaker* (1961), held that the hospital was negligent. When the staff accepted the patient, having been warned of the woman's suicidal tendencies, they assumed a special duty to care for the woman. They were required not only to treat the patient's injuries but also to prevent her from self-inflicted harm. The fact that the hospital segregated the woman from all others who could help her was particularly compelling. Because of the knowledge of the woman's past suicide attempt, putting the woman in a room with only a small peep-hole in which to observe her and in the charge of a nurse with 12 other patients caused the hospital to become liable. The hospital simply did not provide the woman reasonable care in proportion to her needs. In addition, the hospital itself supplied the means by which the woman committed suicide (i.e., the plastic tubing).

As previous cases demonstrate, liability will often depend on the facts of the case. However, three significant factors are to be considered: first, whether the victim of suicide was in, or recently released from, a hospital; second, whether the victim's therapist was a psychiatrist and third, whether the therapist was another type of health care practitioner. A study of these factors should indicate the future trend of liability for counselors and psychologists.

Standard of Care of a Hospital

Legal liability for the suicide of a patient is most often a hospital problem (Berman & Cohen-Sandler, 1982). One reason for this is that hospitals have more money—the so-called "deep pockets" theory. A prospective plaintiff simply has a better chance of getting more money from a hospital than he/she would from an individual. Also, juries are generally less sympathetic to large institutions, such as hospitals, than they are to individual psychiatrists, counselors, or other practitioners. This factor is important to keep in mind because it may be a factor in the future for counselors and psychologists. If they are in a school, the school district has "deep pockets" which may induce plaintiffs to sue the counselor. Also, as previously stated, counselors and psychologists now receive third party payments and often have malpractice insurance. This further induces law suits against them.

Hospitals are legally liable because they have "custodial care" over the suicide victim (Howell, 1978). When a hospital admits a patient with suicidal tendencies, it assumes responsibility for the suicidal behavior (Kjervik, 1984; Schwartz, 1971). As discussed earlier, the hospital now has a duty to use ordinary care to prevent the suicide (Howell, 1978). Therefore, if its doctors and other staff are negligent, the hospital will be liable.

Case Study

A voluntary patient in a psychiatric center escaped from an unlocked ward. He later attempted suicide by jumping in front of a car. He, subsequently, brought a law suit against the hospital, claiming that the hospital staff negligently treated and supervised him.

The court, in *Koenigsmark v. State* (1981), held that the patient not be awarded damages. Due to the fact that the patient's mental condition was continually going "up and down," the court found that the hospital took the reasonable precautions necessary to prevent the patient from escaping. It, therefore, could not be liable for any resulting injuries from the patient's attempted suicide, or if successful, for the patient's suicidal death.

A hospital will not be liable for the suicidal death of a patient when the victim's act was independent of the hospital's duty to prevent the suicide (Kjervik, 1984). For example, when a patient escapes from a hospital that made reasonable attempts to prevent the escape (again judged from the jury's notion of common sense), the hospital will not be responsible for the victim's subsequent suicide. If the victim's escape is an independent act, then the hospital's duty to prevent it is relieved. In legal terminology, the victim's act was the independent (or superceding) cause of his/her own death. Therefore, a third party, like the hospital, is not liable.

The courts will not hold a hospital liable, when a custodial relationships is not established. In this situation, the hospital has not assumed the special duty of care.

Case Study

A woman went to a hospital emergency room and the attending doctor referred her to the hospital psychiatrist. The psychiatrist talked with her and she pointed a gun at him. He grabbed the gun and when he found it unloaded, returned it to her "in order to establish rapport." From the interview, he discovered that the woman wanted to break a drug habit. Deciding that she needed prolonged treatment, he escorted her to the admissions desk. He left her to fill out the proper forms while he went to call her husband. The woman left the desk without completing the admissions process. Later, a janitor found her dead in a hospital bathroom from a self-inflicted bullet wound.

The court, in *Charouleau v. Charity Hospital of Louisiana at New Orleans* (1975), held that since no outward manifestations was observed in the woman's behavior to indicate a risk of suicide, the hospital was not liable. The hospital had not, at that point, assumed any special duty to prevent the woman's suicide. The admissions procedures were not, of themselves, negligent. Therefore, the hospital was not liable.

Health care practitioners in the hospital setting will also avoid liability for the suicide of a patient when the hospital is running an open psychiatric ward. In this situation, the therapeutic value of the "open door" approach outweighs the risk of suicide (Klein, 1983). This type of therapy more closely approximated that found in the treatment of suicidal patients outside the hospital. Therefore, the hospital does not have the same duty to protect the patient from himself/herself. The courts have not wished to penalize this type of therapy (Kjervik, 1984). However, the hospital staff must still decide whether placing the patient in an open ward is in conformity with sound professional judgment. In other words, a future jury must still find the decision reasonable.

Case Study

A man with a long history of mental disease was a voluntary patient in a mental hospital's open ward. He left the hospital ward and threw himself under a subway train. His widow sued claiming that the hospital's negligence in allowing her husband to escape caused his death.

The court, in *Lichtenstein v. Montefiore Hospital and Medical Center* (1977), held that the hospital's actions were not automatically negligent. The man was in a hospital and "not a maximum security prison, or a bank vault, or a closely guarded military installation." The court further held that "the man's nurse was a nurse, not a sentinel."

Again, it appears that liability is less direct when psychologists and counselors lack custodial control over the patient or client. Thus, the future liability of psychologists and counselors may rest on the degree to which health care practitioners began to assume custodial responsibility for clients.

Standard of Care Applied to Psychiatrists

Of all the health care practitioners and therapists treating patients with suicidal tendencies, psychiatrists are usually the ones that get sued (Berman & Cohen-Sandler, 1982). Very rarely are other health care practitioners part of a law suit. Perhaps the reason for this is again "deep pockets." Other health care practitioners usually lack the assets of their medical counterparts and historically have lacked insurance coverage. Psychiatrists also get sued because usually psychiatrists are in charge of treatment teams, both inside and outside the hospital environment. Thus, the health care hierarchy maintains psychiatrists in a position where they are more likely to be sued.

Even so, the law generally does not hold psychiatrists responsible for the suicide of their patients when treating them outside the hospital environment. So far, the courts have recognized that a psychiatrist, working with patients outside the hospital setting, does not have the physical control over the patient necessary to prevent the suicide. In fact, Berman and Cohen-Sandler (1982) reported that from 1970-1980 only three court cases occurred for outside the hospital context in which the family members sued health care practitioners for the suicide of their loved one. Of these three, only one was won by the family members.

Case Study

A psychiatrist prescribed various "psychiatric drugs" to a patient with schizophrenia "of the moderate to mild form." In addition, the patient received sleeping pills from a general practitioner. The patient overdosed on the pills and his wife found him dead the next morning. The wife sued claiming that the psychiatrist failed to diagnose her husband's mental condition adequately. She alleged that her husband was incapable of managing his own affairs and may have taken the sleeping pills thinking that they would enhance his mental conditions.

The court, in *Runyon v. Reid* (1973), held that no reason existed to believe that the victim did not know what he was doing when he committed suicide. In addition the court noted that the psychiatrist could not be held liable as the patient was not in a confined hospital setting where the psychiatrist could restrain his actions.

This standard will assuredly pertain to psychologists and counselors in the future. Like psychiatrists, they usually lack custodial care over patients and simply do not have the same duty as a hospital.

Although few cases exist in which psychiatrists have been responsible outside the hospital environment, several situations could occur in which liability may occur in the future. These situations may cause psychologists and counselors liability as well. For instance, a psychiatrist may be held liable for a gross error in judgment as to whether a patient should be confined or hospitalized (Schwartz, 1971; Kjervik, 1984). In this situation, the imminence of the suicide must be clear enough that any reasonable psychiatrist or psychologist or counselor would see the danger and order confinement. Schwartz (1971) gave an example of a situation where liability may occur. When a very depressed client cannot sleep, has lost the desire to eat, is effectively unable to function in society, and has made several serious suicide attempts, the practitioner may be responsible for the patient's suicidal death if he/she had an opportunity to hospitalize the patient and failed to do so.

One way in which a psychiatrist may be held liable for suicide where a psychologist or counselor cannot be is when the psychiatrist prescribes the drugs that the patient uses in the suicide. If he/she prescribed the drugs negligently, the law may hold him/her accountable (Litman, 1967; Schwartz, 1971). Because psychologists do not have the power to prescribe drugs, they will not be in danger from this type of suit. However, a psychologist may be liable in the same way a psychiatrist would be if he/she intentionally or negligently discloses a patient's confidential communication, and because of this, the patient kills himself/herself (Schwartz, 1971). As of yet, the courts have not been sympathetic to this type of case. The general tendency is to allow for the psychiatrist's professional judgment as to the need of disclosure in a situation. Courts will probably extend this standard to future cases involving psychologists or counselors.

Case Study

A woman, in the process of a divorce, left her children without arranging for their care and entered a mental hospital. A psychiatrist began therapy with her. During the course of the therapy the woman related her past history of suicide attempts and current depression and suicidal feelings. The psychiatrist determined that the woman needed extended treatment. The woman, however, left the hospital against his advice.

Subsequently, at the woman's divorce trial, the custody of the children became the main issue. The husband asked the psychiatrist to write a letter to the judge as to the wife's mental state. The psychiatrist wrote a letter suggesting further evaluation and observation of the woman's fitness as a parent and ability to care for her children. The woman then sued the psychiatrist for breach of contract and invasion of privacy.

The court in *Werner v. Kliewer* (1985), held that the psychiatrist was not liable for his action. The woman did not have grounds to sue because the only persons that saw the letter were the judge and the parties to the divorce action. Therefore, the woman's reputation was not damaged. Also, the truth of the statements made in the letter was not at issue.

A psychiatrist and psychologist or counselor may even have a duty to disclose information that he/she obtains from a patient. This is when there is the possibility of danger to a third party (*Tarasoff v. Regents of the University of California et al.*, 1976). However, as yet this duty to inform has not been extended to situations where a person may be a danger only to himself/herself (Berman & Cohen-Sandler, 1982). Thus, at the present time, the practitioner will not be liable for not disclosing patient confidences. This is apparently even where the patient involved is an adolescent and the parents sue claiming that they should have been informed of the danger.

Case Study

An adolescent girl was under the care of a psychiatrist. During the course of the treatment, the psychiatrist determined that the young woman may be suicidal and he recorded this conclusion in his notes. Soon after, the young woman succumbed to a self-inflicted overdose of pills.

The parents sued the psychiatrist claiming that he failed to prevent the suicide and that he had a duty to warn them of their daughter's condition.

The court, in *Bellah v. Greenson* (1978), held that the psychiatrist did not have the same duty to prevent the woman's suicide in an outpatient setting as in the hospital setting.

Therefore, he had not breached a special duty to care for the woman and was not responsible for her death. Further, the court held that the psychiatrist was not required to inform third parties. The court reasoned that the value of confidentiality outweighed the value of informing. The court specifically rejected the suggestion that it extend the *Tarasoff* duty to inform where the danger is only that a party will inflict injury to himself/herself (as opposed to when the danger is to third parties).

Because psychologists, counselors, and other practitioners have interpreted *Tarasoff* as applying to them, the above standard should apply to them as well.

Several authors have predicted that psychiatrist liability in out-patient settings probably will increase in the future (Schwartz, 1971; Knuth, 1979). The assumption can be made that the same will be true of psychologists and counselors. Future cases against psychiatrists, psychologists, and counselors may be based on three factors: (1) the existence of a therapist-patient relationship, (2) knowledge on the part of the therapist that the patient was likely to attempt suicide, and (3) the therapist's failure to take appropriate measures (Knuth, 1979; *Bella v. Greenson*, 1978). For the present, however, liability for the suicidal death of patient is still a hospital problem (Berman & Cohen-Sandler, 1982).

Standard of Care Applied to Other Health Care Practitioners

Like psychologists and counselors, other health care practitioners to date do not have the same risk of being held liable for the suicidal death of their patients or clients as hospitals and psychiatrists. Non-medical health care practitioners are held to a different standard than psychiatrists. Again, psychiatrists have a duty to use "reasonable professional judgment." Other health care practitioners, on the other hand, must only meet the same standard of reasonableness as anyone else. In other words, they will be liable only when they have acted very negligently in the performance of their duties. However, in a few situations a non-medical health care practitioner may be liable or cause the hospital to be liable.

Case Study

A patient in a hospital had a long history of instability and suicide attempts. On the day before her suicide attempt, the patient told a hospital staff member of her specific plan to commit suicide. The staff member did not inform the supervising psychiatrist of the patient's communications. Subsequently, the patient jumped off the roof of a near-by parking garage as she had planned and communicated.

The court, in *Huntley v. State* (1984), held that this was not a case of medical malpractice, with the propriety of medical (psychiatric) judgment in question. Rather, at issue was the negligence of the staff member in not informing the staff psychiatrist. Thus, the hospital was liable, not for malpractice, but for the negligence of a staff member.

In the future, liability may be extended to other health care practitioners with more frequency. Non-psychiatrists are taking greater and greater responsibility in the treatment of difficult mental health problems. In fact, liability may extend at nearly the same rate that insurance companies increase covering treatment by non-psychiatrist health care practitioners.

Legal Considerations Special to Suicide Attempt

Several of the previous cases illustrate that suicide attempters can sue their therapists for the injuries caused by the attempt. However, there are other legal considerations of adolescent attempted suicide about which health care practitioners and school counselors should be aware that have nothing to do with being sued. These are situations in which the courts may get involved with the adolescent after a suicide attempt.

Although the courts today generally do not criminally punish suicide attempters they may commit the attempter to a mental hospital (Wright, 1975). Most states have statutes that allow their courts to commit a person, judged to be a danger to himself/herself, to the state mental hospital. This is most especially true with adolescents who are wards of the court (e.g., Arizona Revised Statutes 8-242.01). When an adolescent attempts suicide, and the attempt is serious enough to demand hospitalization, a state or county agency and/or a state or county hospital staff may evaluate the adolescent. If this evaluation reveals that the suicide attempt is serious, the evaluators may recommend a hearing to commit the adolescent to the state hospital. The important point is that a health care practitioner, psychologist, or counselor must be aware of the possibility that his/her patient may be civilly committed.

Many state hospital systems are too small and under-funded to handle many mental health problems. This includes adolescent mental health problems. In situations in which a mental health care practitioner or school counselor believes that the patient needs commitment but has parents that can not afford a private facility, then the practitioner or counselor must diligently try to locate the resources that do exist in the state mental health system. To locate these resources, a health care practitioner or counselor may need to contact state agencies and mental hospitals. In some situations state mental hospital space is so limited that the only way to help a serious case is for the court to order commitment.

Often after a suicide attempt requiring hospitalization, a state or county agency may evaluate the adolescent attempter. If not contacted after the attempted suicide of an adolescent patient or client, the health care practitioner or school counselor should contact the appropriate evaluating team or agency. His/her comments to them may be invaluable. In addition, the evaluation team may decide that the best procedure would be for the health care practitioner or counselor to maintain treatment.

When a health care practitioner or counselor has a patient or client attempt suicide, the therapist must know his/her legal resources. If mental hospitalization is necessary, the therapist may be the one that must find what is available. Often the right channels in administrative agencies and the state court systems can assure a patient or client these limited resources. The limitation of a chapter prevent informing the health care practitioner or counselor about what should be done in every situation. All states are different and the procedures in each continually change. Thus, the situation may arise in which the therapist not only needs to but also must find what is available for the patient or client.

IMPLICATIONS

The question of how to treat a potential suicide is an open question (Klein & Glover, 1983). Health care practitioners may use any number of reasonable alternatives when treating patients. A variety of treatment approaches appear promising. If the health care professional acts responsibly and professionally, a court probably will not find him/her negligent. However, nothing can be done to stop people from suing and as the previous cases demonstrate, any number of situations can happen where liability can occur. With this in mind, health care practitioners and institutions can do several things during treatment to avoid law suits (Litman, 1967; Berman & Cohen-Sandler, 1983):

1. In an emergency situation, avoid displaying any contemptuous attitude toward a suicide attempter. A statement like, "Next time cut vertically instead of horizontally and you will get the main artery" would not impress a jury should the attempter later become a suicide victim.
2. Document actions fully and professionally. This should include the practitioner's assessment of the risks involved with a particular course of treatment and his/her reasons for following it. The reasonable professional judgment standard will protect the practitioner from liability if he/she clearly used reasonable professional judgment. A client's records can be used as evidence in a trial and can show that his/her therapist did the best that could be done in the situation.
3. The practitioner always should consult with colleagues on suicide cases. The common sense of a juror says that "two heads are better than one." If a practitioner's colleagues supported the decisions at the time, then negligence is harder to prove. Consultation with colleagues would impress the jury and demonstrate that the patient's suicidal act was independent and could not be stopped.
4. Staff communication must be good. Bad communication between and among "professionals" on a case will negatively impress a future juror. Poor communication is a factor that any non-professional juror, using common sense, would identify as showing negligence.

5. A practitioner must not forget to deal with the family. This is true during the treatment of a potential suicide victim and after a completed suicide. Postvention treatment has a dual purpose. First, it facilitates the family's resolution of grief and should be offered as a matter of humane treatment. Second, the family's contact with the therapist helps prevent the hasty, emotion-driven decision to begin a malpractice law suit.

REFERENCES

Books and Articles

Batt, J., & Bastien, C.P. (1983). Suicide as a compensable claim under workers' compensation statutes: A guide for the lawyer and the psychiatrist. *West Virginia Law Review, 86*, 369-92.

Berman, A.L., & Cohen-Sandler, R. (1982) Suicide and the standard of care: Optimal vs. acceptable. *Suicide and Life Threatening Behavior, 12(2), 114-22.*

Berman, A.L., & Cohen-Sandler, R. (1983). Suicide and malpractice: Expert testimony and the standard of care. Professional Psychology: Research and Practice, 14(1), 6-19.

Drukteinis, A.M. (1985). Psychiatric perspectives on civil liability for suicide. *Bulletin of the American Academy of Psychiatry Law, 13*(1), 71-83.

Howell, J.A. (1978). Suicide and causation. *Arizona State Law Journal*, 573-615.

Kjervik, D.K. (1984). The psychotherapists' duty to act reasonably to prevent suicides: A proposal to allow rational suicide. *Behavioral Sciences and the Law*, 2(2), 207-18.

Klein, J.I., & Glover, S.I. (1983). Psychiatric malpractice. *International Journal of Law and Psychiatry, 6*(2), 131-58.

Knuth, M.O. (1979). Civil liability for suicide. *Loyola of Los Angeles Law Review, 12*, 967-99.

Kolb, L. (1977). *Modern clinical psychiatry*. Philadelphia, PA: Saunders.

Litman, R.E. (1967). Medical legal aspects of suicide. *Washburn Law Journal, 6*, 395-401.

Marzen, J.T., O'Dowd, M.K., Crone, D., & Balch, T.J. (1985). Suicide: A constitutional right? *Duquesne Law Review, 24*(1), 1-242.

Prosser, W., Keeton, W.P., Dobbs, D.B., Keeton, R.E., & Owen, D.G. (1984). *Prosser and Keeton on the Law of Torts,* (5th ed.). St. Paul: West.

Schwartz, V.E. (1971). Civil liability for causing suicide: A synthesis of law and psychiatry. *Vanderbilt Law Review, 24*(2), 217-55.

Slawson, P., & Flynn, E.E. (1977). Hospital liability for suicide: A regional survey. *Bulletin of the American Academy of Psychiatry and the Law, 29,* 29-33.

Wright, D.M. (1975). Criminal aspects of suicide in the United States. *North Carolina Central Law Journal, 7,* 156-63.

Statutes and Cases

Arizona Revised Statutes 8-242.01.

Modal Penal Code 210.5(2).

Bella v. Greenson, 146 California Reporter 535 (App. 1978).

Blue Shield of Virginia v. McCready, 457 U.S. 465 (1982).

Bogust v. Iverson, 10 Wisconsin 2d 129, 102 N.W.2d 228 (1960).

Charouleau v. Charity Hospital of Louisiana at New Orleans, 319 So.2d 464 (La. App., 1975), Cert. denied, 323 So. 2d 137 (La. 1975).

Fernandez v. Baruch, 52 N.J. 127, 244 A.2d 109 (1968).

Fiederlein v. City of New York Health, Etc., 437 N.Y.S.2d 321 (1981).

Huntley v. State, 476 N.R.S.2d 99 (Ct.App. 1984).

Kent v. Whitaker, 364 P.2d 556 (Wis. 1961).

Koenigsmark v. State, 437 N.Y.S.2d 745 (1981).

Lichtenstein v. Montefiore Hospital and Medical Center, 392 N.Y.S.2d 18 (1977).

Meier v. Ross General Hospital, 71 Cal. Rptr. 903, 445 P.2d 519 (1968).

Mutual Life Insurance Co. v. Terry, 15 Wall. 580 (1973).

Runyon v. Reid, 510 P.2d 943 (Okl., 1973).

Tarasoff v. Regents of the University of California et al., 17 Cal.3d 425, 551 P.2d 334 (1976).

Werner v. Kliewer, 238 Kan. 289, 710 P.2d 1250 (1985).

INDEX

C

D

E

F

G

H

I

J

K

L

M

N

O

P

S

T

U

V

W

Y

Z

ABOUT THE AUTHORS

Dave Capuzzi

Dave Capuzzi, Ph.D., Past President (1986-87) of the American Association for Counseling and Development, is a Professor of Counselor Education at Portland State University in Portland, Oregon. Prior to affiliating with Portland State University in 1978, he served in faculty positions at Florida State University, Our Lady of the Lake University of San Antonio, and the University of Wyoming.

Dr. Capuzzi's publications have appeared in journals such as *Counselor Education and Supervision, Counseling and Values, Humanistic Education and Development* and the *Journal for Specialists in Group Work.* From 1980 to 1984, he served as editor of *The School Counselor.* Dr. Capuzzi authored a number of textbook chapters and monographs on the topic of preventing adolescent suicide and was co-editor and author, with Dr. Larry Golden, of *Helping Families Help Children; Family Interventions with School Related Problems*, a textbook published in 1986.

Dr. Capuzzi has won several awards for his contributions of service and expertise to a number of professional groups. Among those were the Human Rights Award of the South Carolina Association for Counseling and Development, the Leona Tyler Award of the Oregon Counseling Association, the Outstanding Service Award of the Western Region of the American Association for Counseling and Development, and the Silver Award for Editorial Excellence of the Society of National Association Publications.

A sought after keynoter and plenary speaker for professional conferences and institutes, Dr. Capuzzi also has served in a variety of consultancies with school districts and community agencies interested in initiating counseling and intervention strategies for the prevention of adolescent suicide. He has facilitated the development of suicide prevention, crisis management and post-vention programs in communities in twenty-three states and is committed to working with youth at-risk for suicide.

During a recent interview Capuzzi stated: "*Preventing Adolescent Suicide* is an outgrowth of my work with a variety of communities all over the country. The escalation of the adolescent suicide rate is indicative of the desperation and alienation experienced by young people in America. Our schools and our communities cannot fail to intervene in what I consider to be, along with AIDS, one of the greatest threats in this century to adolescents in the United States."

Larry Golden

Dr. Larry Golden is a professor in the counseling and guidance program at the University of Texas at San Antonio. He is also a psychologist and specializes in counseling with children and adolescents. He regularly consults with school districts on such topics as brief family interventions and drop-out prevention.

Previous books are *Psychotherapeutic Techniques in School Psychology* (1984) and *Helping Famlies Help Children: Family Interventions with School-Related Problems* (1986). Dr. Golden has published articles on ethics, family assessment, play therapy, social learning, and suicide prevention. He received the Professional Writing Award from the Texas Association for Counseling and Development in 1986 for his research with families. In 1987, Dr. Golden was awarded a Professional Enhancement Grant by the American Association for Counseling and Development to fund the Parent Consultation Center, a project that provides preventive mental health services, such as, parenting skills workshops, family support groups, and brief consultation.

Dr. Golden received his bachelors degree from the University of Miami, masters degree from the City College of New York, and Ph.D, from Arizona State University. Dr. Golden began his career as a classroom teacher in the public schools of Dade County, Florida. Previous academic posts were director of the Marriage and Family Therapy program at Our Lady of the Lake University in San Antonio and Associate Professor of Psychology at Texas Women's University.